ACCA

13

TERRITORY INSPECTION DEPARTMENT

NATSUME ONO

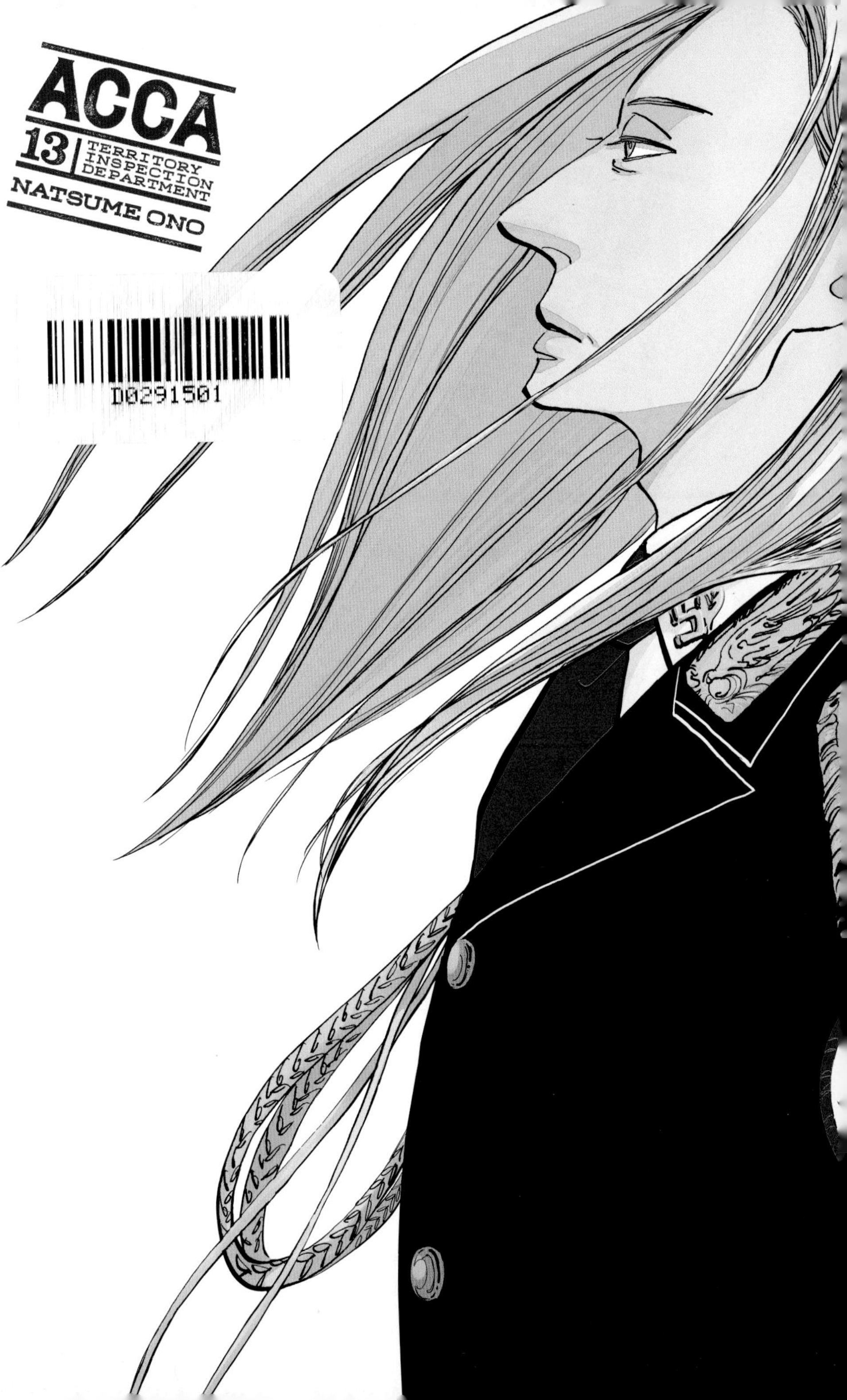

ACCA 13 TERRITORY INSPECTION DEPARTMENT

CONTENTS

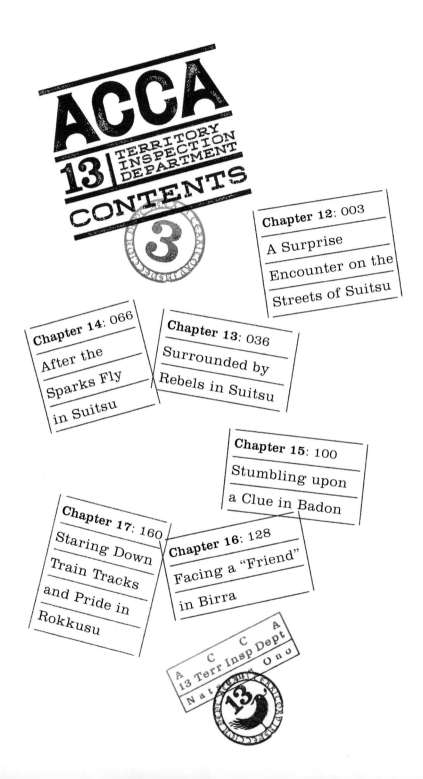

Chapter 12: 003
A Surprise Encounter on the Streets of Suitsu

Chapter 13: 036
Surrounded by Rebels in Suitsu

Chapter 14: 066
After the Sparks Fly in Suitsu

Chapter 15: 100
Stumbling upon a Clue in Badon

Chapter 16: 128
Facing a "Friend" in Birra

Chapter 17: 160
Staring Down Train Tracks and Pride in Rokkusu

ACCA 13 Terr Insp Dept   Natsume Ono

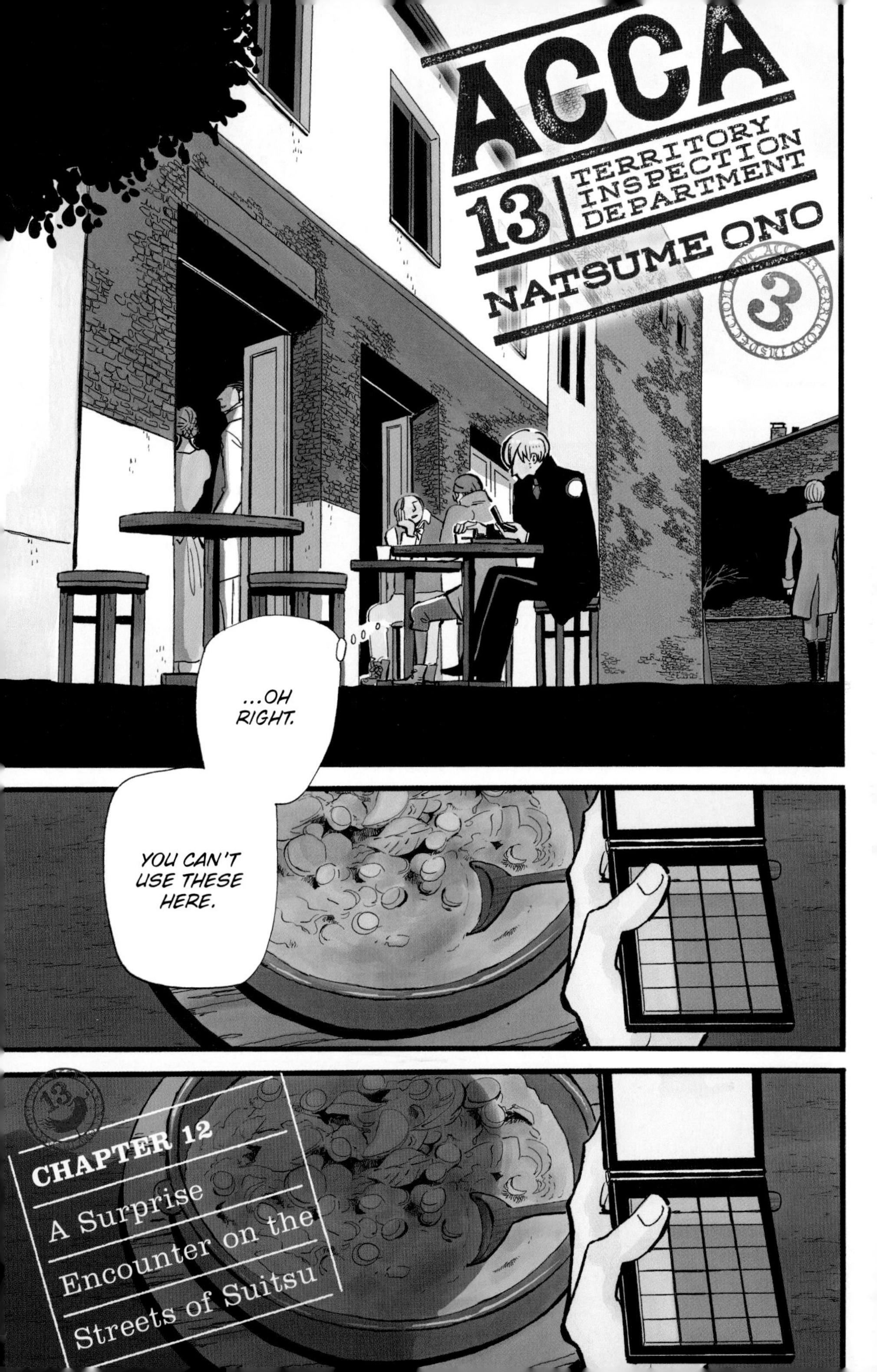
ACCA
13 TERRITORY INSPECTION DEPARTMENT
NATSUME ONO
3
...OH RIGHT.
YOU CAN'T USE THESE HERE.
CHAPTER 12
A Surprise Encounter on the Streets of Suitsu

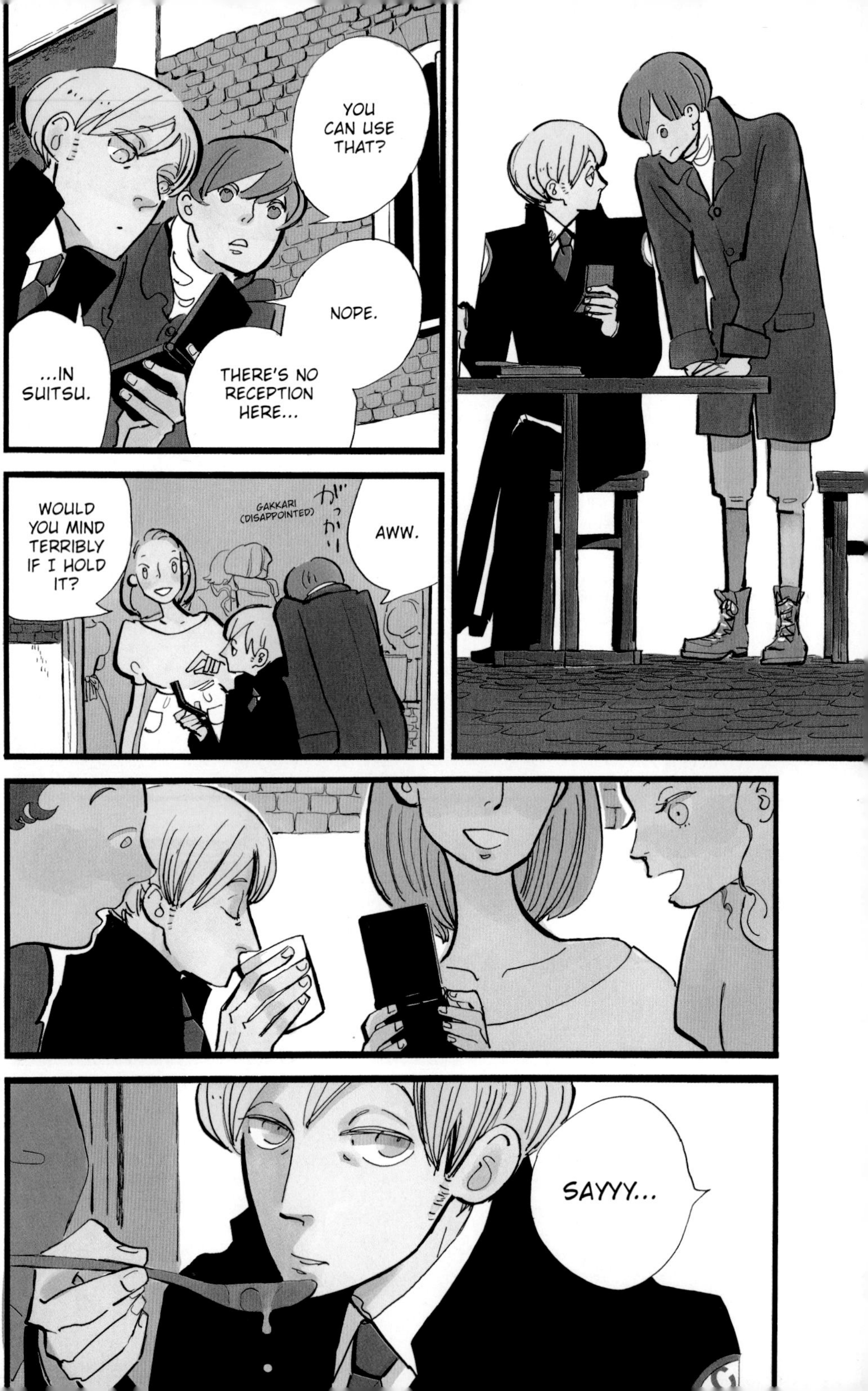
YOU CAN USE THAT?
NOPE.
THERE'S NO RECEPTION HERE...
...IN SUITSU.
AWW.
がっかり
GAKKARI (DISAPPOINTED)
WOULD YOU MIND TERRIBLY IF I HOLD IT?
SAYYY...

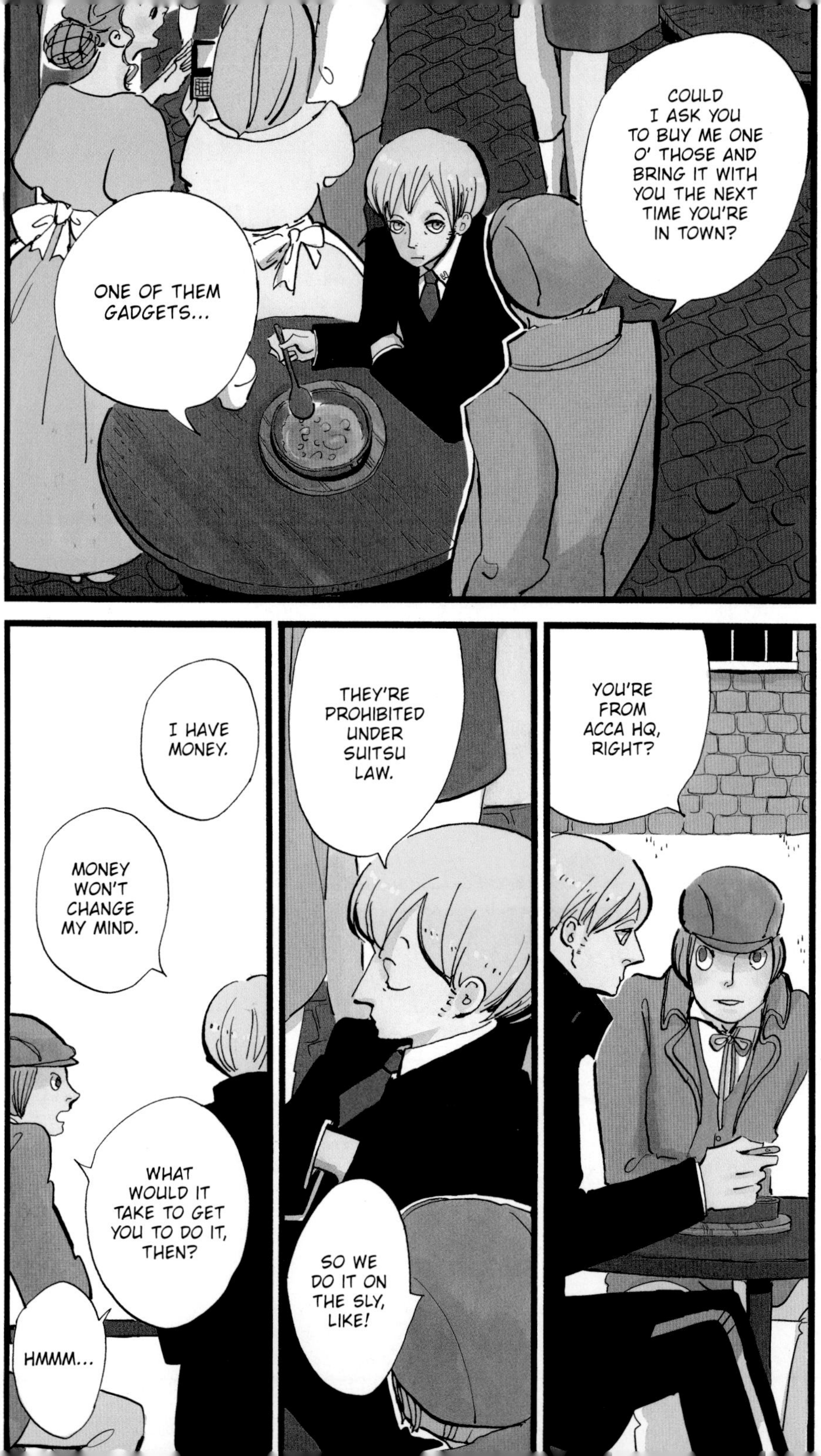
COULD I ASK YOU TO BUY ME ONE O' THOSE AND BRING IT WITH YOU THE NEXT TIME YOU'RE IN TOWN?
ONE OF THEM GADGETS...
YOU'RE FROM ACCA HQ, RIGHT?
THEY'RE PROHIBITED UNDER SUITSU LAW.
SO WE DO IT ON THE SLY, LIKE!
I HAVE MONEY.
MONEY WON'T CHANGE MY MIND.
WHAT WOULD IT TAKE TO GET YOU TO DO IT, THEN?
HMMM...

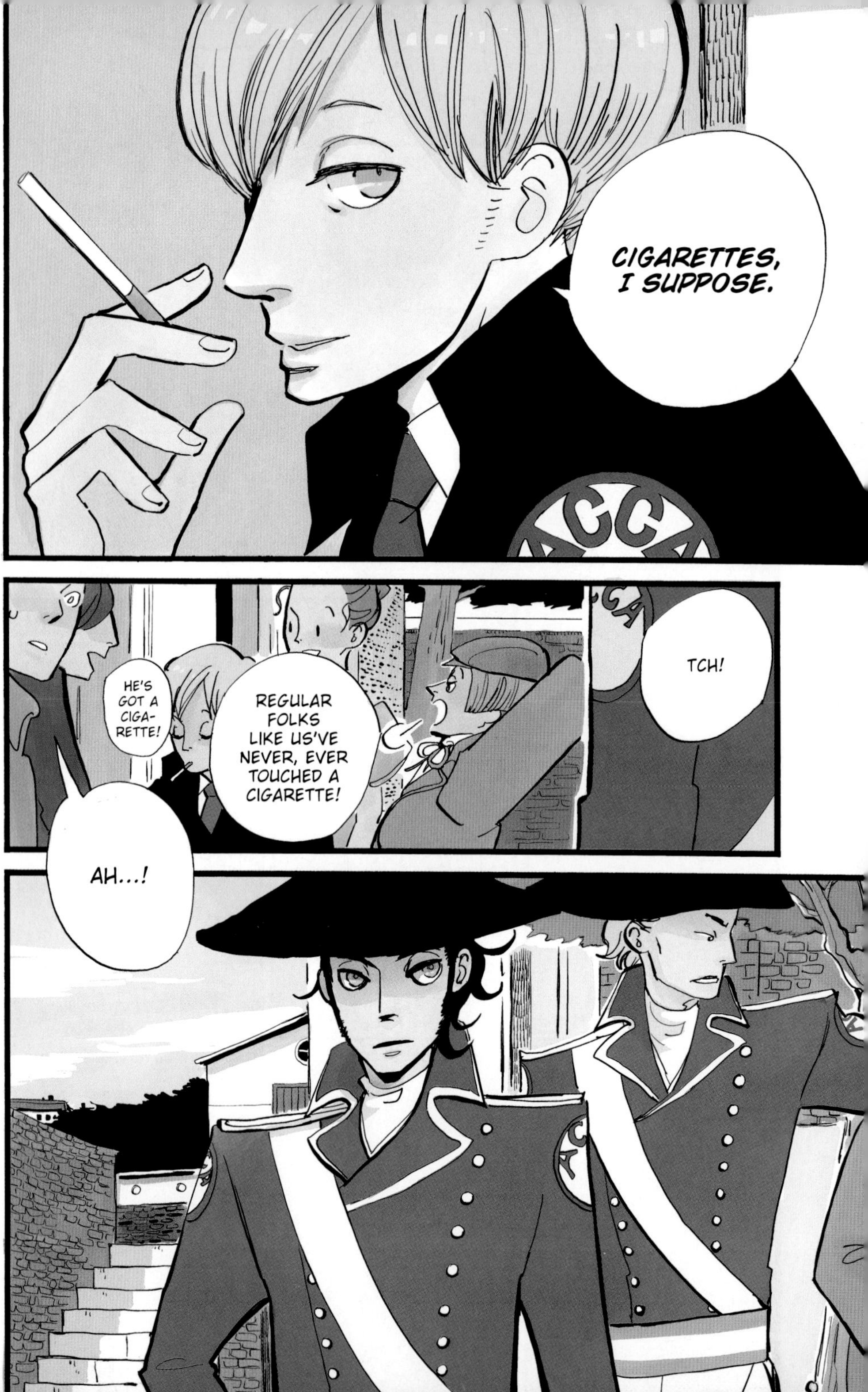
CIGARETTES, I SUPPOSE.
TCH!
REGULAR FOLKS LIKE US'VE NEVER, EVER TOUCHED A CIGARETTE!
HE'S GOT A CIGA-RETTE!
AH...!

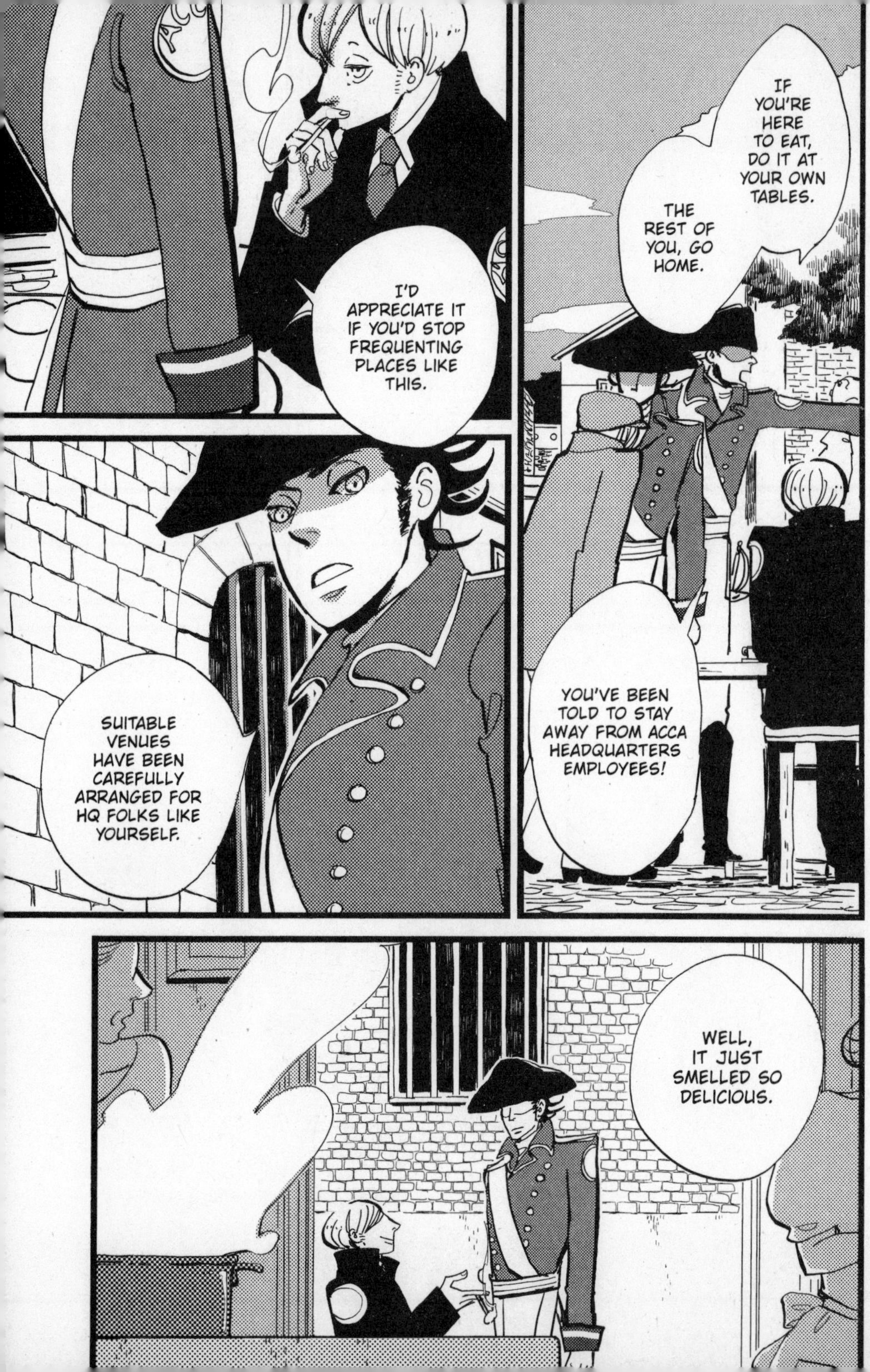
IF YOU'RE HERE TO EAT, DO IT AT YOUR OWN TABLES.
THE REST OF YOU, GO HOME.
YOU'VE BEEN TOLD TO STAY AWAY FROM ACCA HEADQUARTERS EMPLOYEES!
I'D APPRECIATE IT IF YOU'D STOP FREQUENTING PLACES LIKE THIS.
SUITABLE VENUES HAVE BEEN CAREFULLY ARRANGED FOR HQ FOLKS LIKE YOURSELF.
WELL, IT JUST SMELLED SO DELICIOUS.

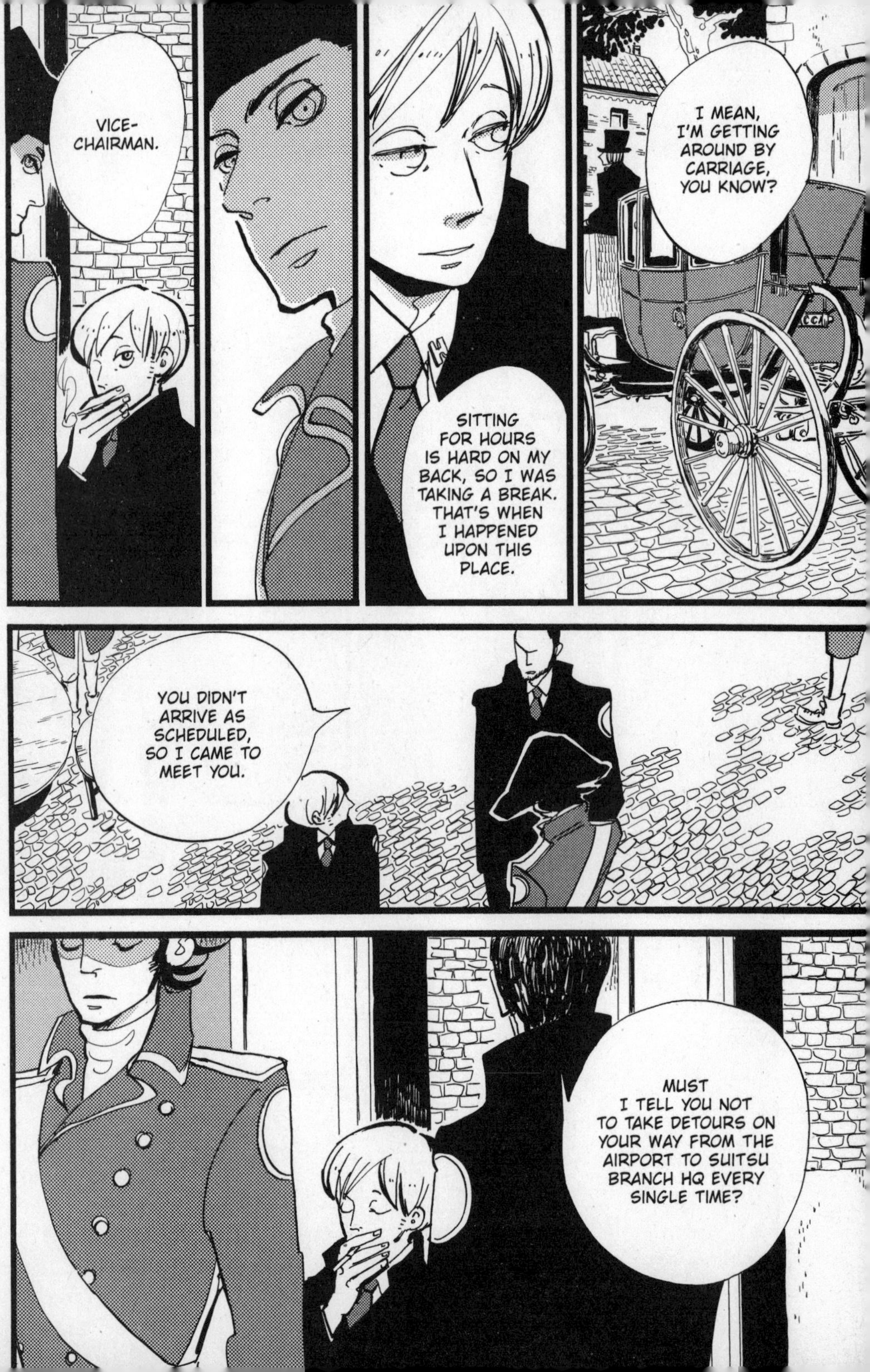
I MEAN, I'M GETTING AROUND BY CARRIAGE, YOU KNOW?
SITTING FOR HOURS IS HARD ON MY BACK, SO I WAS TAKING A BREAK. THAT'S WHEN I HAPPENED UPON THIS PLACE.
VICE-CHAIRMAN.
YOU DIDN'T ARRIVE AS SCHEDULED, SO I CAME TO MEET YOU.
MUST I TELL YOU NOT TO TAKE DETOURS ON YOUR WAY FROM THE AIRPORT TO SUITSU BRANCH HQ EVERY SINGLE TIME?

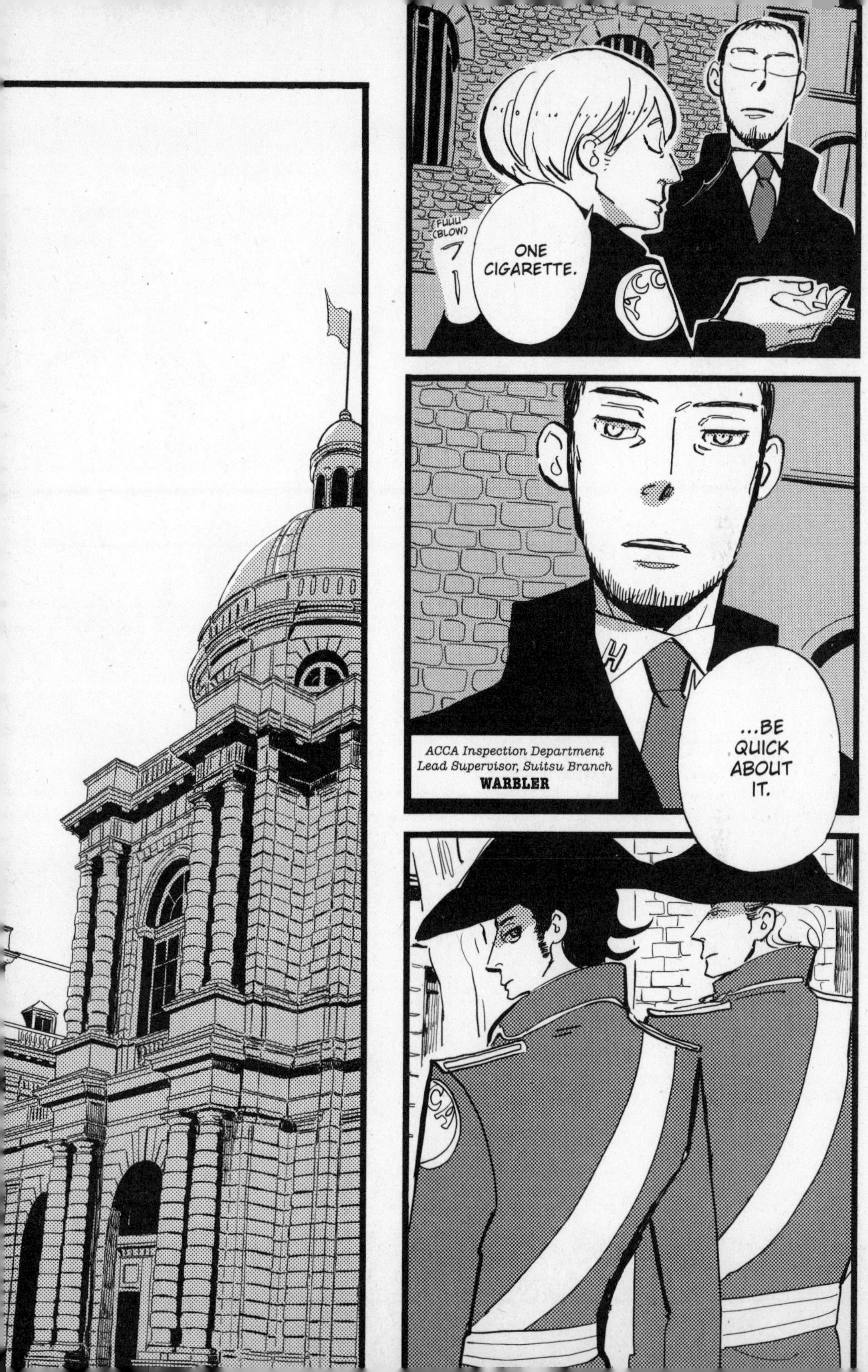
ONE CIGARETTE.
FUUU (BLOW)
ACCA Inspection Department Lead Supervisor, Suitsu Branch WARBLER
...BE QUICK ABOUT IT.

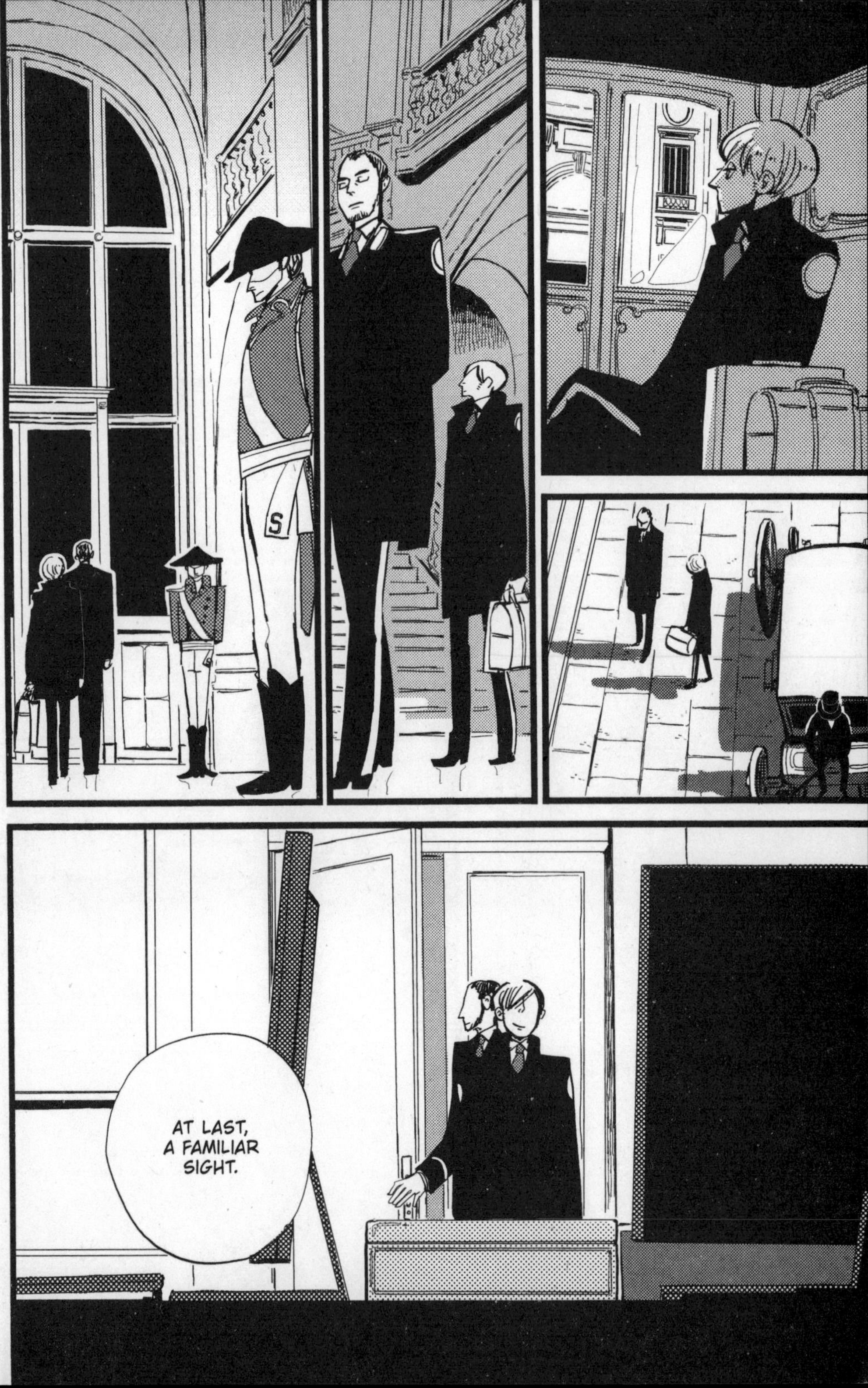
AT LAST,
A FAMILIAR
SIGHT.

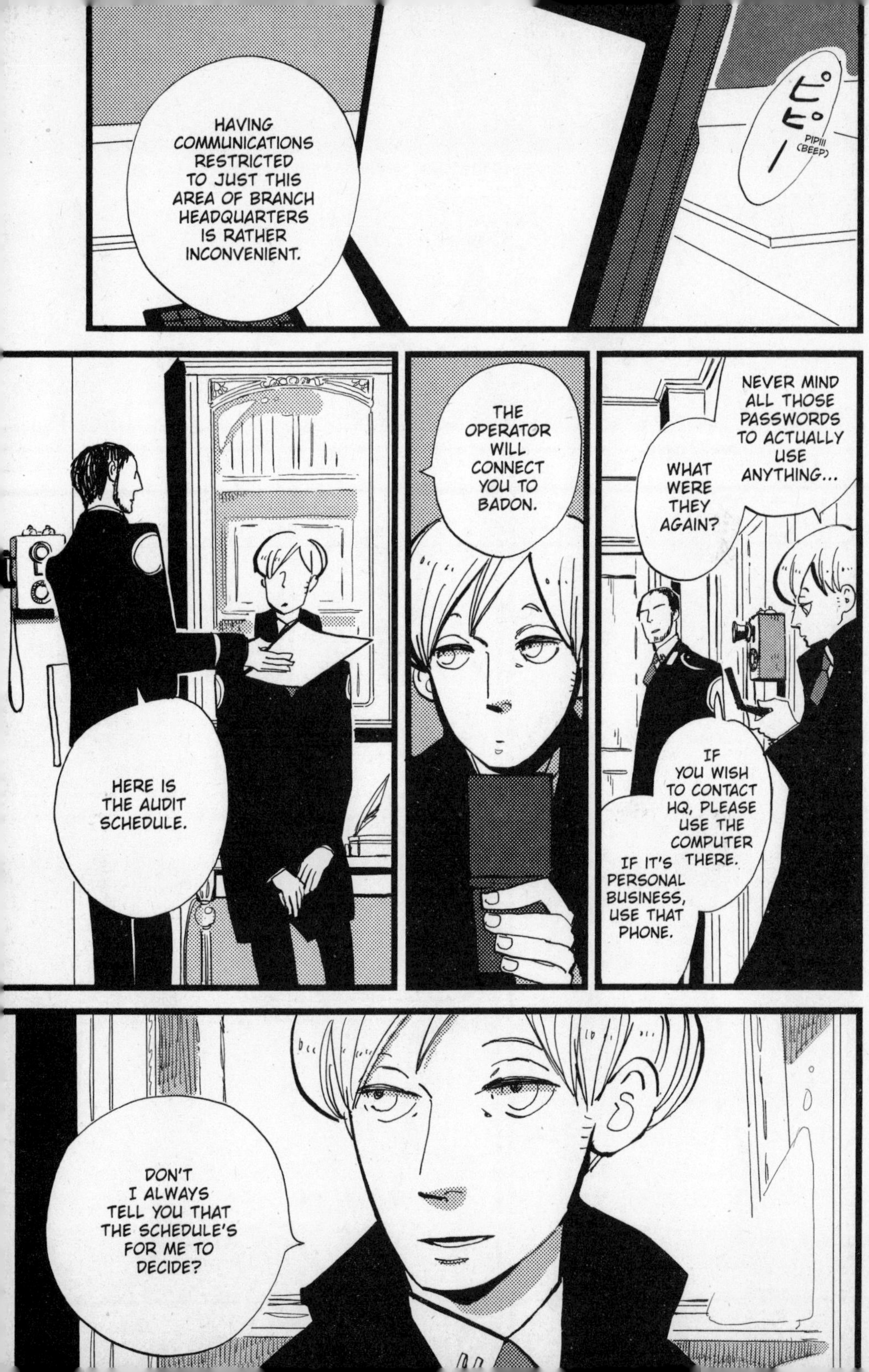
ピピー
PIPIII (BEEP)
HAVING COMMUNICATIONS RESTRICTED TO JUST THIS AREA OF BRANCH HEADQUARTERS IS RATHER INCONVENIENT.
NEVER MIND ALL THOSE PASSWORDS TO ACTUALLY USE ANYTHING...
WHAT WERE THEY AGAIN?
IF YOU WISH TO CONTACT HQ, PLEASE USE THE COMPUTER THERE.
IF IT'S PERSONAL BUSINESS, USE THAT PHONE.
THE OPERATOR WILL CONNECT YOU TO BADON.
HERE IS THE AUDIT SCHEDULE.
DON'T I ALWAYS TELL YOU THAT THE SCHEDULE'S FOR ME TO DECIDE?

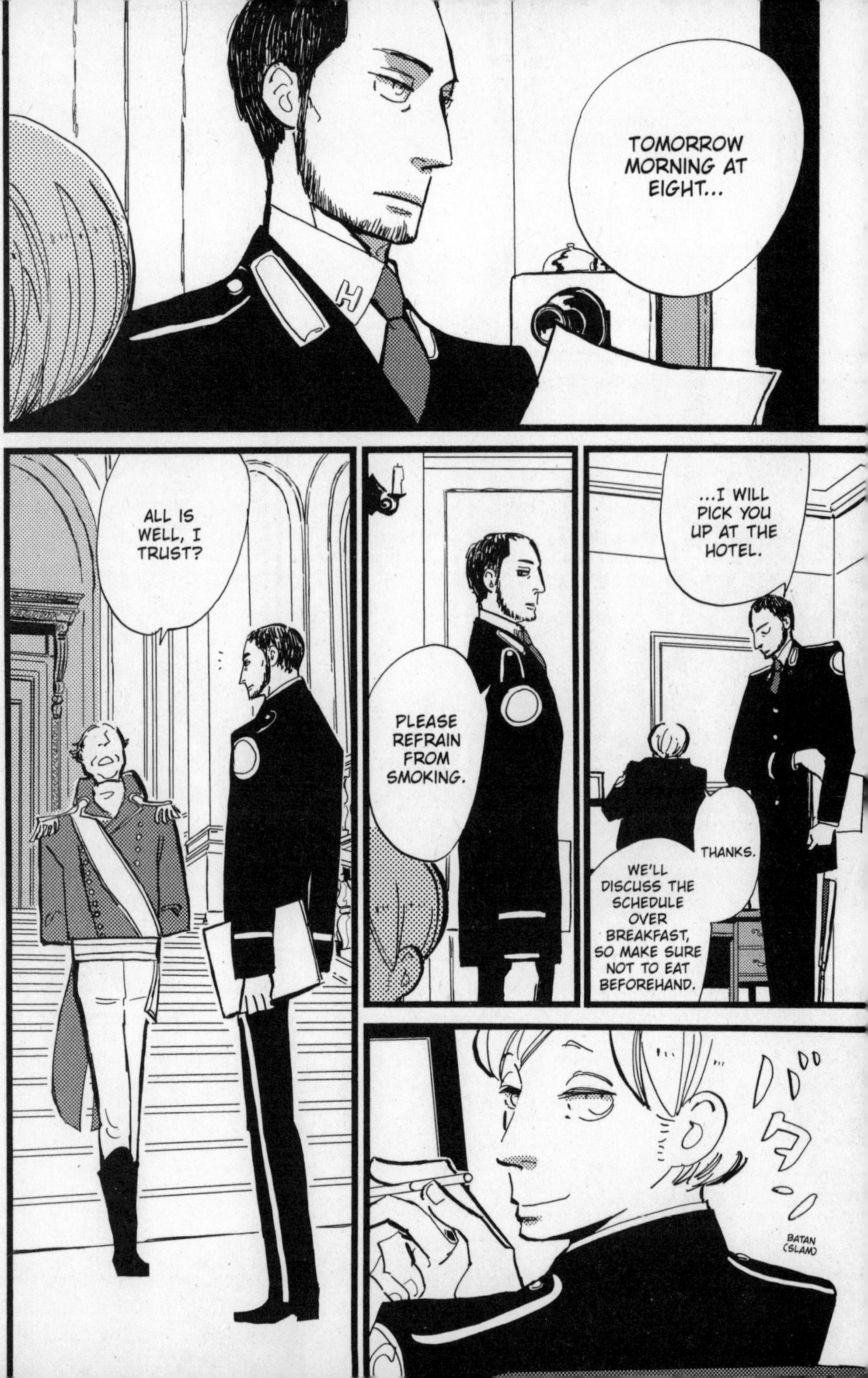
TOMORROW MORNING AT EIGHT...
...I WILL PICK YOU UP AT THE HOTEL.
THANKS.
WE'LL DISCUSS THE SCHEDULE OVER BREAKFAST, SO MAKE SURE NOT TO EAT BEFOREHAND.
PLEASE REFRAIN FROM SMOKING.
BATAN (SLAM)
ALL IS WELL, I TRUST?

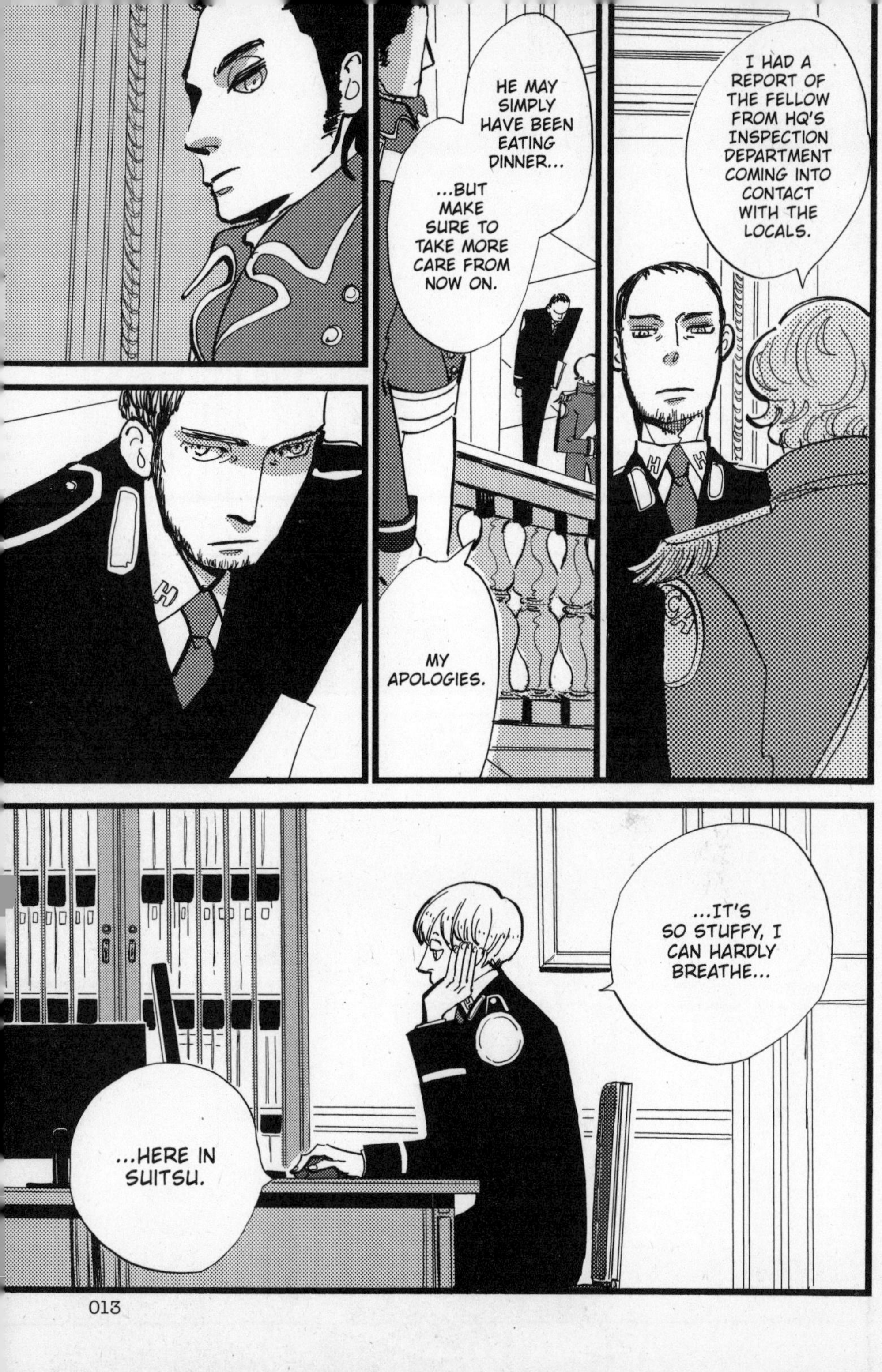
I HAD A REPORT OF THE FELLOW FROM HQ'S INSPECTION DEPARTMENT COMING INTO CONTACT WITH THE LOCALS.
HE MAY SIMPLY HAVE BEEN EATING DINNER...
...BUT MAKE SURE TO TAKE MORE CARE FROM NOW ON.
MY APOLOGIES.
...IT'S SO STUFFY, I CAN HARDLY BREATHE...
...HERE IN SUITSU.

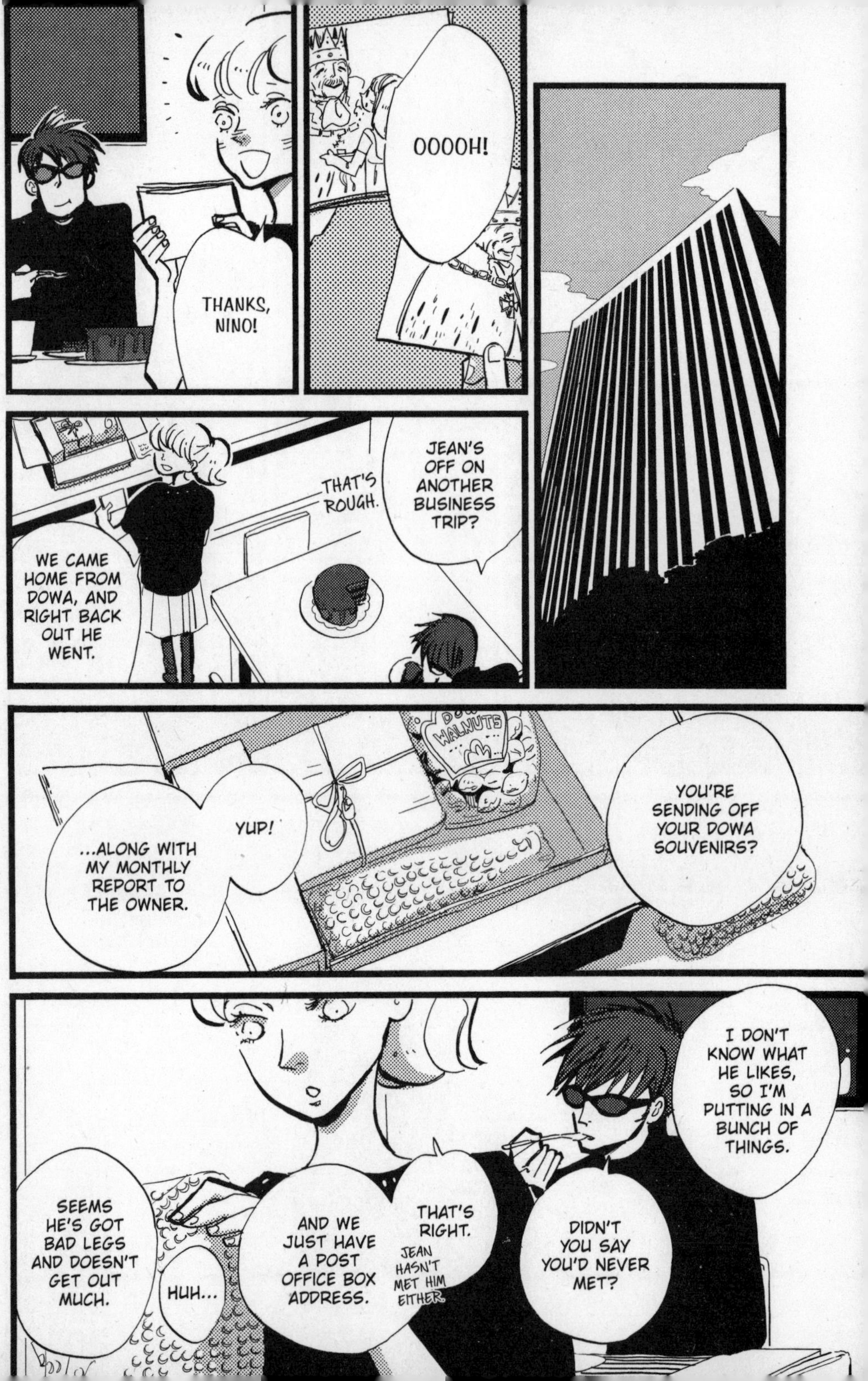
OOOOH!
THANKS, NINO!
JEAN'S OFF ON ANOTHER BUSINESS TRIP?
THAT'S ROUGH.
WE CAME HOME FROM DOWA, AND RIGHT BACK OUT HE WENT.
YOU'RE SENDING OFF YOUR DOWA SOUVENIRS?
WALNUTS
YUP!
...ALONG WITH MY MONTHLY REPORT TO THE OWNER.
I DON'T KNOW WHAT HE LIKES, SO I'M PUTTING IN A BUNCH OF THINGS.
DIDN'T YOU SAY YOU'D NEVER MET?
THAT'S RIGHT.
JEAN HASN'T MET HIM EITHER.
AND WE JUST HAVE A POST OFFICE BOX ADDRESS.
HUH...
SEEMS HE'S GOT BAD LEGS AND DOESN'T GET OUT MUCH.

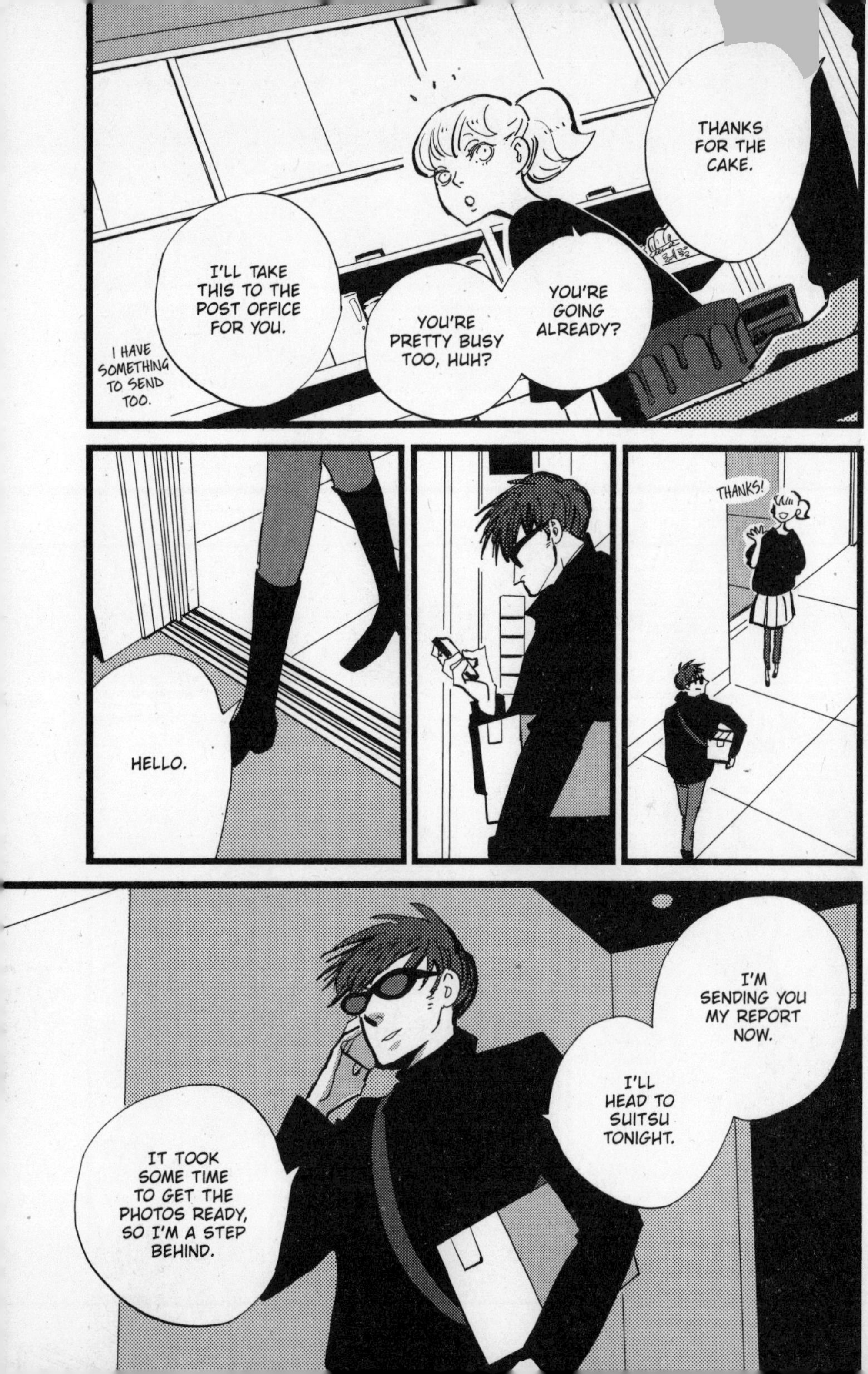
THANKS FOR THE CAKE.
YOU'RE GOING ALREADY?
YOU'RE PRETTY BUSY TOO, HUH?
I'LL TAKE THIS TO THE POST OFFICE FOR YOU.
I HAVE SOMETHING TO SEND TOO.
THANKS!
HELLO.
I'M SENDING YOU MY REPORT NOW.
I'LL HEAD TO SUITSU TONIGHT.
IT TOOK SOME TIME TO GET THE PHOTOS READY, SO I'M A STEP BEHIND.

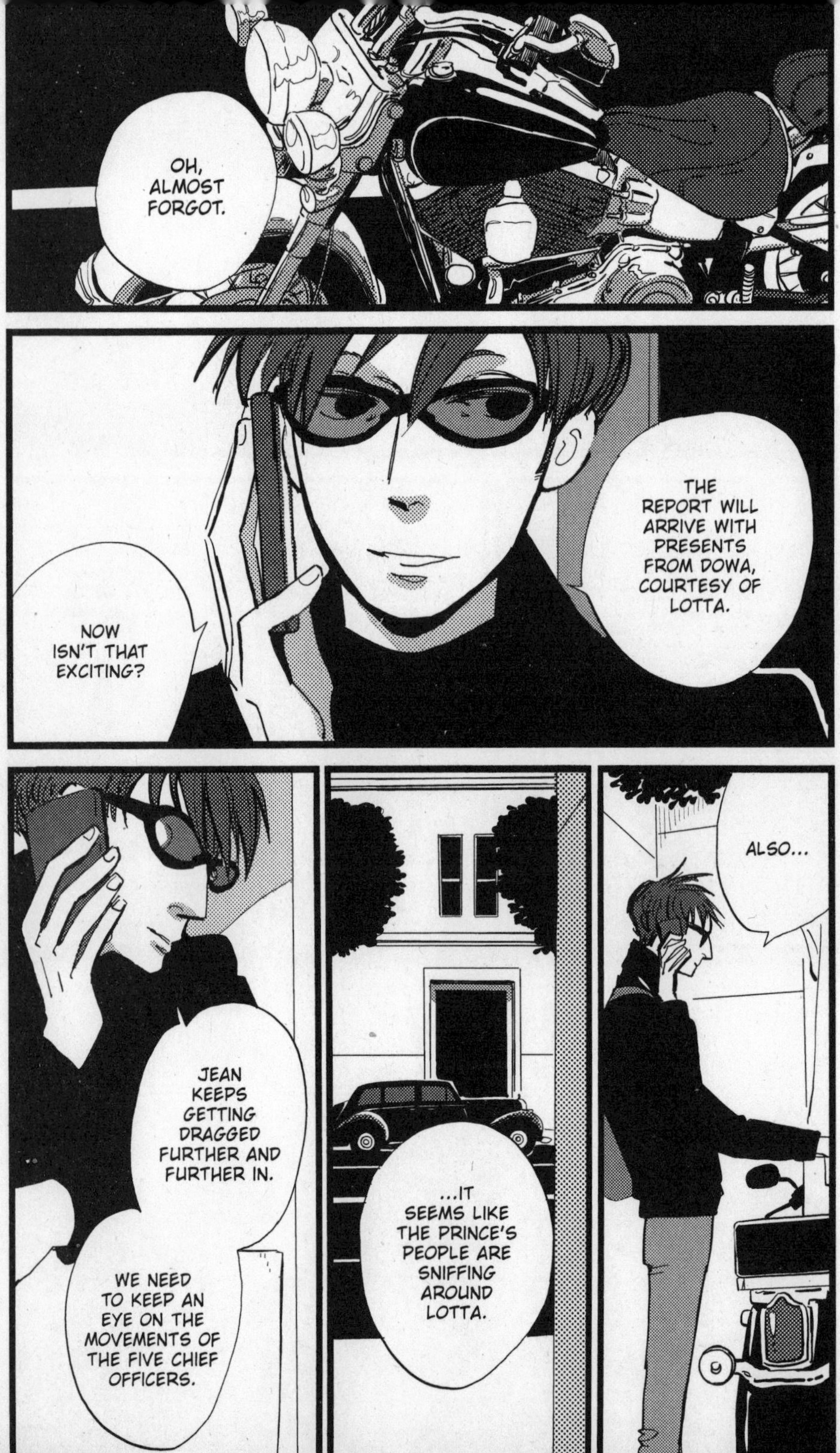
OH, ALMOST FORGOT.
THE REPORT WILL ARRIVE WITH PRESENTS FROM DOWA, COURTESY OF LOTTA.
NOW ISN'T THAT EXCITING?
ALSO...
...IT SEEMS LIKE THE PRINCE'S PEOPLE ARE SNIFFING AROUND LOTTA.
JEAN KEEPS GETTING DRAGGED FURTHER AND FURTHER IN.
WE NEED TO KEEP AN EYE ON THE MOVEMENTS OF THE FIVE CHIEF OFFICERS.

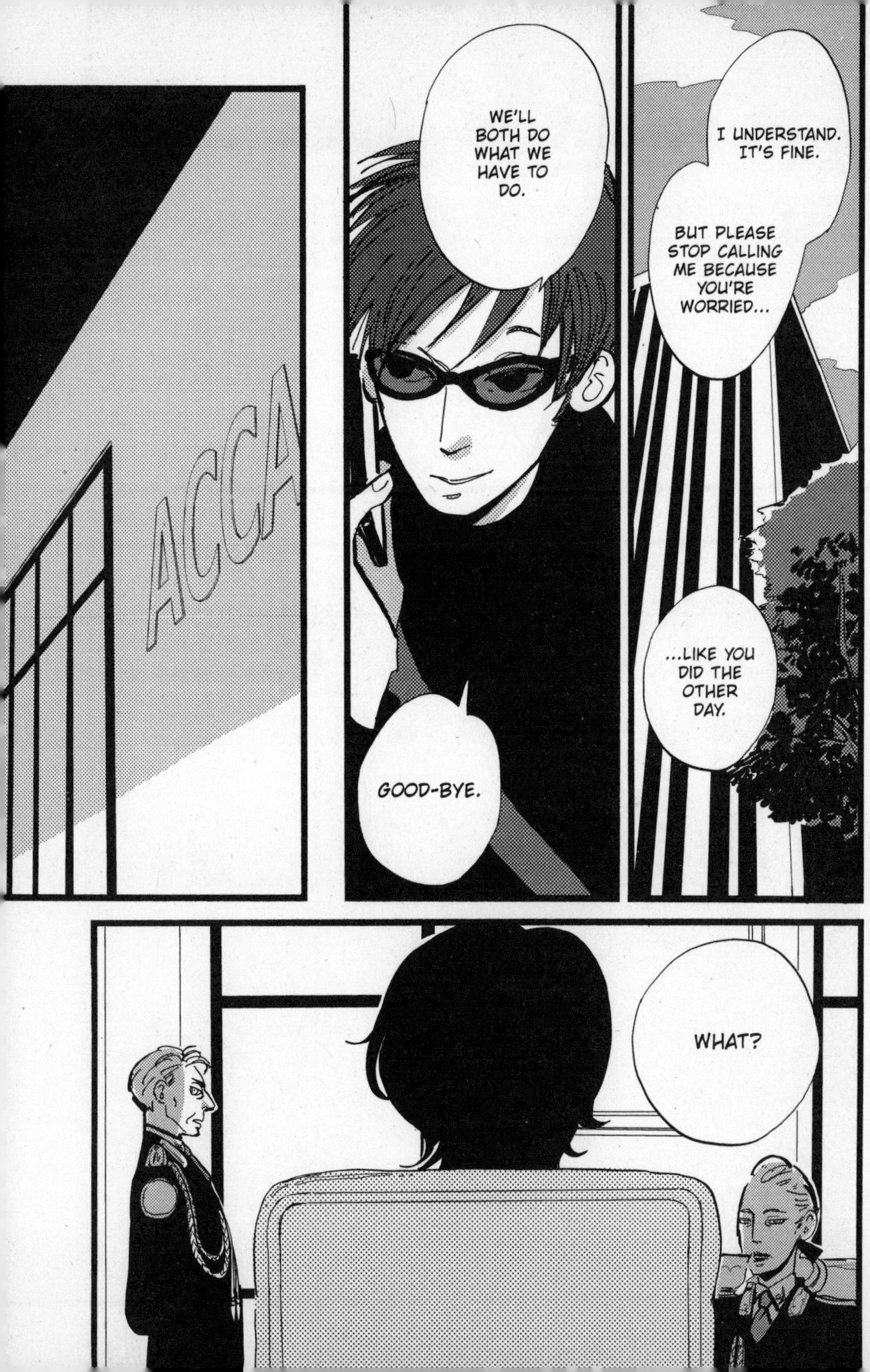
I UNDERSTAND. IT'S FINE.
BUT PLEASE STOP CALLING ME BECAUSE YOU'RE WORRIED...
...LIKE YOU DID THE OTHER DAY.
WE'LL BOTH DO WHAT WE HAVE TO DO.
GOOD-BYE.
ACCA
WHAT?

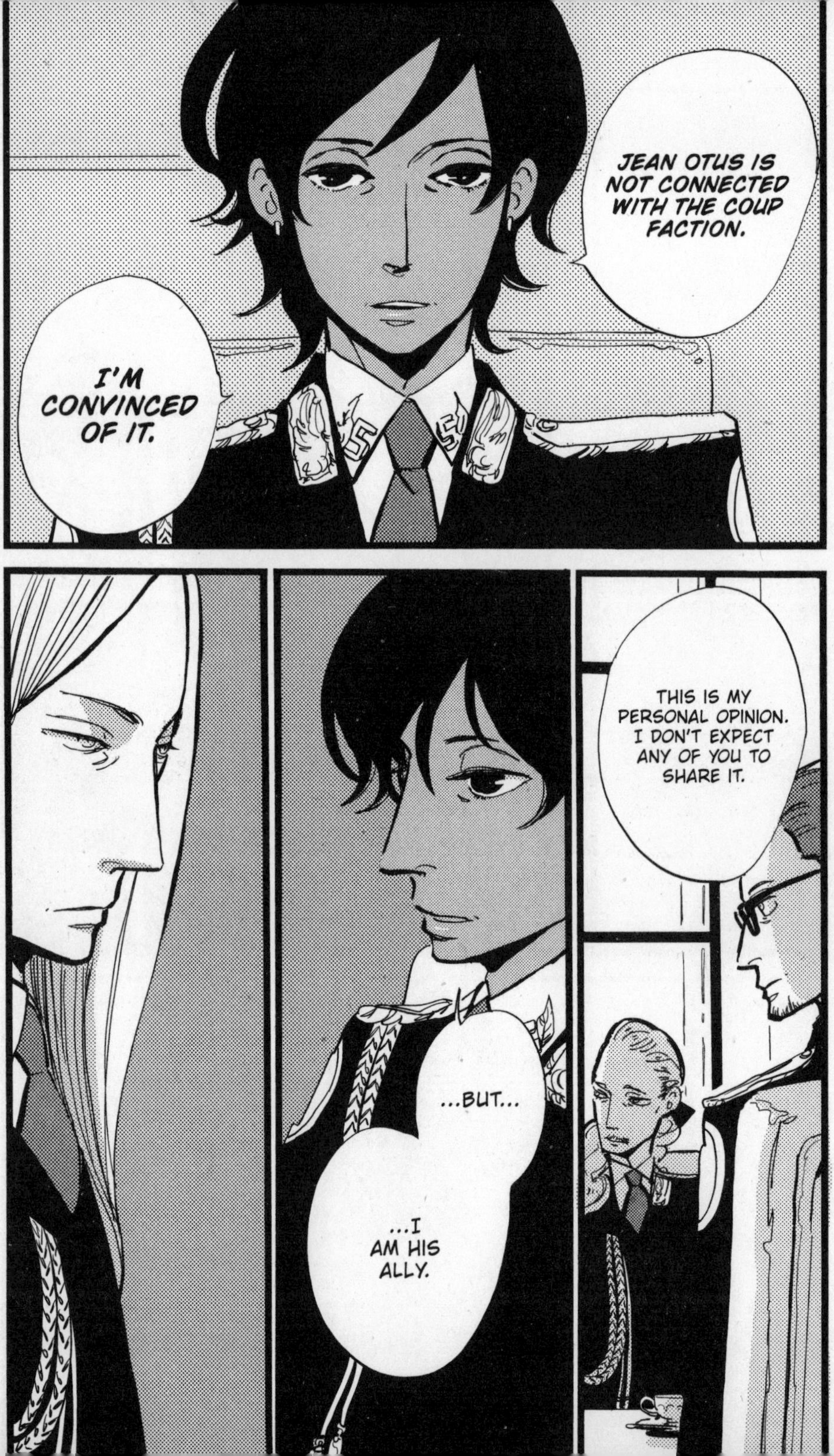
JEAN OTUS IS NOT CONNECTED WITH THE COUP FACTION.
I'M CONVINCED OF IT.
THIS IS MY PERSONAL OPINION. I DON'T EXPECT ANY OF YOU TO SHARE IT.
...BUT...
...I AM HIS ALLY.

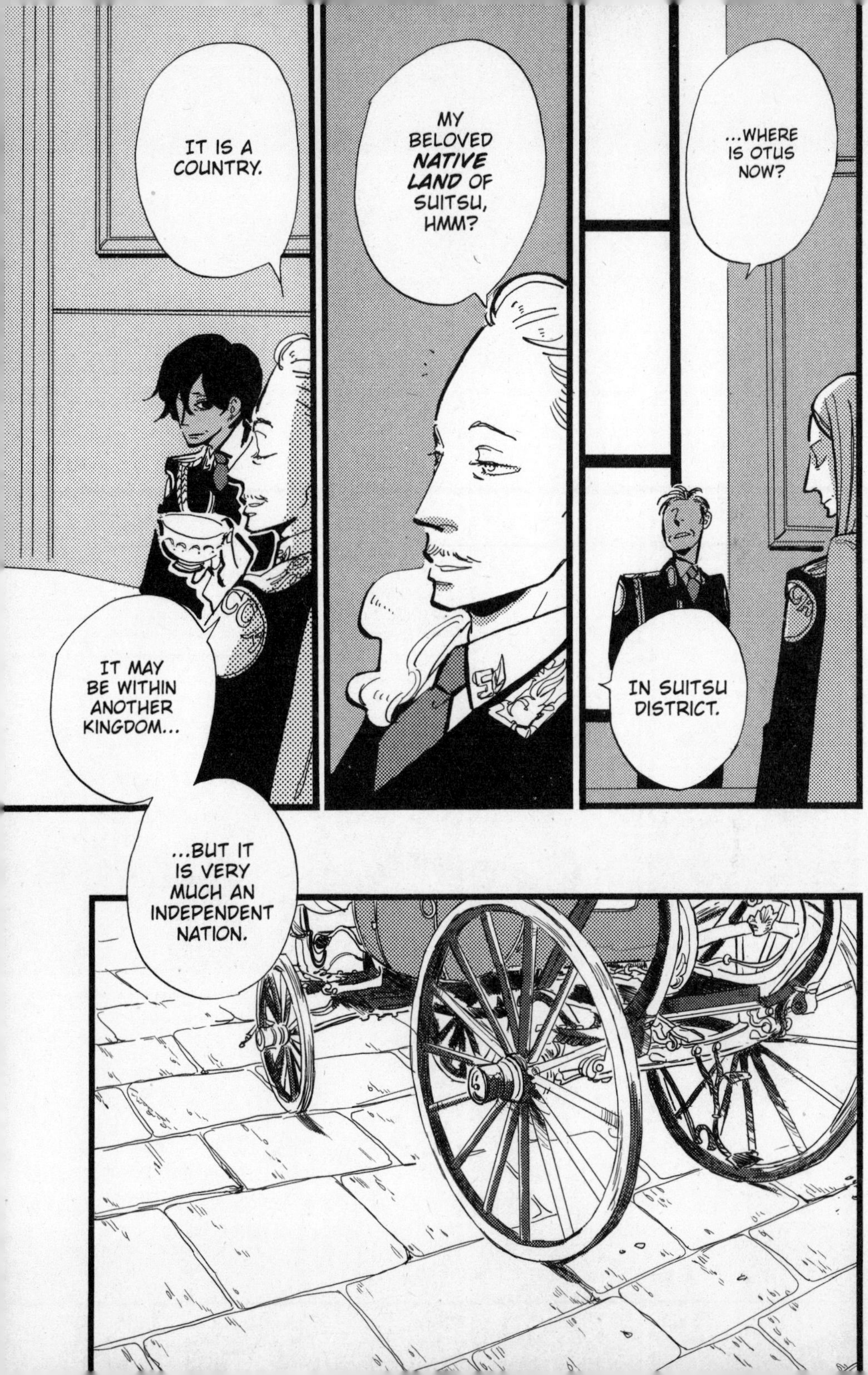
...WHERE IS OTUS NOW?
IN SUITSU DISTRICT.
MY BELOVED NATIVE LAND OF SUITSU, HMM?
IT IS A COUNTRY.
IT MAY BE WITHIN ANOTHER KINGDOM...
...BUT IT IS VERY MUCH AN INDEPENDENT NATION.

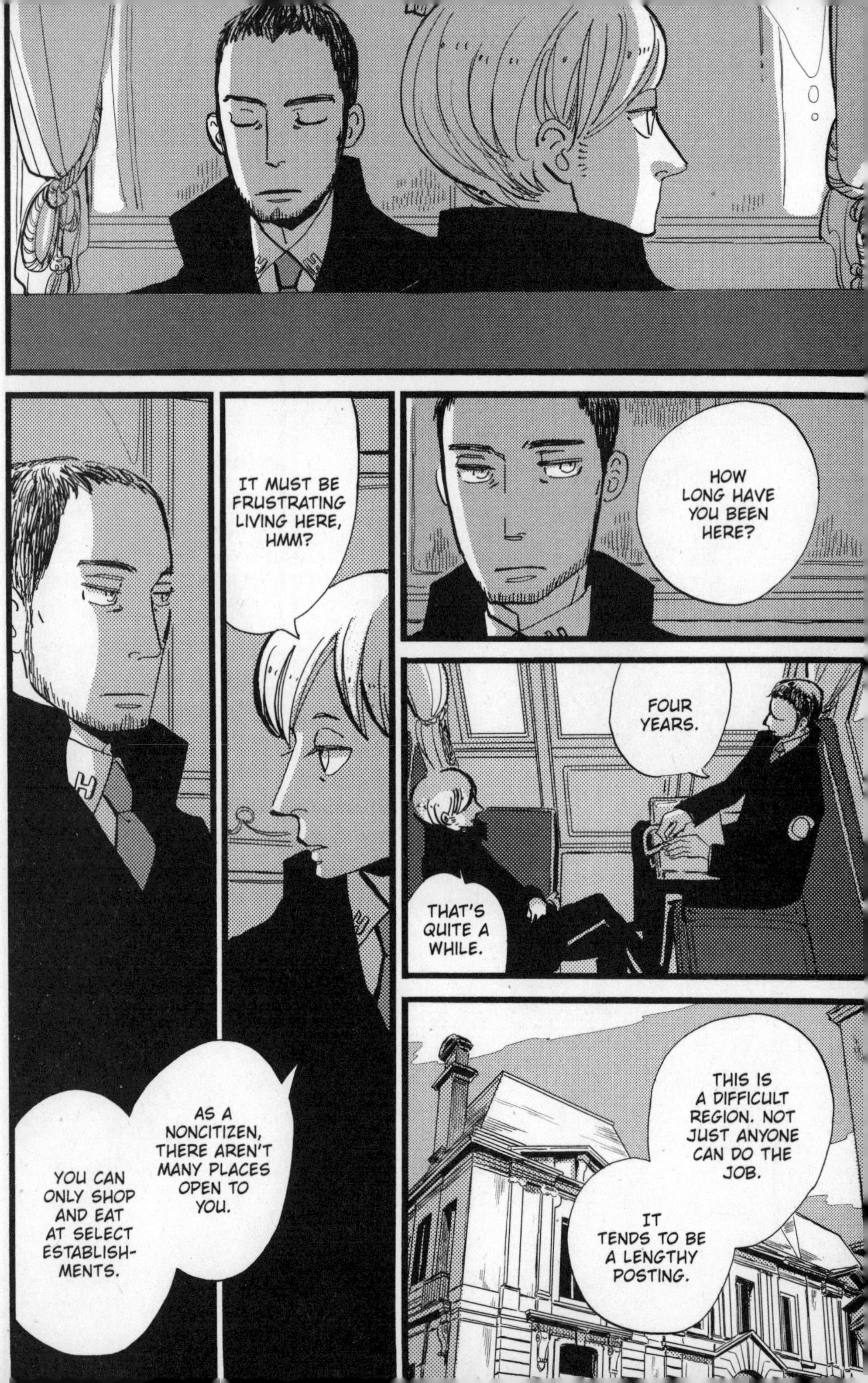
HOW LONG HAVE YOU BEEN HERE?
FOUR YEARS.
THAT'S QUITE A WHILE.
THIS IS A DIFFICULT REGION. NOT JUST ANYONE CAN DO THE JOB.
IT TENDS TO BE A LENGTHY POSTING.
IT MUST BE FRUSTRATING LIVING HERE, HMM?
AS A NONCITIZEN, THERE AREN'T MANY PLACES OPEN TO YOU.
YOU CAN ONLY SHOP AND EAT AT SELECT ESTABLISH-MENTS.

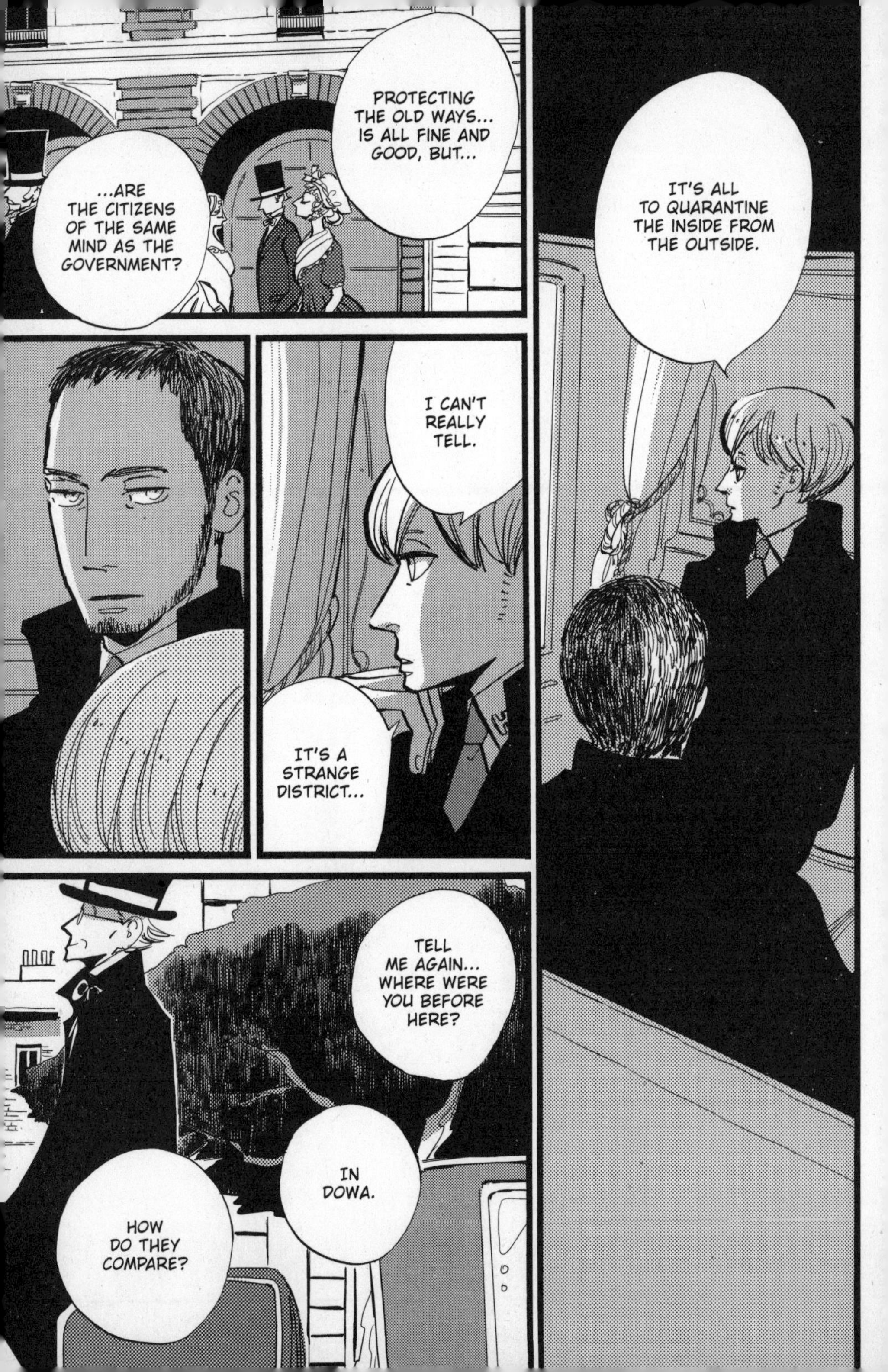
IT'S ALL TO QUARANTINE THE INSIDE FROM THE OUTSIDE.
PROTECTING THE OLD WAYS... IS ALL FINE AND GOOD, BUT...
...ARE THE CITIZENS OF THE SAME MIND AS THE GOVERNMENT?
I CAN'T REALLY TELL.
IT'S A STRANGE DISTRICT...
TELL ME AGAIN... WHERE WERE YOU BEFORE HERE?
IN DOWA.
HOW DO THEY COMPARE?

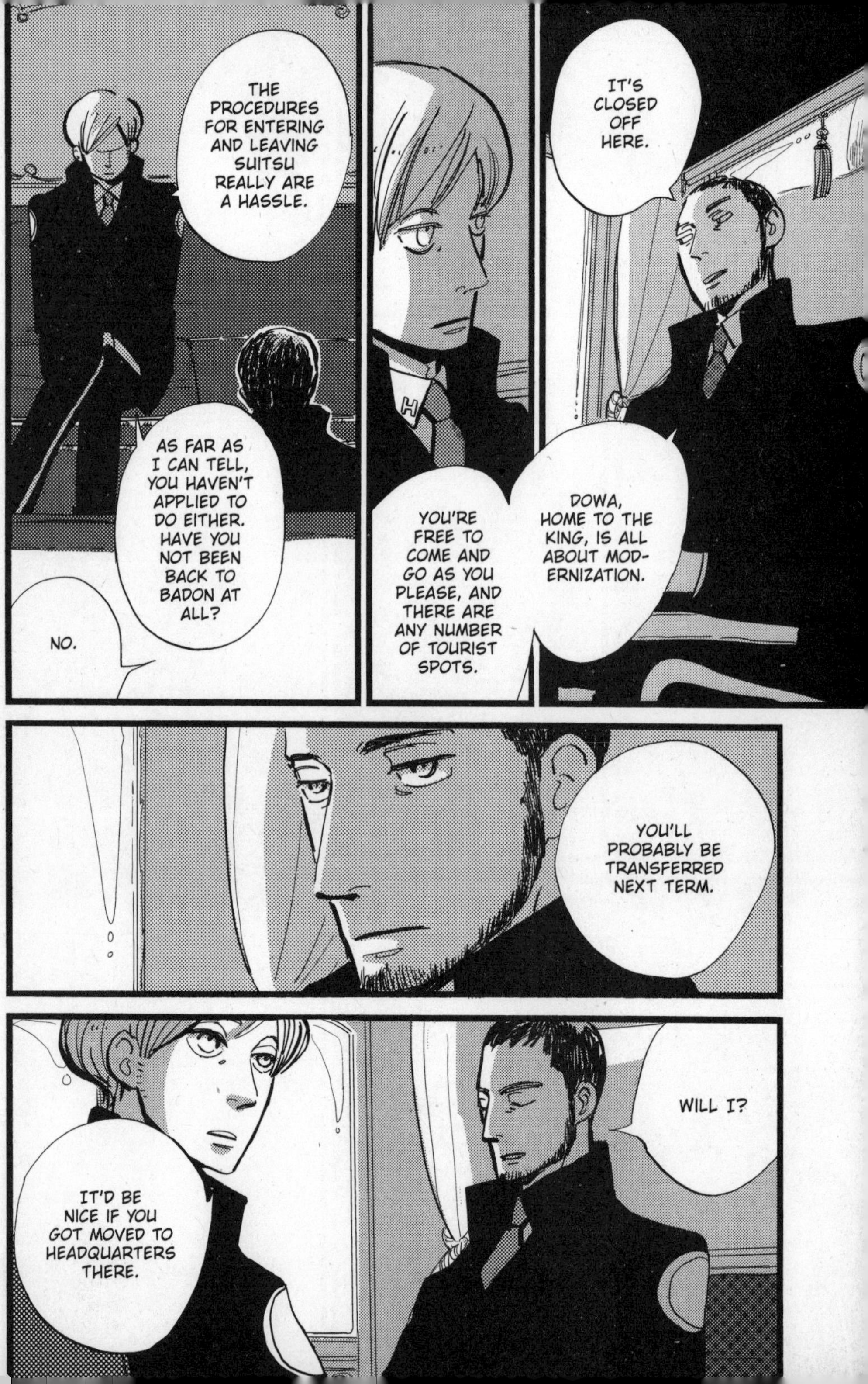
IT'S CLOSED OFF HERE.
DOWA, HOME TO THE KING, IS ALL ABOUT MOD-ERNIZATION.
YOU'RE FREE TO COME AND GO AS YOU PLEASE, AND THERE ARE ANY NUMBER OF TOURIST SPOTS.
THE PROCEDURES FOR ENTERING AND LEAVING SUITSU REALLY ARE A HASSLE.
AS FAR AS I CAN TELL, YOU HAVEN'T APPLIED TO DO EITHER. HAVE YOU NOT BEEN BACK TO BADON AT ALL?
NO.
YOU'LL PROBABLY BE TRANSFERRED NEXT TERM.
WILL I?
IT'D BE NICE IF YOU GOT MOVED TO HEADQUARTERS THERE.

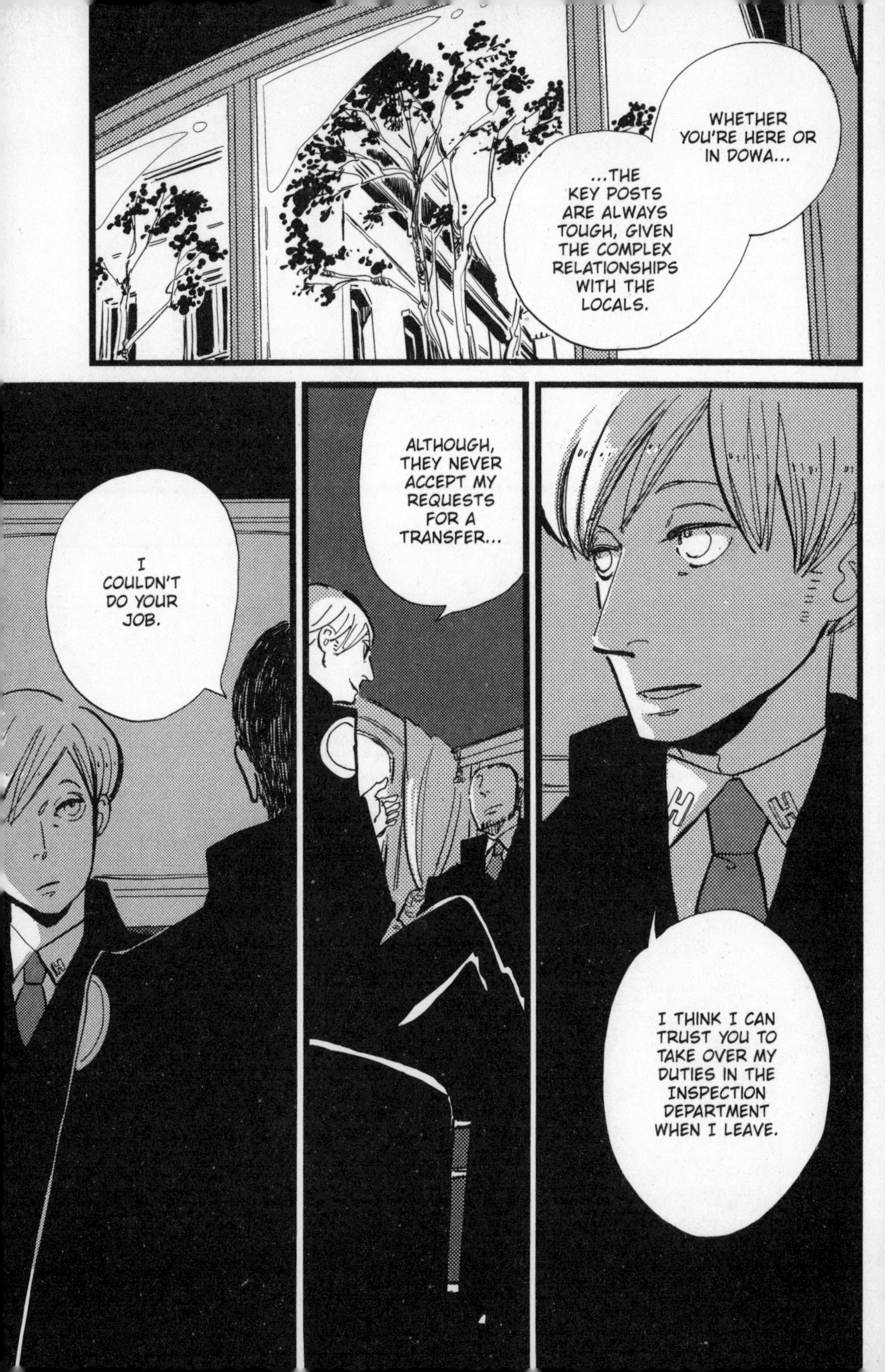
WHETHER YOU'RE HERE OR IN DOWA...
...THE KEY POSTS ARE ALWAYS TOUGH, GIVEN THE COMPLEX RELATIONSHIPS WITH THE LOCALS.
I THINK I CAN TRUST YOU TO TAKE OVER MY DUTIES IN THE INSPECTION DEPARTMENT WHEN I LEAVE.
ALTHOUGH, THEY NEVER ACCEPT MY REQUESTS FOR A TRANSFER...
I COULDN'T DO YOUR JOB.

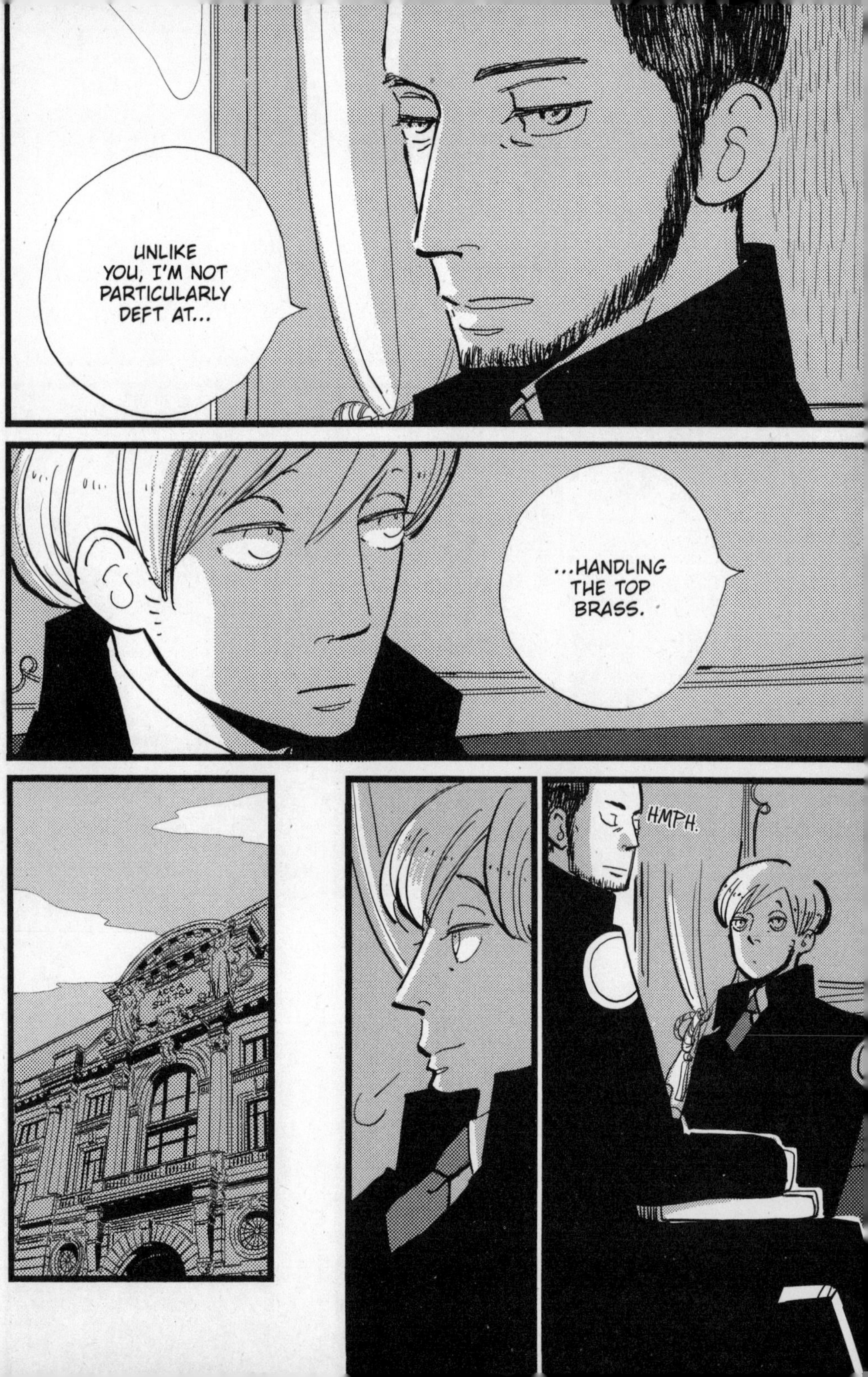
UNLIKE YOU, I'M NOT PARTICULARLY DEFT AT...
...HANDLING THE TOP BRASS.
HMPH.

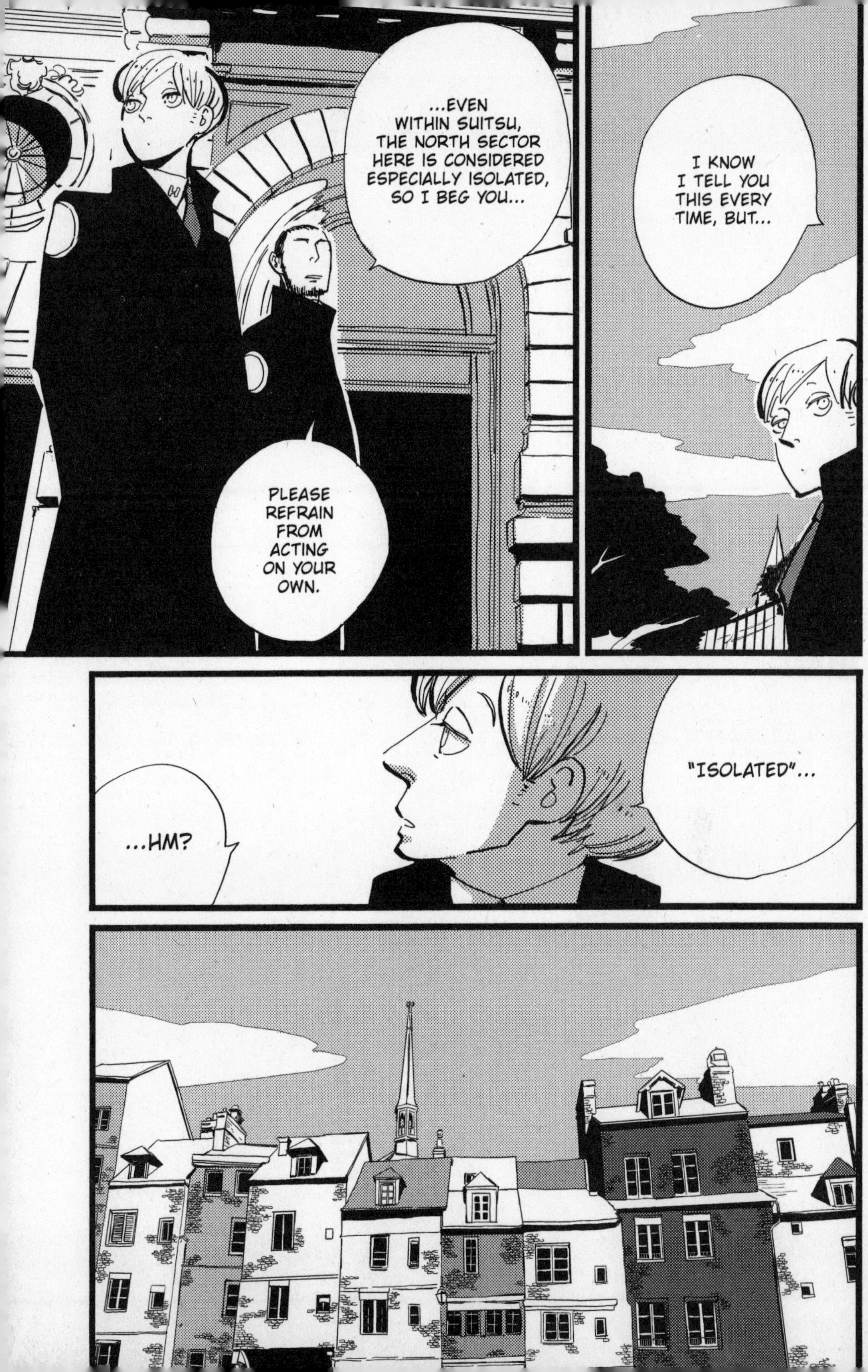
I KNOW I TELL YOU THIS EVERY TIME, BUT...
...EVEN WITHIN SUITSU, THE NORTH SECTOR HERE IS CONSIDERED ESPECIALLY ISOLATED, SO I BEG YOU...
PLEASE REFRAIN FROM ACTING ON YOUR OWN.
"ISOLATED"...
...HM?

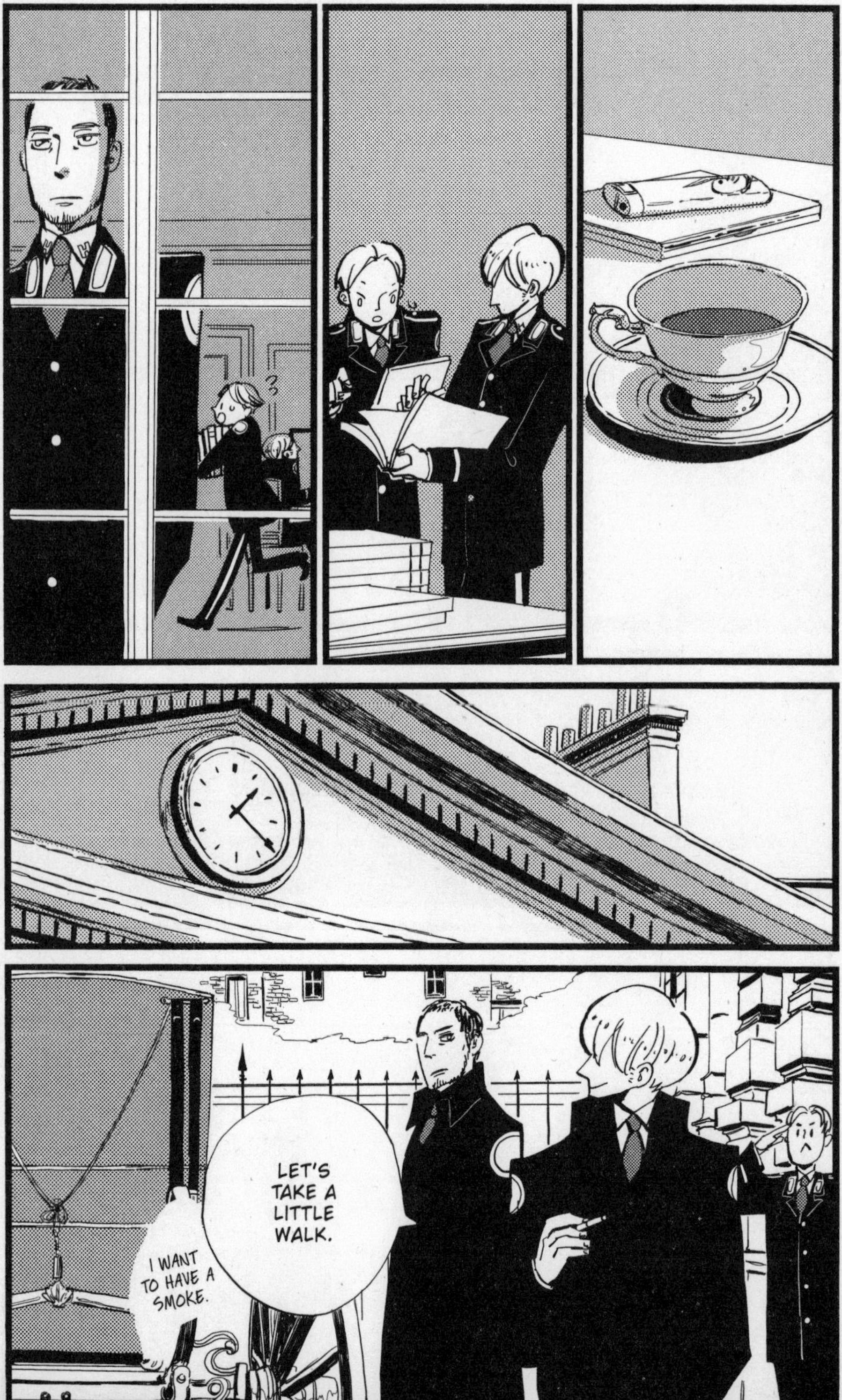
LET'S TAKE A LITTLE WALK.
I WANT TO HAVE A SMOKE.

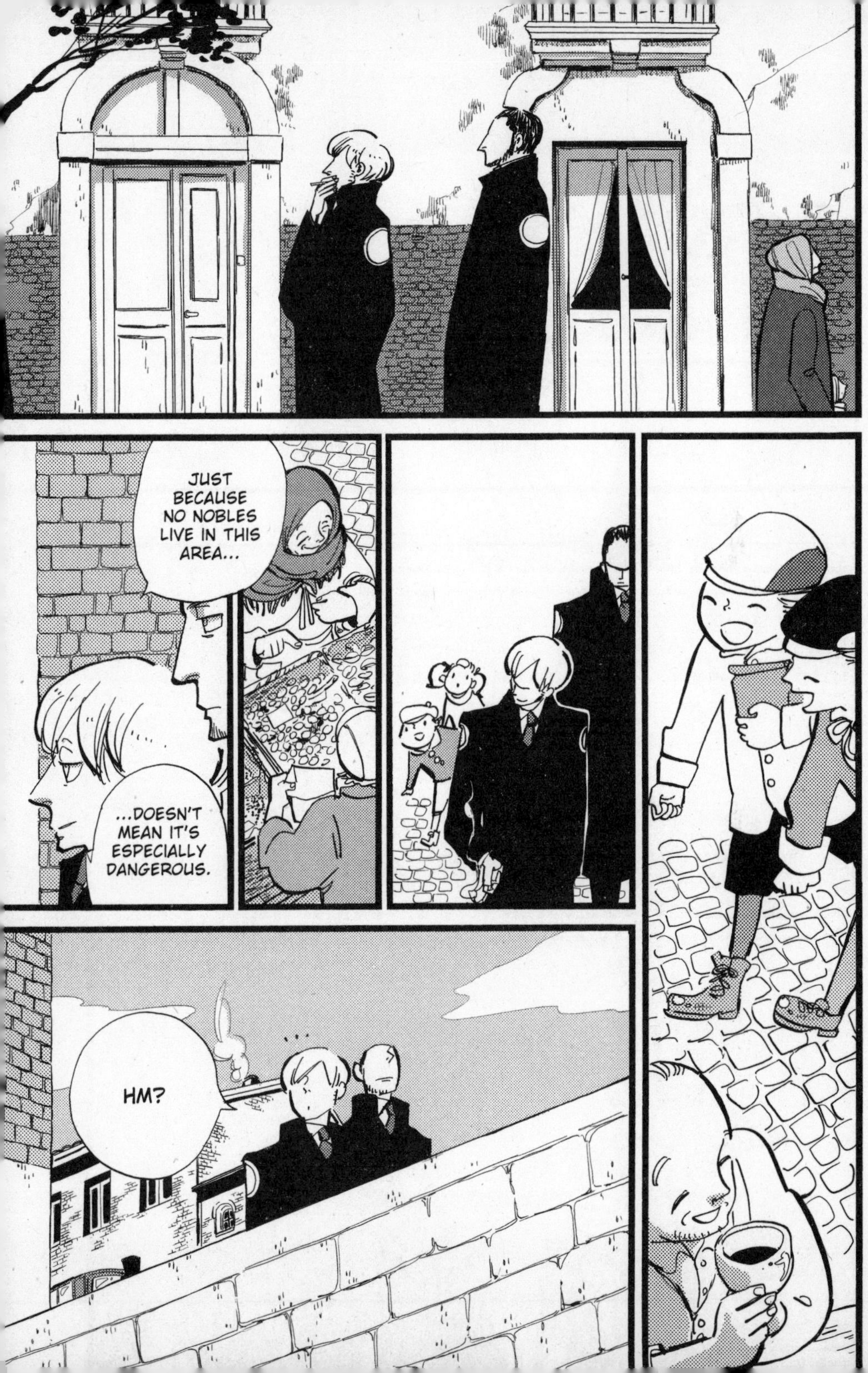
JUST BECAUSE NO NOBLES LIVE IN THIS AREA...
...DOESN'T MEAN IT'S ESPECIALLY DANGEROUS.
HM?

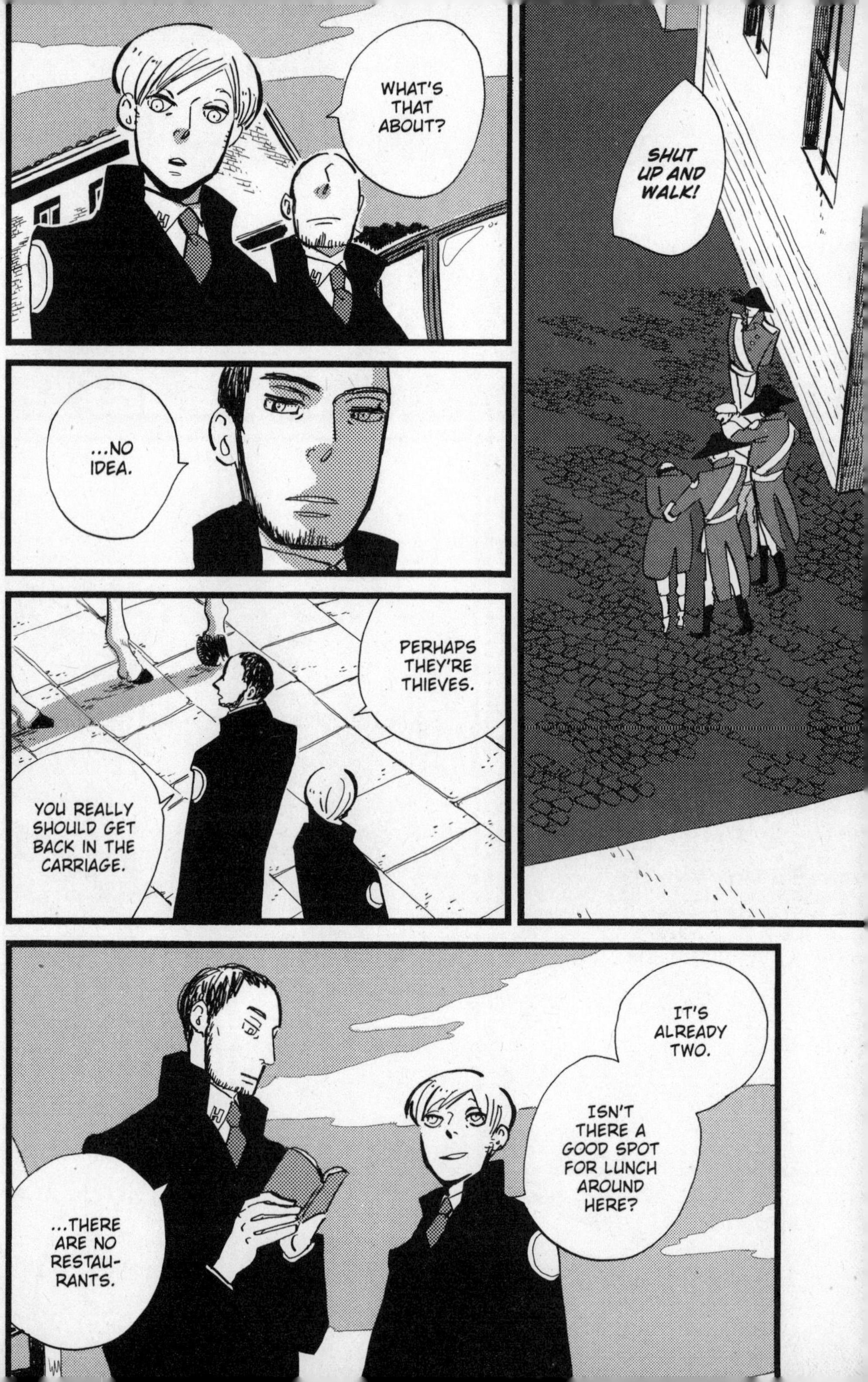
SHUT UP AND WALK!
WHAT'S THAT ABOUT?
...NO IDEA.
PERHAPS THEY'RE THIEVES.
YOU REALLY SHOULD GET BACK IN THE CARRIAGE.
IT'S ALREADY TWO.
ISN'T THERE A GOOD SPOT FOR LUNCH AROUND HERE?
...THERE ARE NO RESTAURANTS.

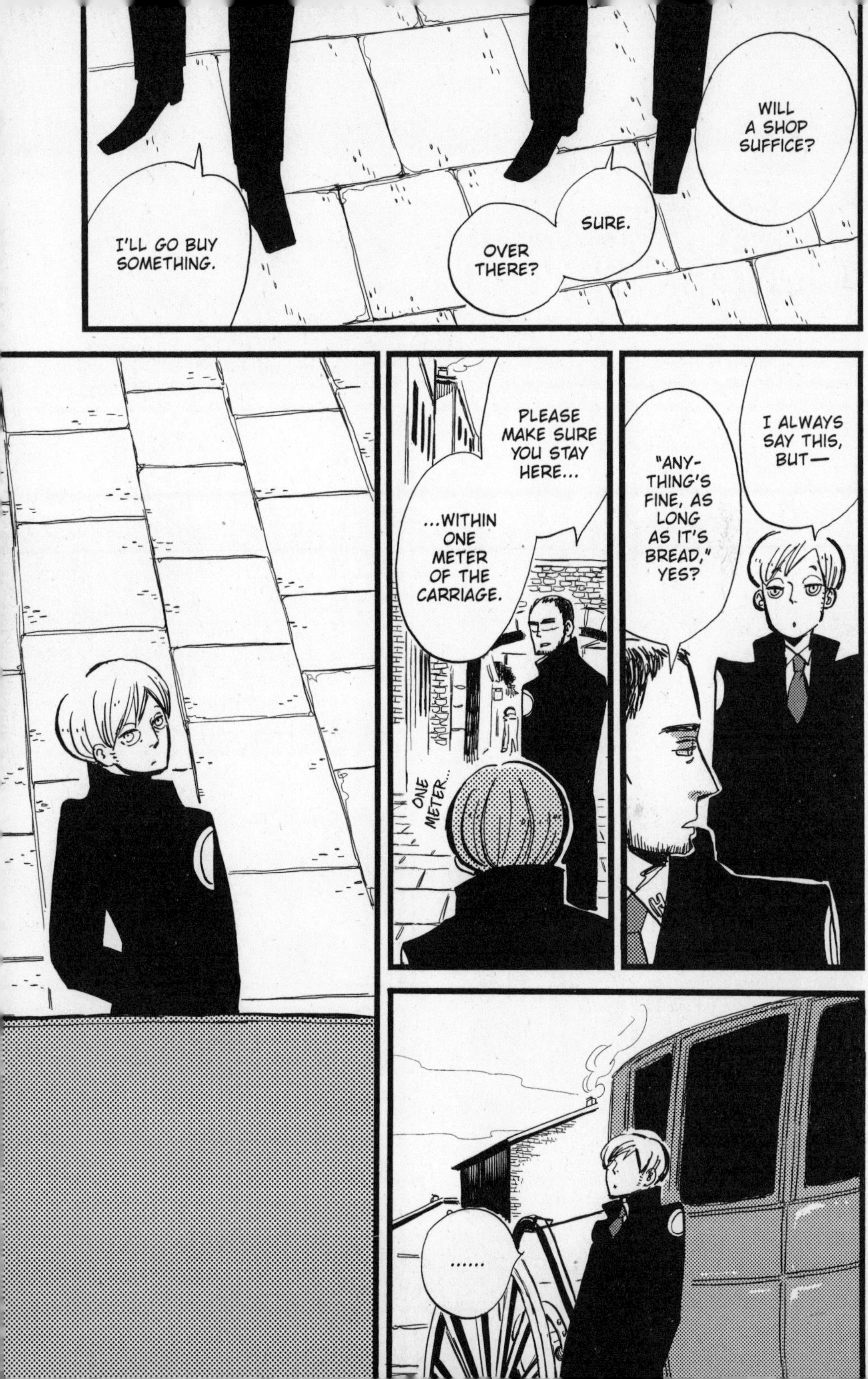
WILL A SHOP SUFFICE?
SURE.
OVER THERE?
I'LL GO BUY SOMETHING.
I ALWAYS SAY THIS, BUT—
"ANY-THING'S FINE, AS LONG AS IT'S BREAD," YES?
PLEASE MAKE SURE YOU STAY HERE...
...WITHIN ONE METER OF THE CARRIAGE.
ONE METER...
......

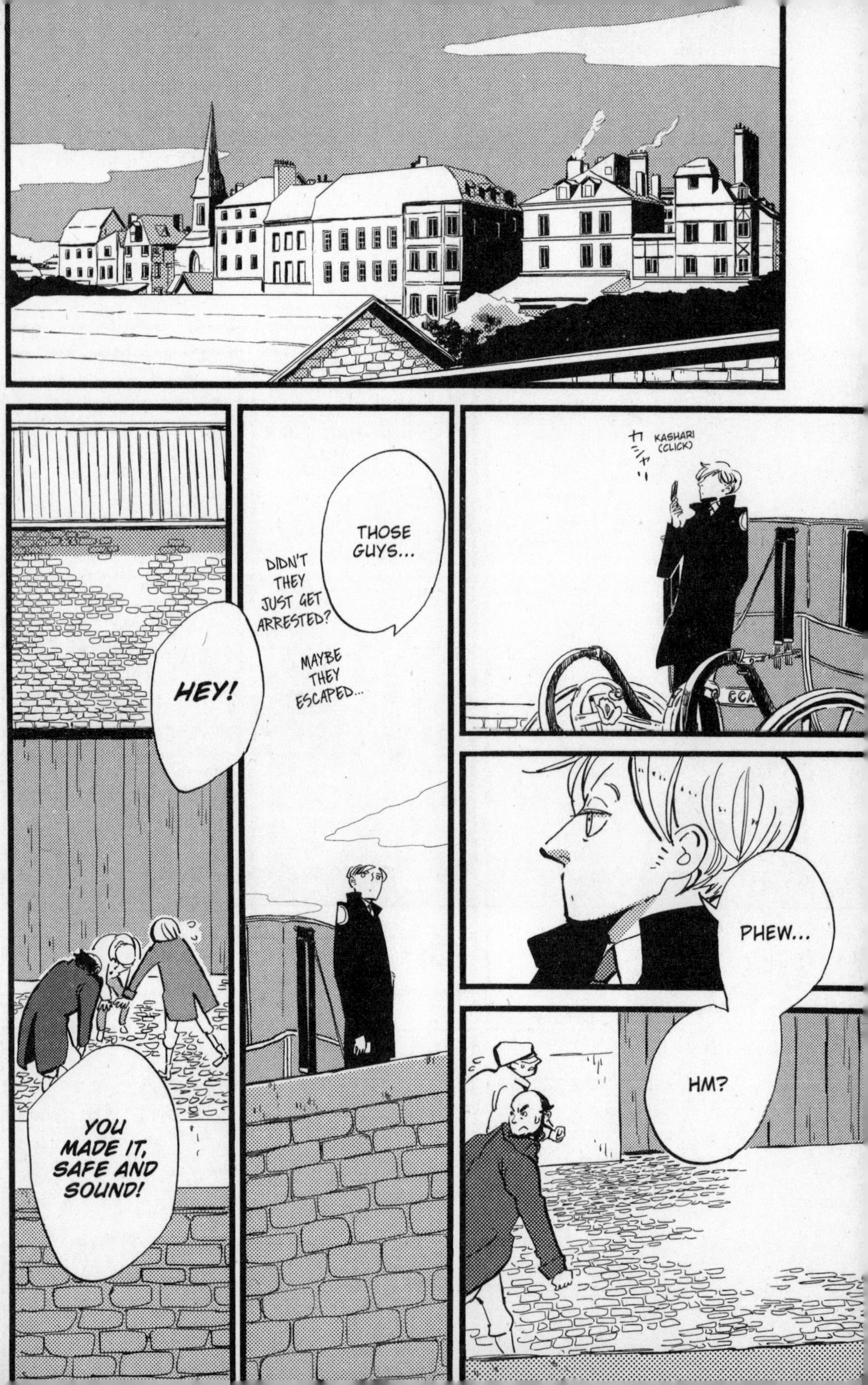
KASHARI (CLICK)
PHEW...
HM?
THOSE GUYS...
DIDN'T THEY JUST GET ARRESTED?
MAYBE THEY ESCAPED...
HEY!
YOU MADE IT, SAFE AND SOUND!

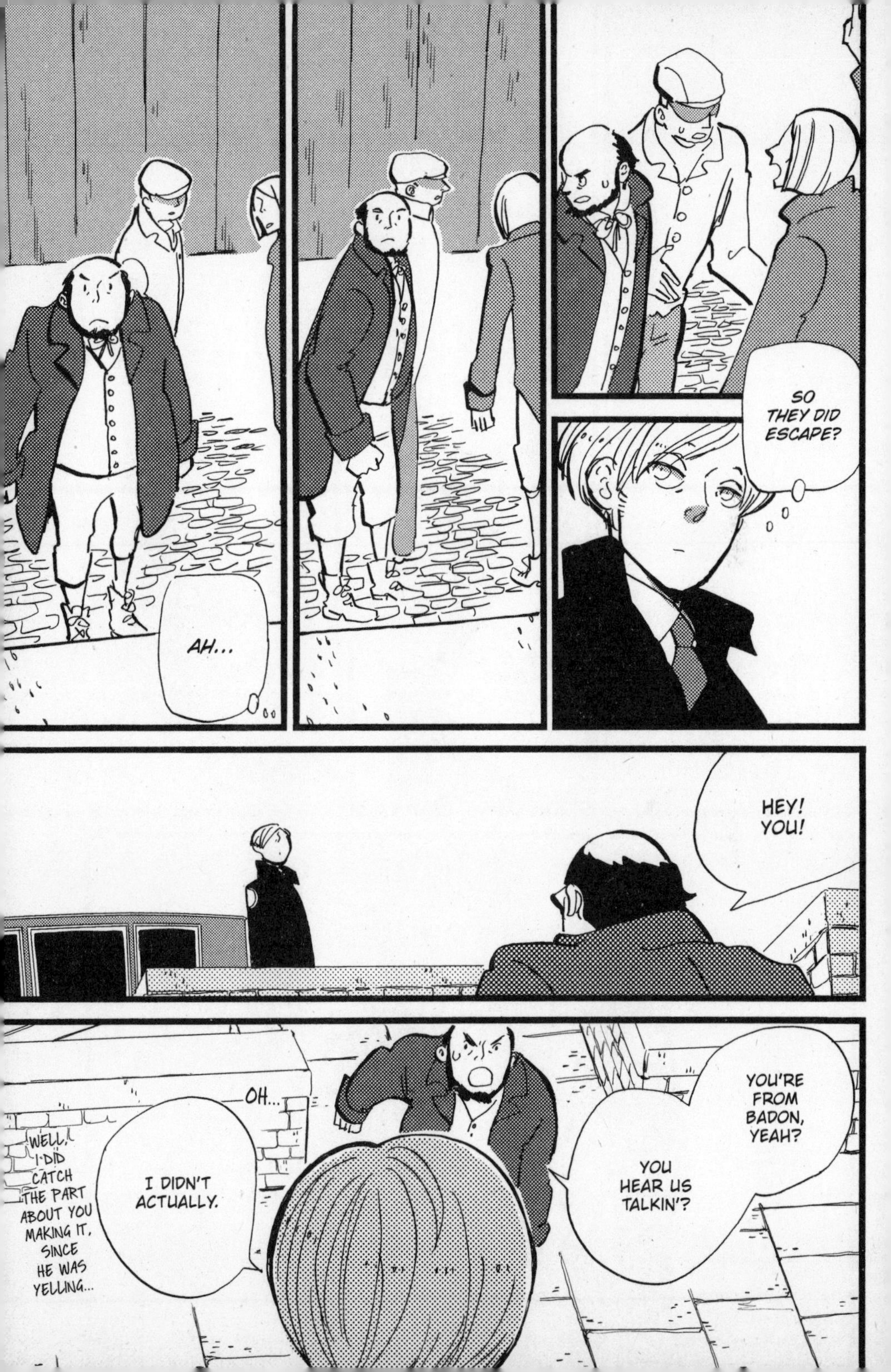
SO THEY DID ESCAPE?
AH...
HEY! YOU!
YOU'RE FROM BADON, YEAH?
YOU HEAR US TALKIN'?
OH...
I DIDN'T ACTUALLY.
WELL, I DID CATCH THE PART ABOUT YOU MAKING IT, SINCE HE WAS YELLING...

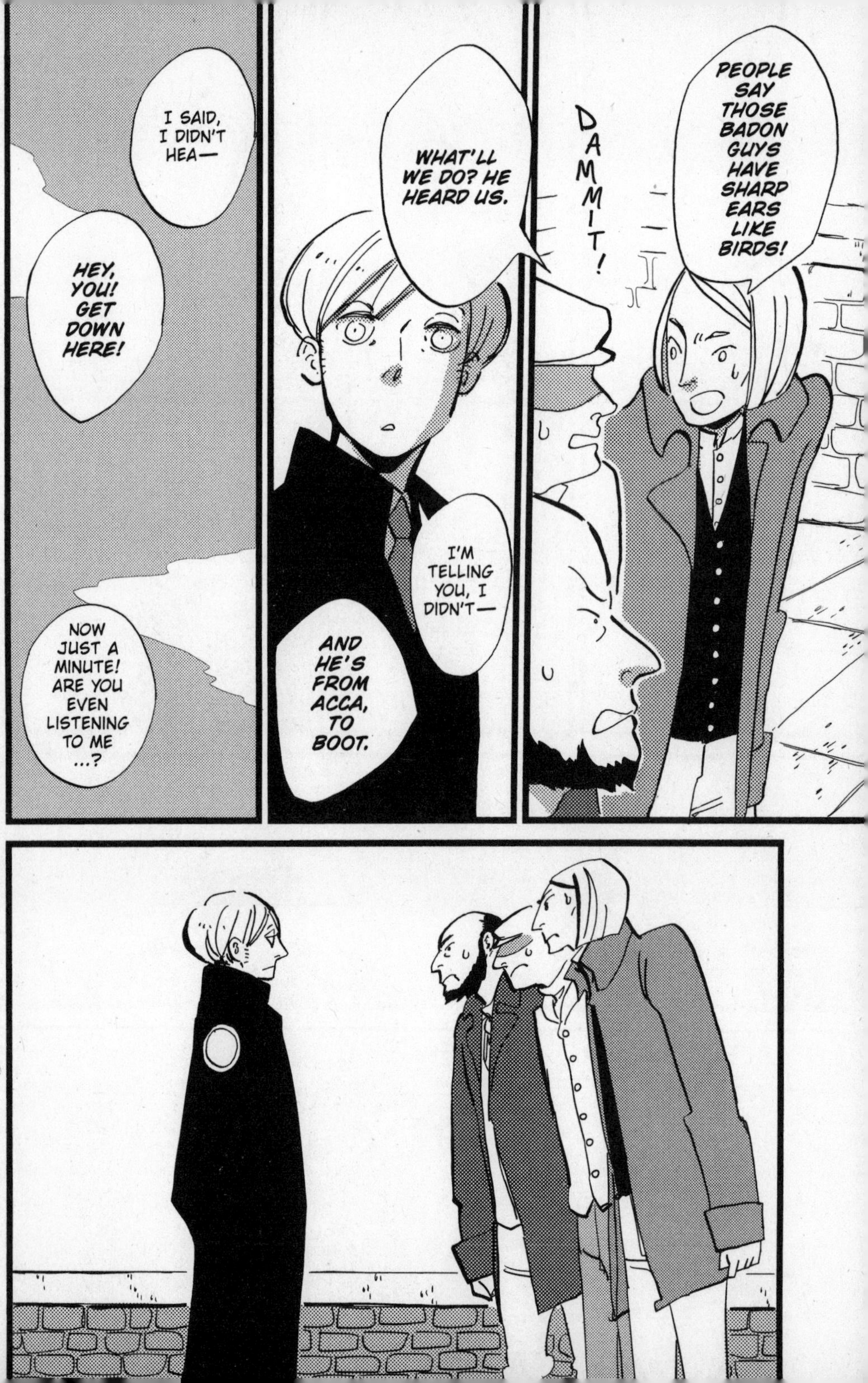
PEOPLE SAY THOSE BADON GUYS HAVE SHARP EARS LIKE BIRDS!
DAMMIT!
WHAT'LL WE DO? HE HEARD US.
I'M TELLING YOU, I DIDN'T—
AND HE'S FROM ACCA, TO BOOT.
I SAID, I DIDN'T HEA—
HEY, YOU! GET DOWN HERE!
NOW JUST A MINUTE! ARE YOU EVEN LISTENING TO ME ...?

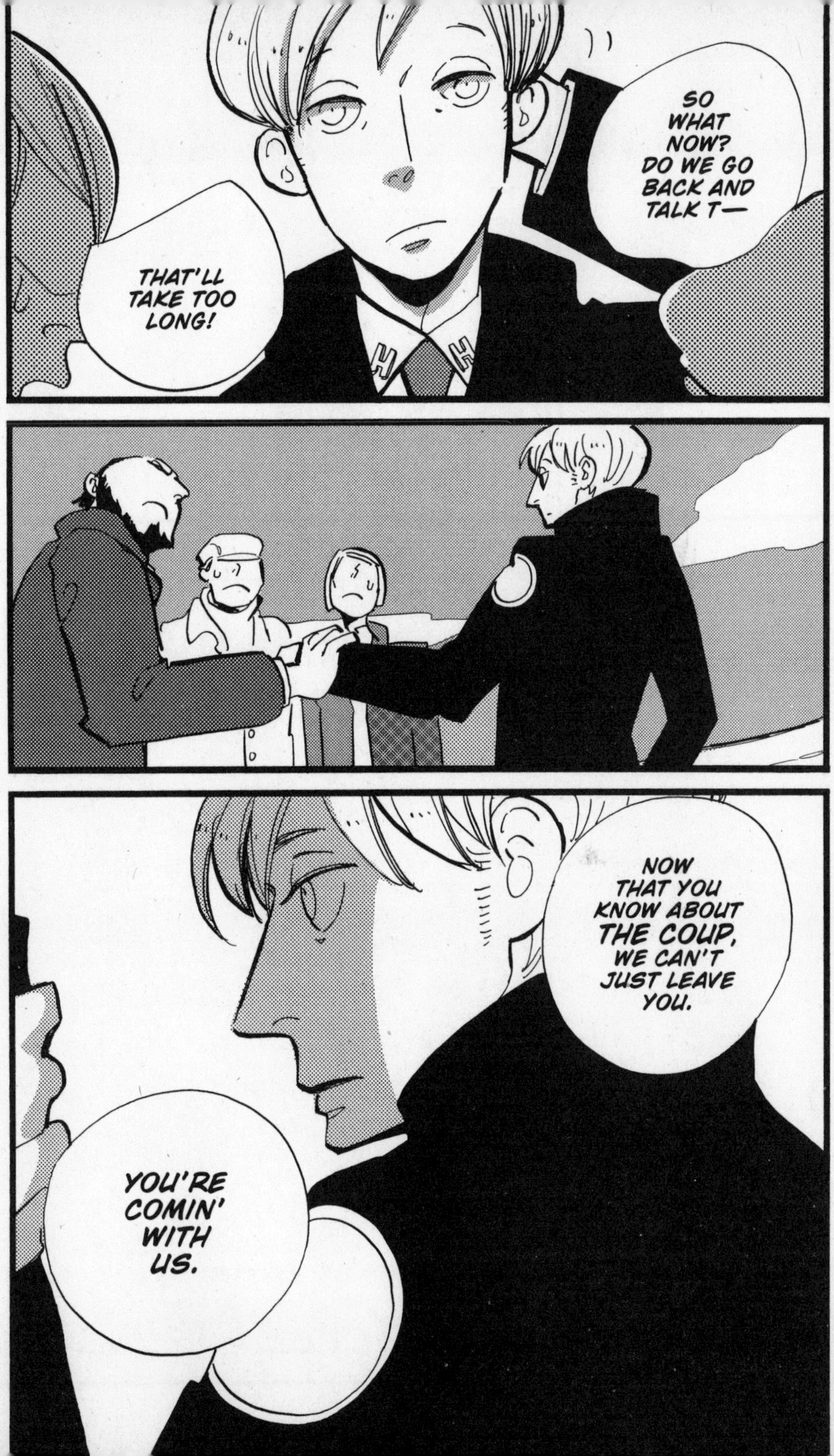
SO WHAT NOW? DO WE GO BACK AND TALK T—
THAT'LL TAKE TOO LONG!
NOW THAT YOU KNOW ABOUT THE COUP, WE CAN'T JUST LEAVE YOU.
YOU'RE COMIN' WITH US.

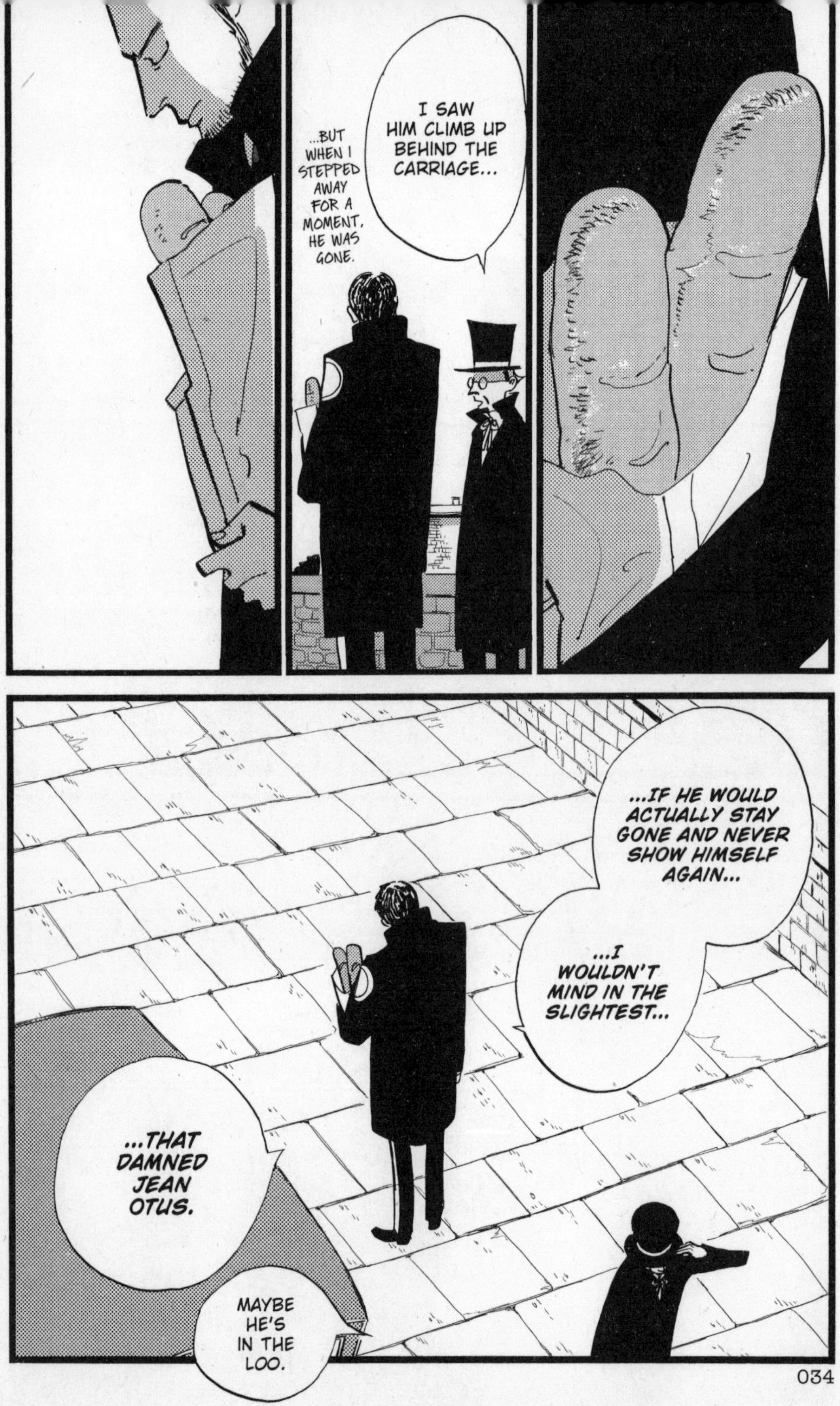
I SAW HIM CLIMB UP BEHIND THE CARRIAGE...
...BUT WHEN I STEPPED AWAY FOR A MOMENT, HE WAS GONE.
...IF HE WOULD ACTUALLY STAY GONE AND NEVER SHOW HIMSELF AGAIN...
...I WOULDN'T MIND IN THE SLIGHTEST...
...THAT DAMNED JEAN OTUS.
MAYBE HE'S IN THE LOO.

CHAPTER 12

A Surprise Encounter on the Streets of Suitsu

ACCA 13 TERRITORY INSPECTION DEPT

PASS

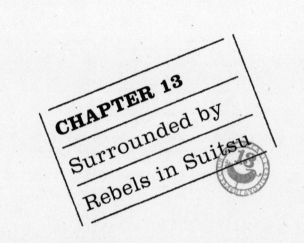

CHAPTER 13

Surrounded by
Rebels in Suitsu

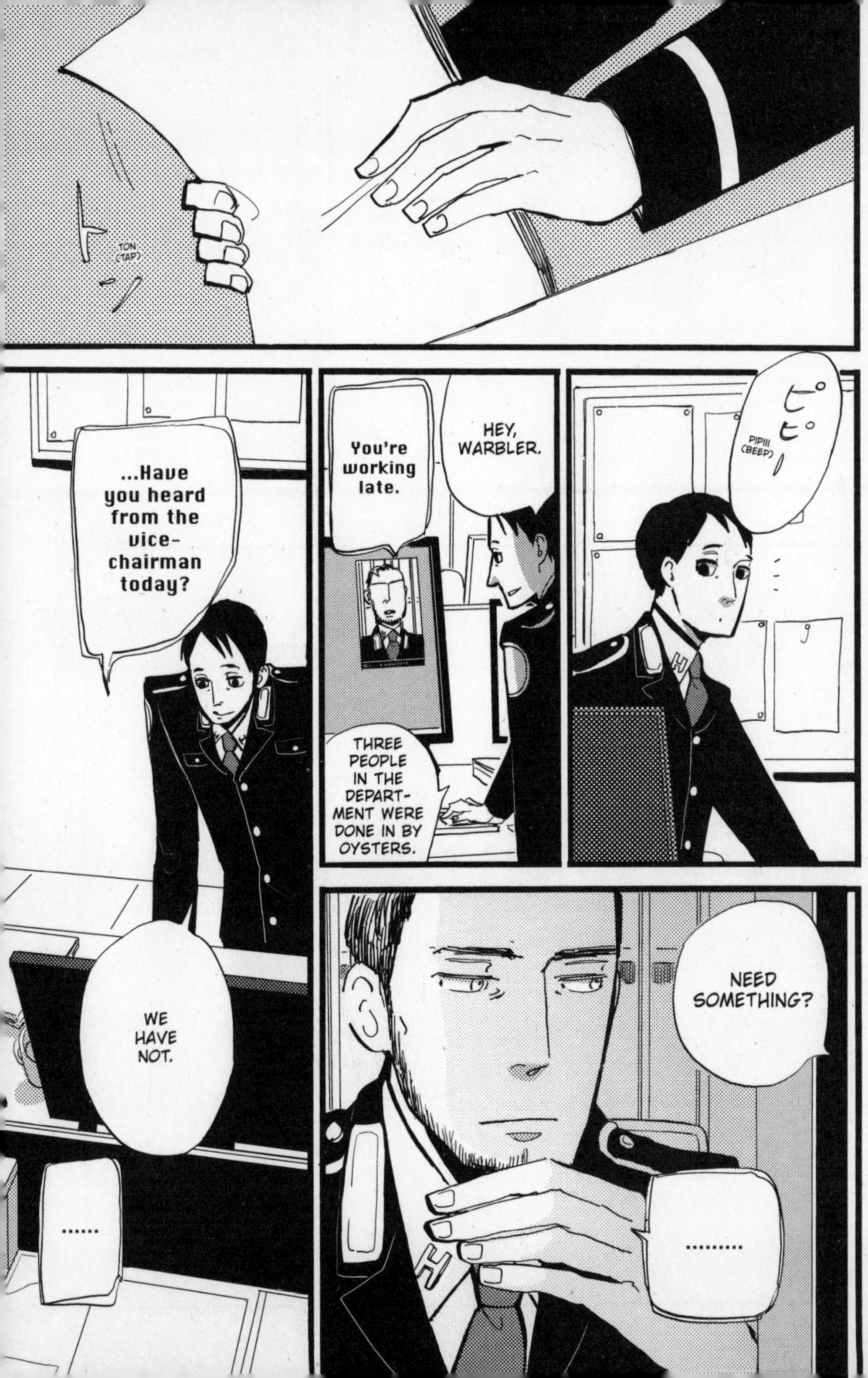
TON (TAP)
ピピー
PIPIII (BEEP)
HEY, WARBLER.
You're working late.
THREE PEOPLE IN THE DEPART-MENT WERE DONE IN BY OYSTERS.
NEED SOMETHING?
....
...Have you heard from the vice-chairman today?
WE HAVE NOT.
......

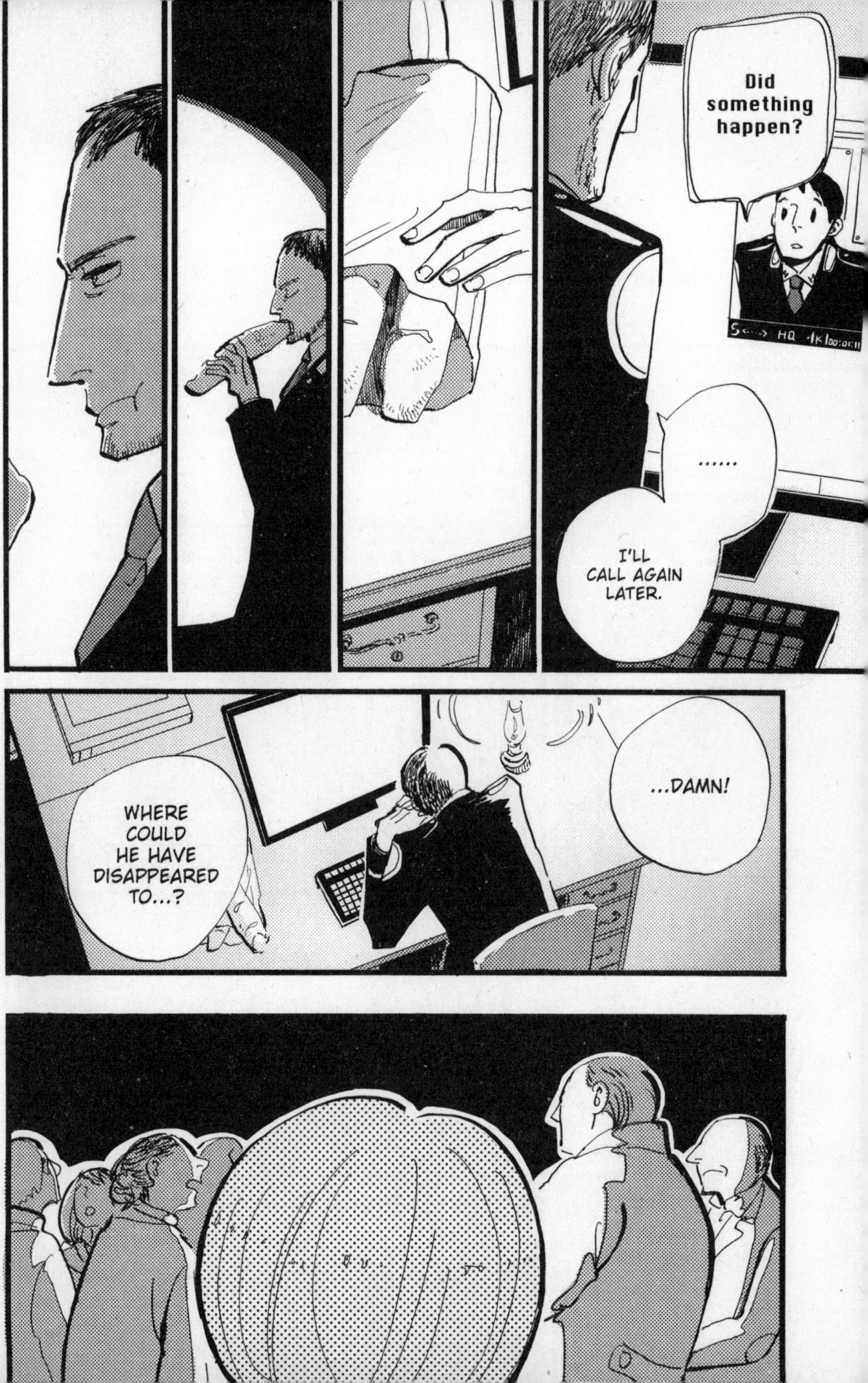
Did something happen?
......
I'LL CALL AGAIN LATER.
...DAMN!
WHERE COULD HE HAVE DISAPPEARED TO...?

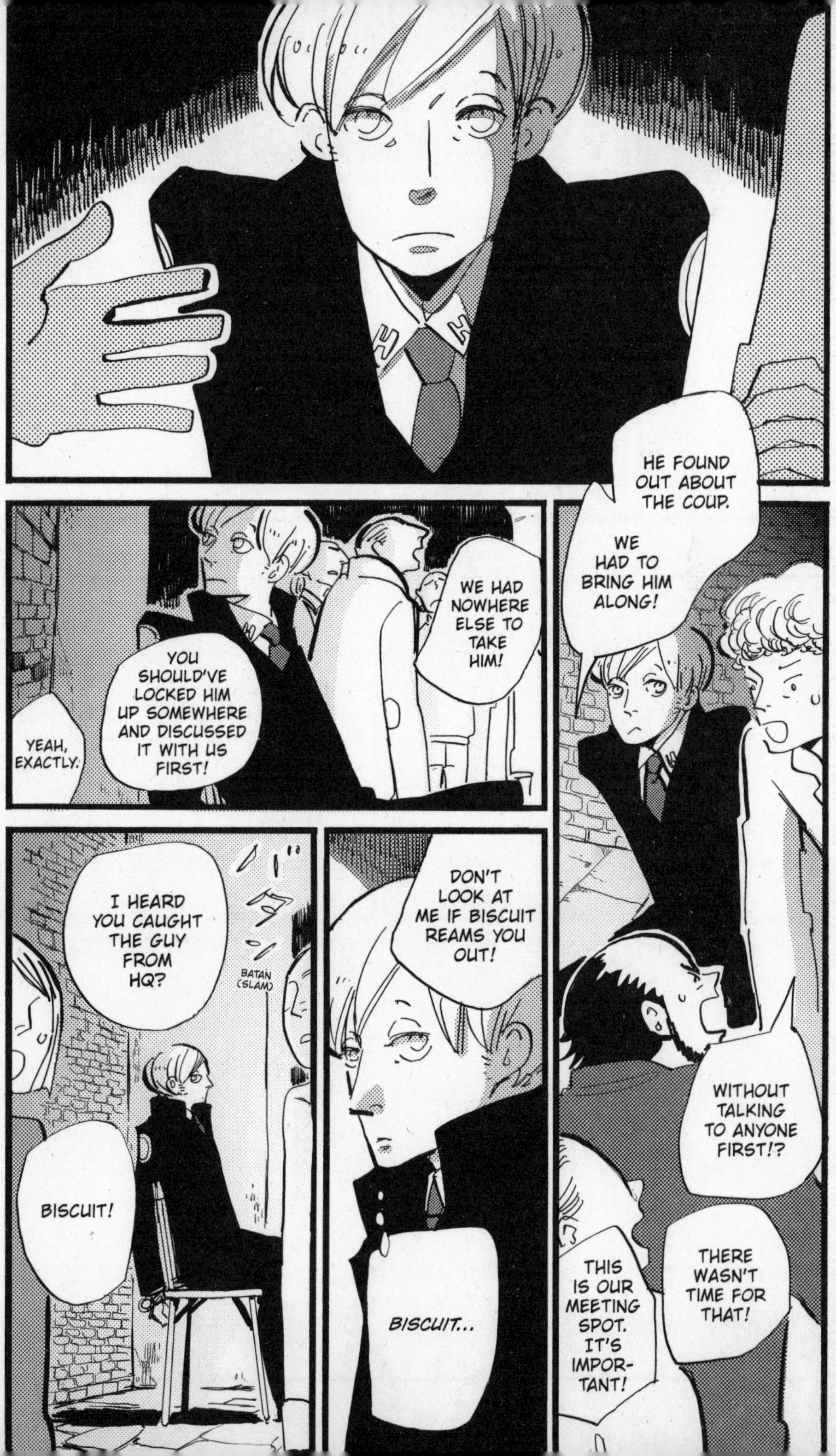
HE FOUND OUT ABOUT THE COUP.
WE HAD TO BRING HIM ALONG!
WITHOUT TALKING TO ANYONE FIRST!?
THERE WASN'T TIME FOR THAT!
THIS IS OUR MEETING SPOT. IT'S IMPOR-TANT!
WE HAD NOWHERE ELSE TO TAKE HIM!
YOU SHOULD'VE LOCKED HIM UP SOMEWHERE AND DISCUSSED IT WITH US FIRST!
YEAH, EXACTLY.
DON'T LOOK AT ME IF BISCUIT REAMS YOU OUT!
BISCUIT...
BATAN (SLAM)
I HEARD YOU CAUGHT THE GUY FROM HQ?
BISCUIT!

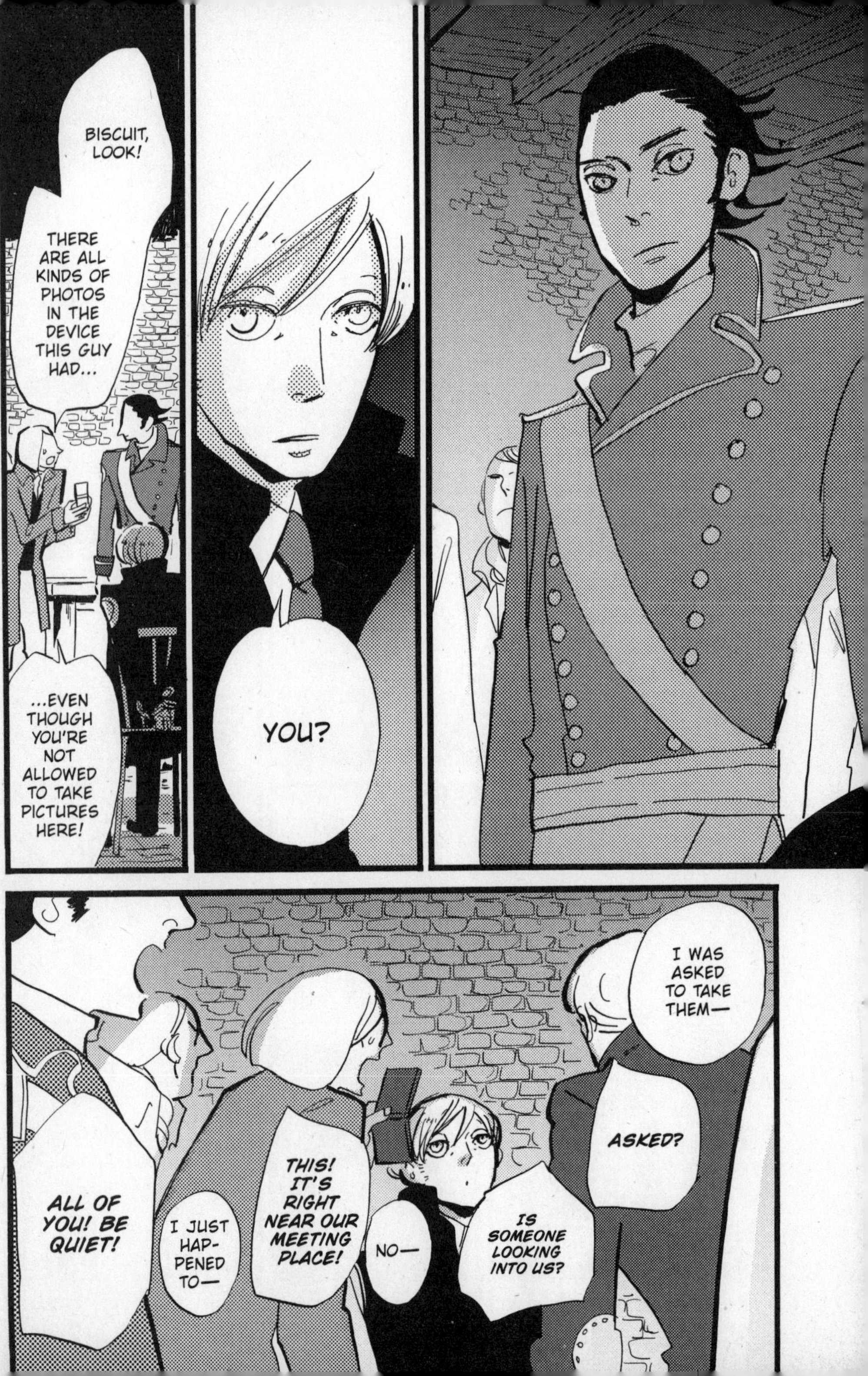
YOU?
BISCUIT, LOOK!
THERE ARE ALL KINDS OF PHOTOS IN THE DEVICE THIS GUY HAD...
...EVEN THOUGH YOU'RE NOT ALLOWED TO TAKE PICTURES HERE!
I WAS ASKED TO TAKE THEM—
ASKED?
IS SOMEONE LOOKING INTO US?
NO—
THIS! IT'S RIGHT NEAR OUR MEETING PLACE!
I JUST HAP-PENED TO—
ALL OF YOU! BE QUIET!

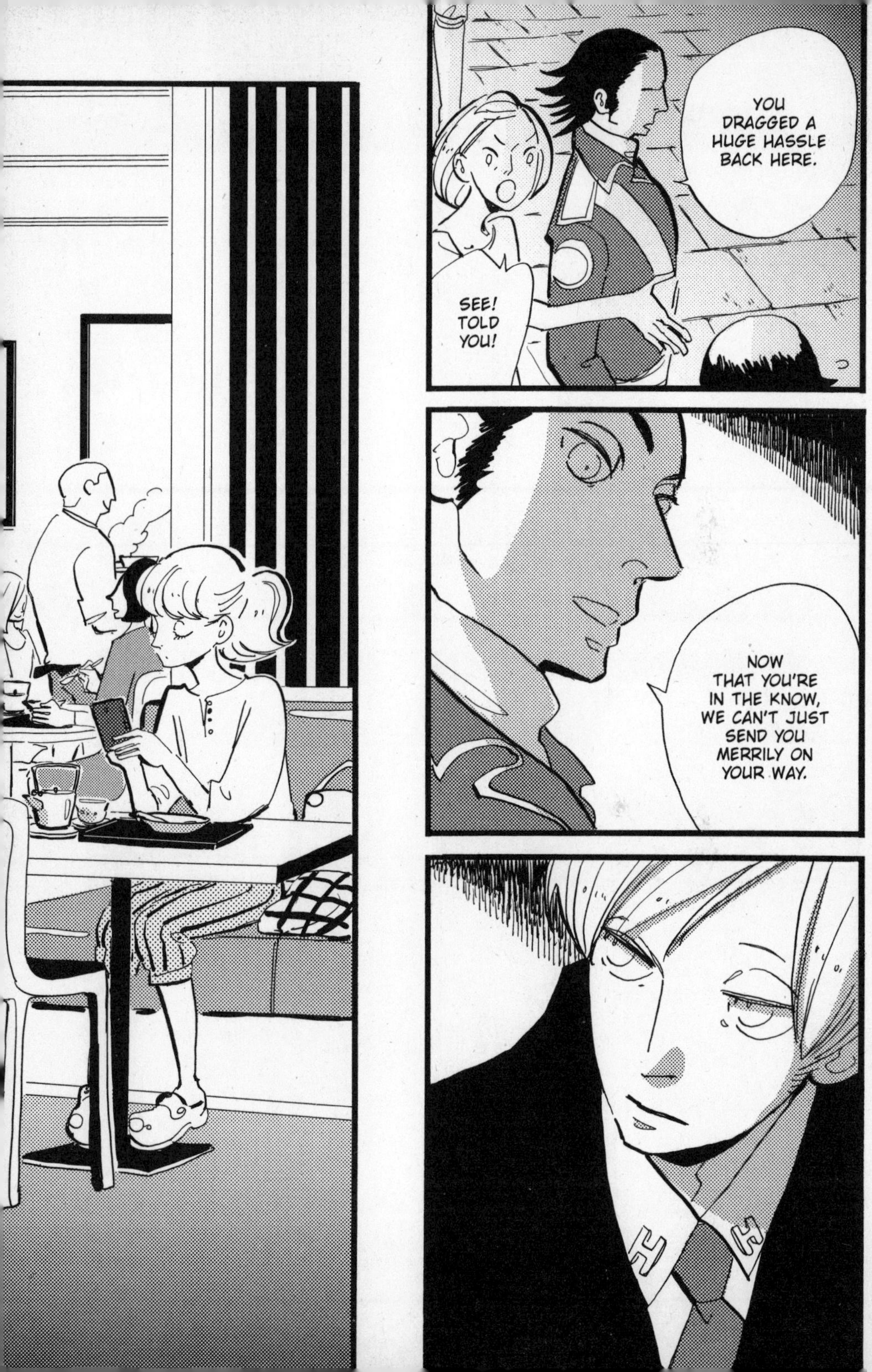
YOU DRAGGED A HUGE HASSLE BACK HERE.
SEE! TOLD YOU!
NOW THAT YOU'RE IN THE KNOW, WE CAN'T JUST SEND YOU MERRILY ON YOUR WAY.

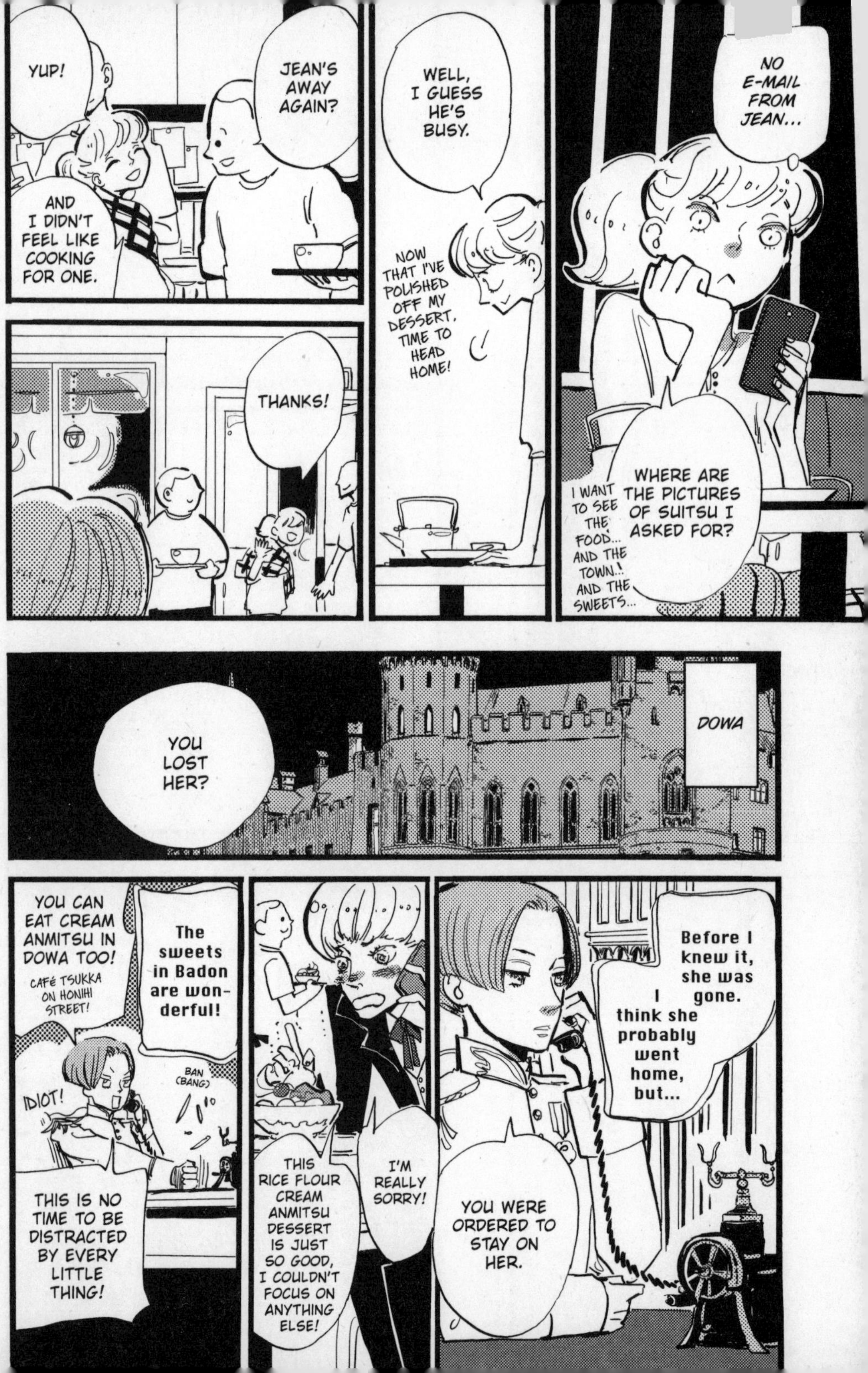
NO E-MAIL FROM JEAN...
WHERE ARE THE PICTURES OF SUITSU I ASKED FOR?
I WANT TO SEE THE FOOD... AND THE TOWN...! AND THE SWEETS...
WELL, I GUESS HE'S BUSY.
NOW THAT I'VE POLISHED OFF MY DESSERT, TIME TO HEAD HOME!
JEAN'S AWAY AGAIN?
YUP!
AND I DIDN'T FEEL LIKE COOKING FOR ONE.
THANKS!
DOWA
YOU LOST HER?
Before I knew it, she was gone. I think she probably went home, but...
YOU WERE ORDERED TO STAY ON HER.
I'M REALLY SORRY!
THIS RICE FLOUR CREAM ANMITSU DESSERT IS JUST SO GOOD, I COULDN'T FOCUS ON ANYTHING ELSE!
The sweets in Badon are wonderful!
YOU CAN EAT CREAM ANMITSU IN DOWA TOO!
CAFÉ TSUKKA ON HONIHI STREET!
BAN (BANG)
IDIOT!
THIS IS NO TIME TO BE DISTRACTED BY EVERY LITTLE THING!

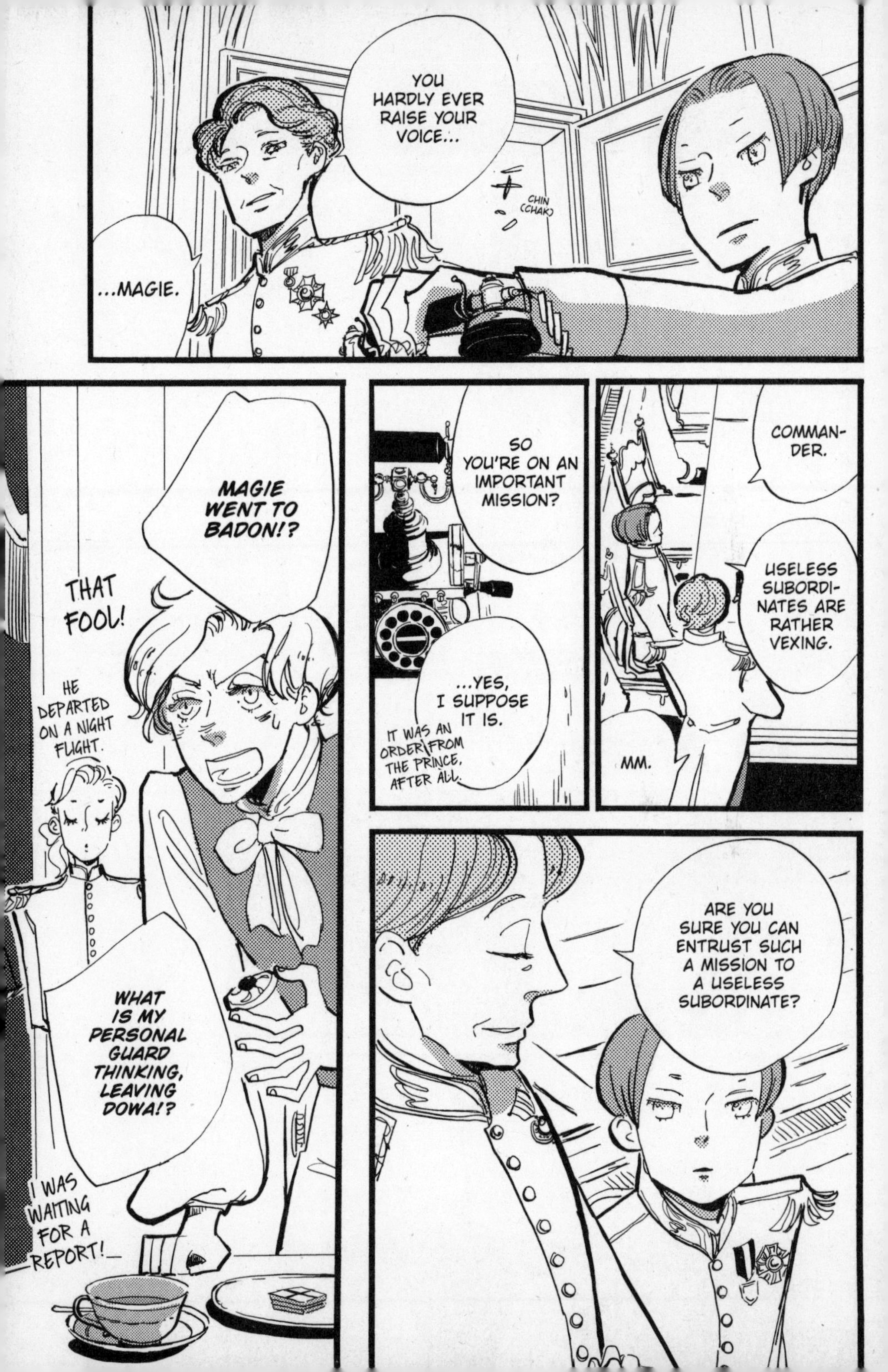
YOU HARDLY EVER RAISE YOUR VOICE...
CHIN (CHAK)
...MAGIE.
COMMANDER.
USELESS SUBORDINATES ARE RATHER VEXING.
MM.
SO YOU'RE ON AN IMPORTANT MISSION?
...YES, I SUPPOSE IT IS.
IT WAS AN ORDER FROM THE PRINCE, AFTER ALL.
ARE YOU SURE YOU CAN ENTRUST SUCH A MISSION TO A USELESS SUBORDINATE?
MAGIE WENT TO BADON!?
THAT FOOL!
HE DEPARTED ON A NIGHT FLIGHT.
WHAT IS MY PERSONAL GUARD THINKING, LEAVING DOWA!?
I WAS WAITING FOR A REPORT!

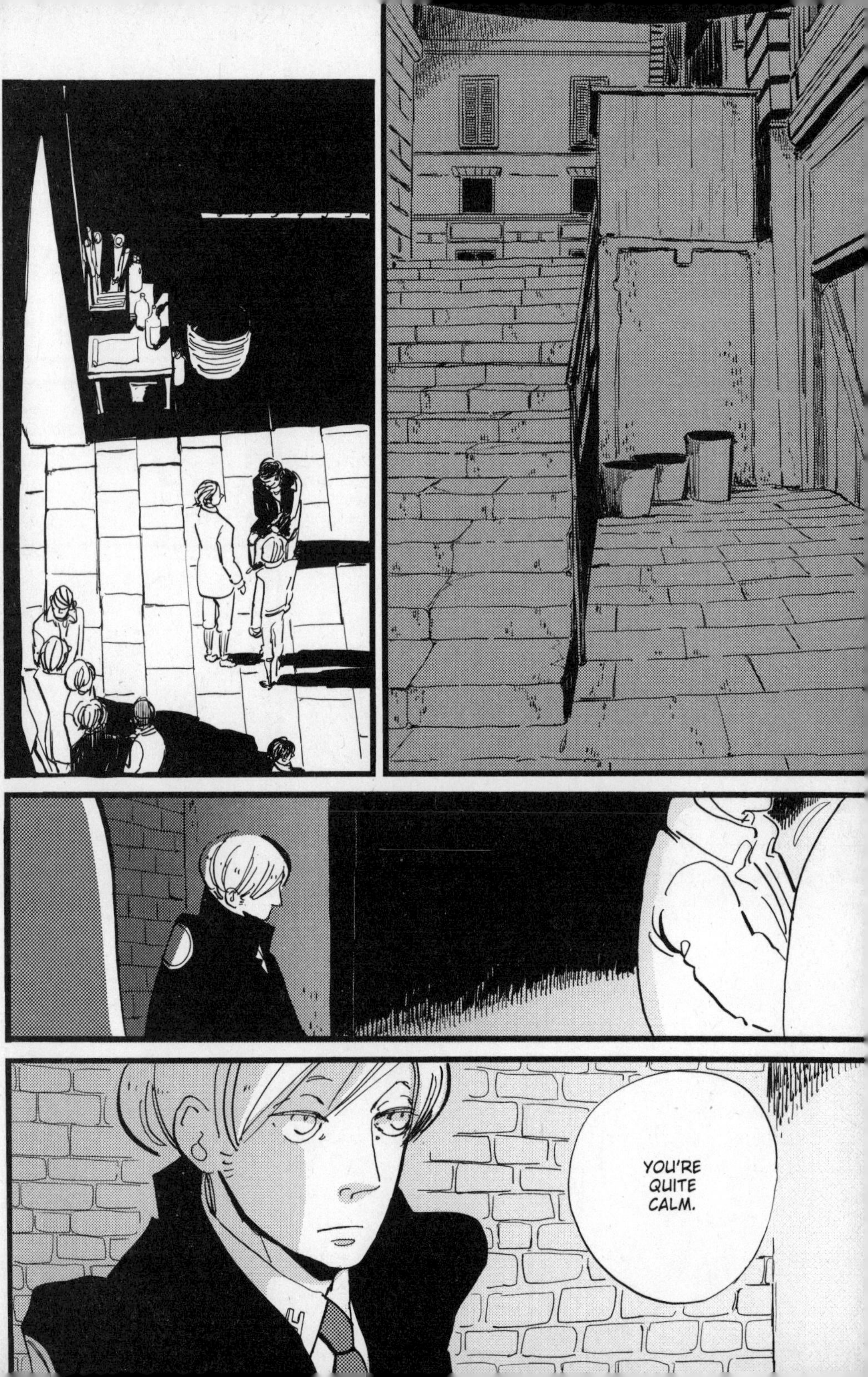
YOU'RE QUITE CALM.

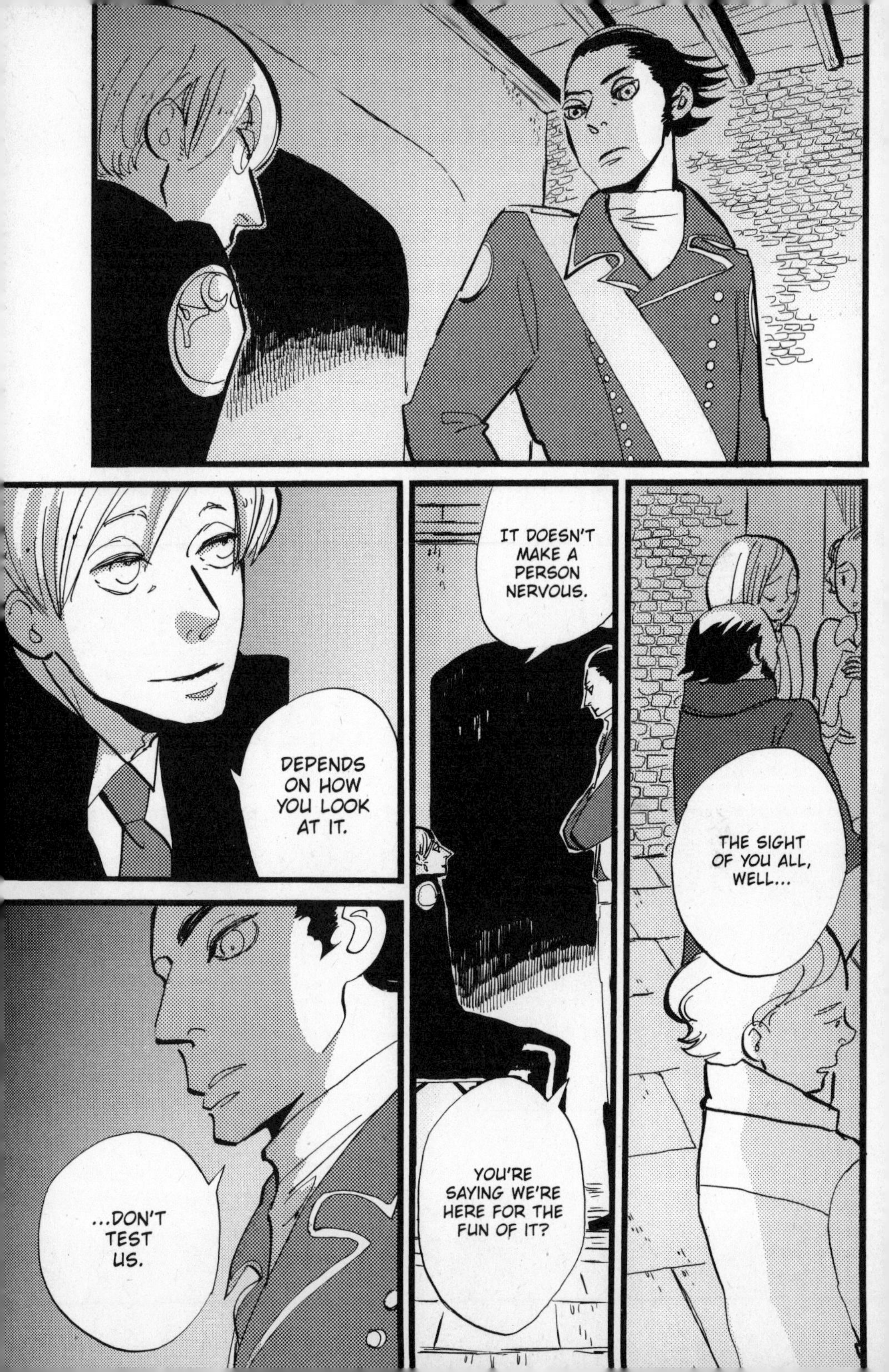
THE SIGHT OF YOU ALL, WELL...
IT DOESN'T MAKE A PERSON NERVOUS.
YOU'RE SAYING WE'RE HERE FOR THE FUN OF IT?
DEPENDS ON HOW YOU LOOK AT IT.
...DON'T TEST US.

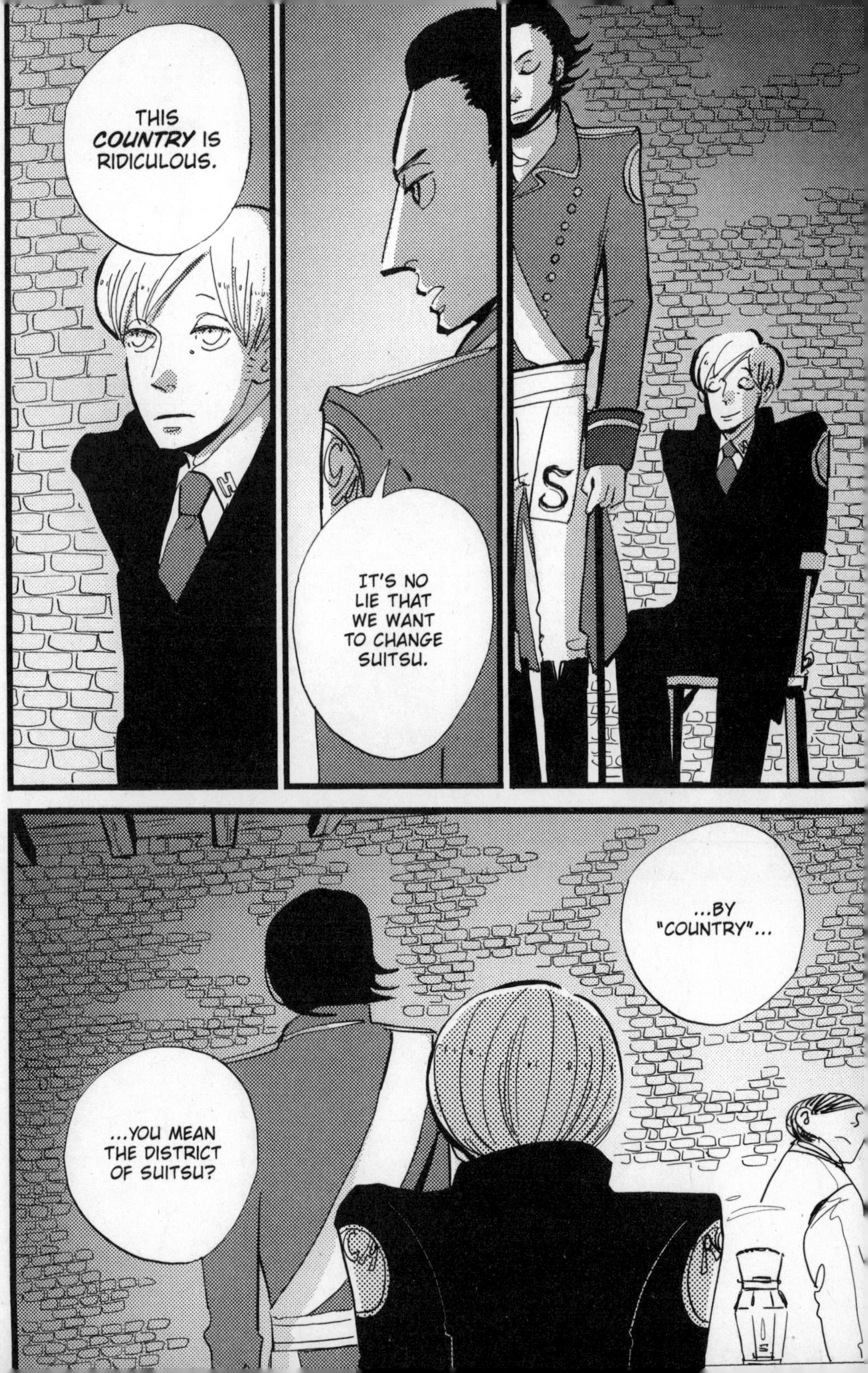
IT'S NO LIE THAT WE WANT TO CHANGE SUITSU.
THIS *COUNTRY* IS RIDICULOUS.
...BY "COUNTRY"...
...YOU MEAN THE DISTRICT OF SUITSU?

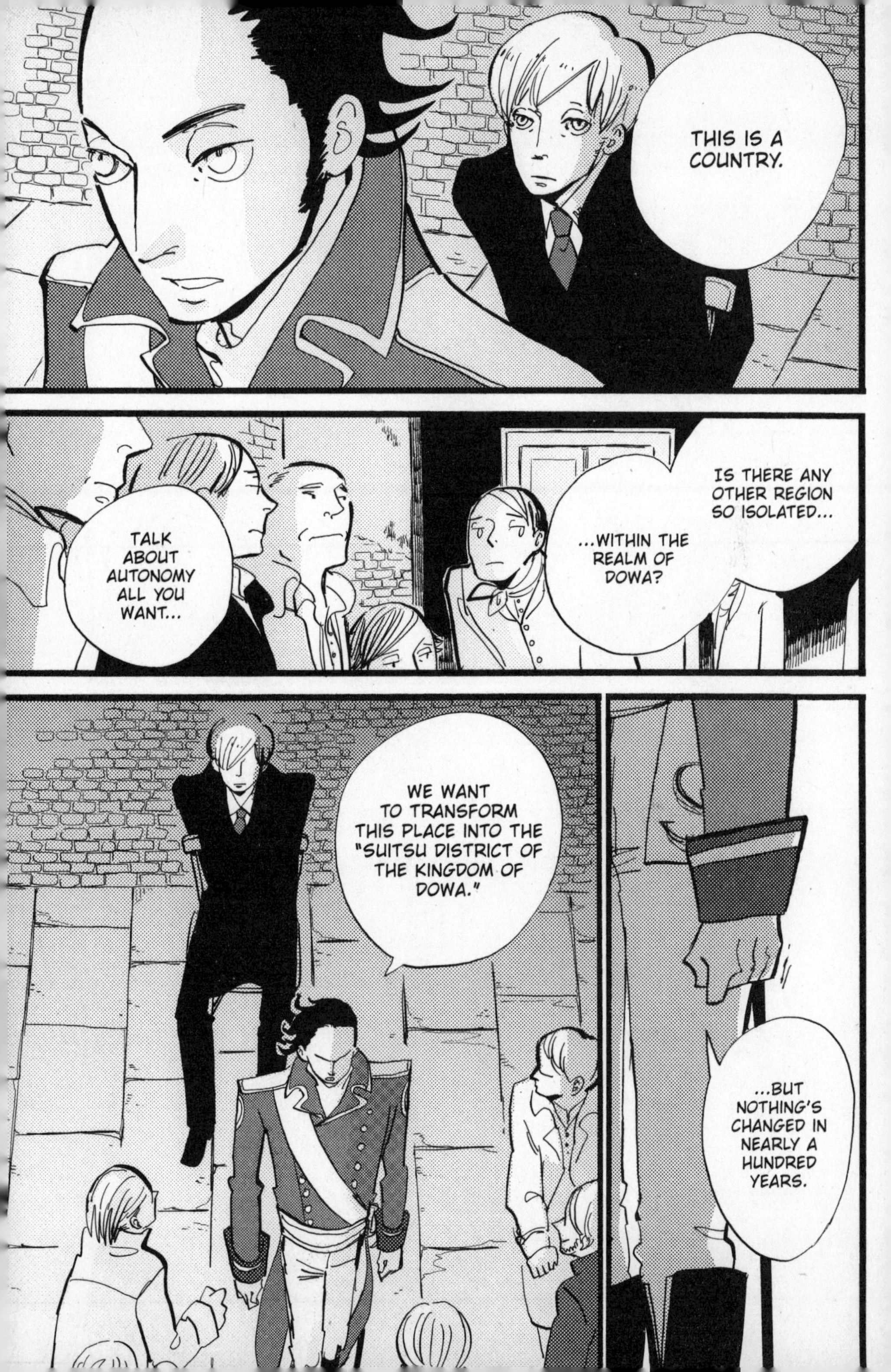
THIS IS A COUNTRY.
IS THERE ANY OTHER REGION SO ISOLATED...
...WITHIN THE REALM OF DOWA?
TALK ABOUT AUTONOMY ALL YOU WANT...
...BUT NOTHING'S CHANGED IN NEARLY A HUNDRED YEARS.
WE WANT TO TRANSFORM THIS PLACE INTO THE "SUITSU DISTRICT OF THE KINGDOM OF DOWA."

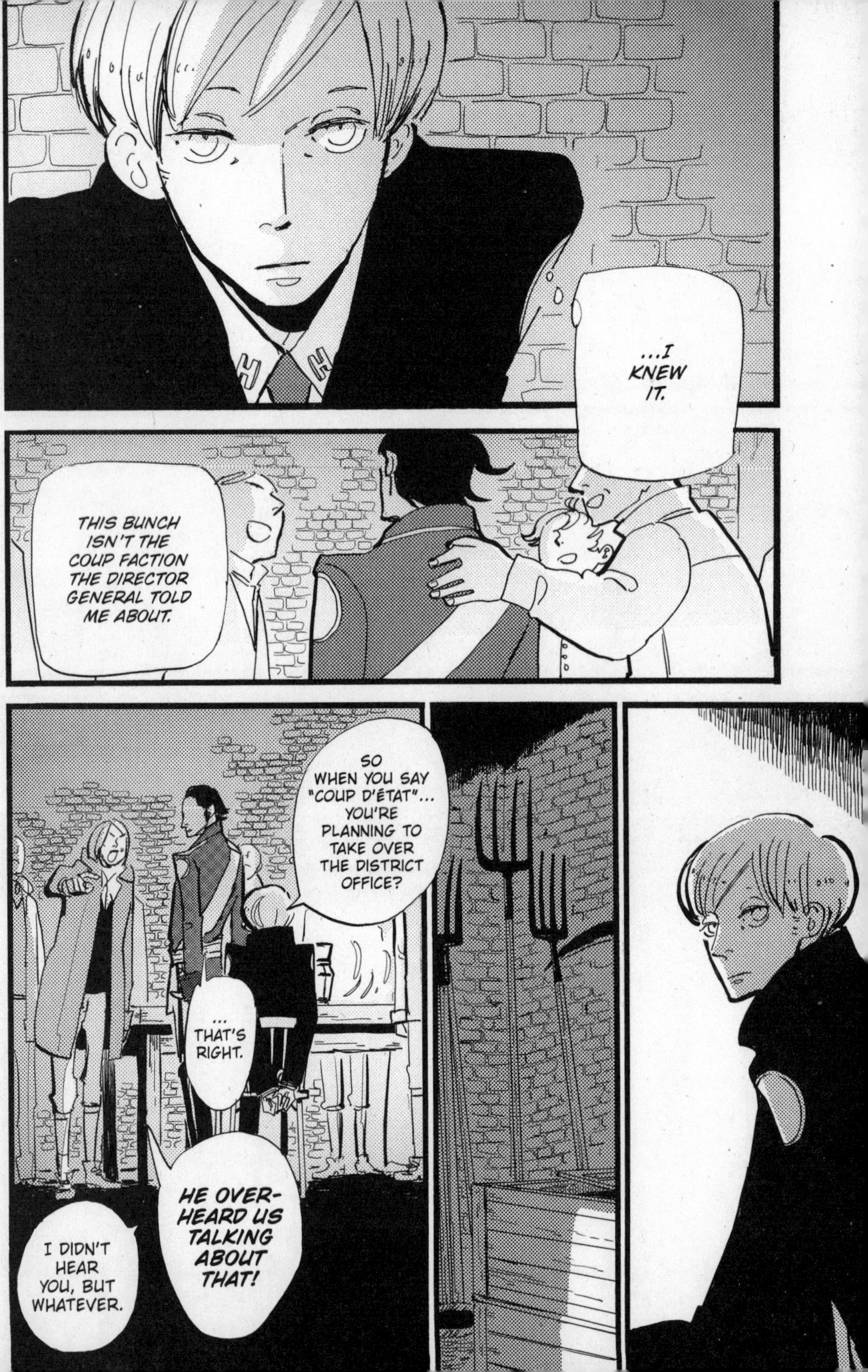
...I KNEW IT.
THIS BUNCH ISN'T THE COUP FACTION THE DIRECTOR GENERAL TOLD ME ABOUT.
SO WHEN YOU SAY "COUP D'ÉTAT"... YOU'RE PLANNING TO TAKE OVER THE DISTRICT OFFICE?
...THAT'S RIGHT.
HE OVER-HEARD US TALKING ABOUT THAT!
I DIDN'T HEAR YOU, BUT WHATEVER.

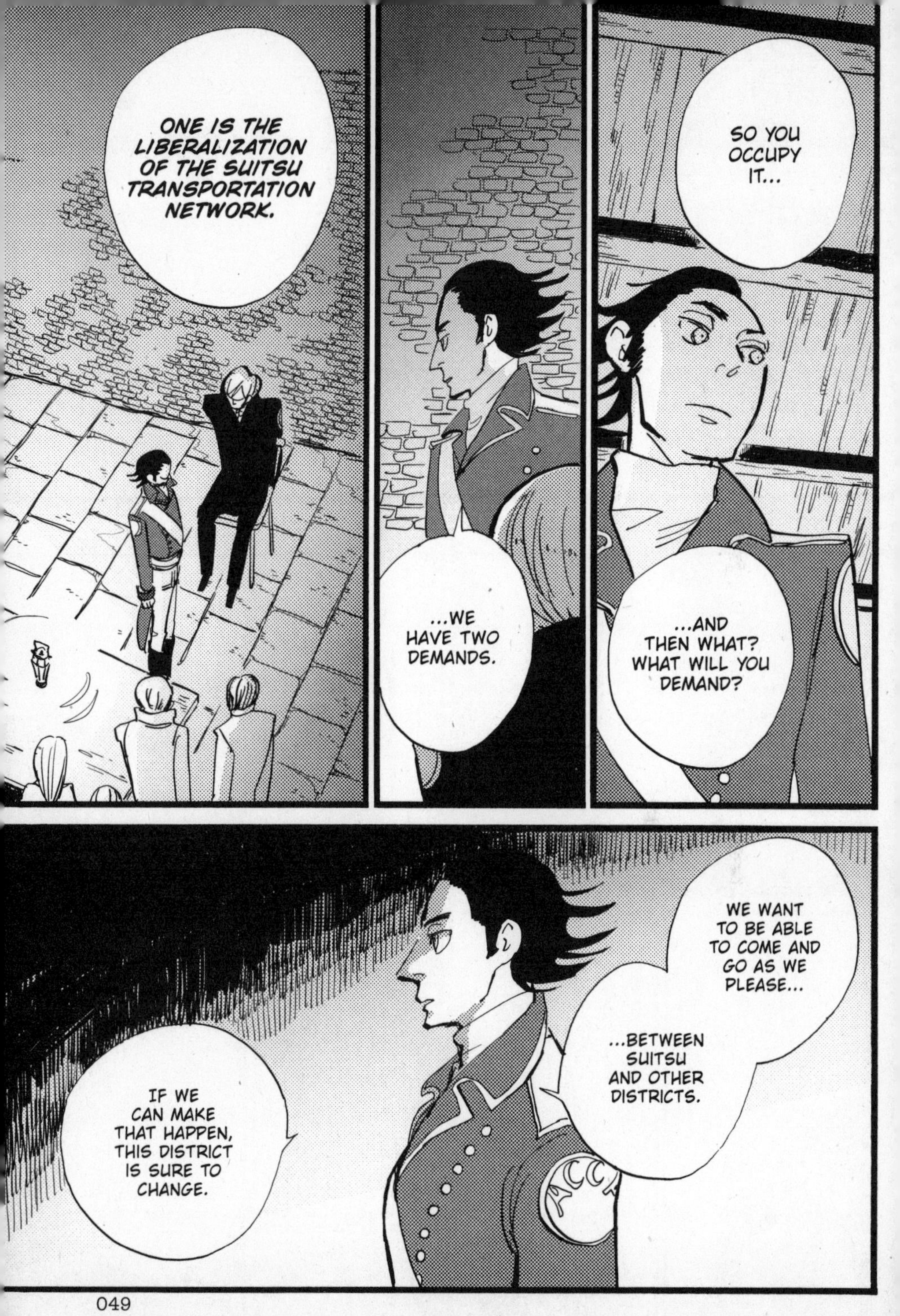
SO YOU OCCUPY IT...
...AND THEN WHAT? WHAT WILL YOU DEMAND?
...WE HAVE TWO DEMANDS.
ONE IS THE LIBERALIZATION OF THE SUITSU TRANSPORTATION NETWORK.
WE WANT TO BE ABLE TO COME AND GO AS WE PLEASE...
...BETWEEN SUITSU AND OTHER DISTRICTS.
IF WE CAN MAKE THAT HAPPEN, THIS DISTRICT IS SURE TO CHANGE.

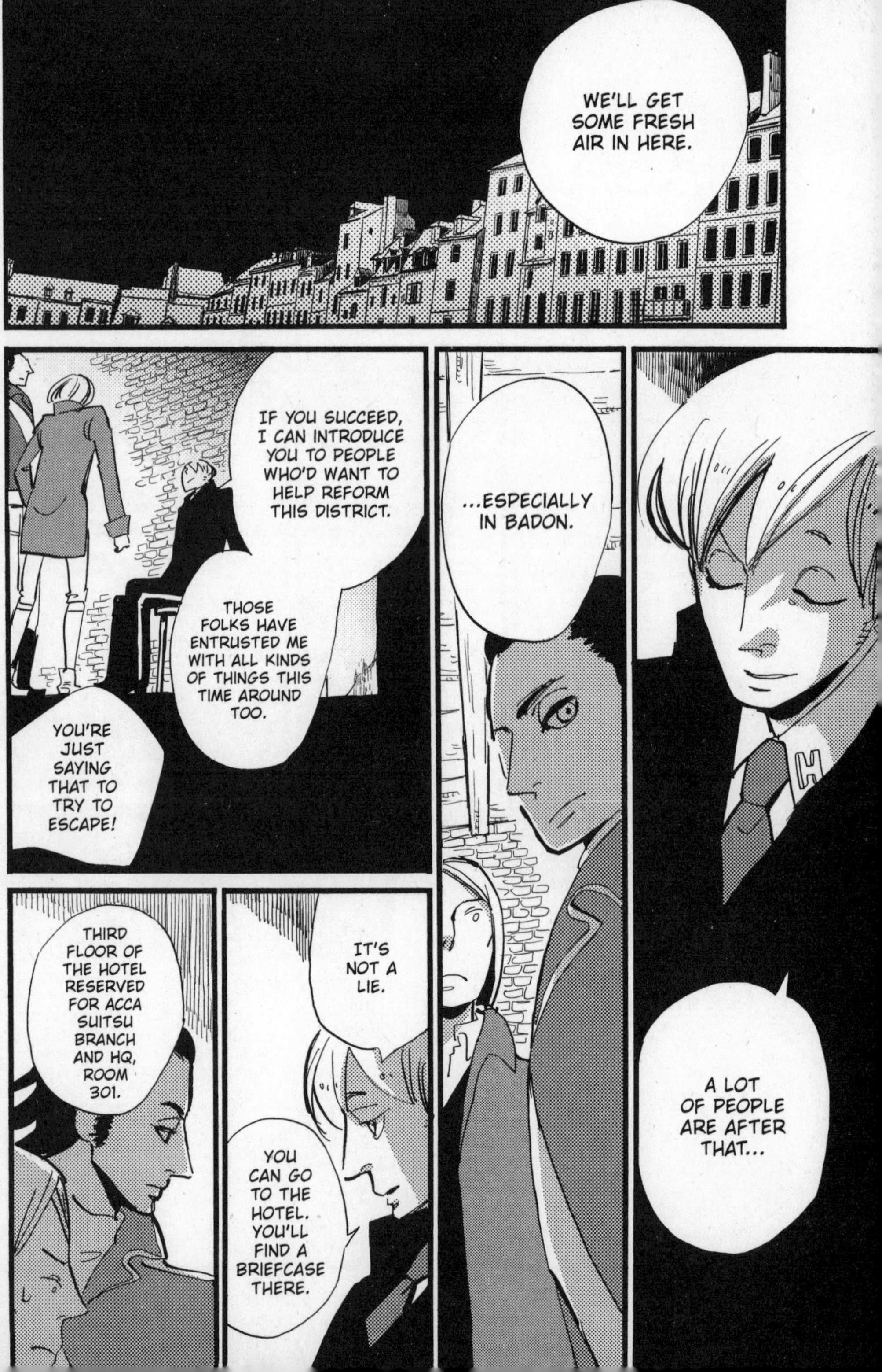
WE'LL GET SOME FRESH AIR IN HERE.
A LOT OF PEOPLE ARE AFTER THAT...
...ESPECIALLY IN BADON.
IF YOU SUCCEED, I CAN INTRODUCE YOU TO PEOPLE WHO'D WANT TO HELP REFORM THIS DISTRICT.
THOSE FOLKS HAVE ENTRUSTED ME WITH ALL KINDS OF THINGS THIS TIME AROUND TOO.
YOU'RE JUST SAYING THAT TO TRY TO ESCAPE!
IT'S NOT A LIE.
YOU CAN GO TO THE HOTEL. YOU'LL FIND A BRIEFCASE THERE.
THIRD FLOOR OF THE HOTEL RESERVED FOR ACCA SUITSU BRANCH AND HQ, ROOM 301.

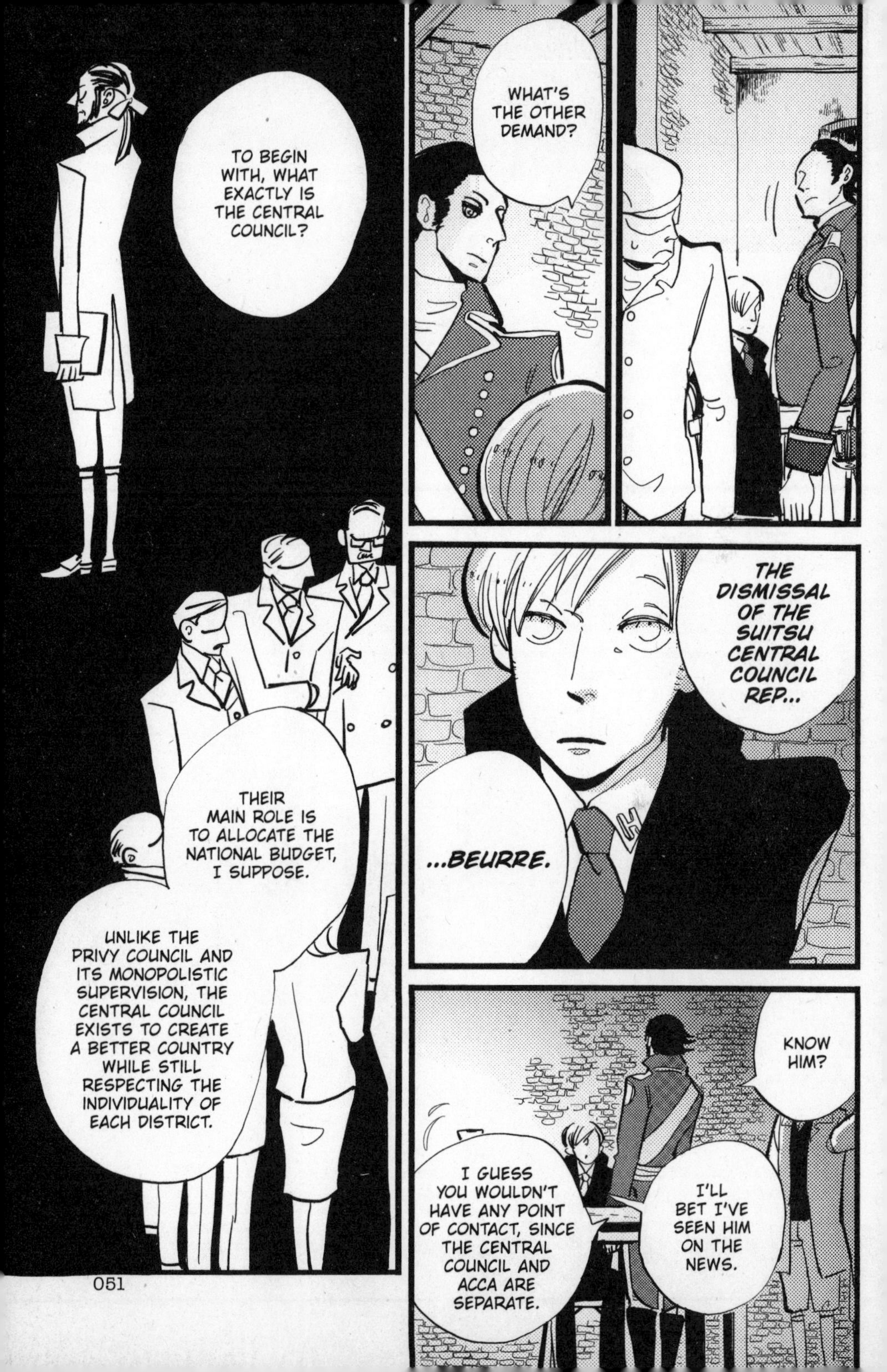
WHAT'S THE OTHER DEMAND?
THE DISMISSAL OF THE SUITSU CENTRAL COUNCIL REP...
...BEURRE.
KNOW HIM?
I'LL BET I'VE SEEN HIM ON THE NEWS.
I GUESS YOU WOULDN'T HAVE ANY POINT OF CONTACT, SINCE THE CENTRAL COUNCIL AND ACCA ARE SEPARATE.
TO BEGIN WITH, WHAT EXACTLY IS THE CENTRAL COUNCIL?
THEIR MAIN ROLE IS TO ALLOCATE THE NATIONAL BUDGET, I SUPPOSE.
UNLIKE THE PRIVY COUNCIL AND ITS MONOPOLISTIC SUPERVISION, THE CENTRAL COUNCIL EXISTS TO CREATE A BETTER COUNTRY WHILE STILL RESPECTING THE INDIVIDUALITY OF EACH DISTRICT.

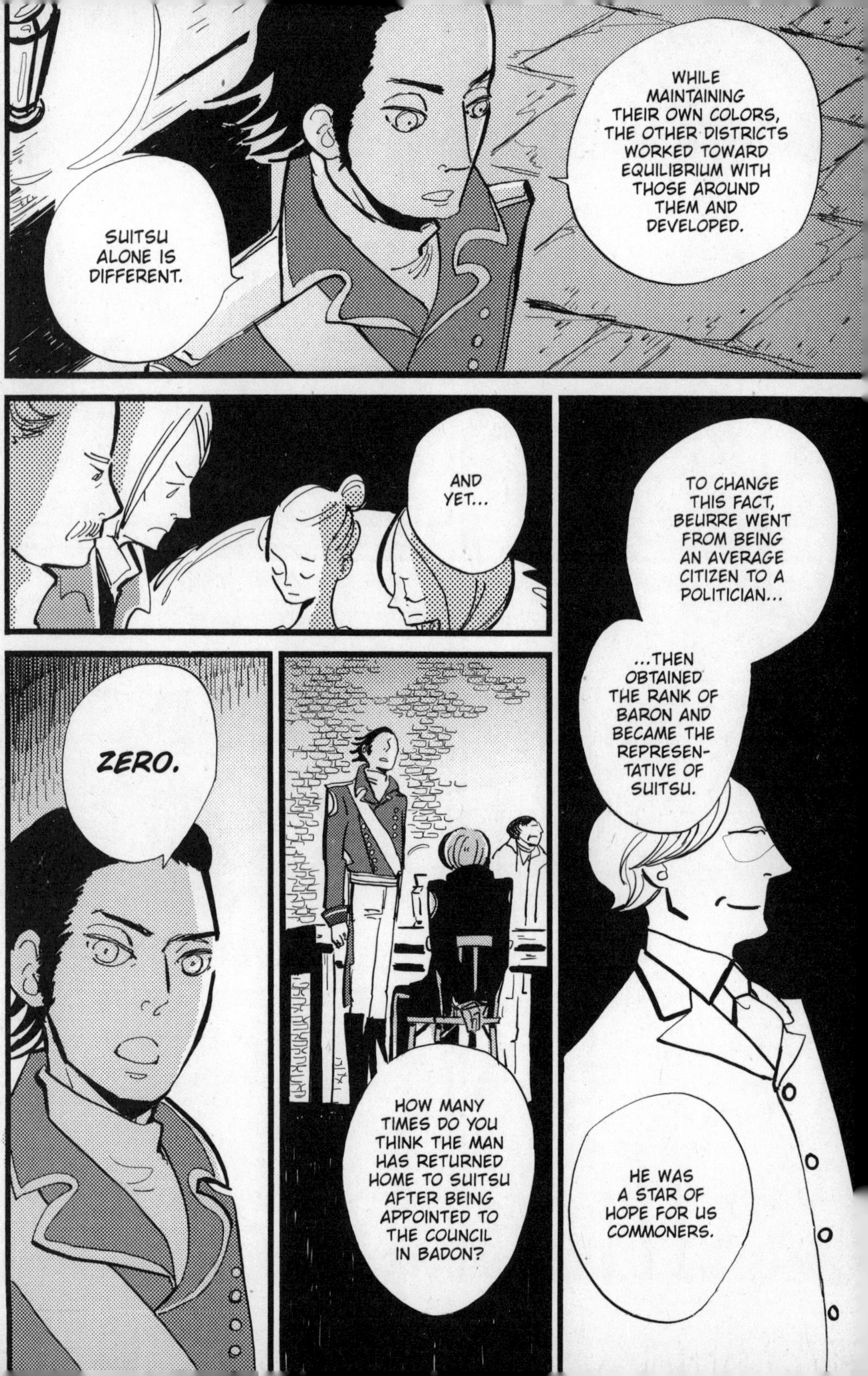
WHILE MAINTAINING THEIR OWN COLORS, THE OTHER DISTRICTS WORKED TOWARD EQUILIBRIUM WITH THOSE AROUND THEM AND DEVELOPED.
SUITSU ALONE IS DIFFERENT.
TO CHANGE THIS FACT, BEURRE WENT FROM BEING AN AVERAGE CITIZEN TO A POLITICIAN...
...THEN OBTAINED THE RANK OF BARON AND BECAME THE REPRESENTATIVE OF SUITSU.
HE WAS A STAR OF HOPE FOR US COMMONERS.
AND YET...
HOW MANY TIMES DO YOU THINK THE MAN HAS RETURNED HOME TO SUITSU AFTER BEING APPOINTED TO THE COUNCIL IN BADON?
ZERO.

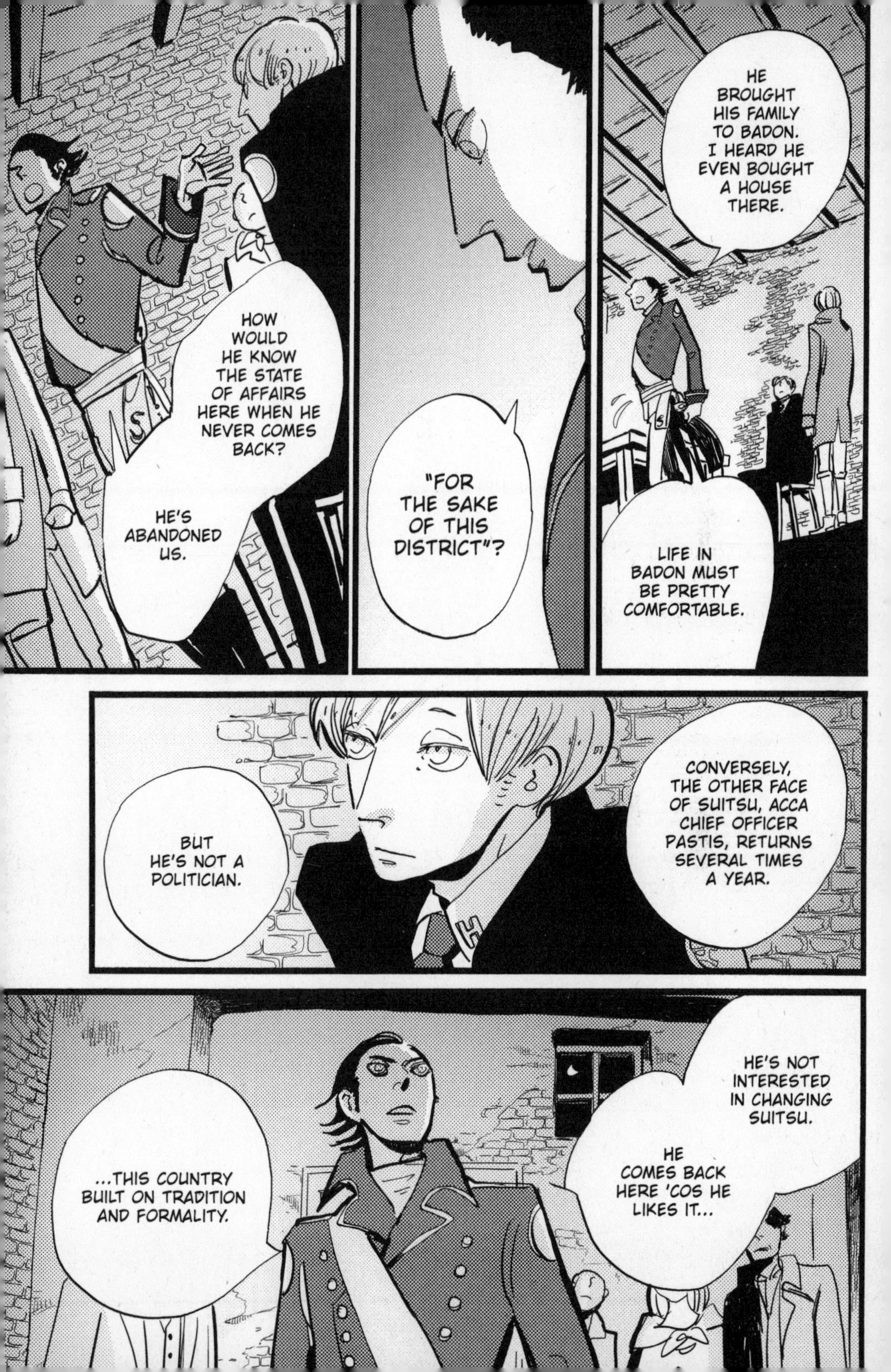
HE BROUGHT HIS FAMILY TO BADON. I HEARD HE EVEN BOUGHT A HOUSE THERE.
LIFE IN BADON MUST BE PRETTY COMFORTABLE.
"FOR THE SAKE OF THIS DISTRICT"?
HOW WOULD HE KNOW THE STATE OF AFFAIRS HERE WHEN HE NEVER COMES BACK?
HE'S ABANDONED US.
CONVERSELY, THE OTHER FACE OF SUITSU, ACCA CHIEF OFFICER PASTIS, RETURNS SEVERAL TIMES A YEAR.
BUT HE'S NOT A POLITICIAN.
HE'S NOT INTERESTED IN CHANGING SUITSU.
HE COMES BACK HERE 'COS HE LIKES IT...
...THIS COUNTRY BUILT ON TRADITION AND FORMALITY.

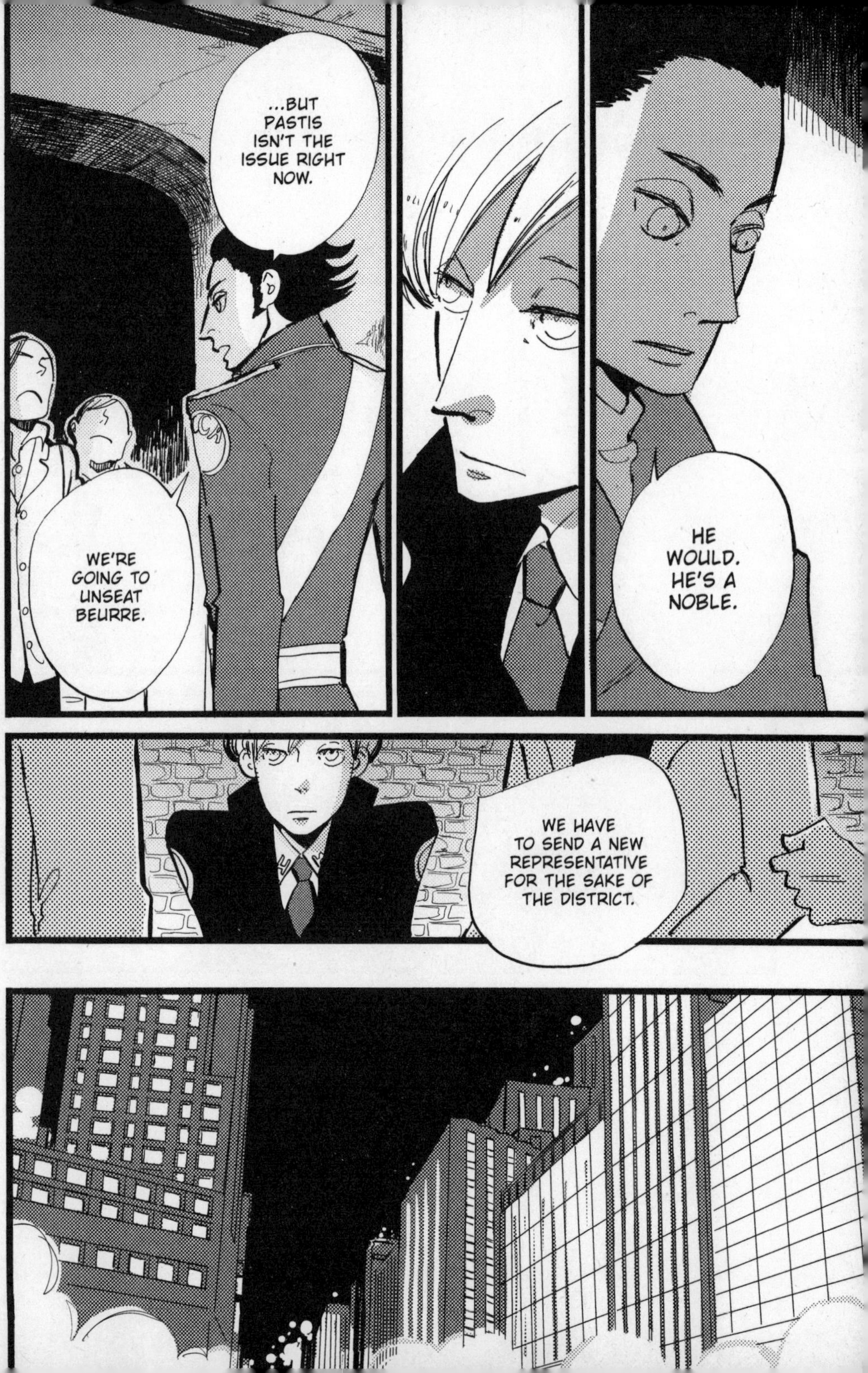
HE WOULD. HE'S A NOBLE.
...BUT PASTIS ISN'T THE ISSUE RIGHT NOW.
WE'RE GOING TO UNSEAT BEURRE.
WE HAVE TO SEND A NEW REPRESENTATIVE FOR THE SAKE OF THE DISTRICT.

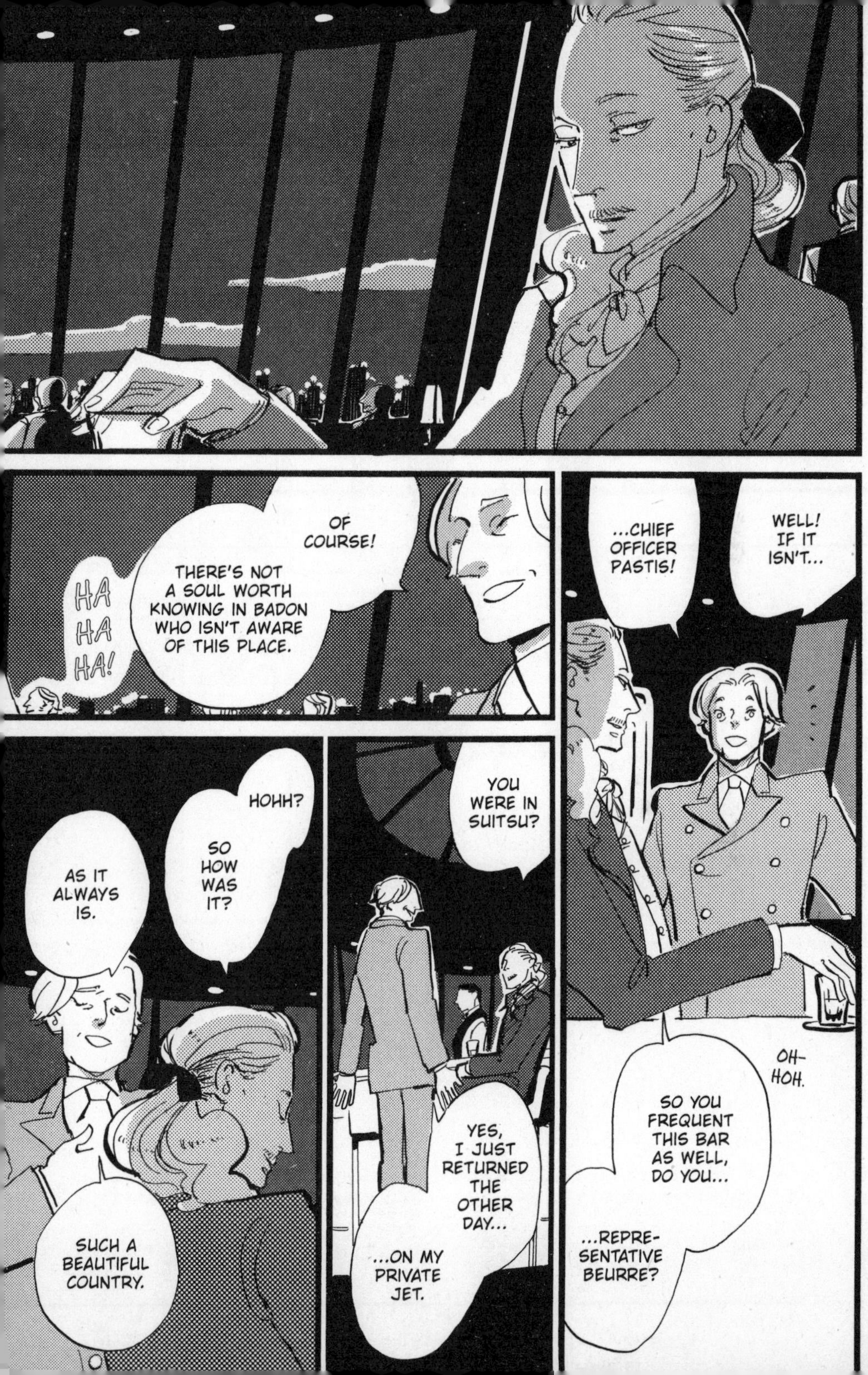
WELL! IF IT ISN'T...
...CHIEF OFFICER PASTIS!
OH-HOH.
SO YOU FREQUENT THIS BAR AS WELL, DO YOU...
...REPRESENTATIVE BEURRE?
OF COURSE!
THERE'S NOT A SOUL WORTH KNOWING IN BADON WHO ISN'T AWARE OF THIS PLACE.
HA HA HA!
YOU WERE IN SUITSU?
YES, I JUST RETURNED THE OTHER DAY...
...ON MY PRIVATE JET.
HOHH?
SO HOW WAS IT?
AS IT ALWAYS IS.
SUCH A BEAUTIFUL COUNTRY.

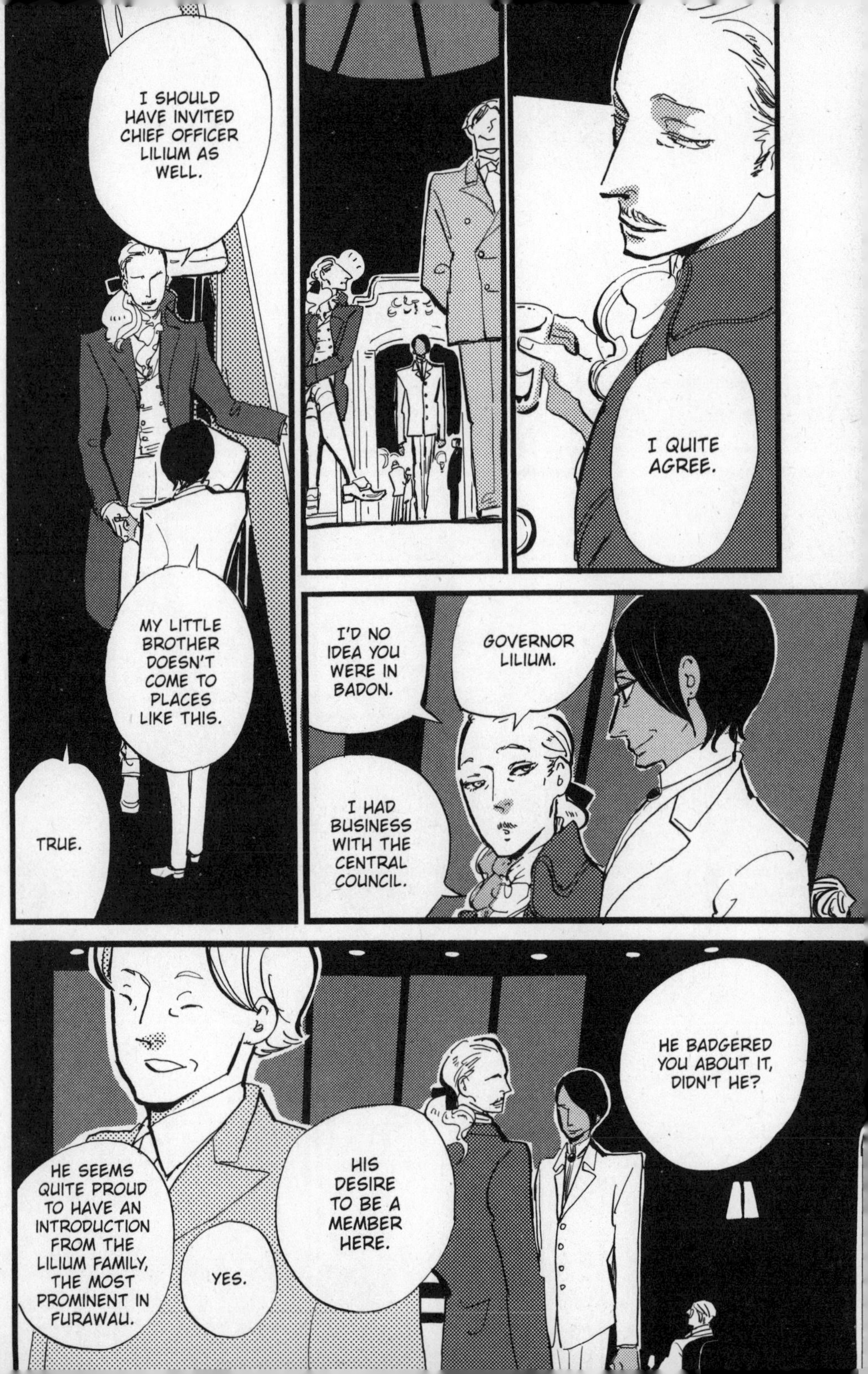
I QUITE AGREE.
GOVERNOR LILIUM.
I'D NO IDEA YOU WERE IN BADON.
I HAD BUSINESS WITH THE CENTRAL COUNCIL.
I SHOULD HAVE INVITED CHIEF OFFICER LILIUM AS WELL.
MY LITTLE BROTHER DOESN'T COME TO PLACES LIKE THIS.
TRUE.
HE BADGERED YOU ABOUT IT, DIDN'T HE?
HIS DESIRE TO BE A MEMBER HERE.
YES.
HE SEEMS QUITE PROUD TO HAVE AN INTRODUCTION FROM THE LILIUM FAMILY, THE MOST PROMINENT IN FURAWAU.

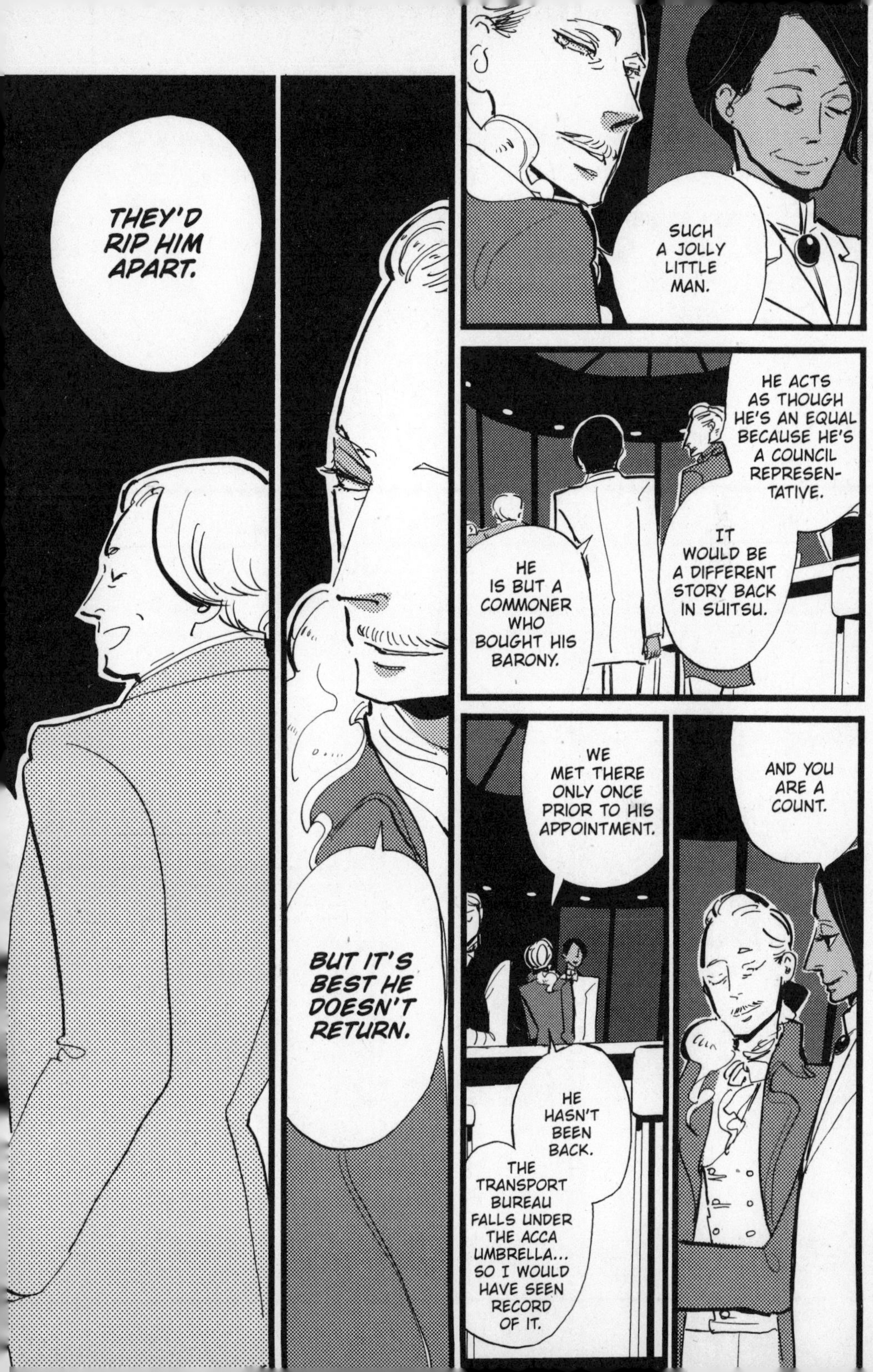

SUCH A JOLLY LITTLE MAN.
HE ACTS AS THOUGH HE'S AN EQUAL BECAUSE HE'S A COUNCIL REPRESEN-TATIVE.
IT WOULD BE A DIFFERENT STORY BACK IN SUITSU.
HE IS BUT A COMMONER WHO BOUGHT HIS BARONY.
AND YOU ARE A COUNT.
WE MET THERE ONLY ONCE PRIOR TO HIS APPOINTMENT.
HE HASN'T BEEN BACK.
THE TRANSPORT BUREAU FALLS UNDER THE ACCA UMBRELLA... SO I WOULD HAVE SEEN RECORD OF IT.
BUT IT'S BEST HE DOESN'T RETURN.
THEY'D RIP HIM APART.

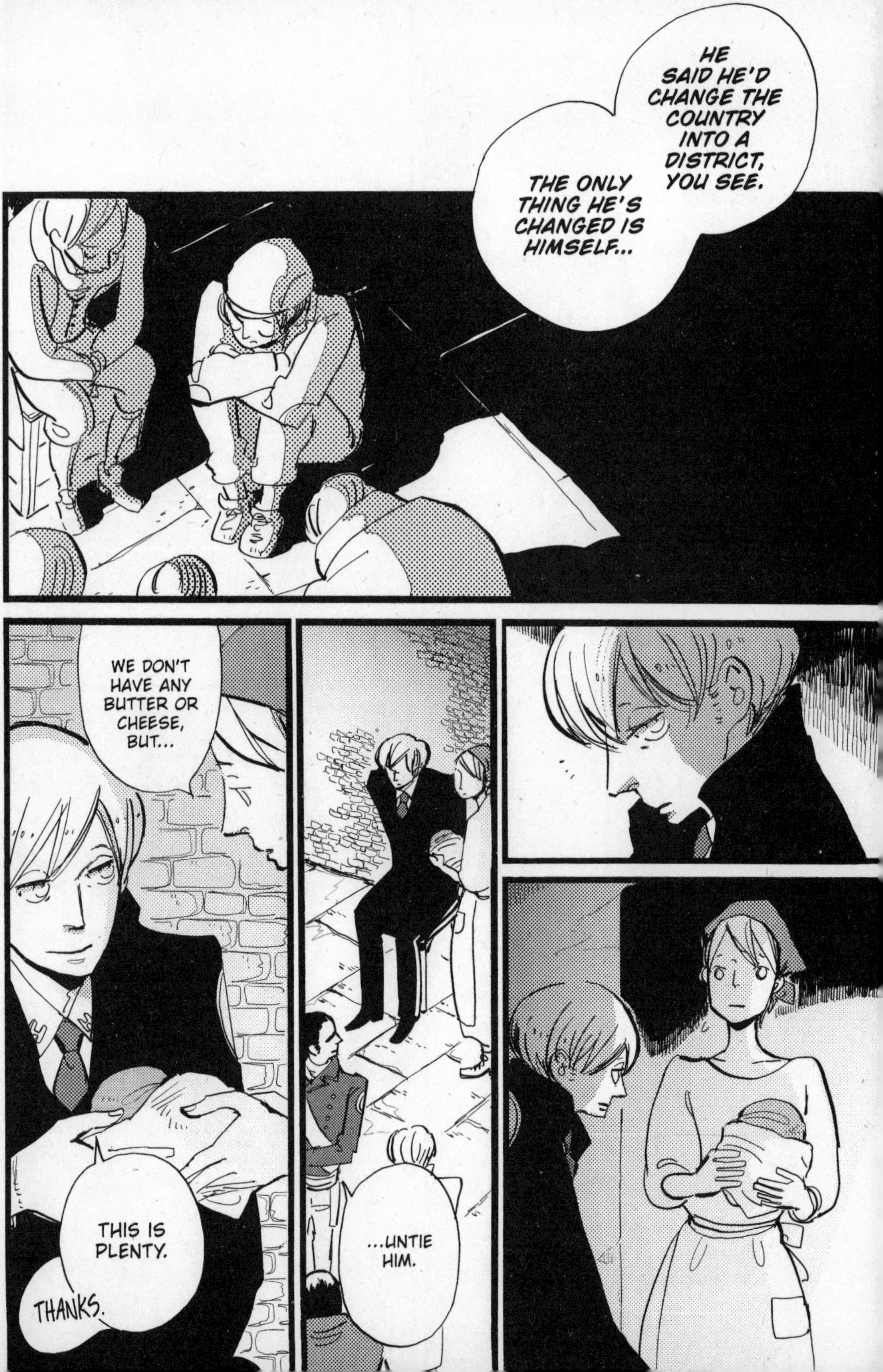
HE SAID HE'D CHANGE THE COUNTRY INTO A DISTRICT, YOU SEE.
THE ONLY THING HE'S CHANGED IS HIMSELF...
...UNTIE HIM.
WE DON'T HAVE ANY BUTTER OR CHEESE, BUT...
THIS IS PLENTY.
THANKS.

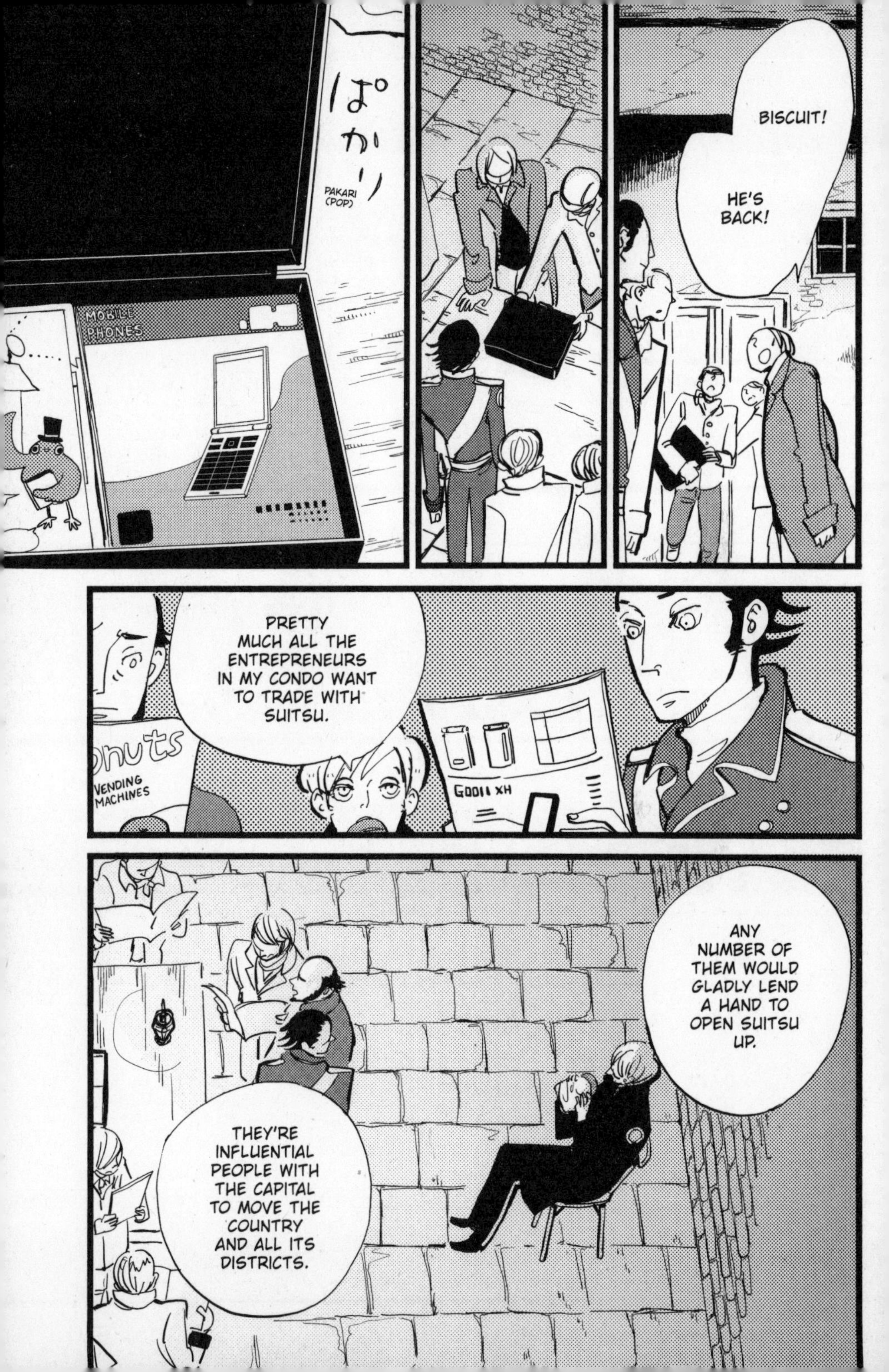
BISCUIT!
HE'S BACK!
ぱかり
PAKARI (POP)
MOBILE PHONES
PRETTY MUCH ALL THE ENTREPRENEURS IN MY CONDO WANT TO TRADE WITH SUITSU.
VENDING MACHINES
ANY NUMBER OF THEM WOULD GLADLY LEND A HAND TO OPEN SUITSU UP.
THEY'RE INFLUENTIAL PEOPLE WITH THE CAPITAL TO MOVE THE COUNTRY AND ALL ITS DISTRICTS.

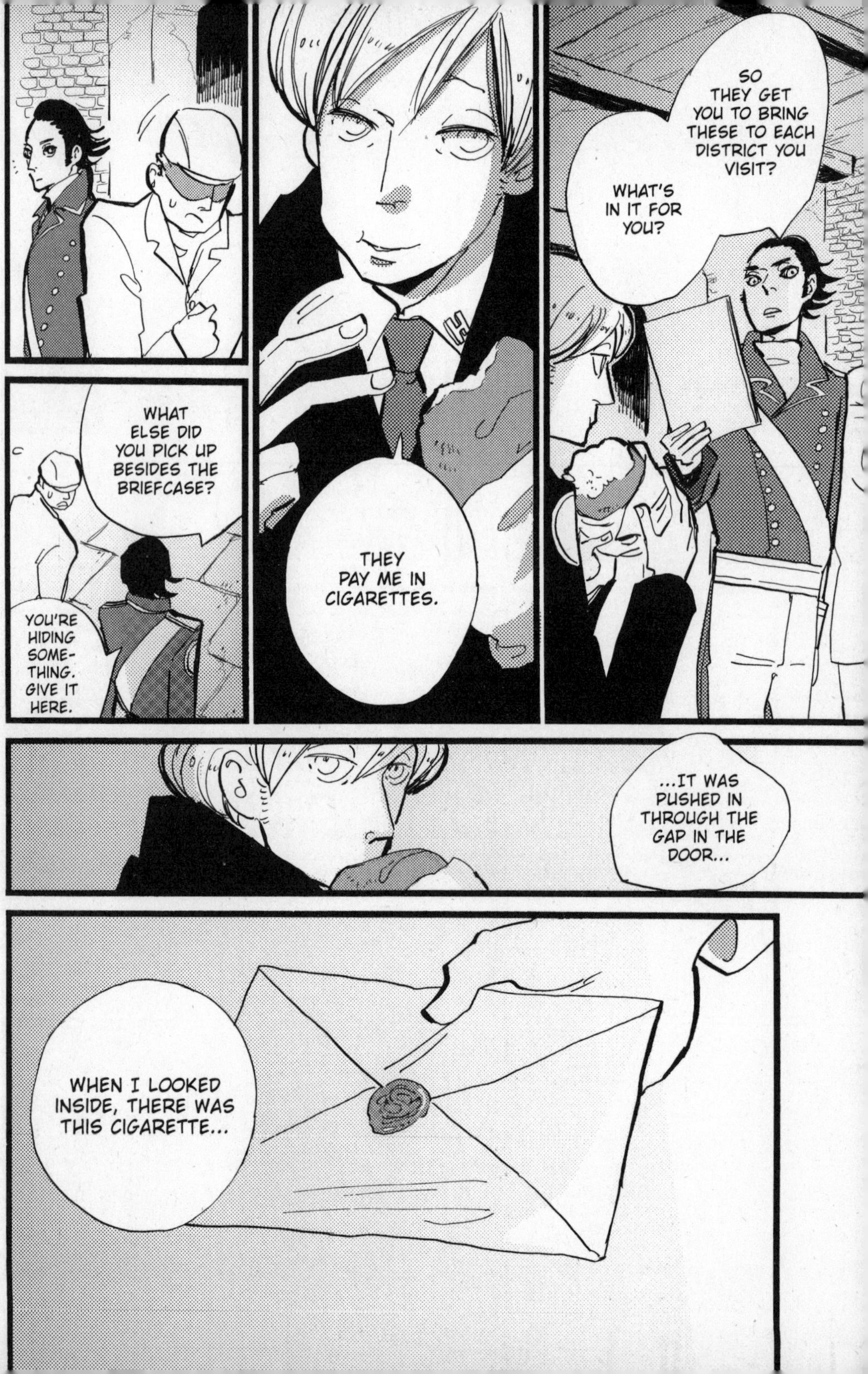
SO THEY GET YOU TO BRING THESE TO EACH DISTRICT YOU VISIT?
WHAT'S IN IT FOR YOU?
THEY PAY ME IN CIGARETTES.
WHAT ELSE DID YOU PICK UP BESIDES THE BRIEFCASE?
YOU'RE HIDING SOME-THING. GIVE IT HERE.
...IT WAS PUSHED IN THROUGH THE GAP IN THE DOOR...
WHEN I LOOKED INSIDE, THERE WAS THIS CIGARETTE...

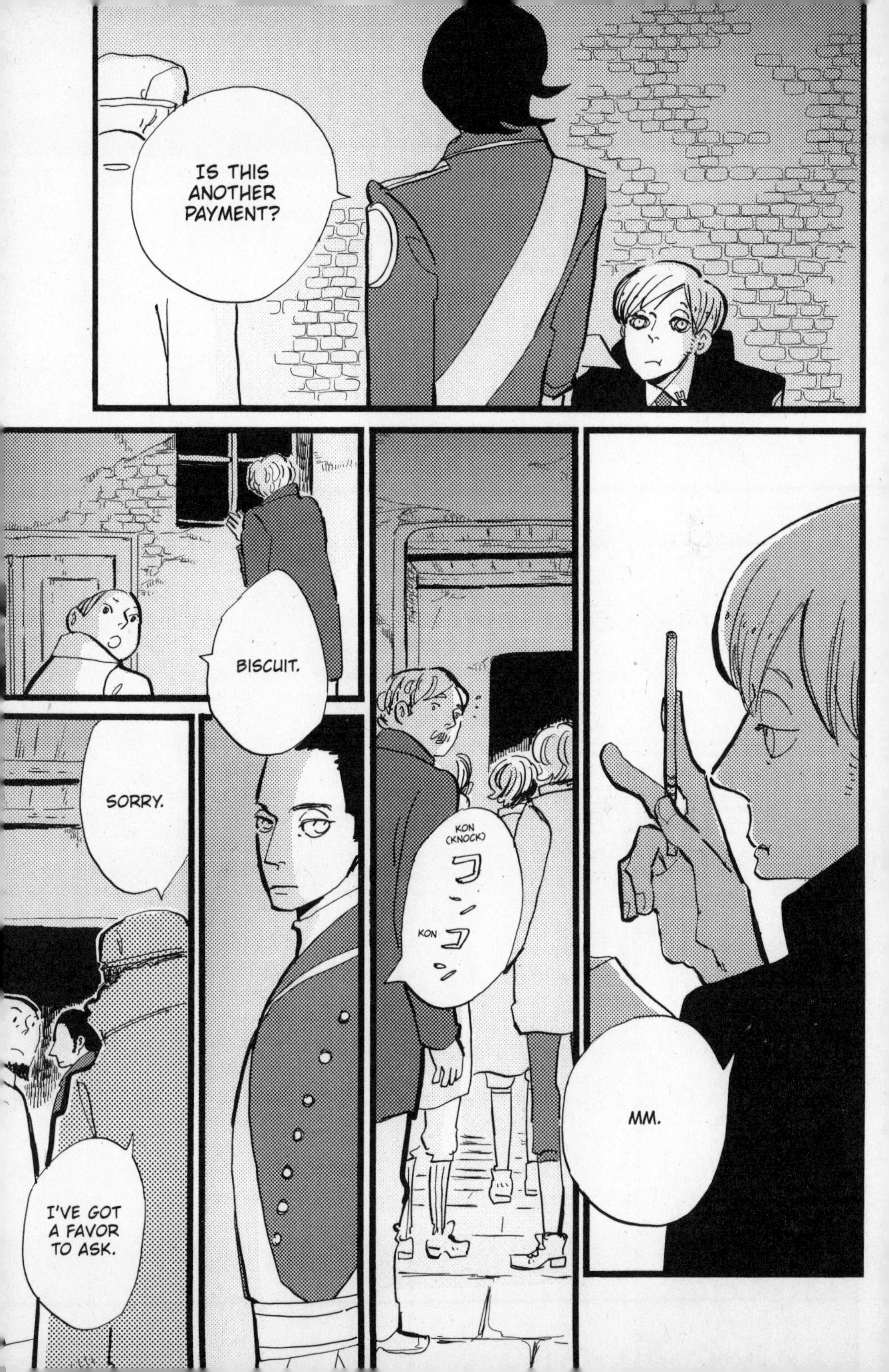
IS THIS ANOTHER PAYMENT?
MM.
KON (KNOCK)
コン
KON
コン
BISCUIT.
SORRY.
I'VE GOT A FAVOR TO ASK.

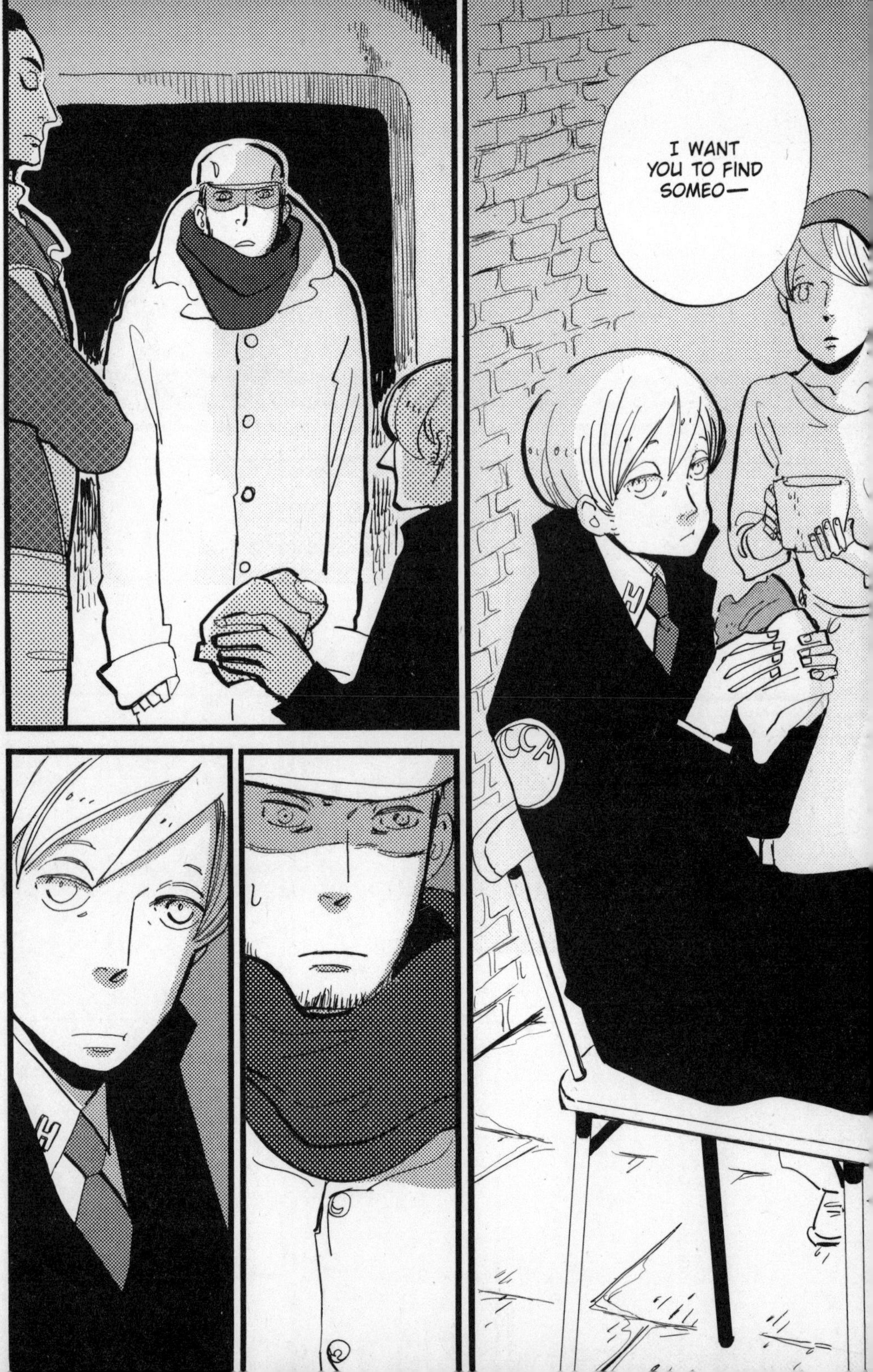
I WANT YOU TO FIND SOMEO—

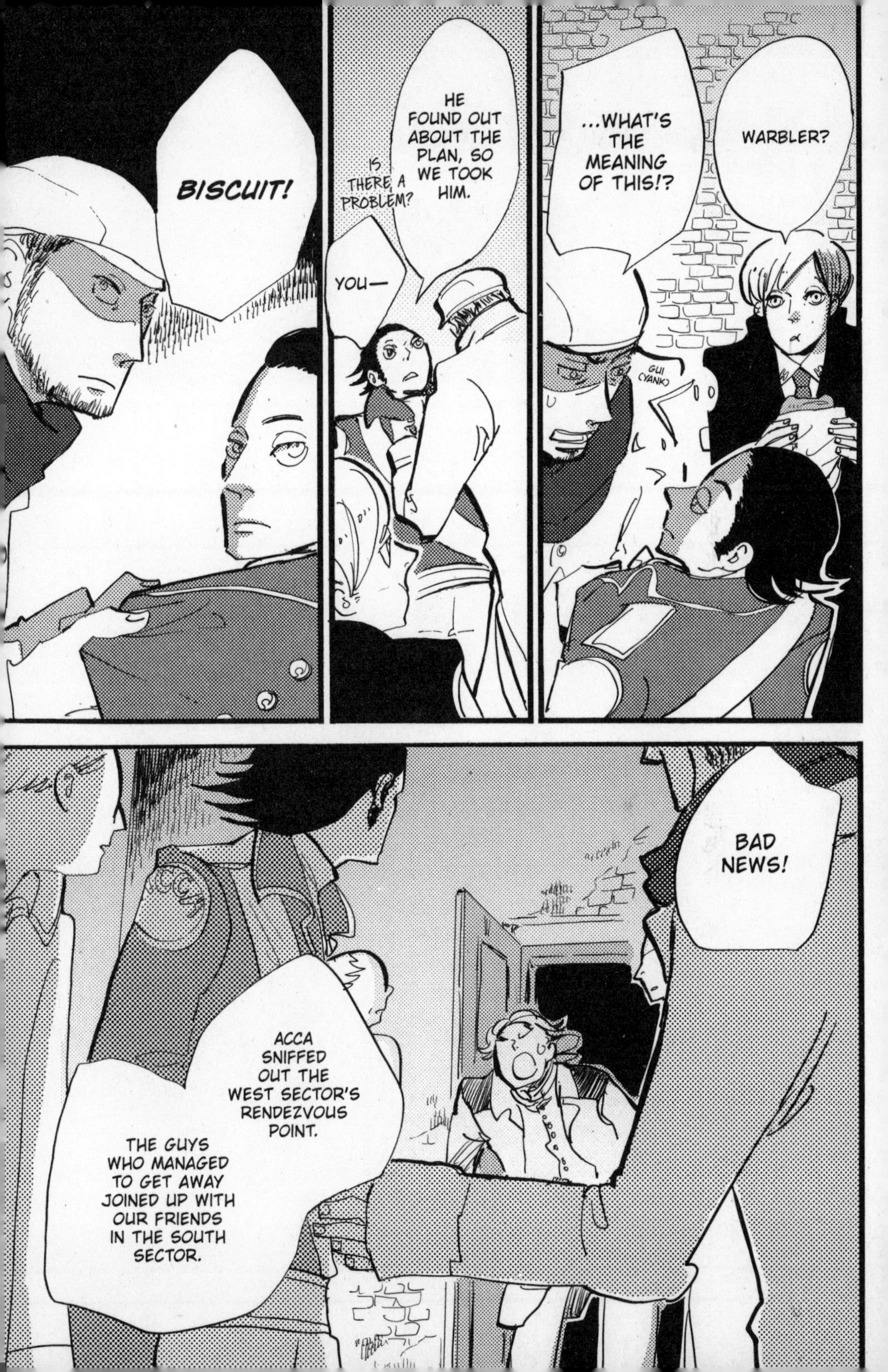

WARBLER?
...WHAT'S THE MEANING OF THIS!?
GUI (YANK)
HE FOUND OUT ABOUT THE PLAN, SO WE TOOK HIM.
IS THERE A PROBLEM?
YOU—
BISCUIT!
BAD NEWS!
ACCA SNIFFED OUT THE WEST SECTOR'S RENDEZVOUS POINT.
THE GUYS WHO MANAGED TO GET AWAY JOINED UP WITH OUR FRIENDS IN THE SOUTH SECTOR.

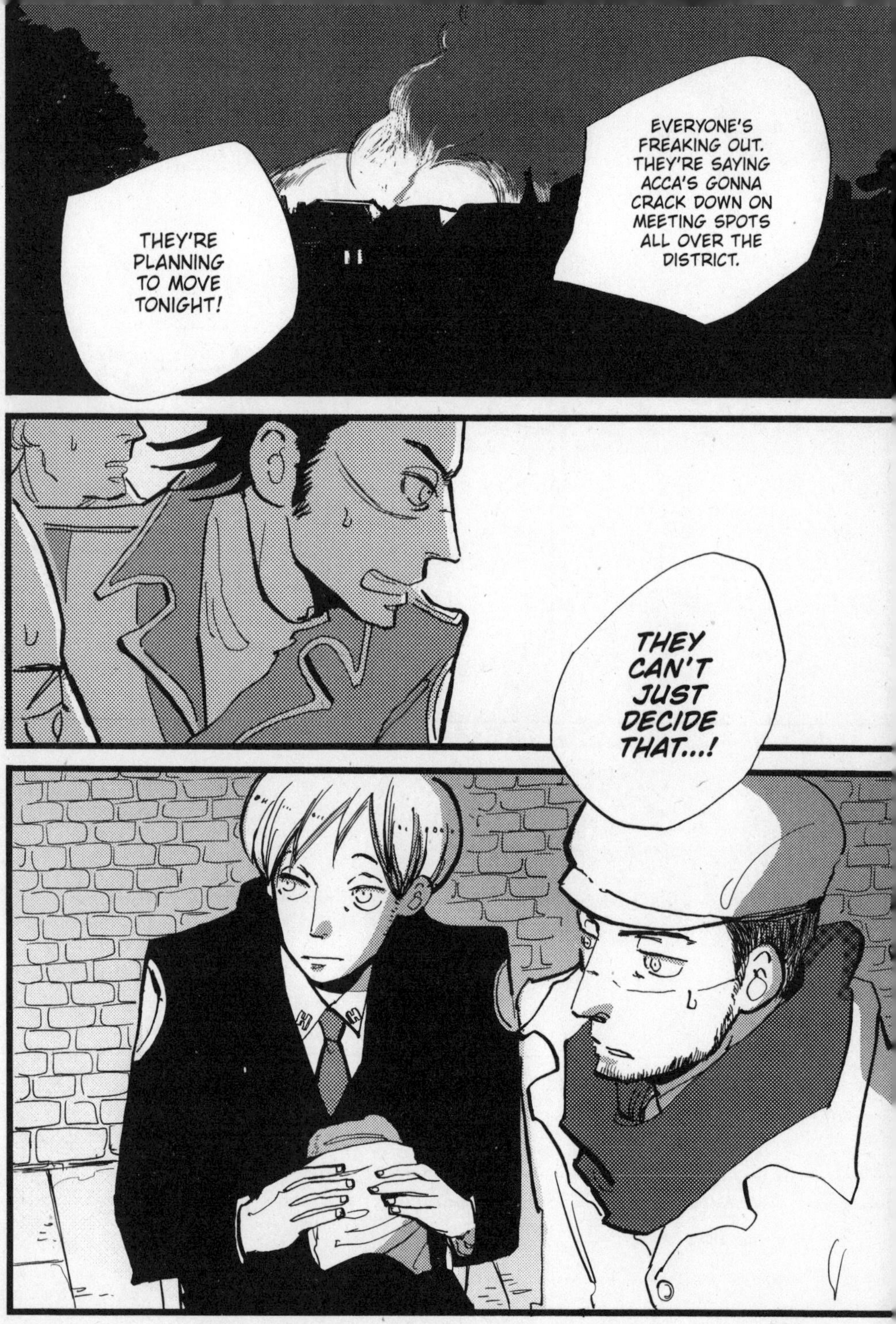
EVERYONE'S FREAKING OUT. THEY'RE SAYING ACCA'S GONNA CRACK DOWN ON MEETING SPOTS ALL OVER THE DISTRICT.
THEY'RE PLANNING TO MOVE TONIGHT!
THEY CAN'T JUST DECIDE THAT...!

CHAPTER 13

Surrounded by Rebels in Suitsu

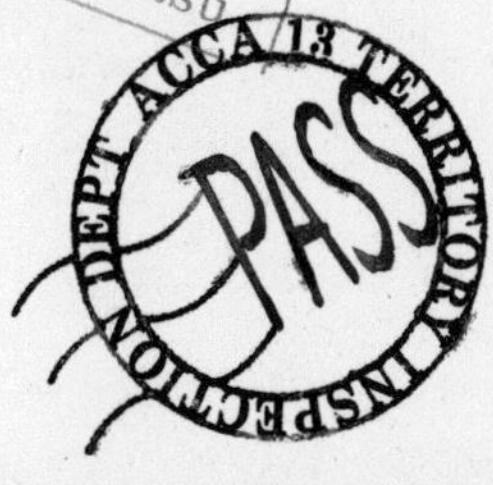
ACCA 13 TERRITORY INSPECTION DEPT
PASS

CHAPTER 14
After the Sparks Fly in Suitsu

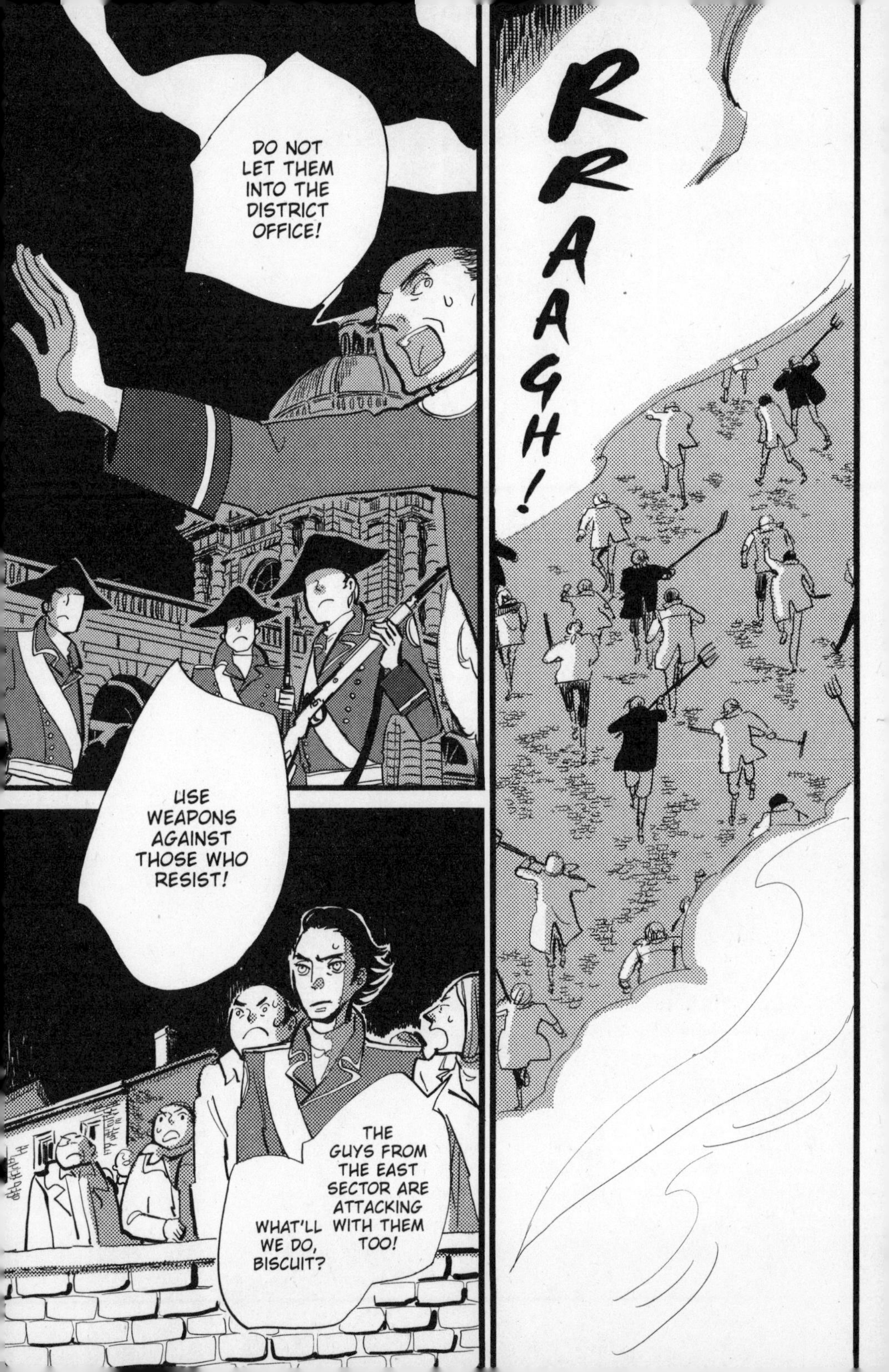
RRAAGH!
DO NOT LET THEM INTO THE DISTRICT OFFICE!
USE WEAPONS AGAINST THOSE WHO RESIST!
THE GUYS FROM THE EAST SECTOR ARE ATTACKING WITH THEM TOO!
WHAT'LL WE DO, BISCUIT?

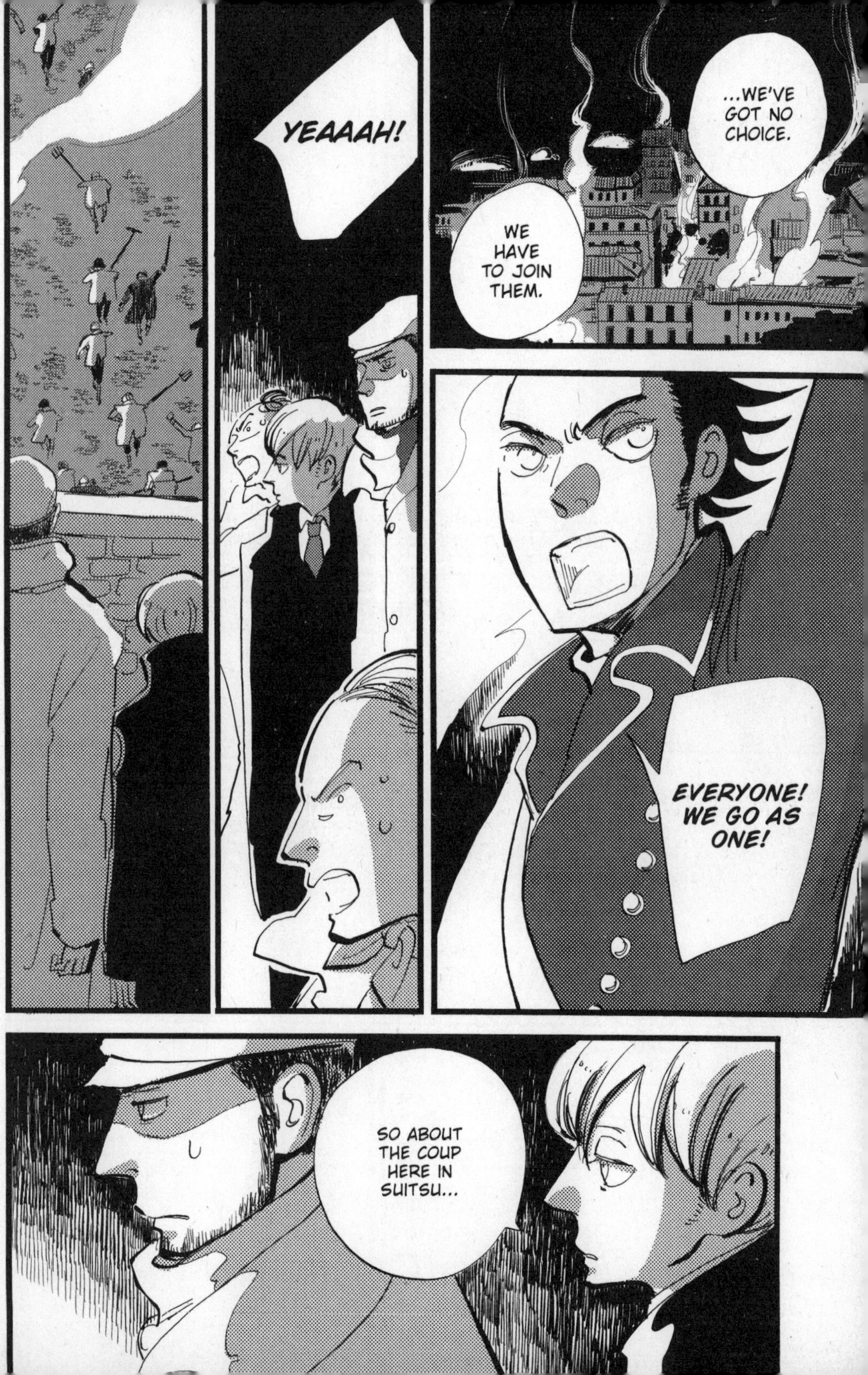
...WE'VE GOT NO CHOICE.
WE HAVE TO JOIN THEM.
EVERYONE! WE GO AS ONE!
YEAAAH!
SO ABOUT THE COUP HERE IN SUITSU...

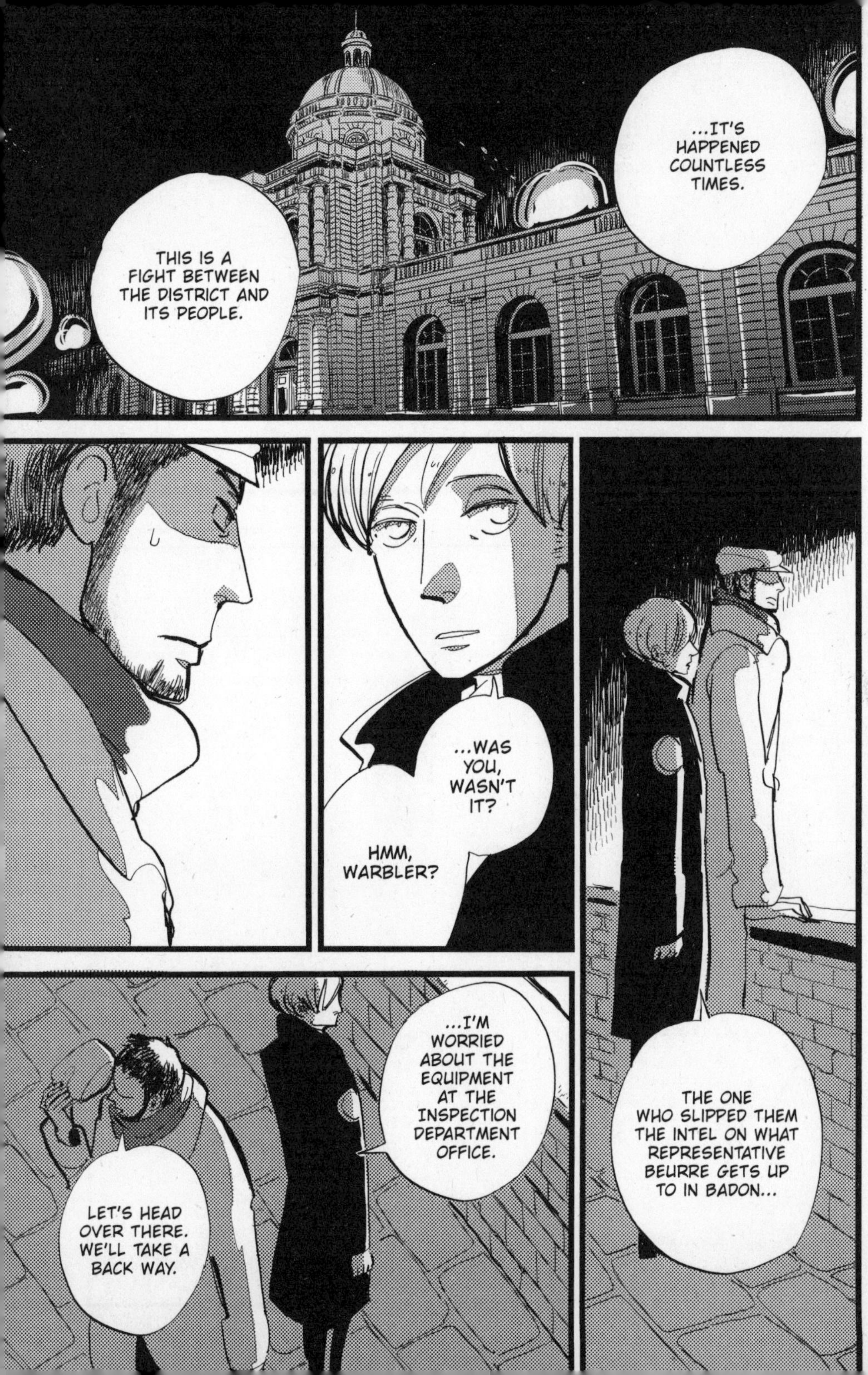
...IT'S HAPPENED COUNTLESS TIMES.
THIS IS A FIGHT BETWEEN THE DISTRICT AND ITS PEOPLE.
THE ONE WHO SLIPPED THEM THE INTEL ON WHAT REPRESENTATIVE BEURRE GETS UP TO IN BADON...
...WAS YOU, WASN'T IT?
HMM, WARBLER?
...I'M WORRIED ABOUT THE EQUIPMENT AT THE INSPECTION DEPARTMENT OFFICE.
LET'S HEAD OVER THERE. WE'LL TAKE A BACK WAY.

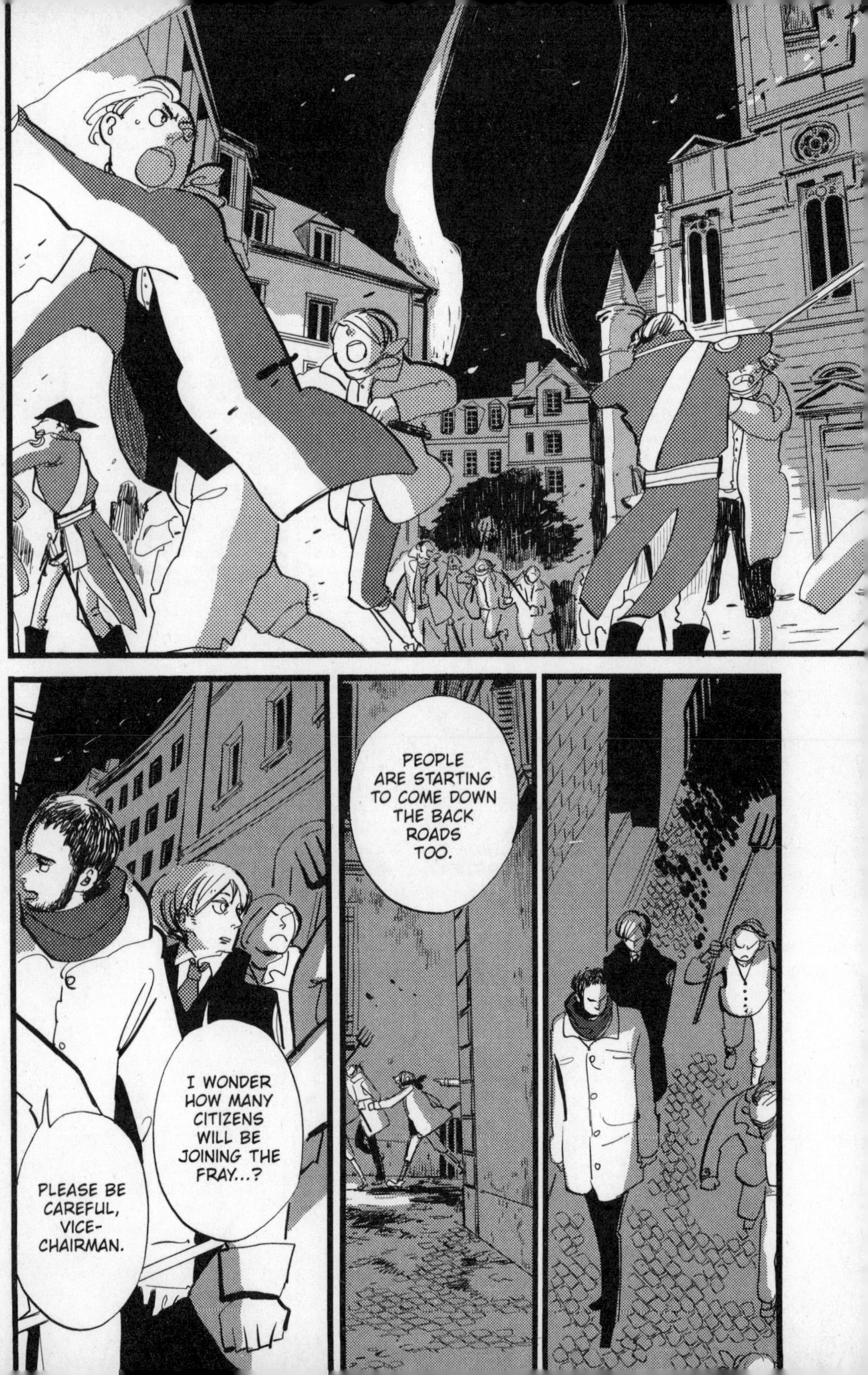
PEOPLE ARE STARTING TO COME DOWN THE BACK ROADS TOO.
I WONDER HOW MANY CITIZENS WILL BE JOINING THE FRAY...?
PLEASE BE CAREFUL, VICE-CHAIRMAN.

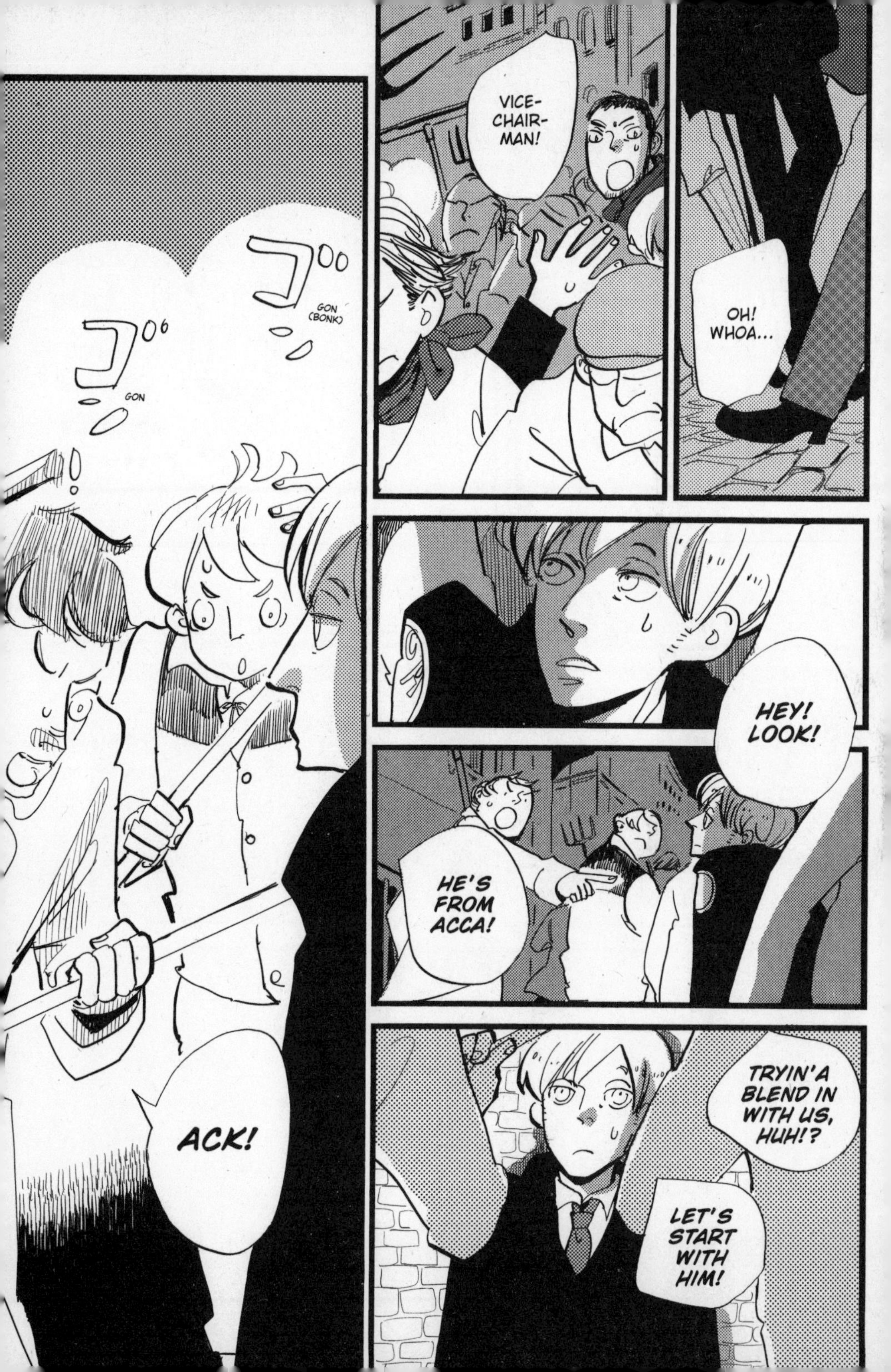
OH! WHOA...
VICE-CHAIRMAN!
HEY! LOOK!
HE'S FROM ACCA!
TRYIN'A BLEND IN WITH US, HUH!?
LET'S START WITH HIM!
コ
GON (BONK)
コ
GON
ACK!

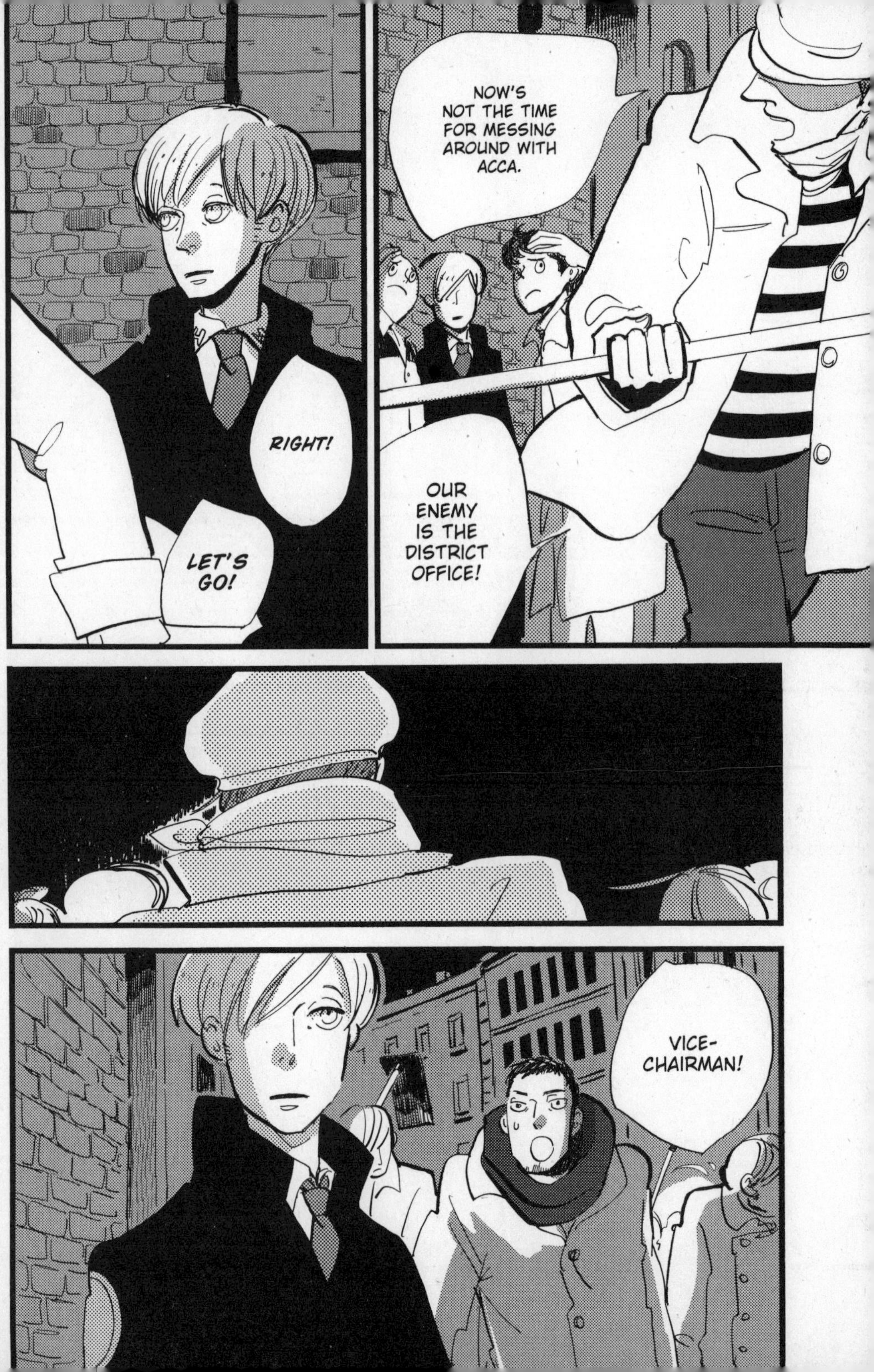
NOW'S NOT THE TIME FOR MESSING AROUND WITH ACCA.
OUR ENEMY IS THE DISTRICT OFFICE!
RIGHT!
LET'S GO!
VICE-CHAIRMAN!

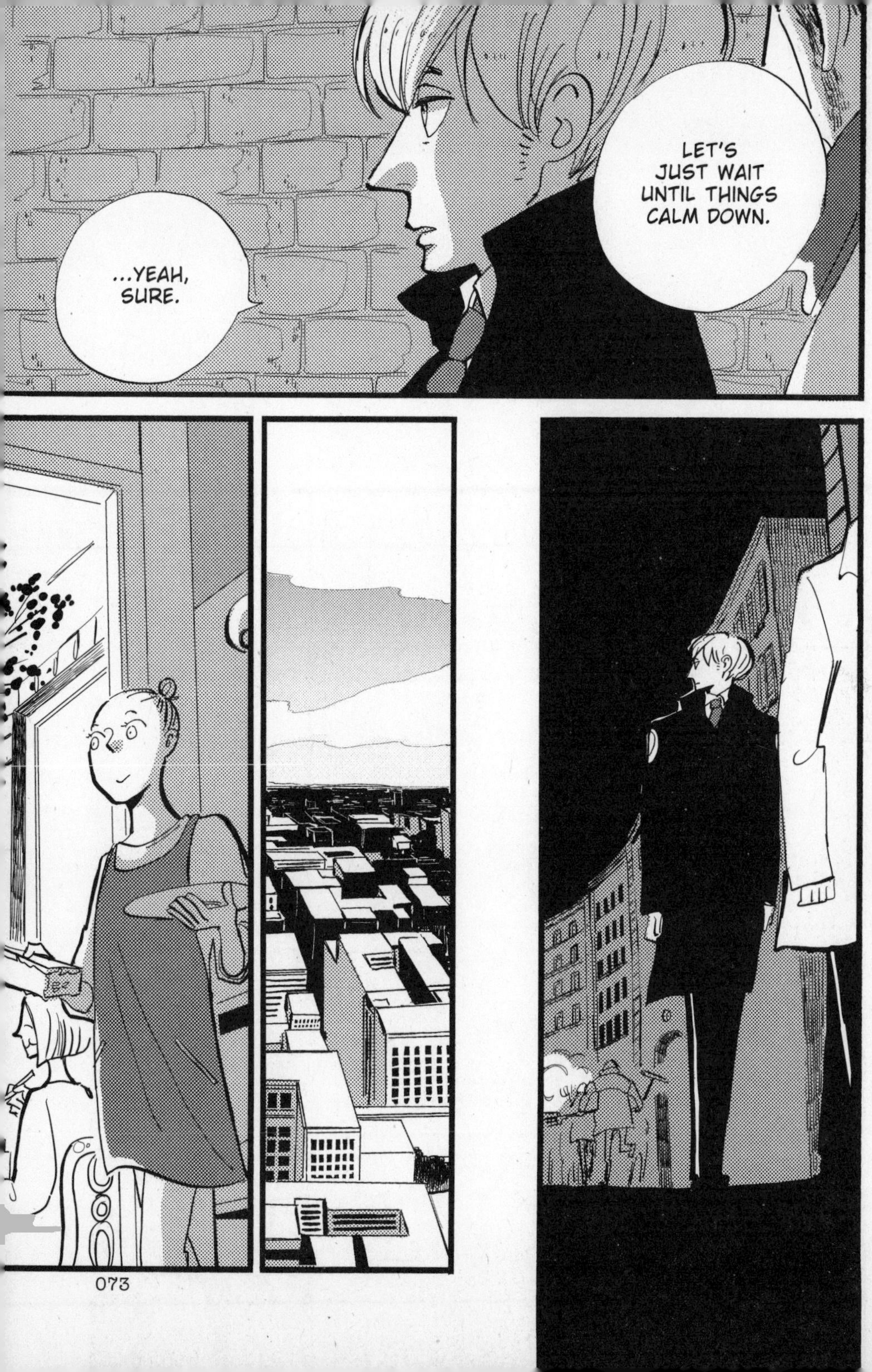
LET'S JUST WAIT UNTIL THINGS CALM DOWN.
...YEAH, SURE.

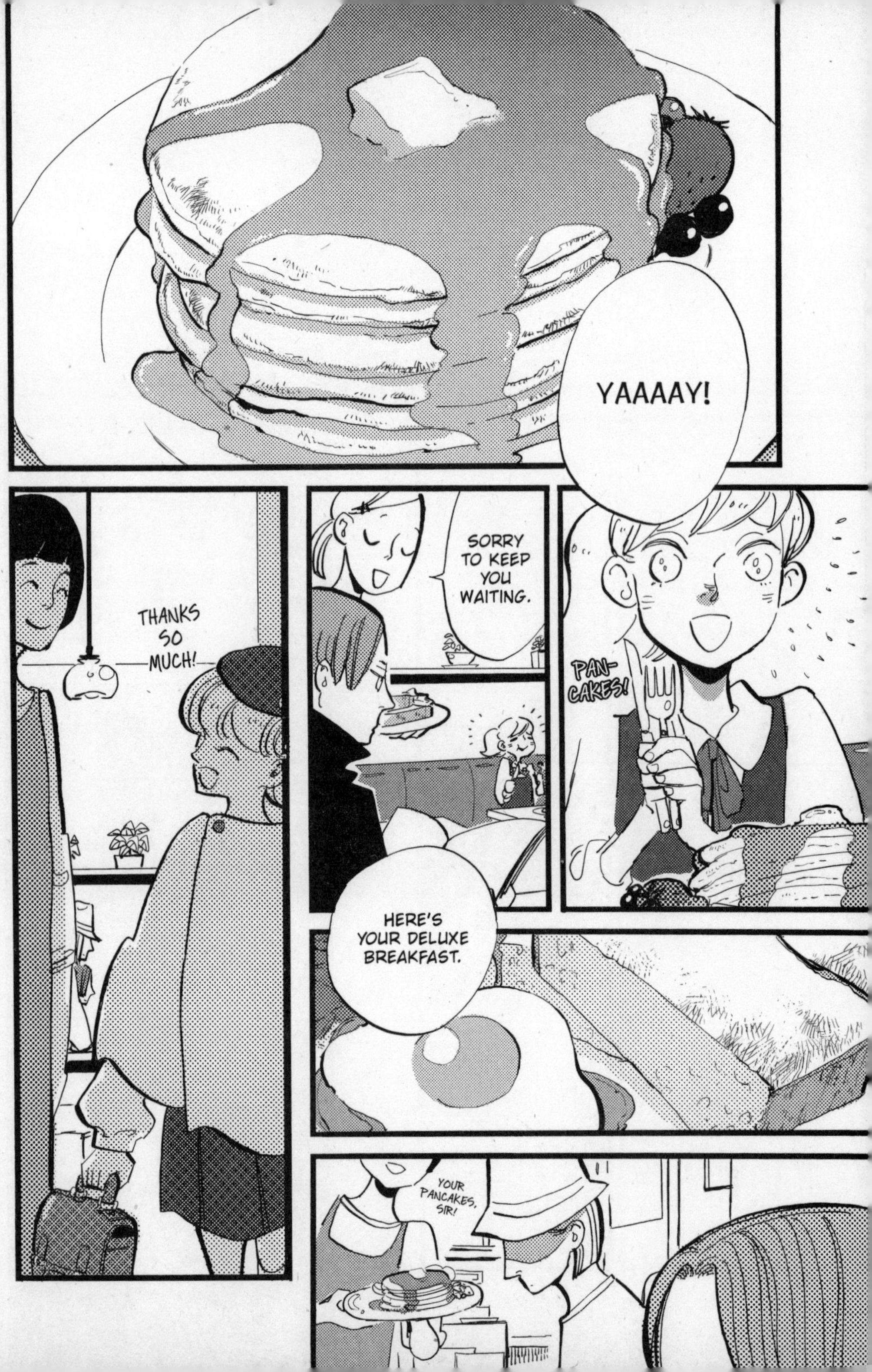
YAAAAY!
PAN-CAKES!
SORRY TO KEEP YOU WAITING.
HERE'S YOUR DELUXE BREAKFAST.
YOUR PANCAKES, SIR!
THANKS SO MUCH!

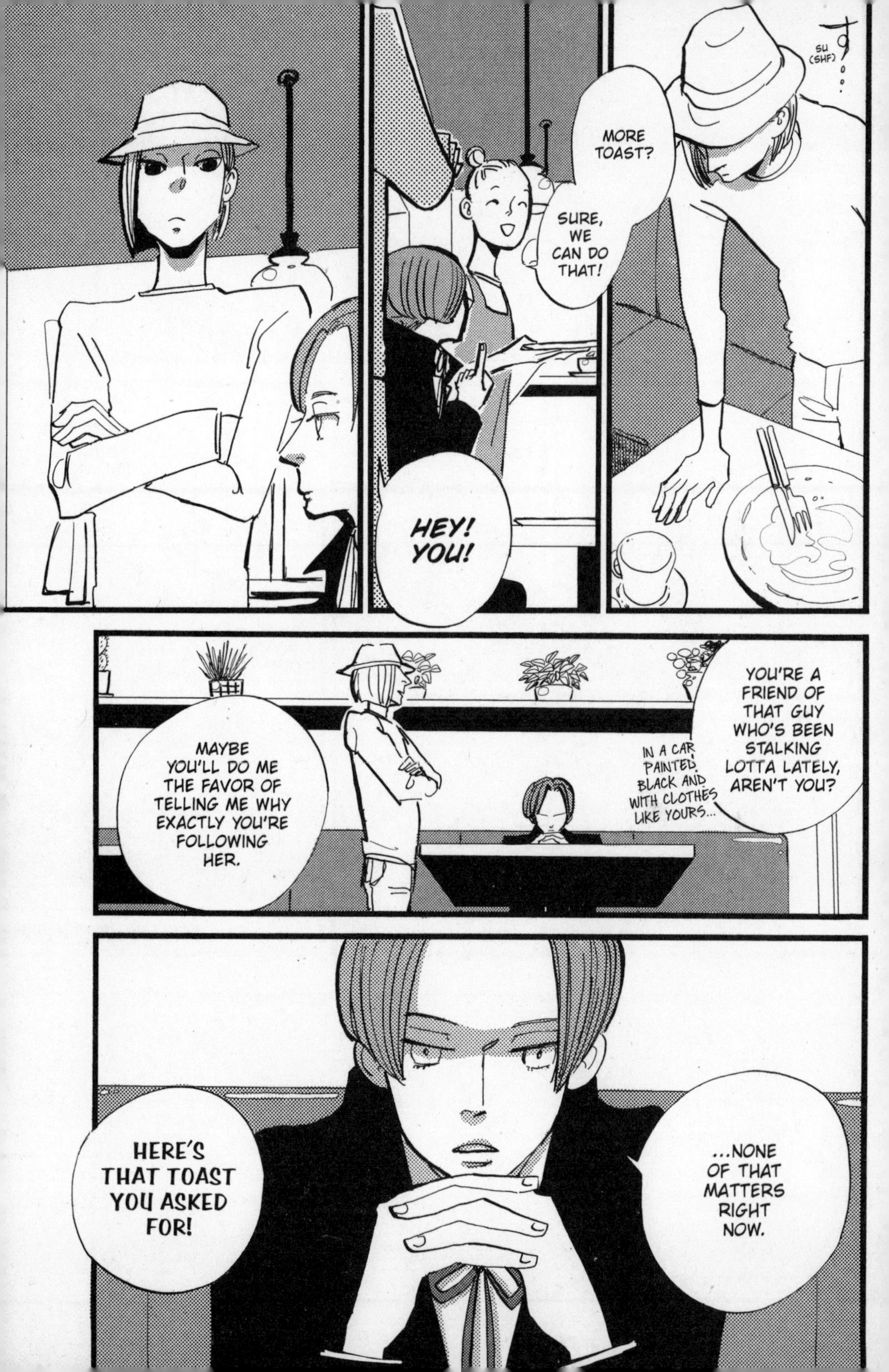
す
SU (SHF)
MORE TOAST?
SURE, WE CAN DO THAT!
HEY! YOU!
YOU'RE A FRIEND OF THAT GUY WHO'S BEEN STALKING LOTTA LATELY, AREN'T YOU?
IN A CAR PAINTED BLACK AND WITH CLOTHES LIKE YOURS...
MAYBE YOU'LL DO ME THE FAVOR OF TELLING ME WHY EXACTLY YOU'RE FOLLOWING HER.
...NONE OF THAT MATTERS RIGHT NOW.
HERE'S THAT TOAST YOU ASKED FOR!

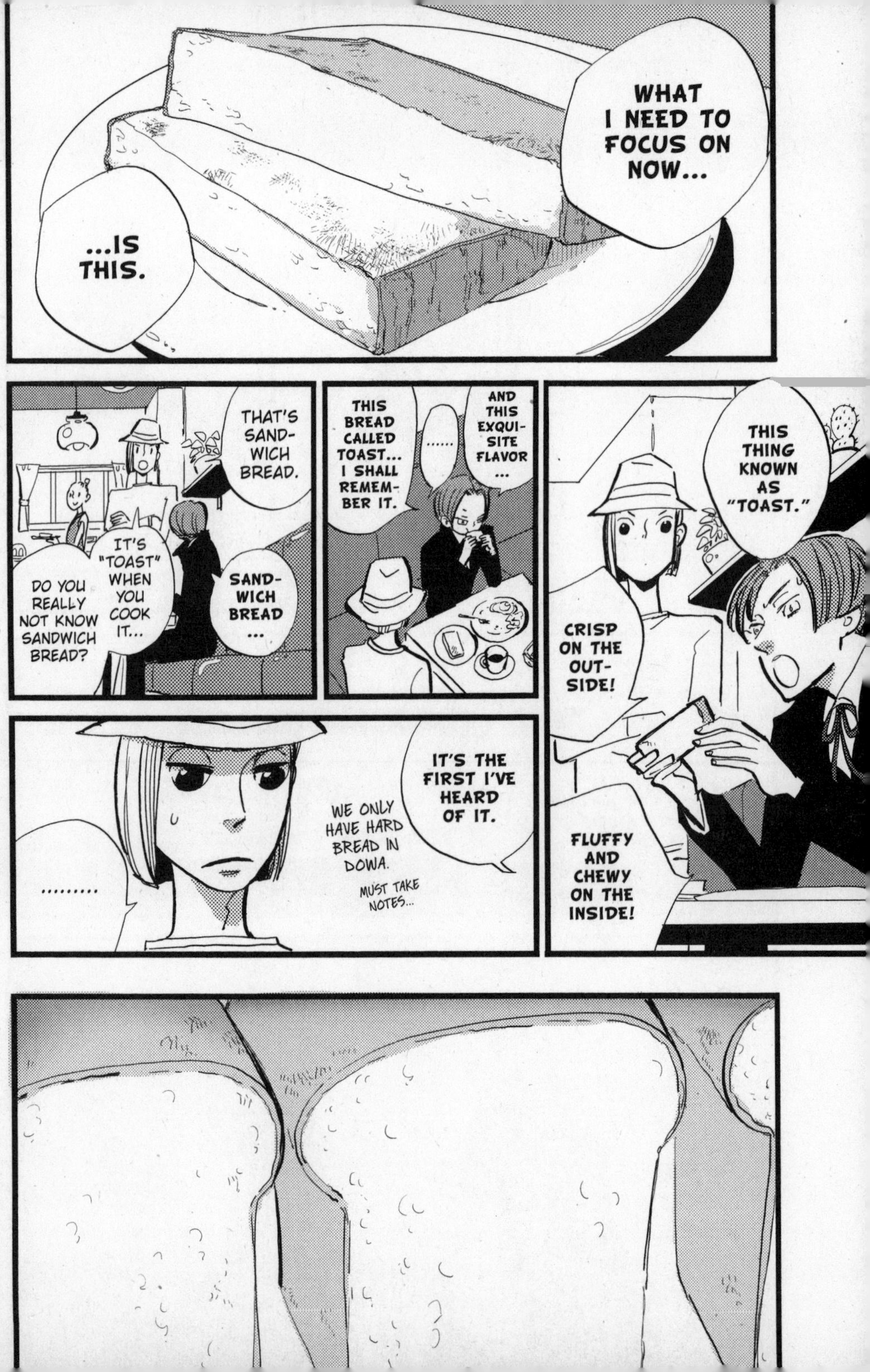
WHAT I NEED TO FOCUS ON NOW...
...IS THIS.
THIS THING KNOWN AS "TOAST."
CRISP ON THE OUTSIDE!
FLUFFY AND CHEWY ON THE INSIDE!
AND THIS EXQUISITE FLAVOR ...
......
THIS BREAD CALLED TOAST... I SHALL REMEMBER IT.
THAT'S SANDWICH BREAD.
SANDWICH BREAD ...
IT'S "TOAST" WHEN YOU COOK IT...
DO YOU REALLY NOT KNOW SANDWICH BREAD?
IT'S THE FIRST I'VE HEARD OF IT.
WE ONLY HAVE HARD BREAD IN DOWA.
MUST TAKE NOTES...
....

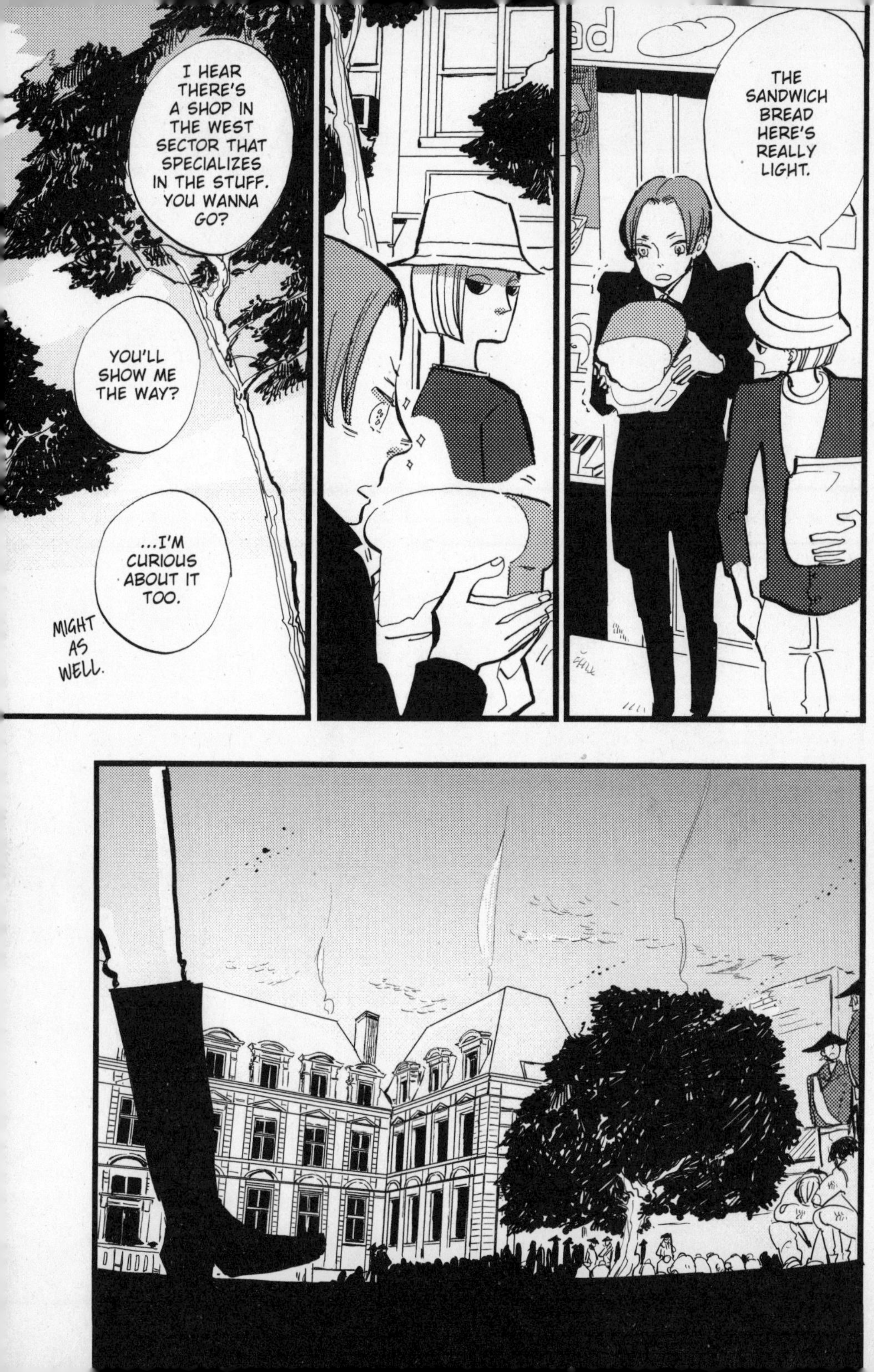
THE SANDWICH BREAD HERE'S REALLY LIGHT.
I HEAR THERE'S A SHOP IN THE WEST SECTOR THAT SPECIALIZES IN THE STUFF. YOU WANNA GO?
YOU'LL SHOW ME THE WAY?
...I'M CURIOUS ABOUT IT TOO.
MIGHT AS WELL.

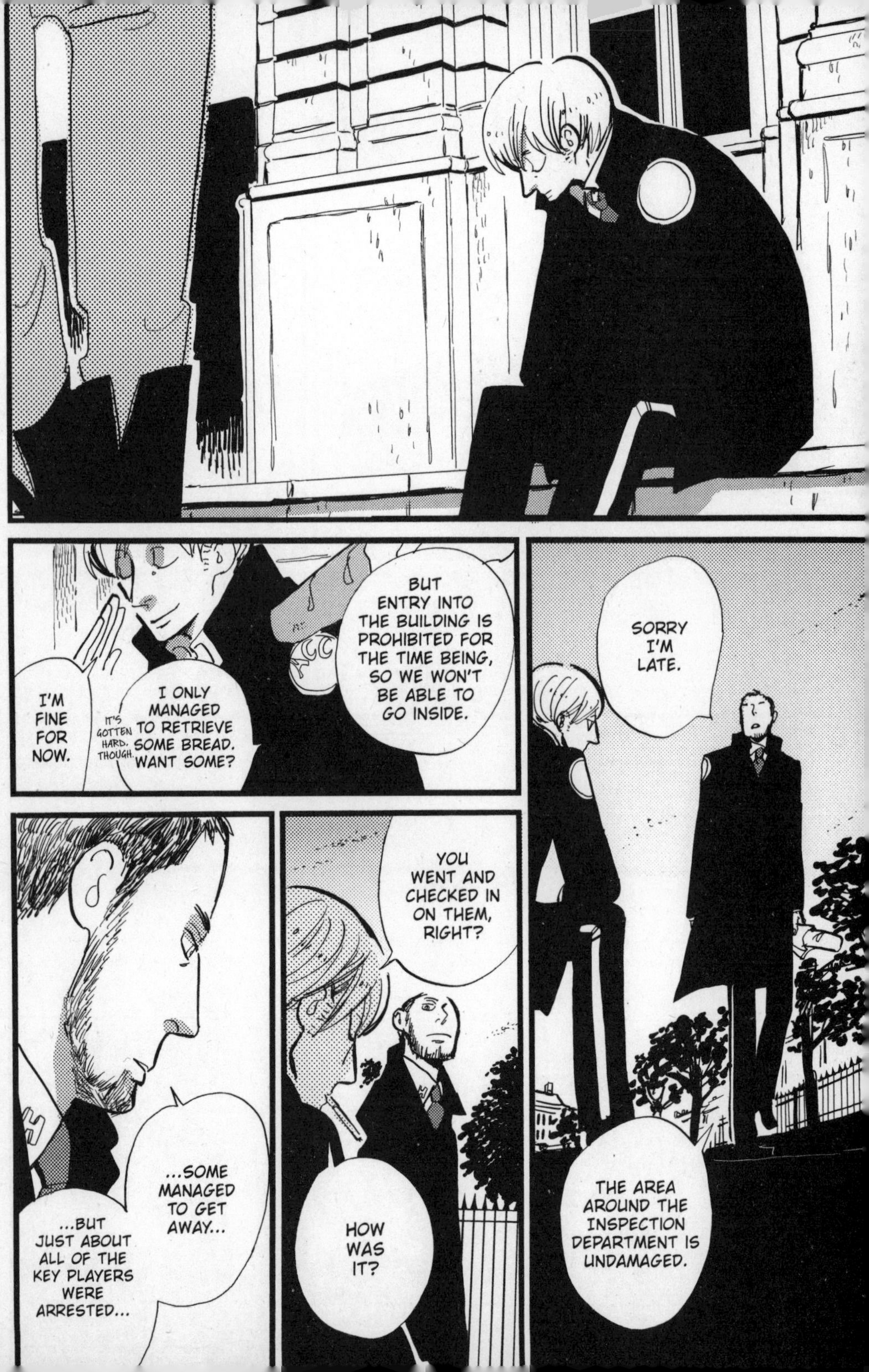
SORRY I'M LATE.
THE AREA AROUND THE INSPECTION DEPARTMENT IS UNDAMAGED.
BUT ENTRY INTO THE BUILDING IS PROHIBITED FOR THE TIME BEING, SO WE WON'T BE ABLE TO GO INSIDE.
I ONLY MANAGED TO RETRIEVE SOME BREAD. WANT SOME?
IT'S GOTTEN HARD, THOUGH.
I'M FINE FOR NOW.
YOU WENT AND CHECKED IN ON THEM, RIGHT?
HOW WAS IT?
...SOME MANAGED TO GET AWAY...
...BUT JUST ABOUT ALL OF THE KEY PLAYERS WERE ARRESTED...

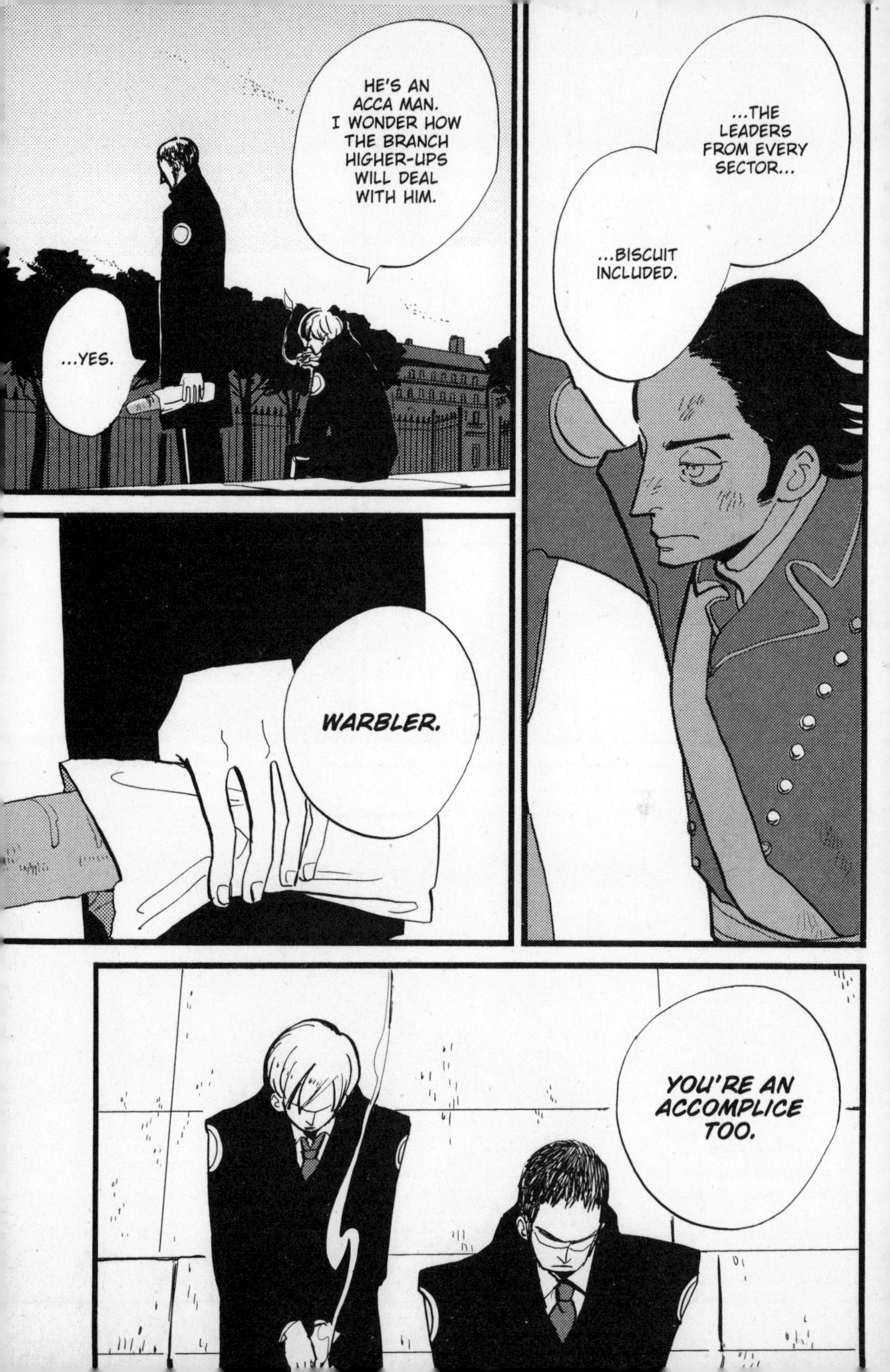
...THE LEADERS FROM EVERY SECTOR...
...BISCUIT INCLUDED.
HE'S AN ACCA MAN. I WONDER HOW THE BRANCH HIGHER-UPS WILL DEAL WITH HIM.
...YES.
WARBLER.
YOU'RE AN ACCOMPLICE TOO.

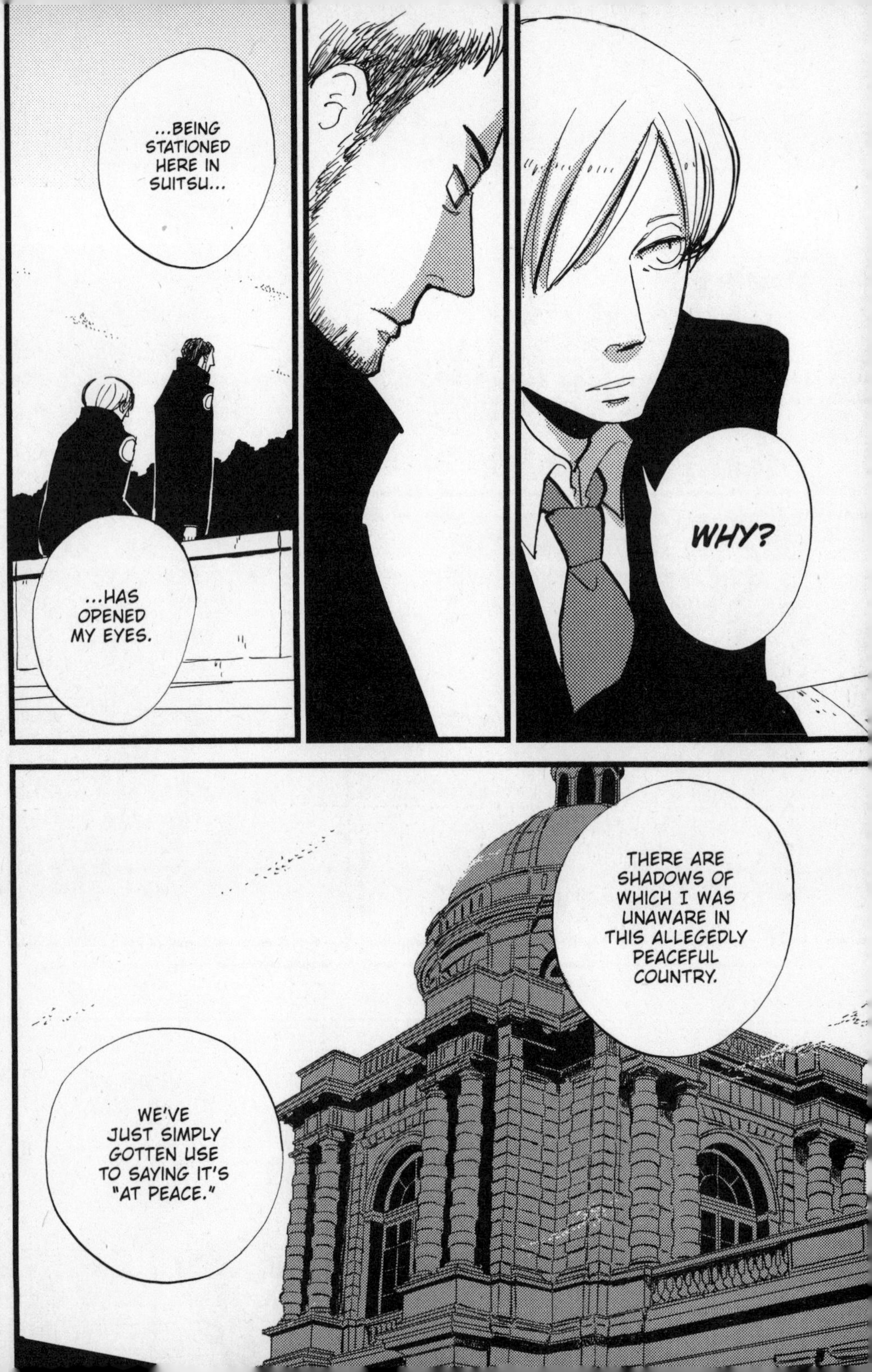
WHY?
...BEING STATIONED HERE IN SUITSU...
...HAS OPENED MY EYES.
THERE ARE SHADOWS OF WHICH I WAS UNAWARE IN THIS ALLEGEDLY PEACEFUL COUNTRY.
WE'VE JUST SIMPLY GOTTEN USE TO SAYING IT'S "AT PEACE."

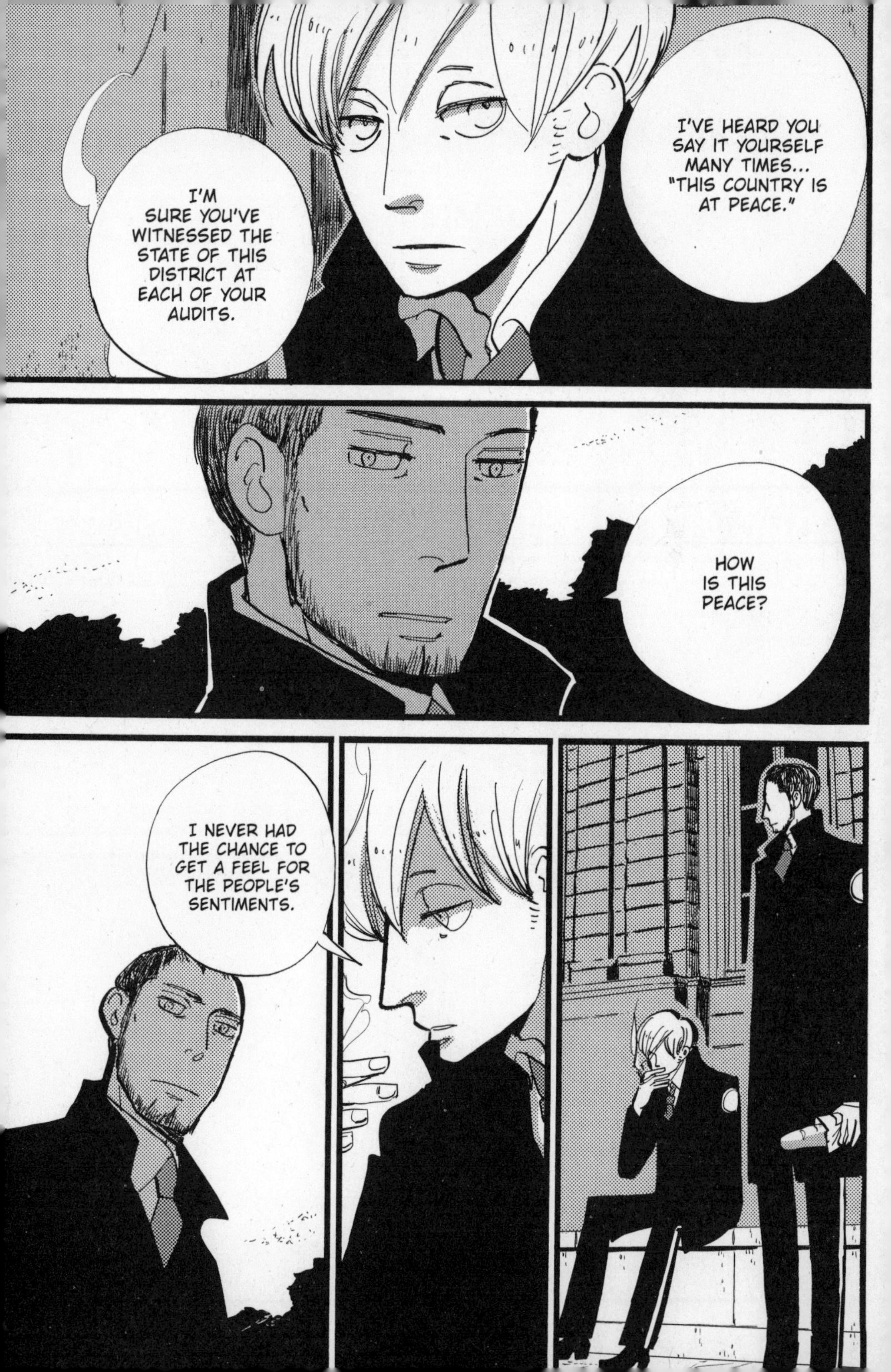
I'VE HEARD YOU SAY IT YOURSELF MANY TIMES... "THIS COUNTRY IS AT PEACE."
I'M SURE YOU'VE WITNESSED THE STATE OF THIS DISTRICT AT EACH OF YOUR AUDITS.
HOW IS THIS PEACE?
I NEVER HAD THE CHANCE TO GET A FEEL FOR THE PEOPLE'S SENTIMENTS.

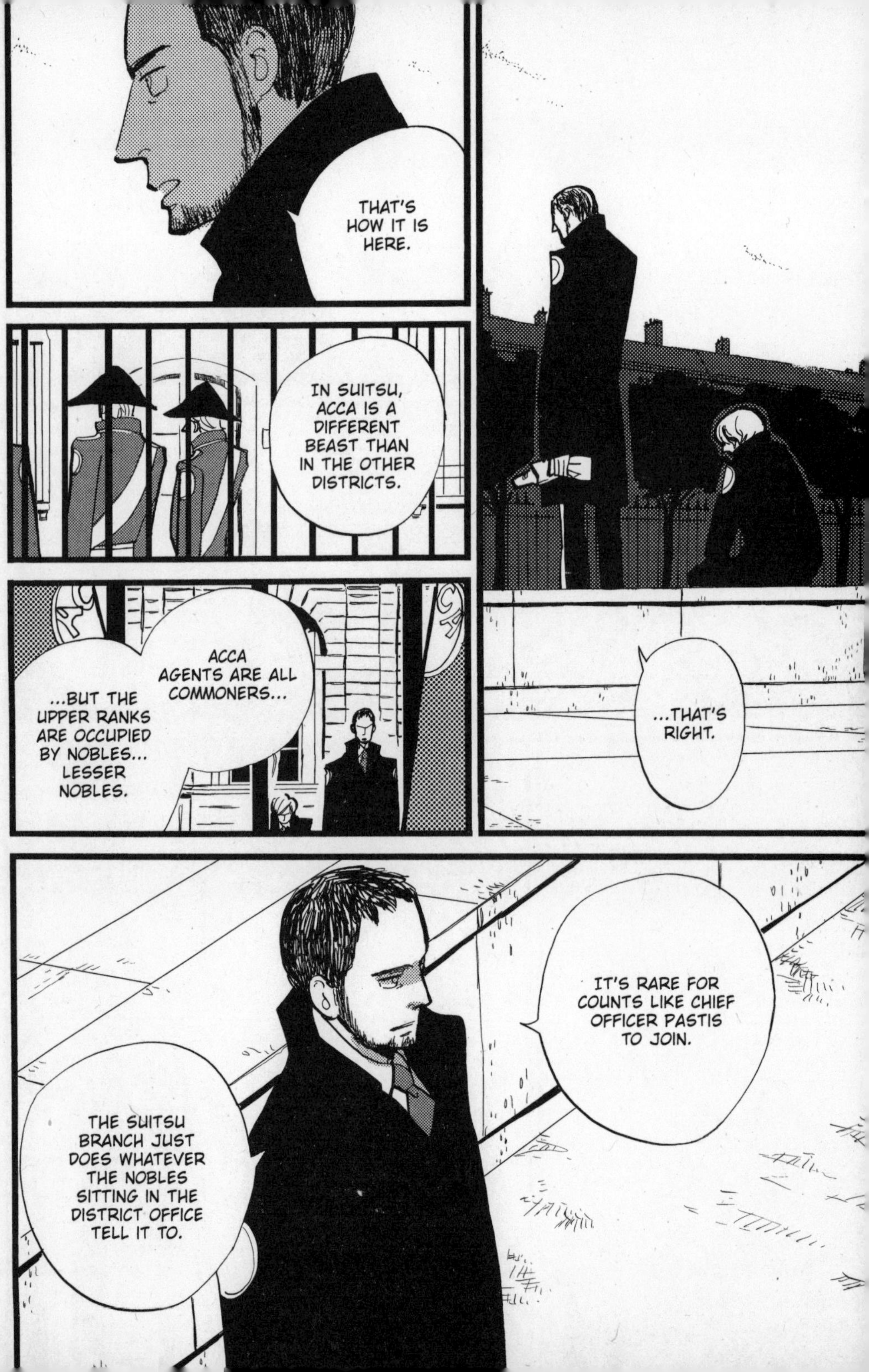
THAT'S HOW IT IS HERE.
IN SUITSU, ACCA IS A DIFFERENT BEAST THAN IN THE OTHER DISTRICTS.
...THAT'S RIGHT.
ACCA AGENTS ARE ALL COMMONERS...
...BUT THE UPPER RANKS ARE OCCUPIED BY NOBLES... LESSER NOBLES.
IT'S RARE FOR COUNTS LIKE CHIEF OFFICER PASTIS TO JOIN.
THE SUITSU BRANCH JUST DOES WHATEVER THE NOBLES SITTING IN THE DISTRICT OFFICE TELL IT TO.

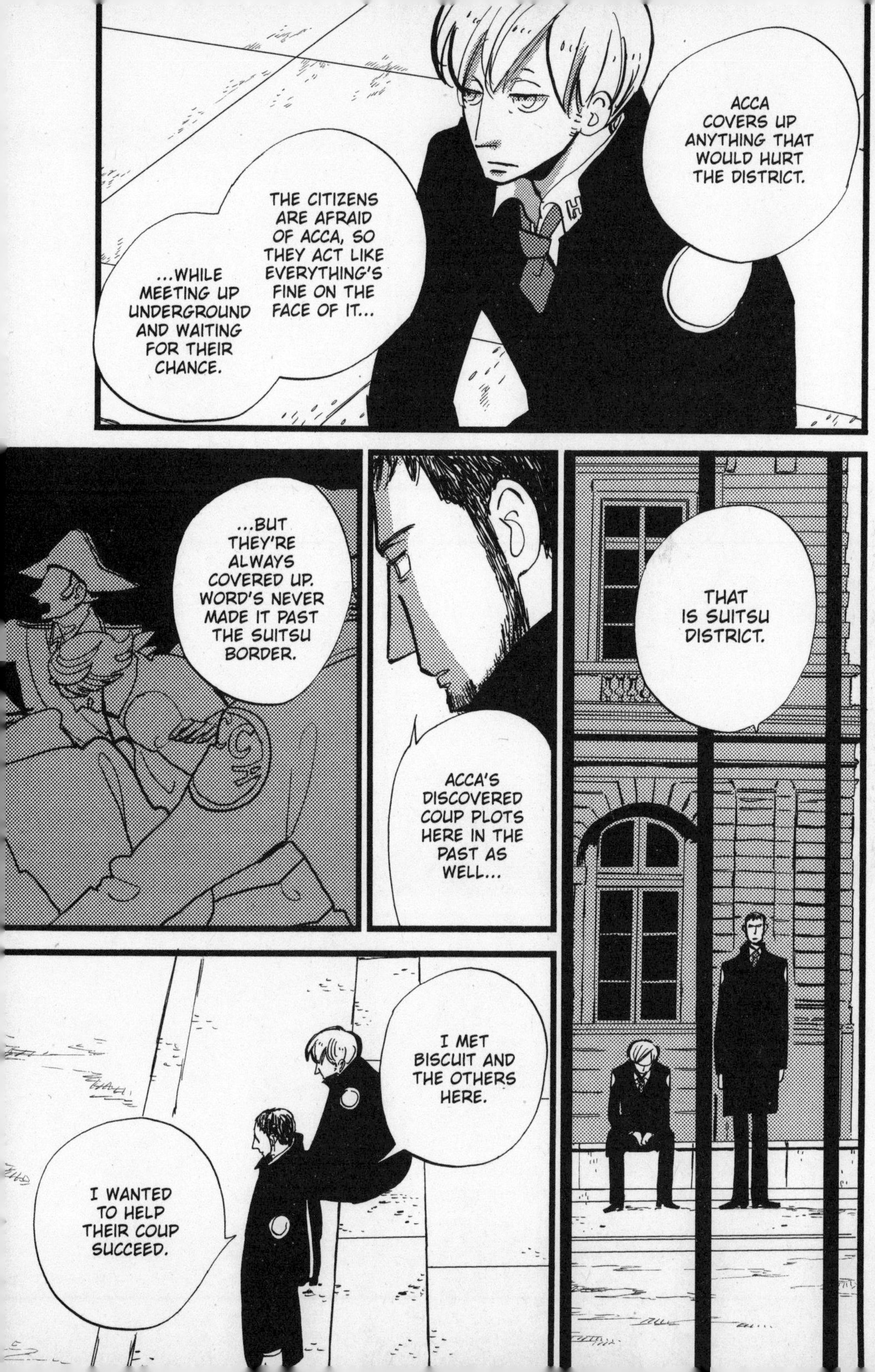
ACCA COVERS UP ANYTHING THAT WOULD HURT THE DISTRICT.
THE CITIZENS ARE AFRAID OF ACCA, SO THEY ACT LIKE EVERYTHING'S FINE ON THE FACE OF IT...
...WHILE MEETING UP UNDERGROUND AND WAITING FOR THEIR CHANCE.
THAT IS SUITSU DISTRICT.
ACCA'S DISCOVERED COUP PLOTS HERE IN THE PAST AS WELL...
...BUT THEY'RE ALWAYS COVERED UP. WORD'S NEVER MADE IT PAST THE SUITSU BORDER.
I MET BISCUIT AND THE OTHERS HERE.
I WANTED TO HELP THEIR COUP SUCCEED.

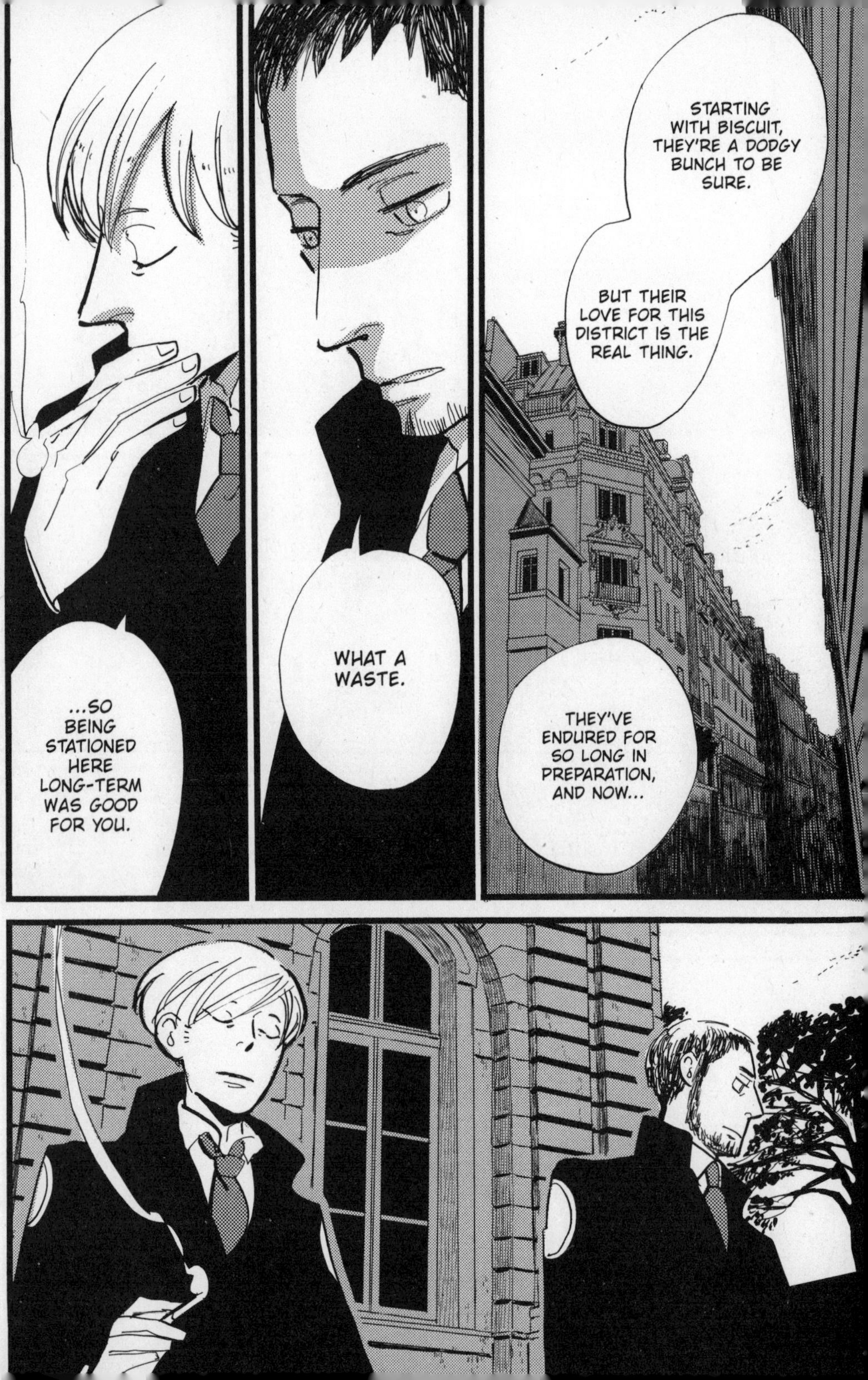
STARTING WITH BISCUIT, THEY'RE A DODGY BUNCH TO BE SURE.
BUT THEIR LOVE FOR THIS DISTRICT IS THE REAL THING.
THEY'VE ENDURED FOR SO LONG IN PREPARATION, AND NOW...
WHAT A WASTE.
...SO BEING STATIONED HERE LONG-TERM WAS GOOD FOR YOU.

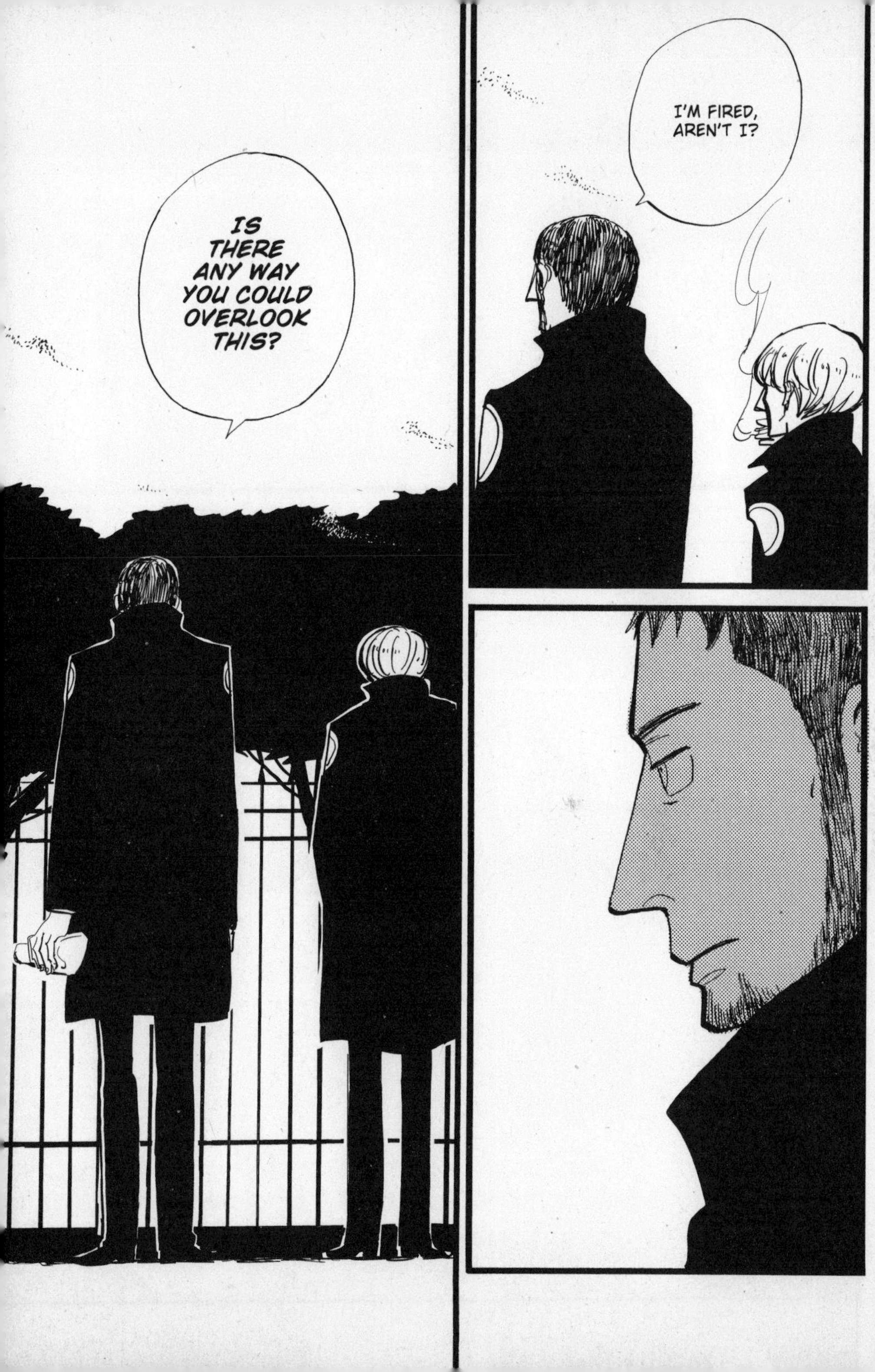
I'M FIRED, AREN'T I?
IS THERE ANY WAY YOU COULD OVERLOOK THIS?

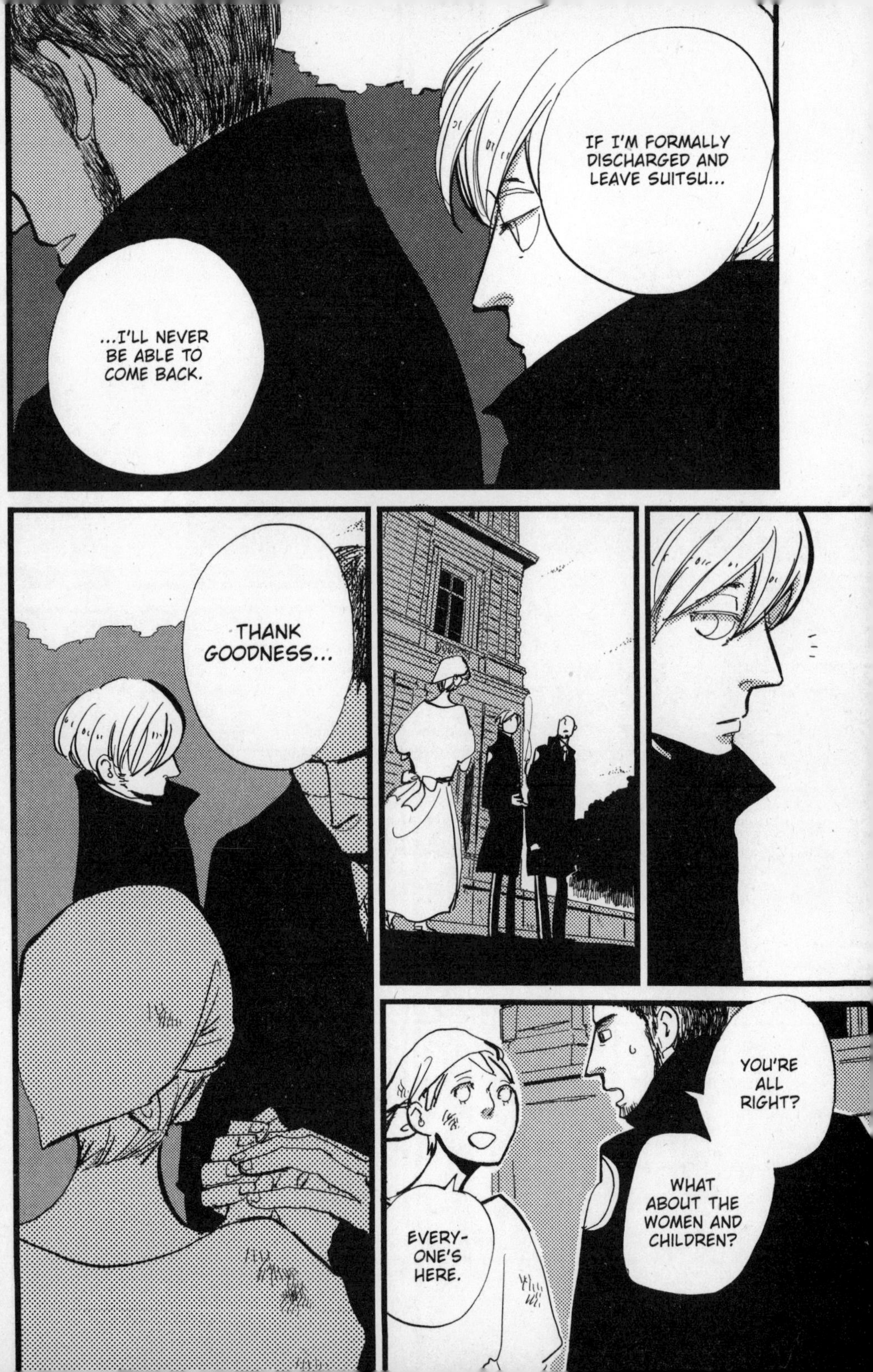
IF I'M FORMALLY DISCHARGED AND LEAVE SUITSU...
...I'LL NEVER BE ABLE TO COME BACK.
YOU'RE ALL RIGHT?
WHAT ABOUT THE WOMEN AND CHILDREN?
EVERY-ONE'S HERE.
THANK GOODNESS...

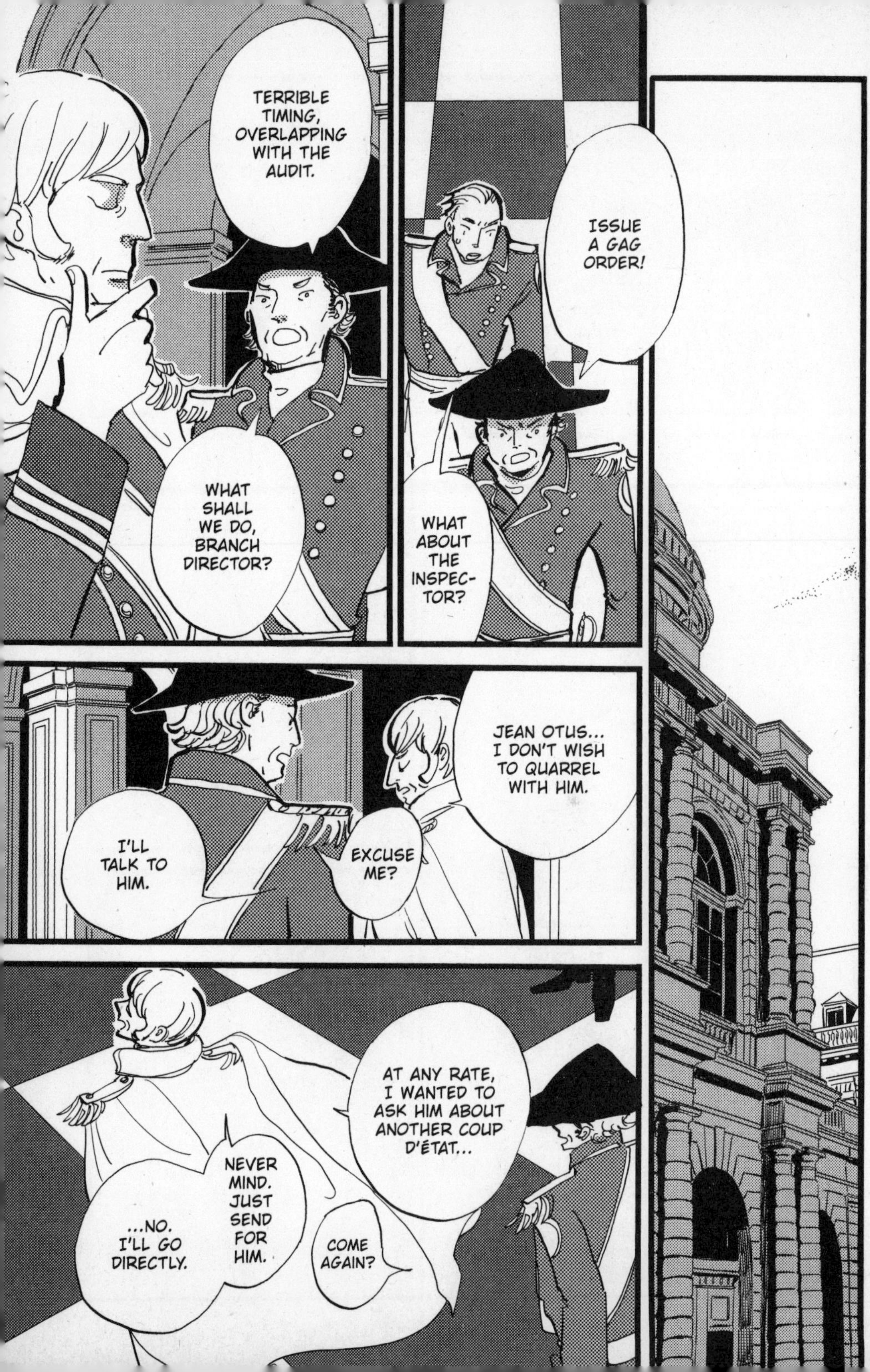
ISSUE A GAG ORDER!
WHAT ABOUT THE INSPECTOR?
TERRIBLE TIMING, OVERLAPPING WITH THE AUDIT.
WHAT SHALL WE DO, BRANCH DIRECTOR?
JEAN OTUS... I DON'T WISH TO QUARREL WITH HIM.
EXCUSE ME?
I'LL TALK TO HIM.
AT ANY RATE, I WANTED TO ASK HIM ABOUT ANOTHER COUP D'ÉTAT...
NEVER MIND. JUST SEND FOR HIM.
COME AGAIN?
...NO. I'LL GO DIRECTLY.

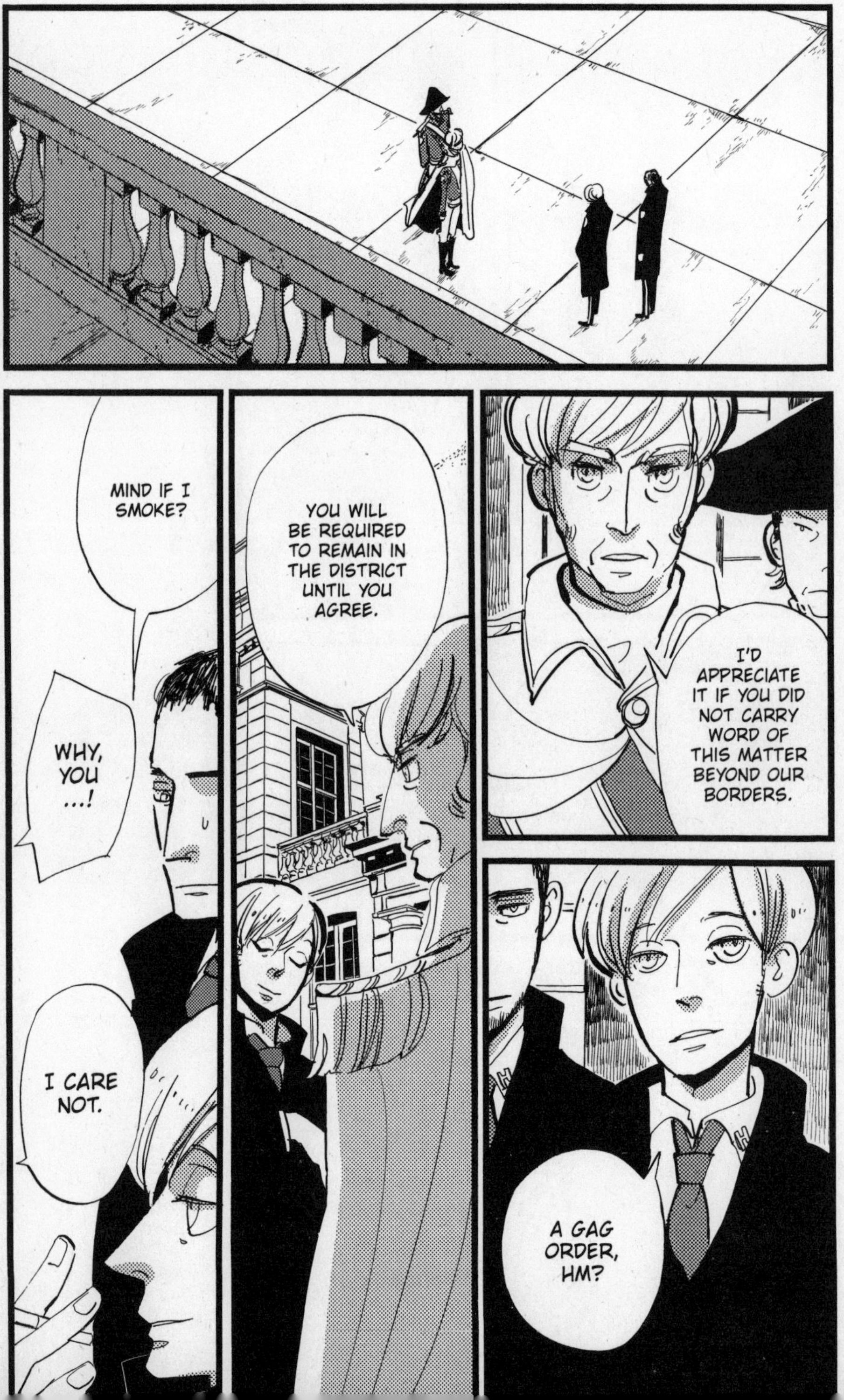
I'D APPRECIATE IT IF YOU DID NOT CARRY WORD OF THIS MATTER BEYOND OUR BORDERS.
A GAG ORDER, HM?
YOU WILL BE REQUIRED TO REMAIN IN THE DISTRICT UNTIL YOU AGREE.
MIND IF I SMOKE?
WHY, YOU ...!
I CARE NOT.

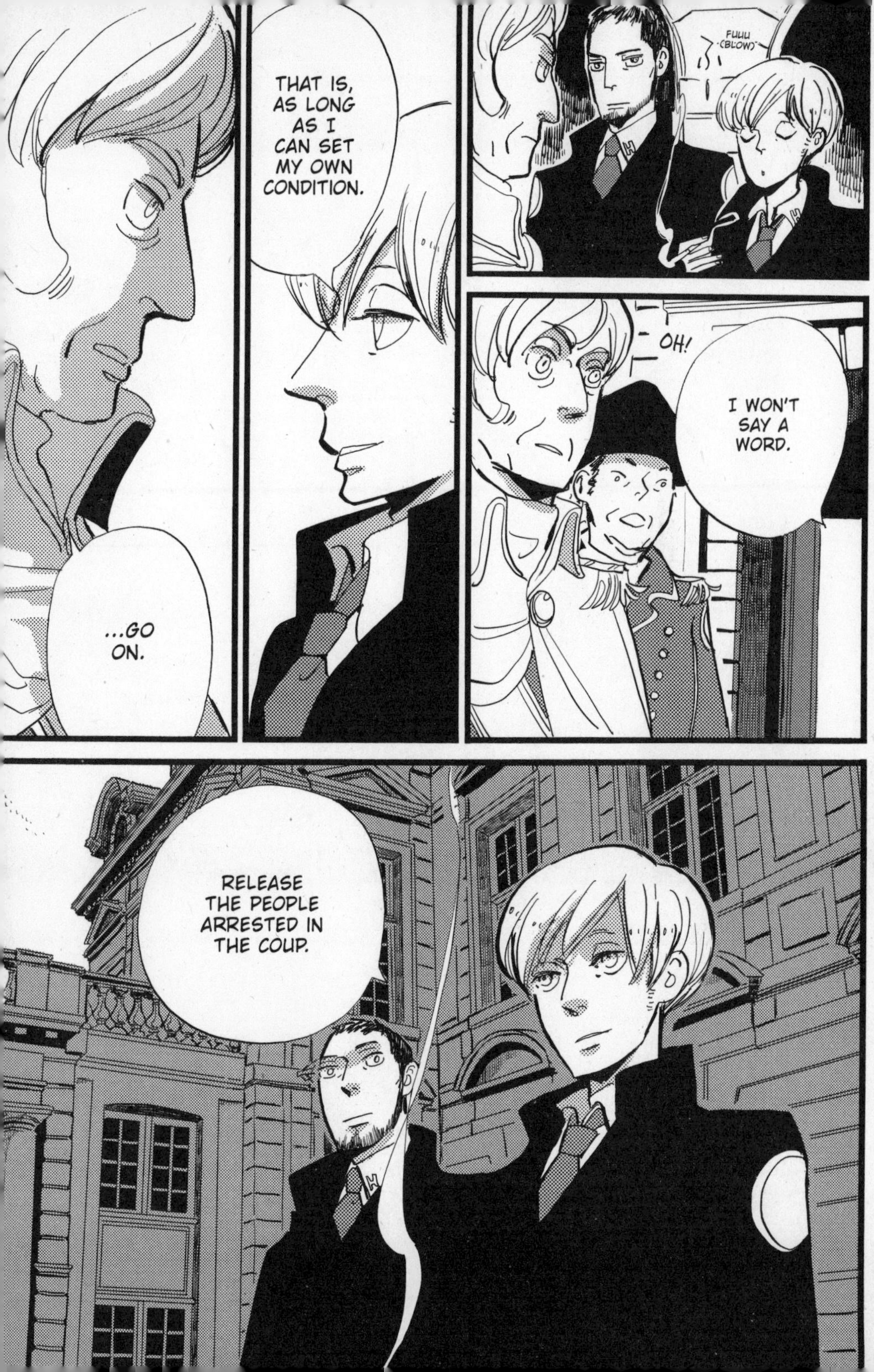
FUUU (BLOW)
OH!
I WON'T SAY A WORD.
THAT IS, AS LONG AS I CAN SET MY OWN CONDITION.
...GO ON.
RELEASE THE PEOPLE ARRESTED IN THE COUP.

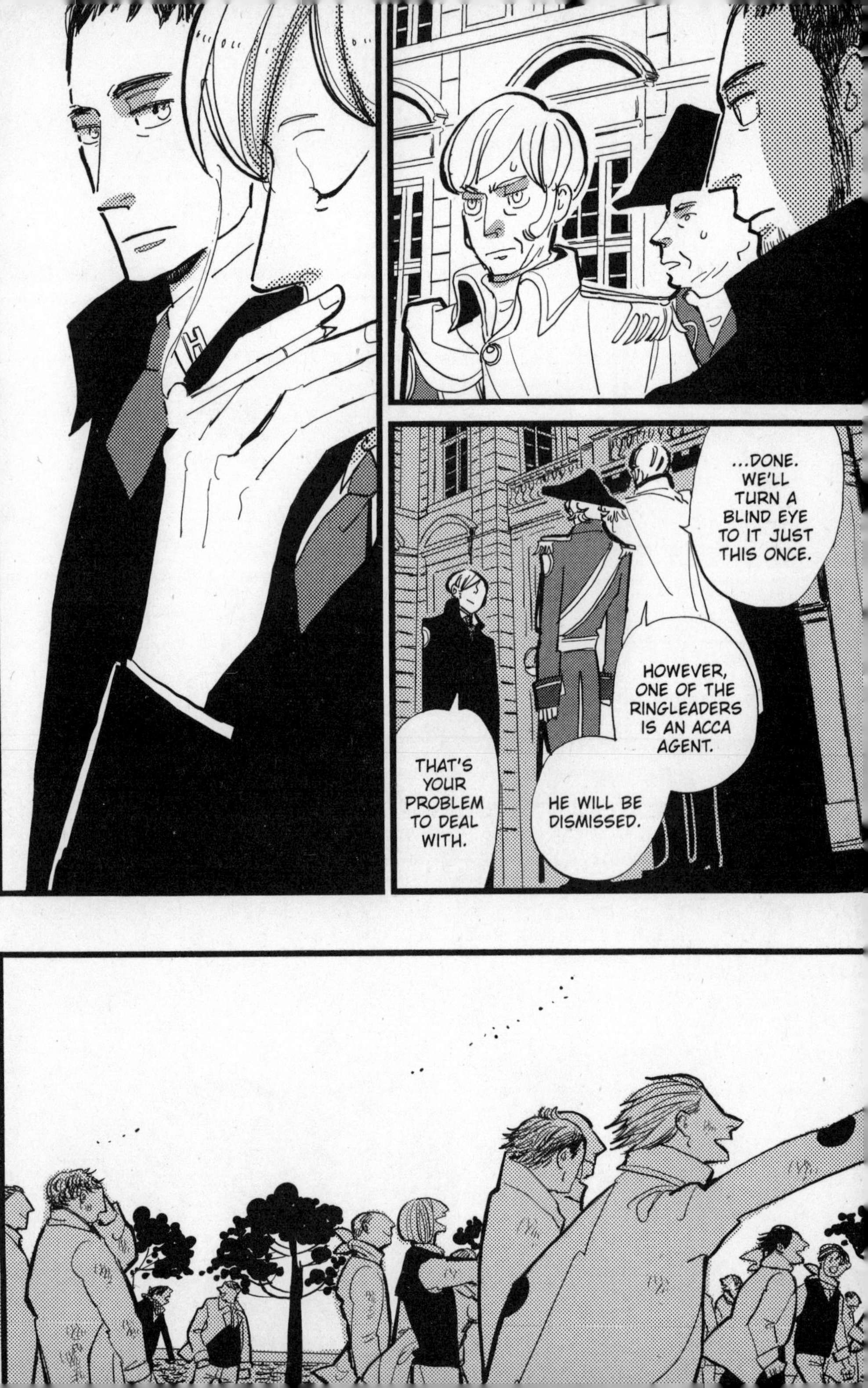
...DONE. WE'LL TURN A BLIND EYE TO IT JUST THIS ONCE.
HOWEVER, ONE OF THE RINGLEADERS IS AN ACCA AGENT.
HE WILL BE DISMISSED.
THAT'S YOUR PROBLEM TO DEAL WITH.

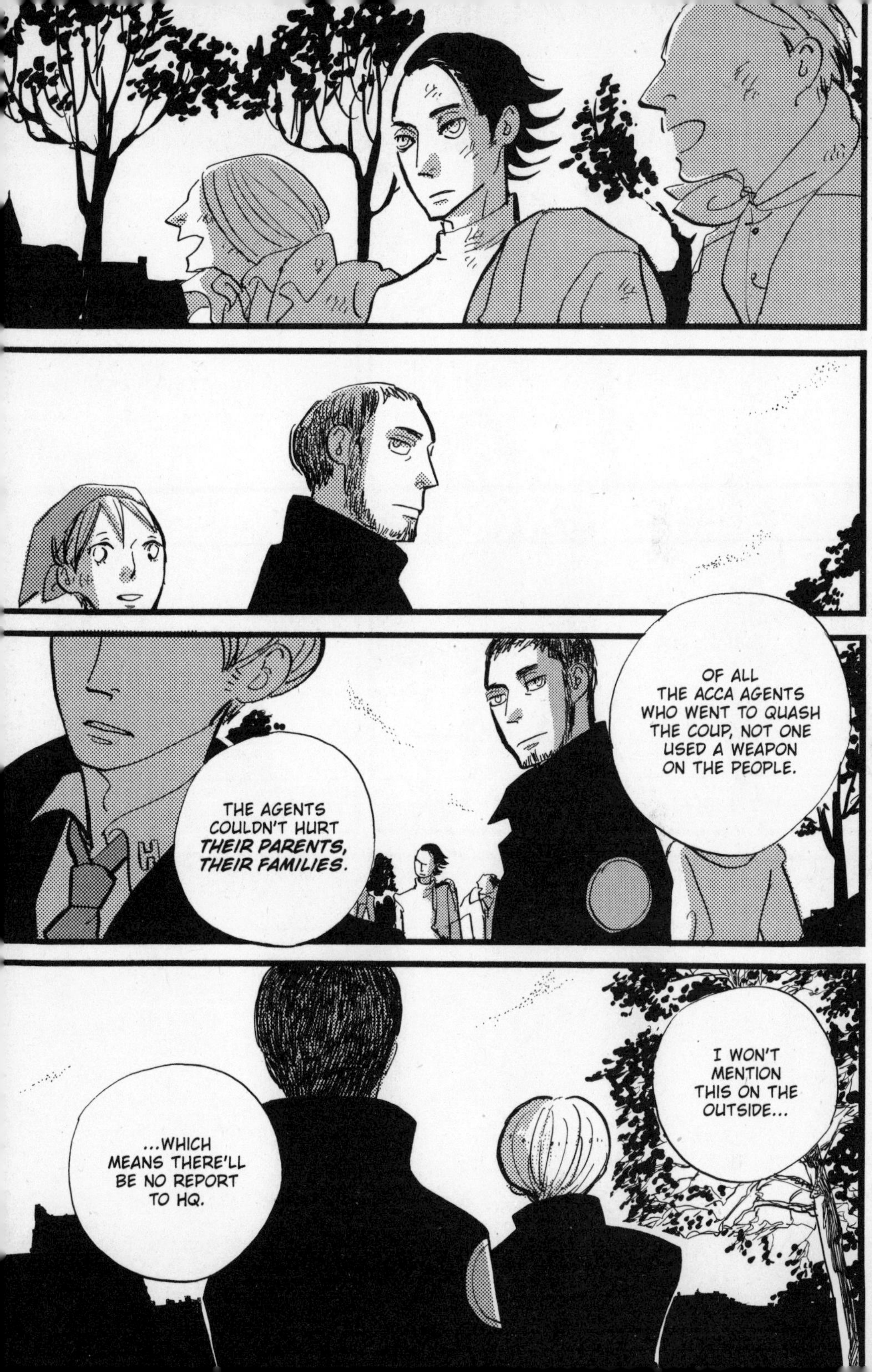
OF ALL THE ACCA AGENTS WHO WENT TO QUASH THE COUP, NOT ONE USED A WEAPON ON THE PEOPLE.
THE AGENTS COULDN'T HURT *THEIR PARENTS, THEIR FAMILIES*.
I WON'T MENTION THIS ON THE OUTSIDE...
...WHICH MEANS THERE'LL BE NO REPORT TO HQ.

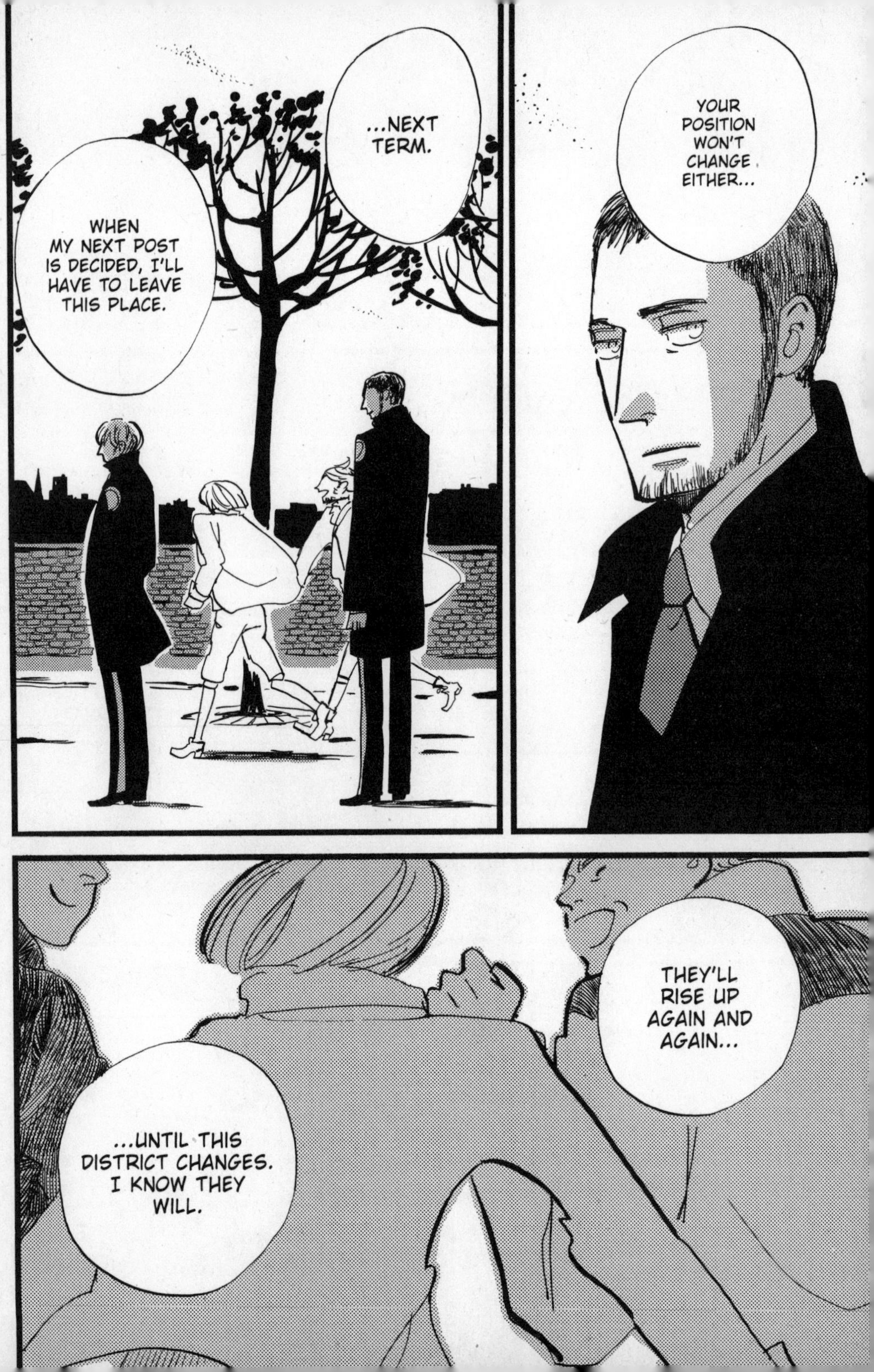
YOUR POSITION WON'T CHANGE EITHER...
...NEXT TERM.
WHEN MY NEXT POST IS DECIDED, I'LL HAVE TO LEAVE THIS PLACE.
THEY'LL RISE UP AGAIN AND AGAIN...
...UNTIL THIS DISTRICT CHANGES. I KNOW THEY WILL.

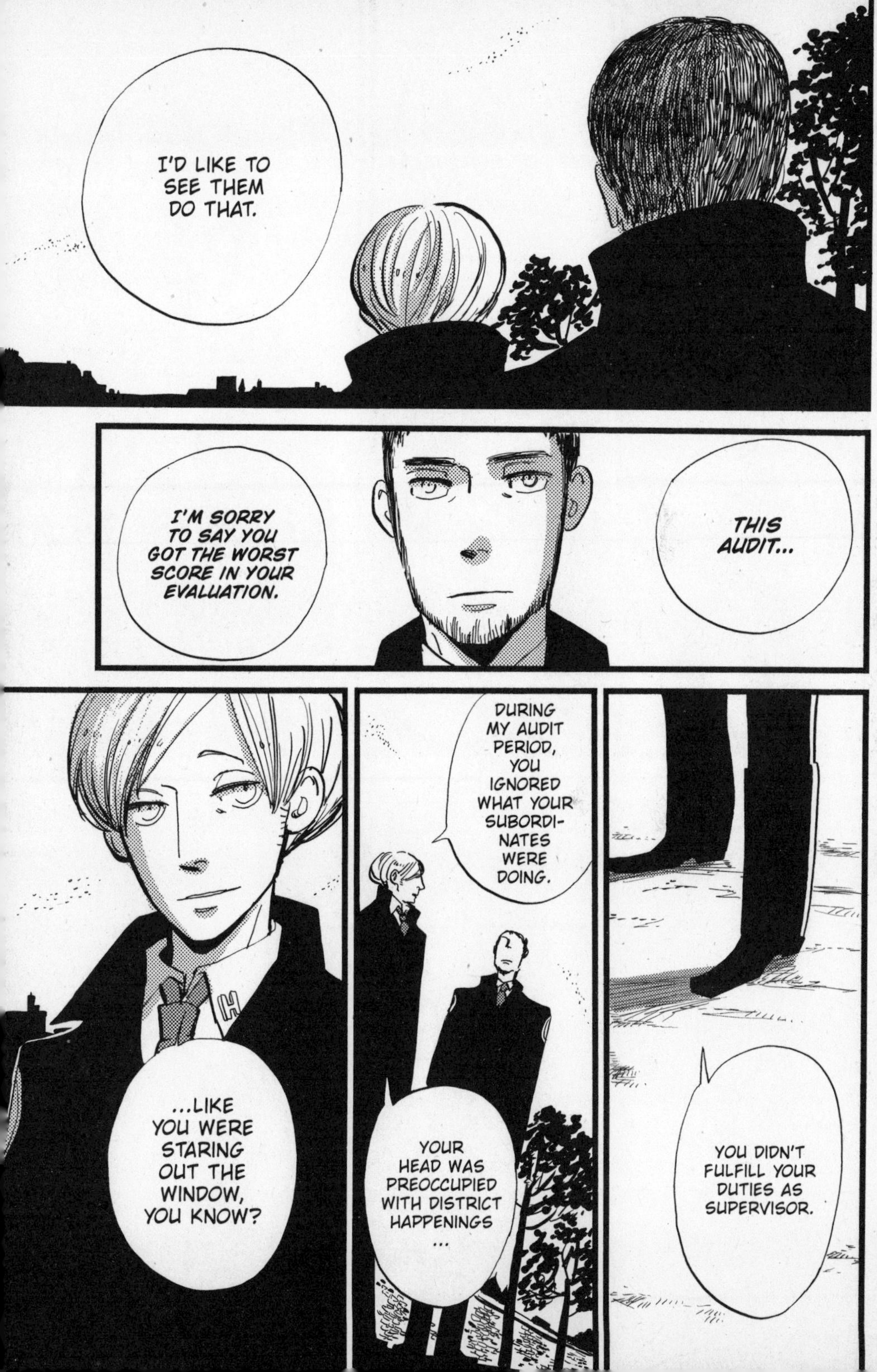
I'D LIKE TO SEE THEM DO THAT.
THIS AUDIT...
I'M SORRY TO SAY YOU GOT THE WORST SCORE IN YOUR EVALUATION.
YOU DIDN'T FULFILL YOUR DUTIES AS SUPERVISOR.
DURING MY AUDIT PERIOD, YOU IGNORED WHAT YOUR SUBORDI-NATES WERE DOING.
YOUR HEAD WAS PREOCCUPIED WITH DISTRICT HAPPENINGS...
...LIKE YOU WERE STARING OUT THE WINDOW, YOU KNOW?

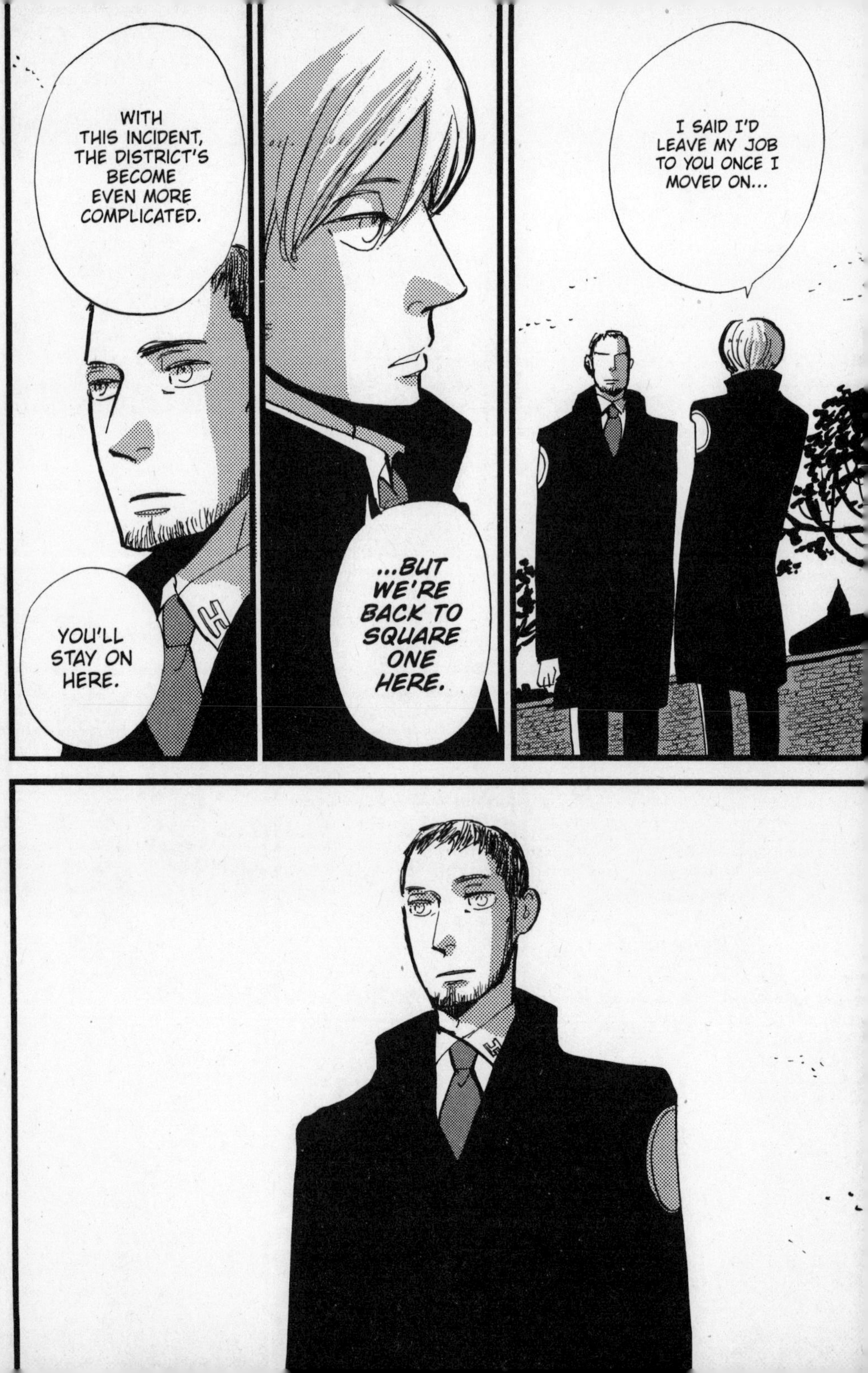
I SAID I'D LEAVE MY JOB TO YOU ONCE I MOVED ON...
...BUT WE'RE BACK TO SQUARE ONE HERE.
WITH THIS INCIDENT, THE DISTRICT'S BECOME EVEN MORE COMPLICATED.
YOU'LL STAY ON HERE.

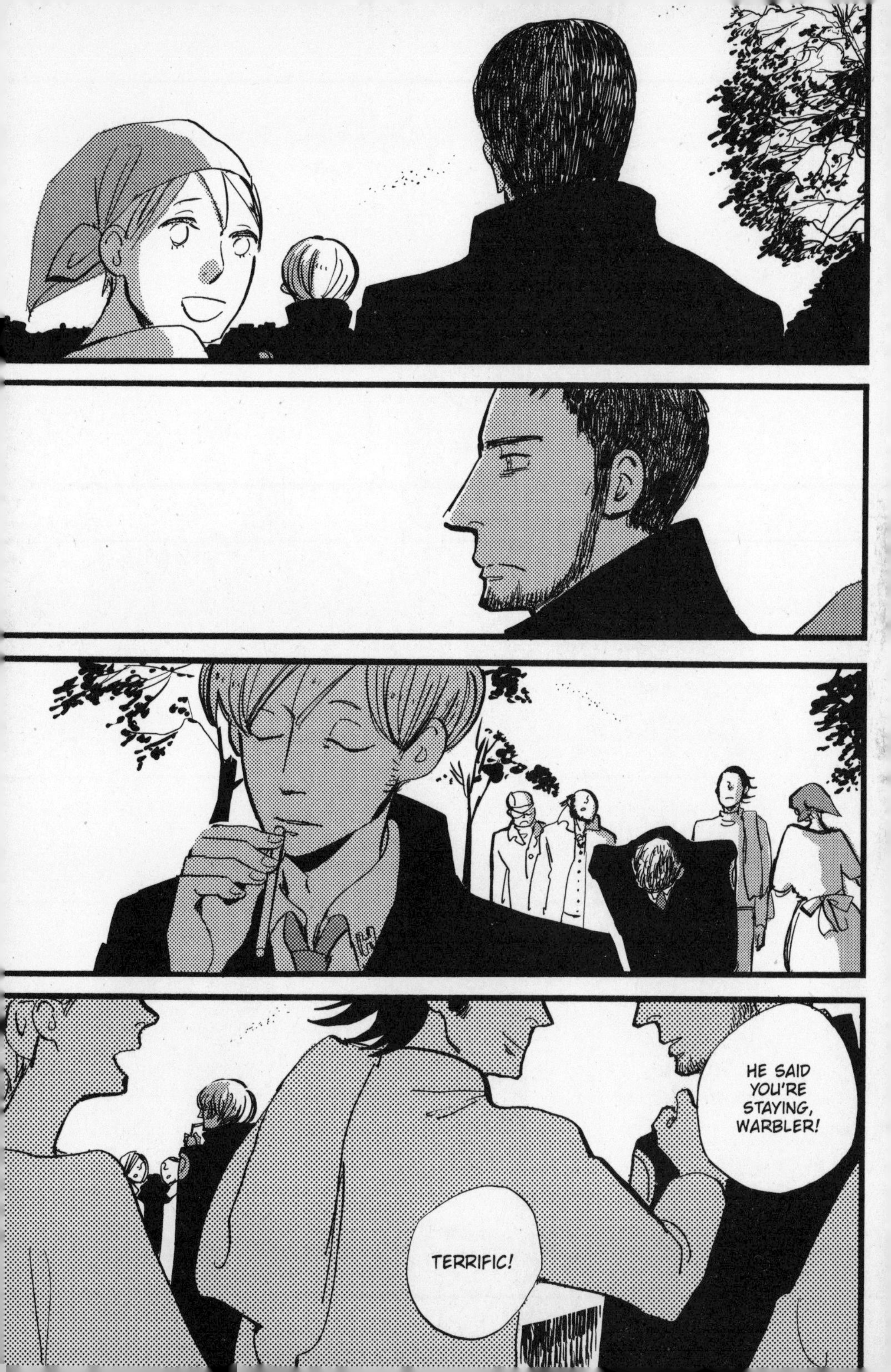
HE SAID YOU'RE STAYING, WARBLER!
TERRIFIC!

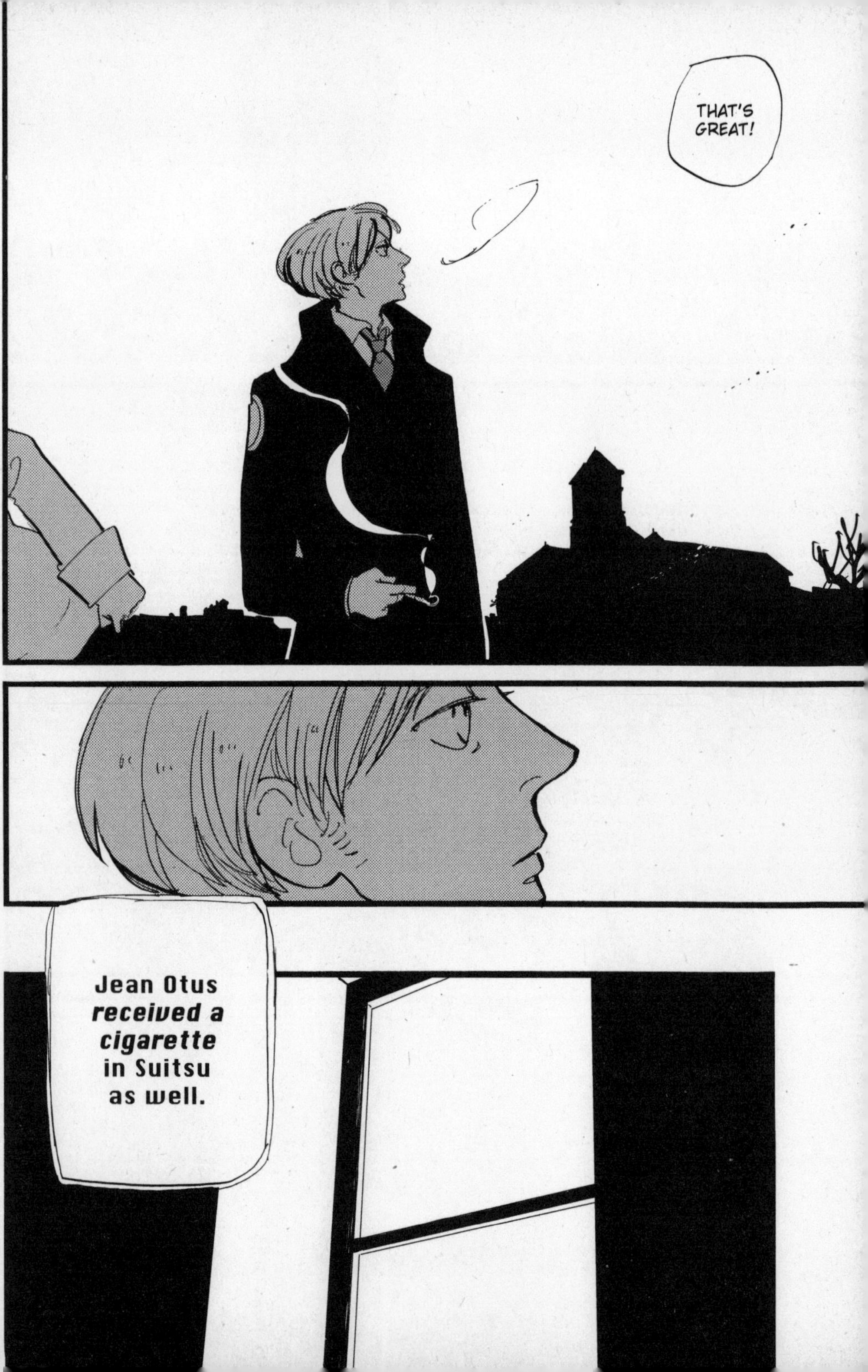
THAT'S GREAT!
Jean Otus *received a cigarette* in Suitsu as well.

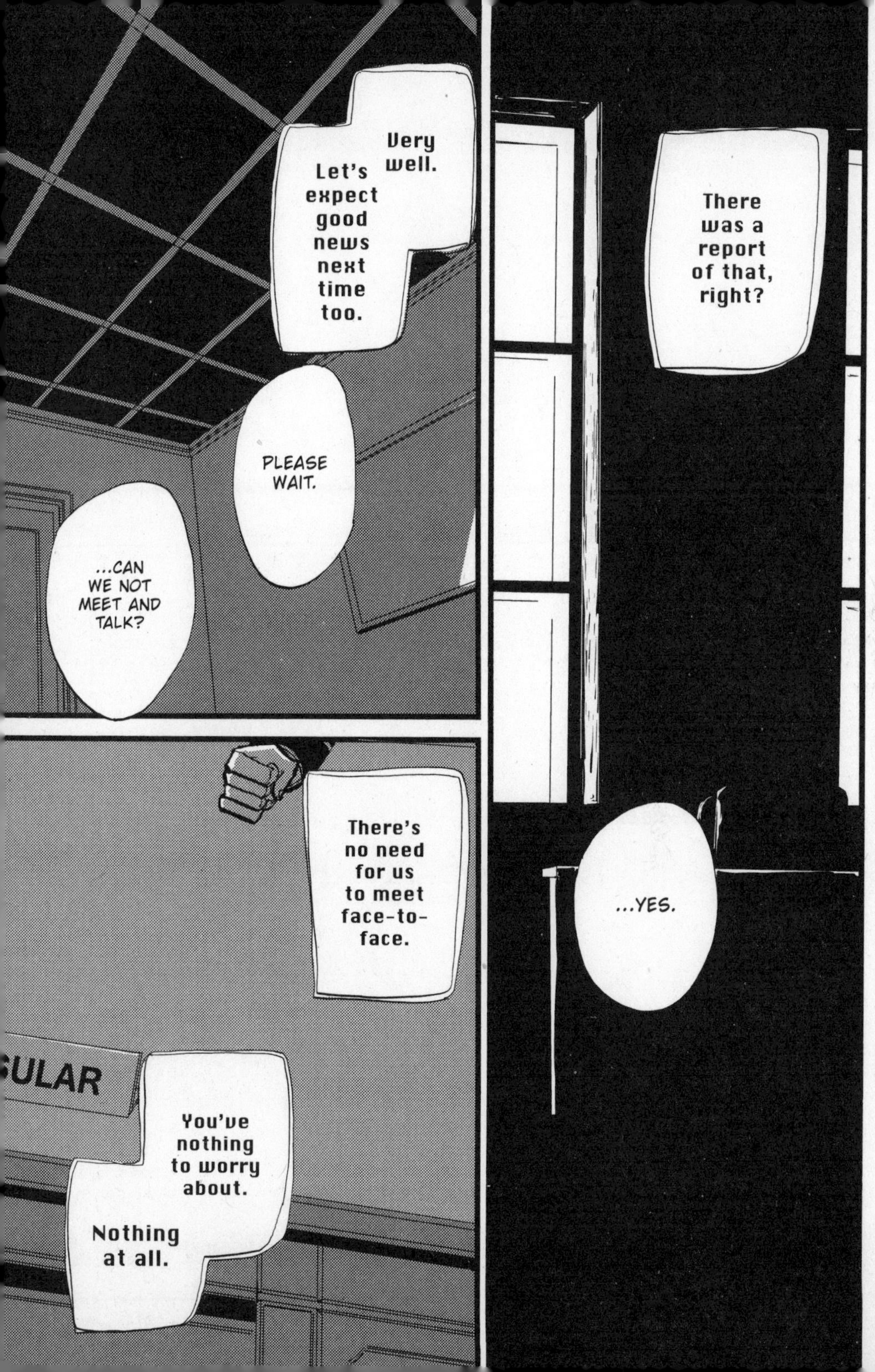
There was a report of that, right?
...YES.
Very well.
Let's expect good news next time too.
PLEASE WAIT.
...CAN WE NOT MEET AND TALK?
There's no need for us to meet face-to-face.
SULAR
You've nothing to worry about.
Nothing at all.

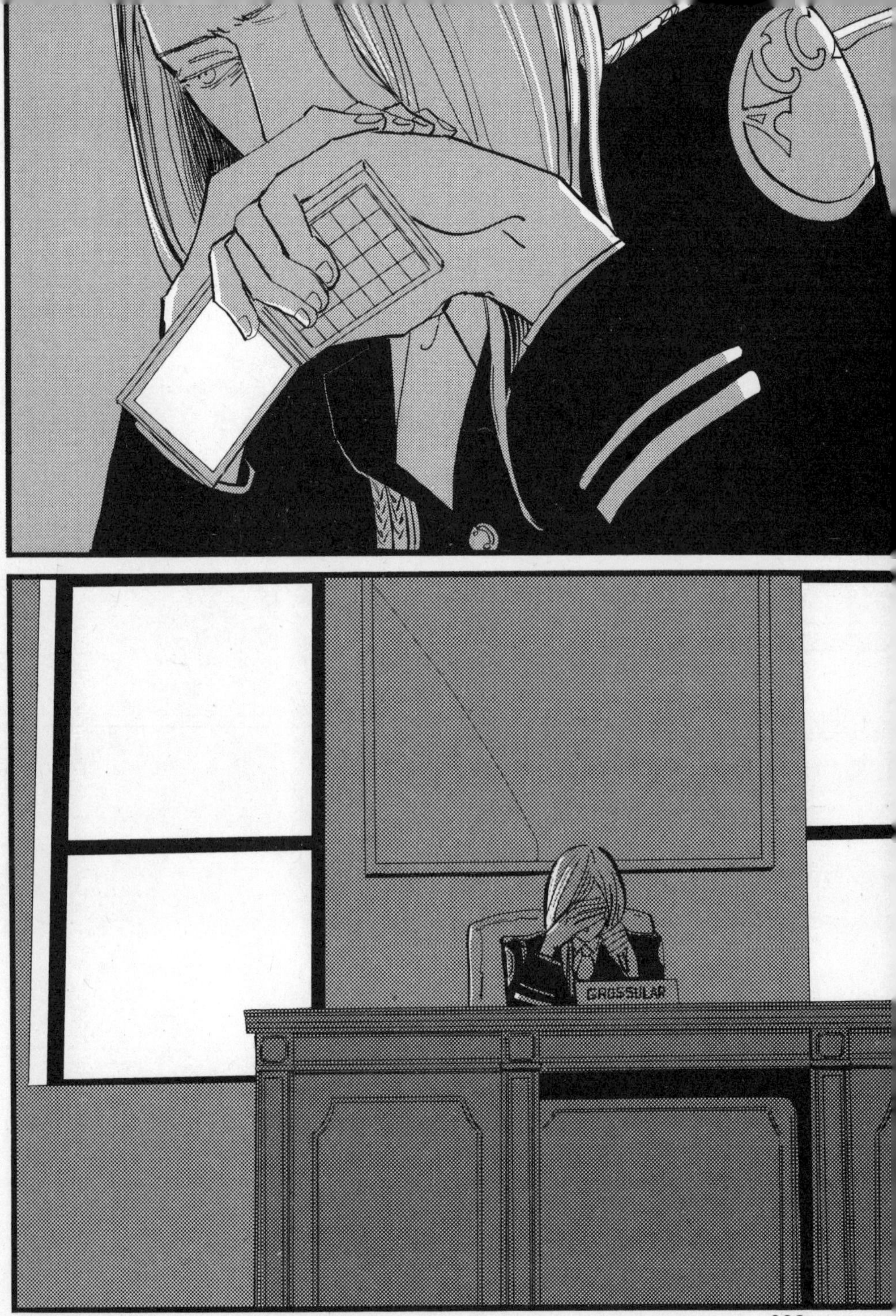
GROSSULAR

ACCA Branch Uniforms | 5

Suitsu District

Because Suitsu District, with its love of traditions and social norms from olden days, is controlled by the nobility, the branch uniforms markedly reflect this aristocratic aesthetic. It is the home district of Pastis, one of the five chief officers.

13

CHAPTER 14
After the
Sparks Fly
in Suitsu

PASS

CHAPTER 15

Stumbling upon a Clue in Badon

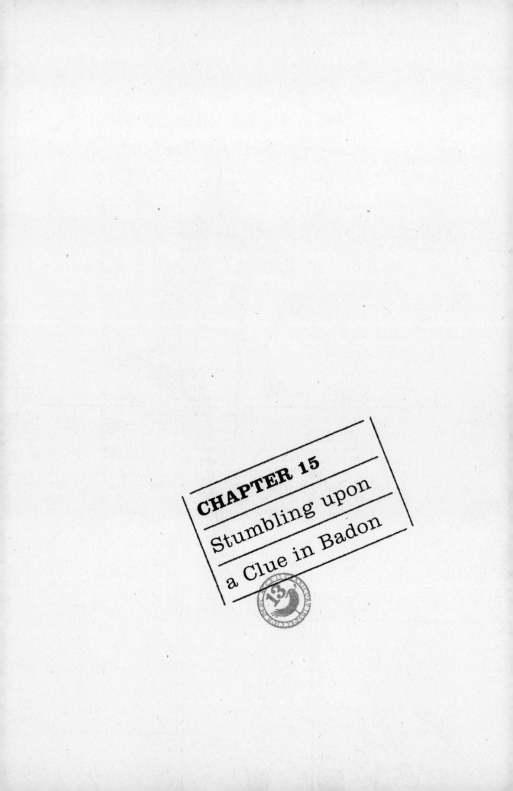

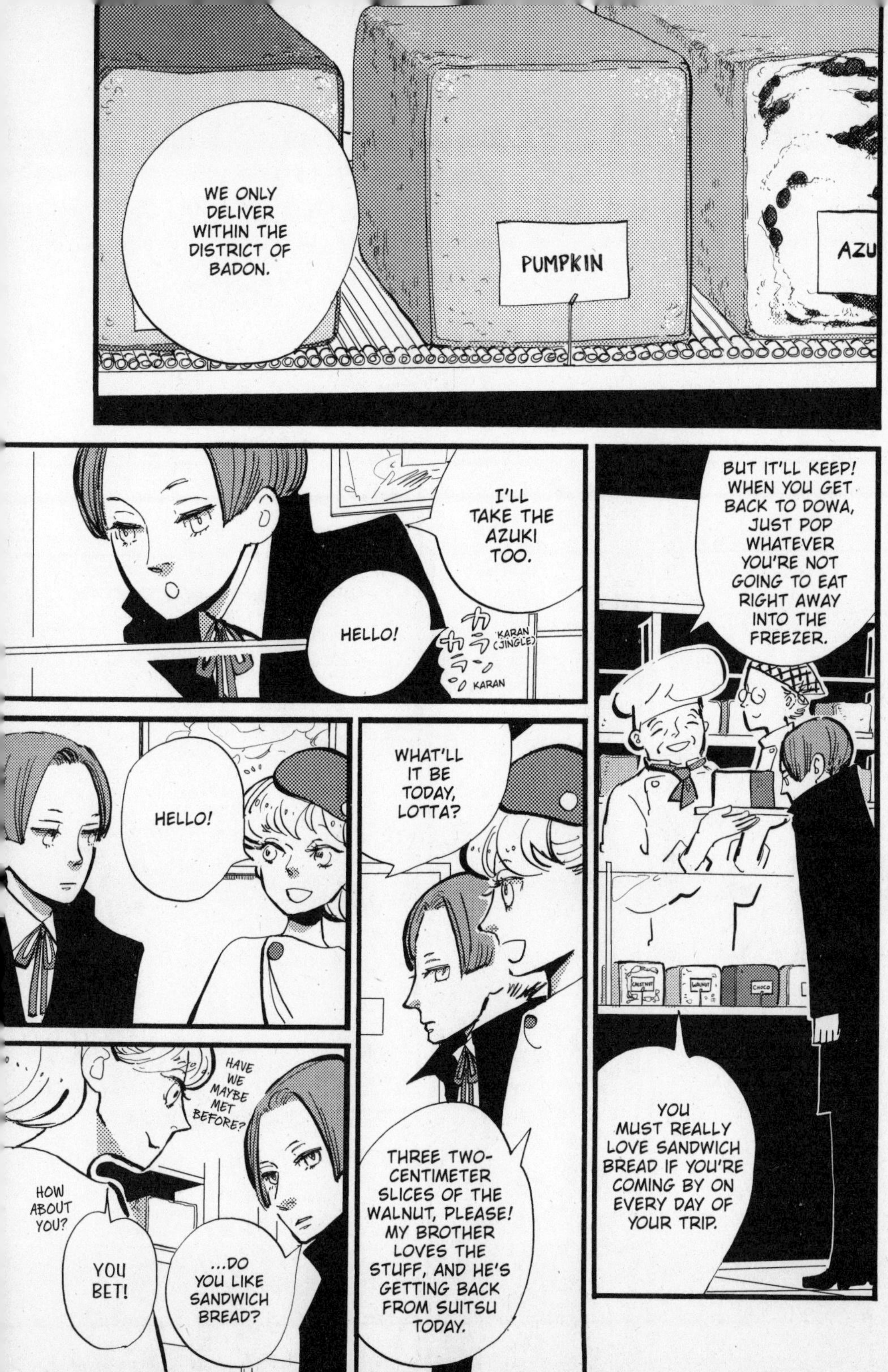
WE ONLY DELIVER WITHIN THE DISTRICT OF BADON.
PUMPKIN
BUT IT'LL KEEP! WHEN YOU GET BACK TO DOWA, JUST POP WHATEVER YOU'RE NOT GOING TO EAT RIGHT AWAY INTO THE FREEZER.
CHESTNUT
WALNUT
CHOCO
YOU MUST REALLY LOVE SANDWICH BREAD IF YOU'RE COMING BY ON EVERY DAY OF YOUR TRIP.
I'LL TAKE THE AZUKI TOO.
KARAN (JINGLE)
KARAN
HELLO!
WHAT'LL IT BE TODAY, LOTTA?
THREE TWO-CENTIMETER SLICES OF THE WALNUT, PLEASE! MY BROTHER LOVES THE STUFF, AND HE'S GETTING BACK FROM SUITSU TODAY.
HELLO!
HAVE WE MAYBE MET BEFORE?
...DO YOU LIKE SANDWICH BREAD?
YOU BET!
HOW ABOUT YOU?

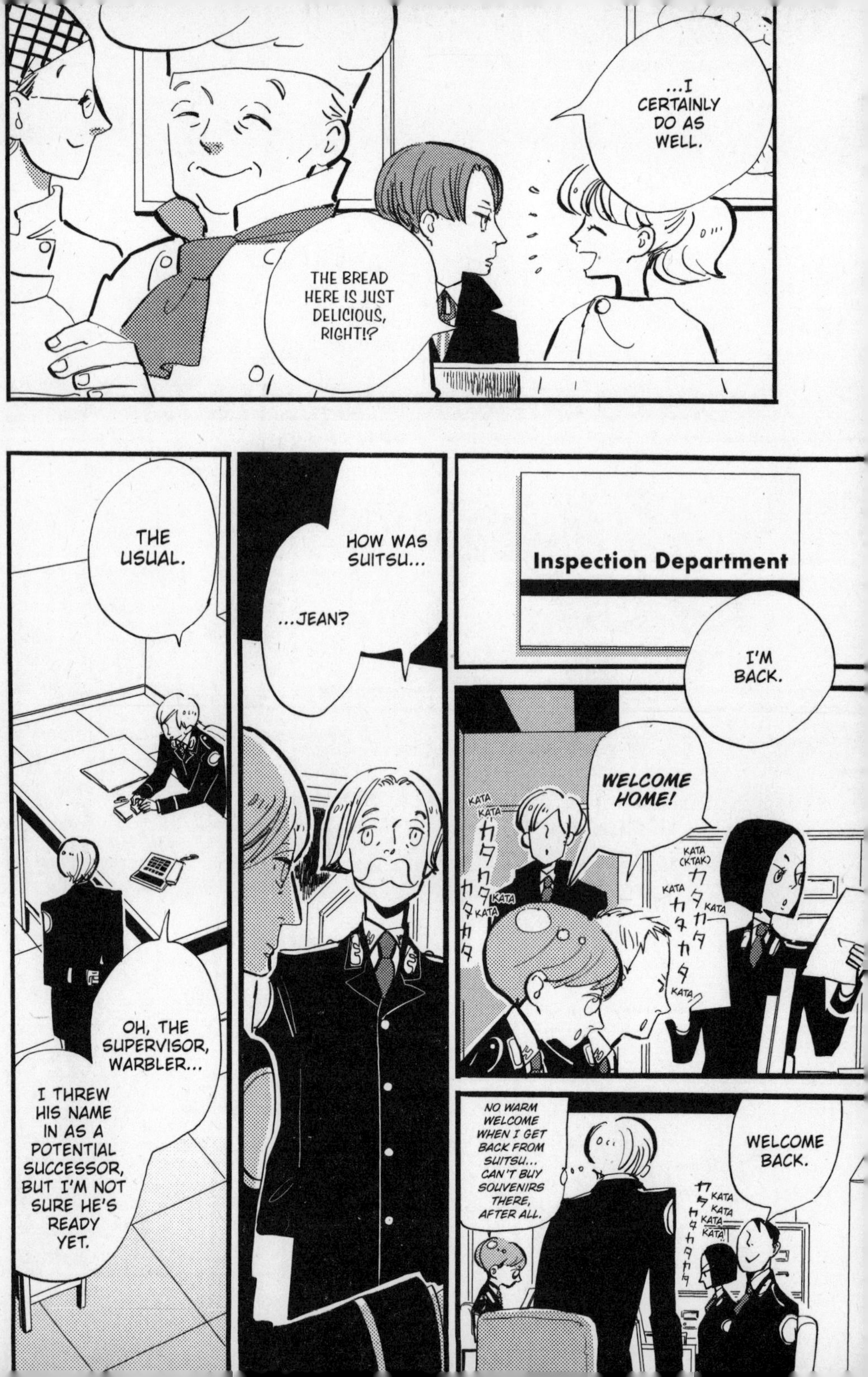
...I CERTAINLY DO AS WELL.
THE BREAD HERE IS JUST DELICIOUS, RIGHT!?
Inspection Department
I'M BACK.
WELCOME HOME!
KATA (KTAK)
KATA KATA KATA KATA
KATA KATA KATA KATA
WELCOME BACK.
KATA KATA KATA KATA
NO WARM WELCOME WHEN I GET BACK FROM SUITSU... CAN'T BUY SOUVENIRS THERE, AFTER ALL.
HOW WAS SUITSU...
...JEAN?
THE USUAL.
OH, THE SUPERVISOR, WARBLER...
I THREW HIS NAME IN AS A POTENTIAL SUCCESSOR, BUT I'M NOT SURE HE'S READY YET.

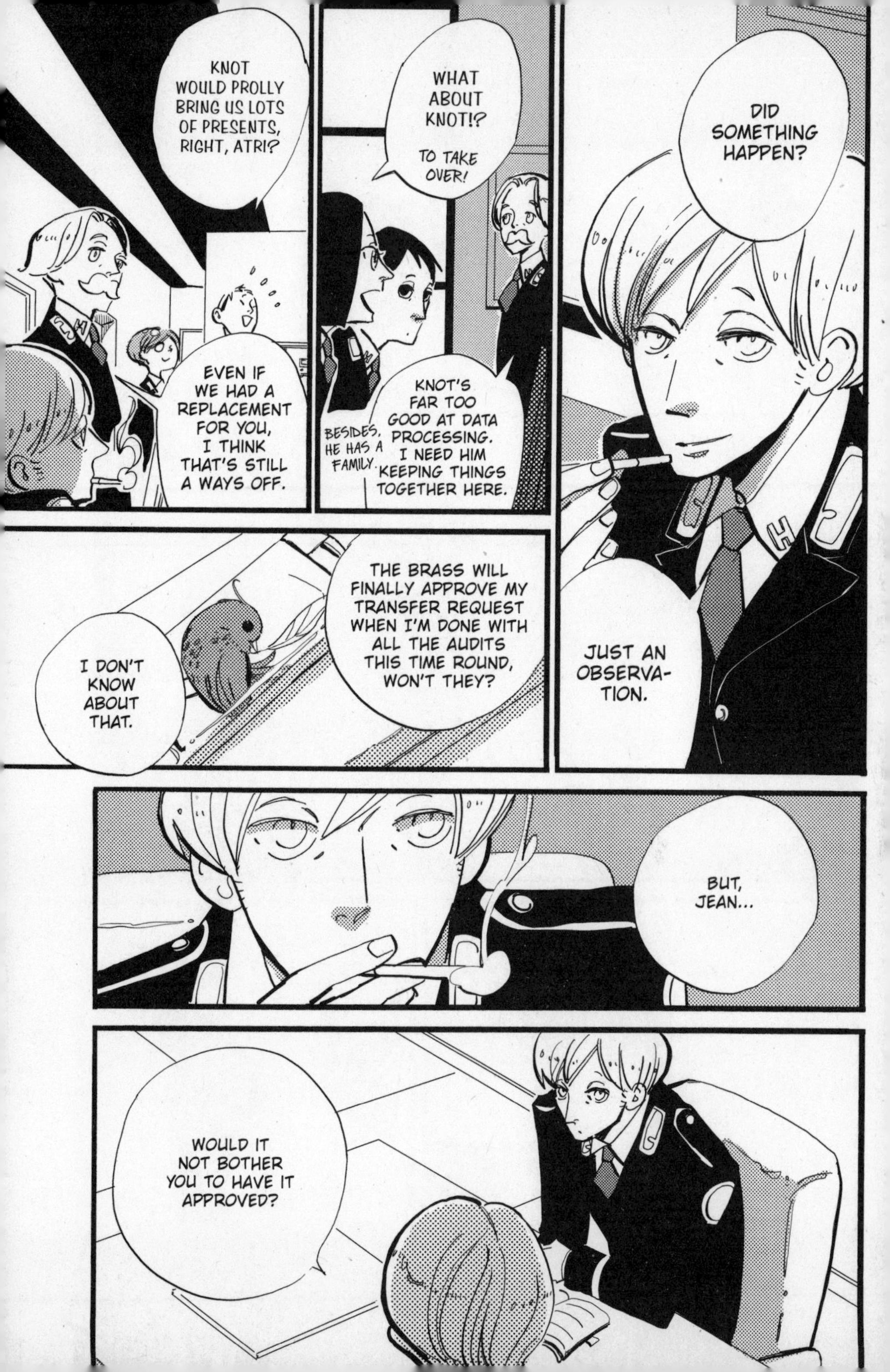
DID SOMETHING HAPPEN?
JUST AN OBSERVATION.
WHAT ABOUT KNOT!?
TO TAKE OVER!
KNOT'S FAR TOO GOOD AT DATA PROCESSING. I NEED HIM KEEPING THINGS TOGETHER HERE.
BESIDES, HE HAS A FAMILY.
KNOT WOULD PROLLY BRING US LOTS OF PRESENTS, RIGHT, ATRI?
EVEN IF WE HAD A REPLACEMENT FOR YOU, I THINK THAT'S STILL A WAYS OFF.
THE BRASS WILL FINALLY APPROVE MY TRANSFER REQUEST WHEN I'M DONE WITH ALL THE AUDITS THIS TIME ROUND, WON'T THEY?
I DON'T KNOW ABOUT THAT.
BUT, JEAN...
WOULD IT NOT BOTHER YOU TO HAVE IT APPROVED?

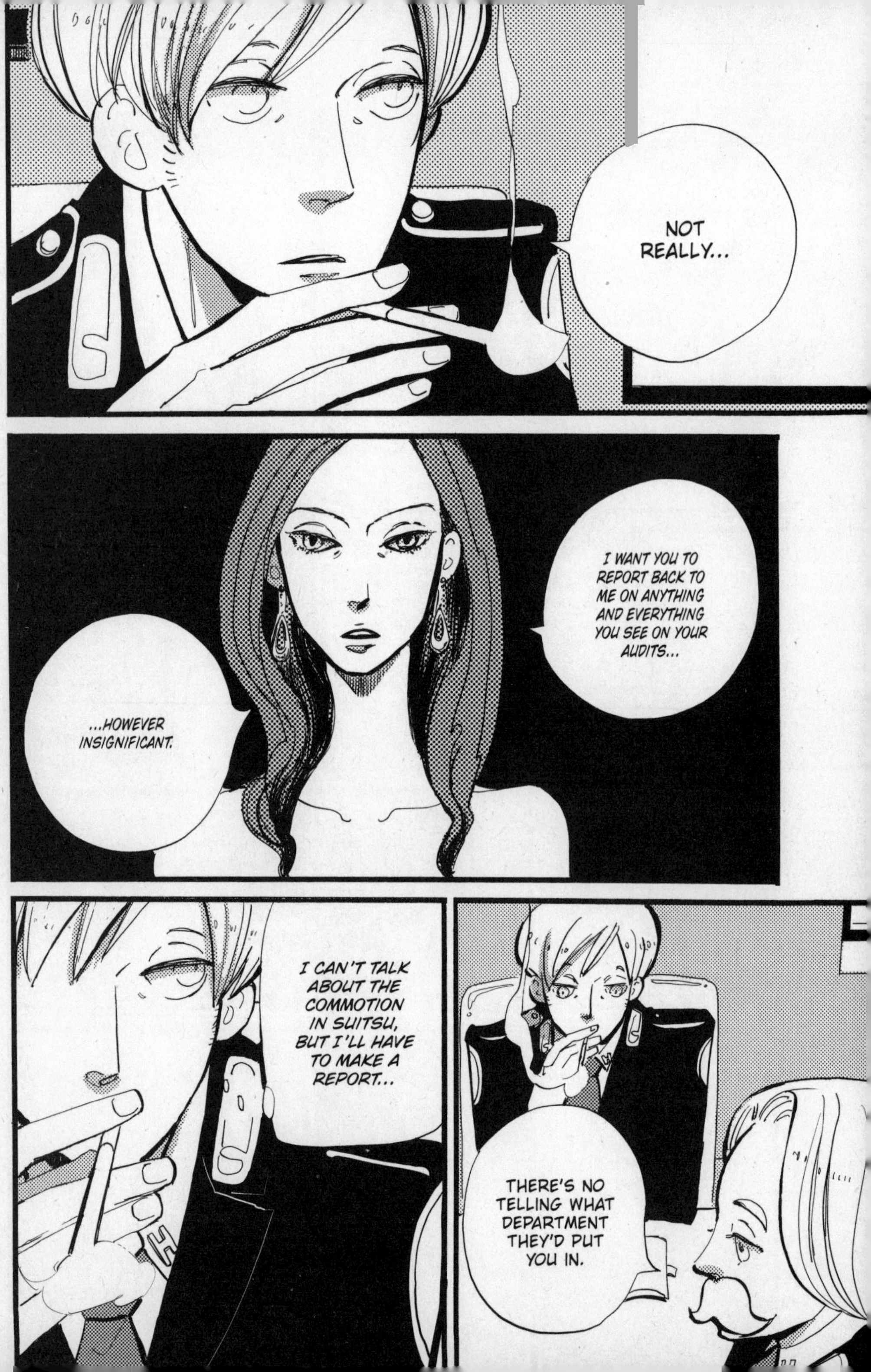
NOT REALLY...
I WANT YOU TO REPORT BACK TO ME ON ANYTHING AND EVERYTHING YOU SEE ON YOUR AUDITS...
...HOWEVER INSIGNIFICANT.
THERE'S NO TELLING WHAT DEPARTMENT THEY'D PUT YOU IN.
I CAN'T TALK ABOUT THE COMMOTION IN SUITSU, BUT I'LL HAVE TO MAKE A REPORT...

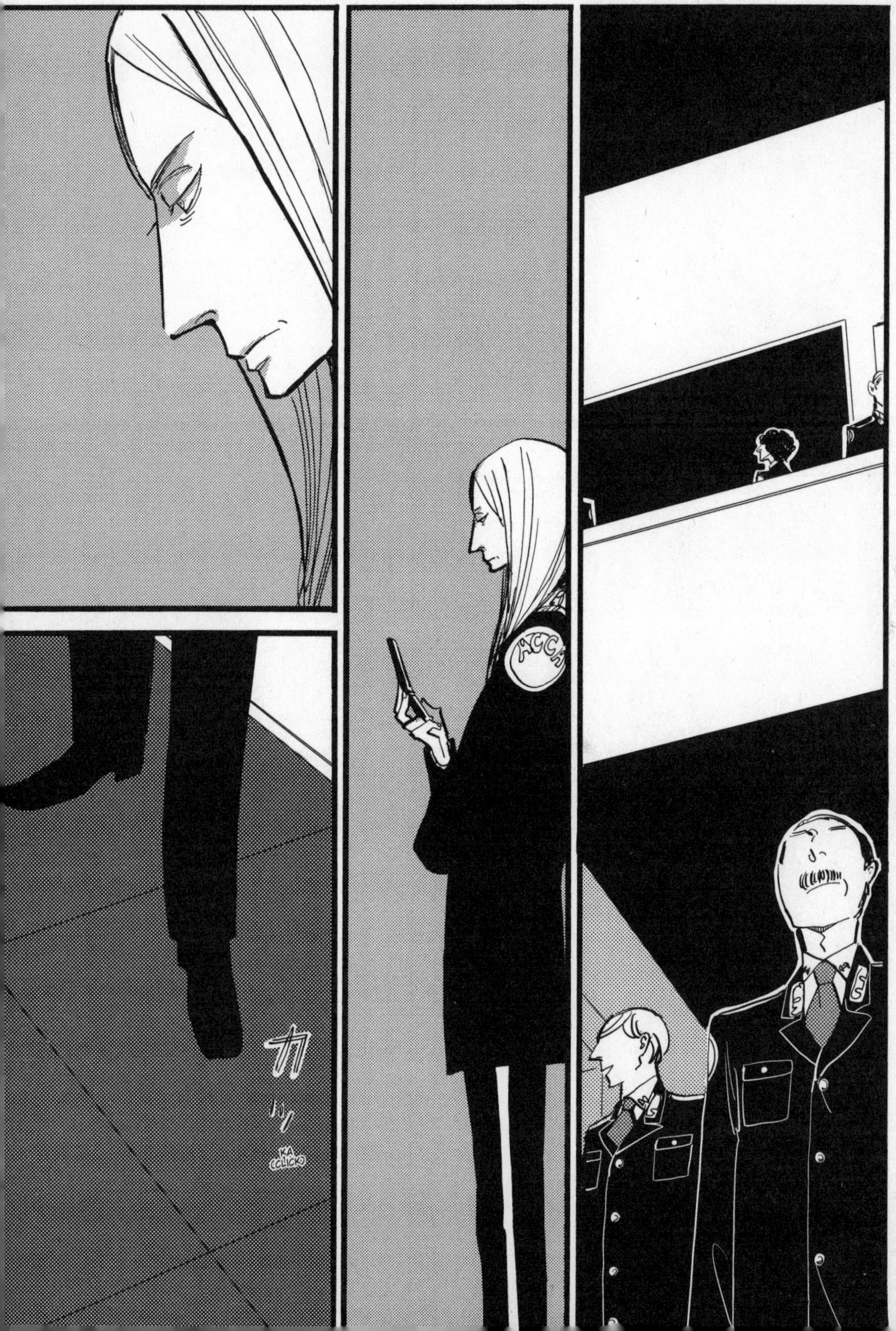
ACCA
カ
チリ
KA (CLICK)

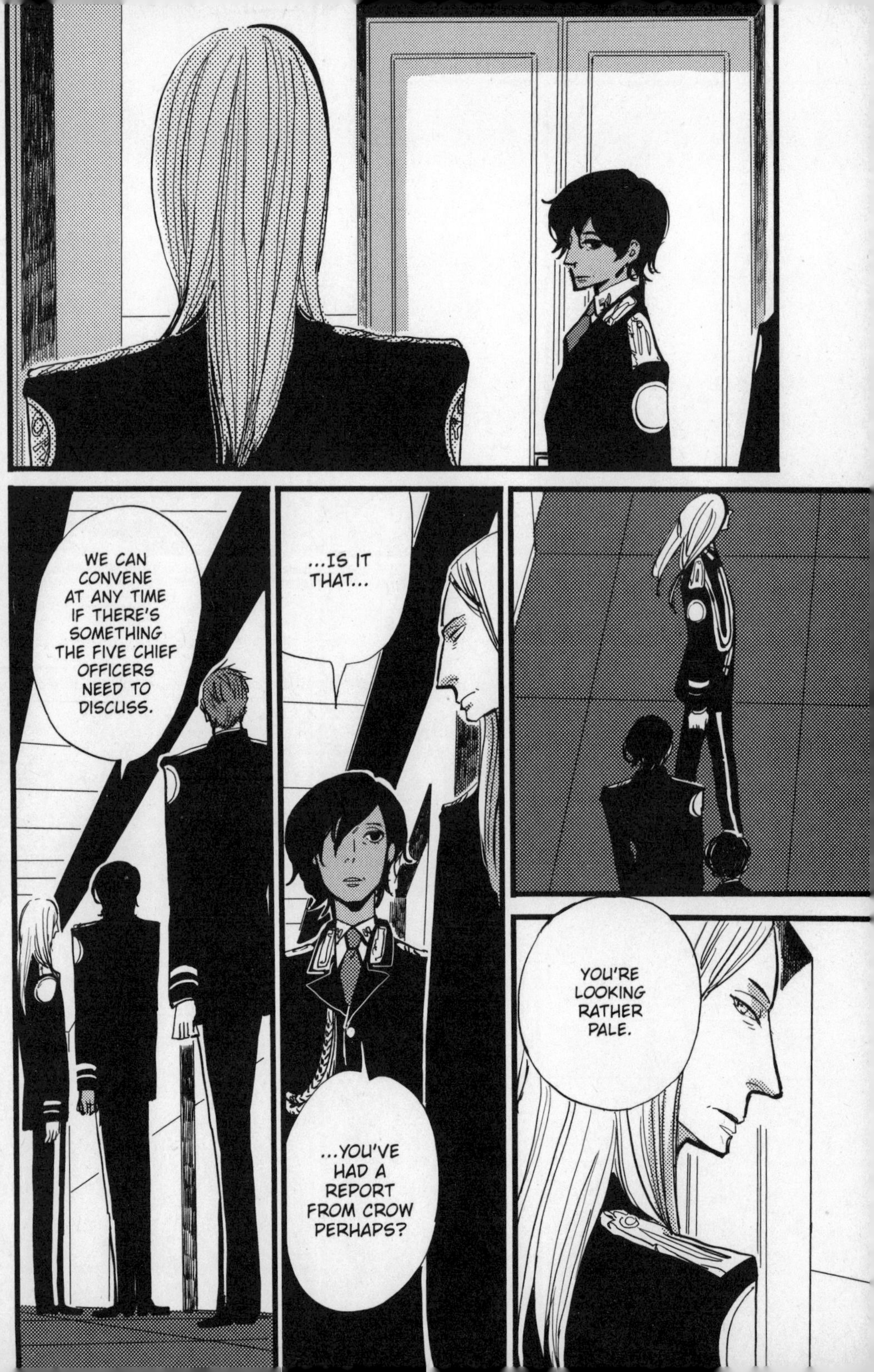
YOU'RE LOOKING RATHER PALE.
...IS IT THAT...
...YOU'VE HAD A REPORT FROM CROW PERHAPS?
WE CAN CONVENE AT ANY TIME IF THERE'S SOMETHING THE FIVE CHIEF OFFICERS NEED TO DISCUSS.

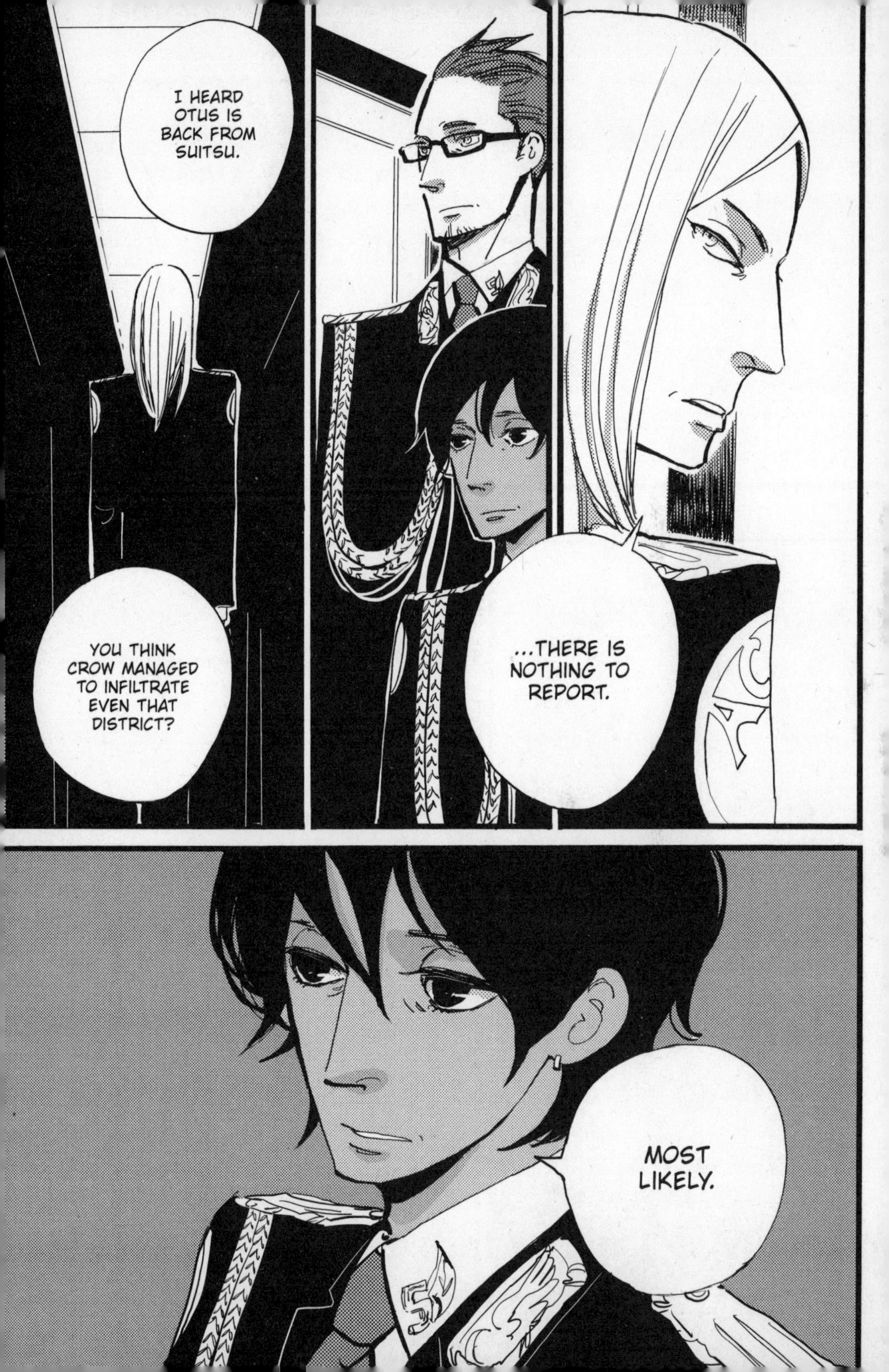
I HEARD OTUS IS BACK FROM SUITSU.
...THERE IS NOTHING TO REPORT.
YOU THINK CROW MANAGED TO INFILTRATE EVEN THAT DISTRICT?
MOST LIKELY.

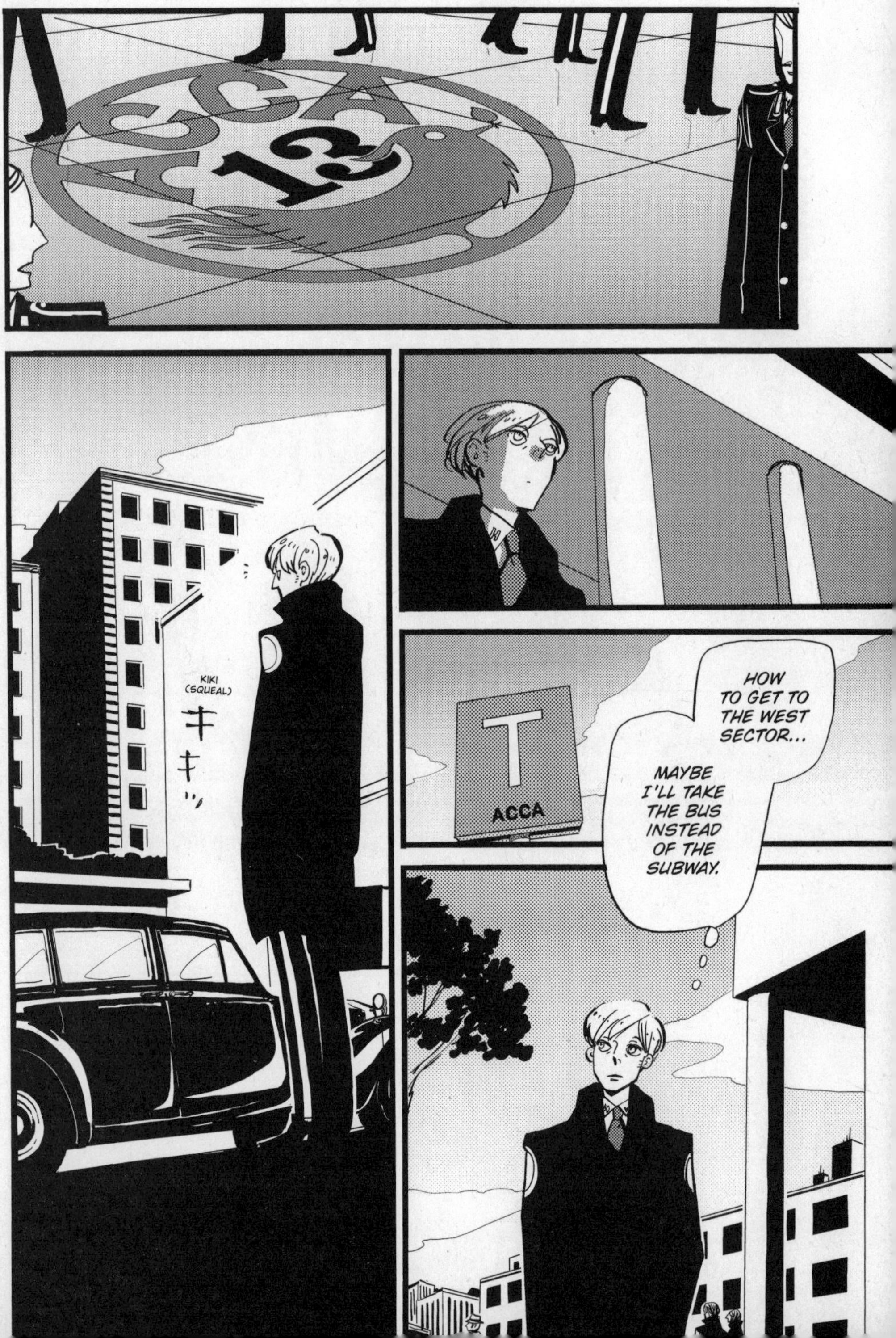

T
ACCA
HOW TO GET TO THE WEST SECTOR...
MAYBE I'LL TAKE THE BUS INSTEAD OF THE SUBWAY.
キキッ
KIKI (SQUEAL)

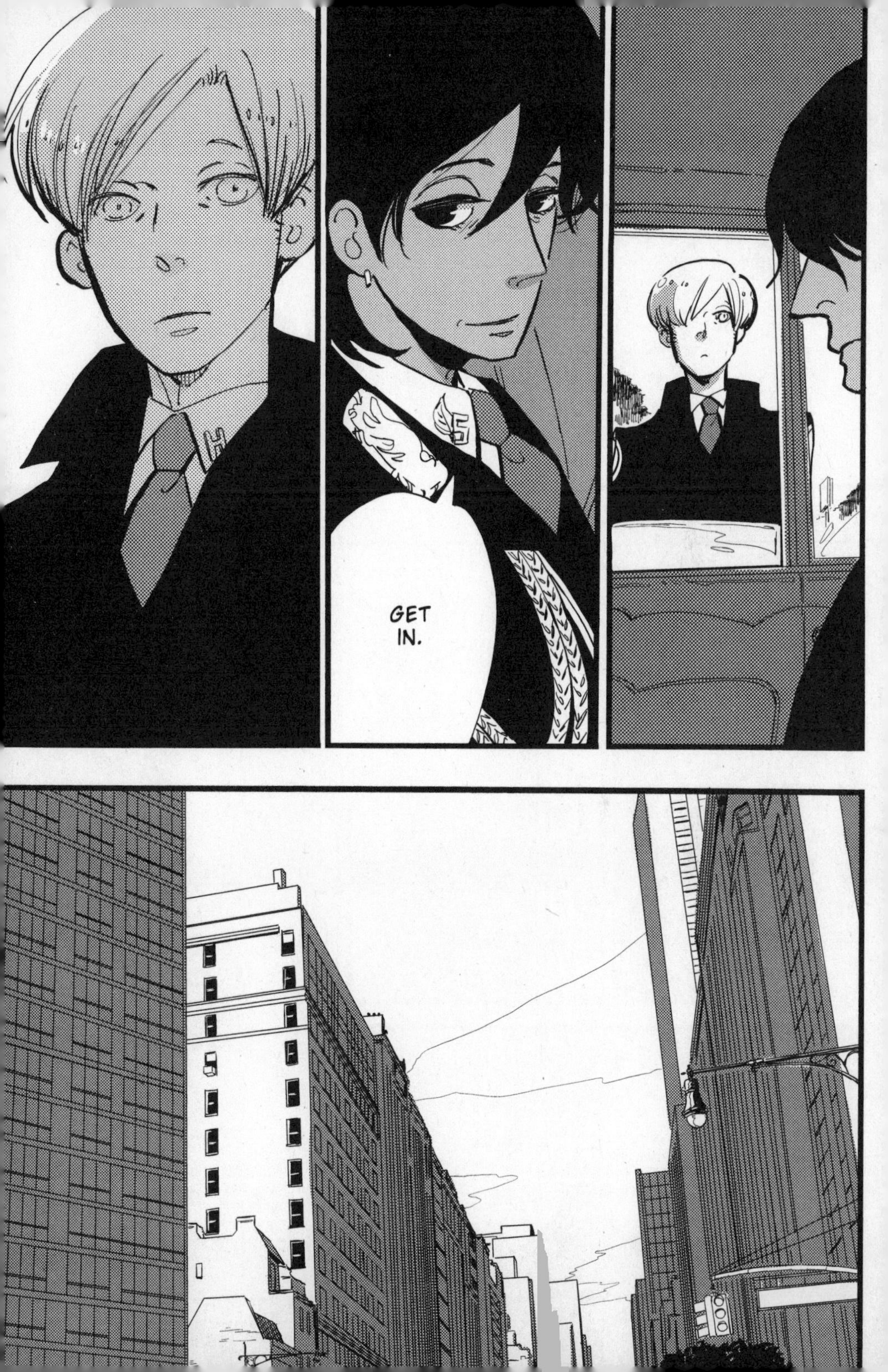
GET IN.

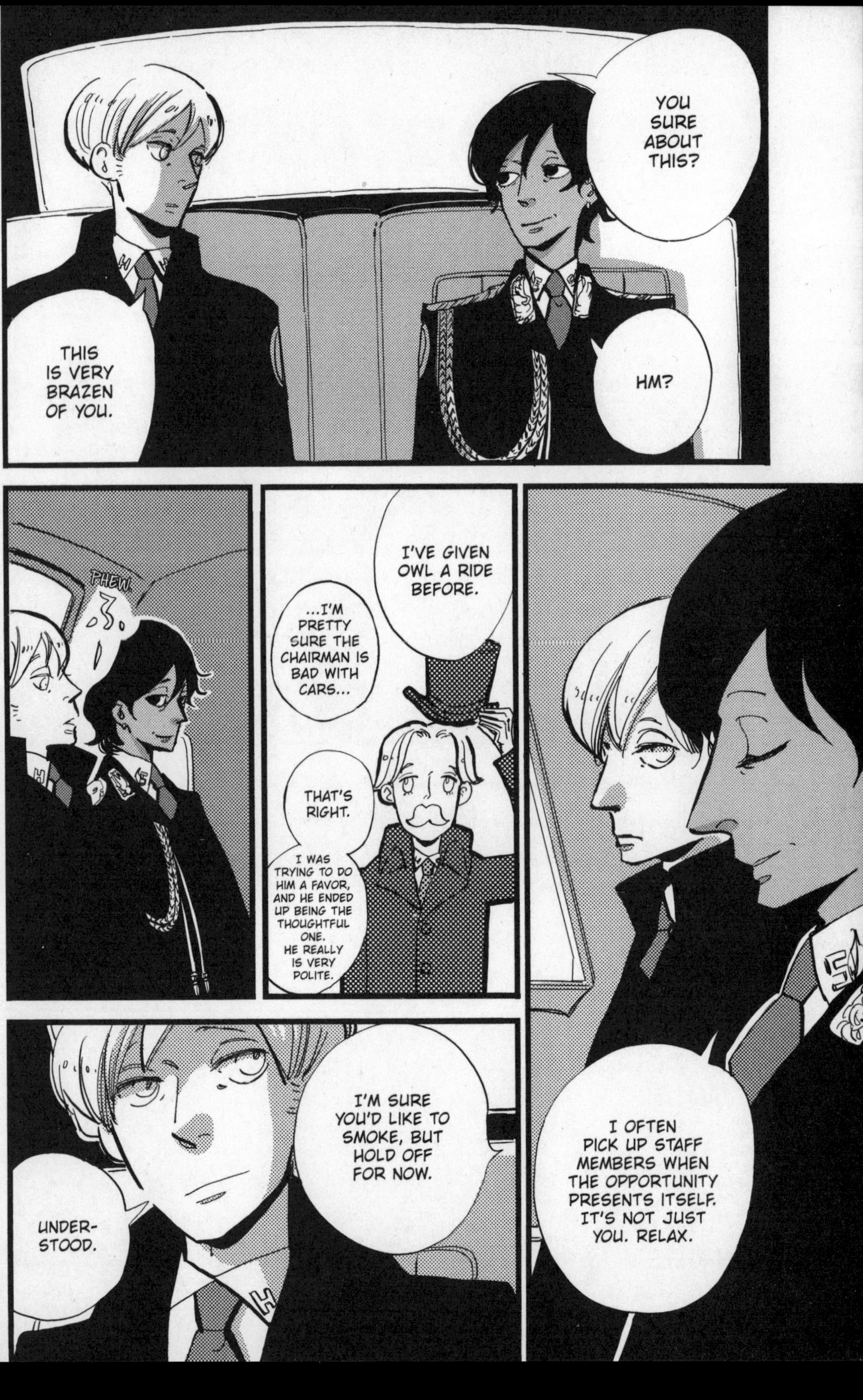
YOU SURE ABOUT THIS?
HM?
THIS IS VERY BRAZEN OF YOU.
I OFTEN PICK UP STAFF MEMBERS WHEN THE OPPORTUNITY PRESENTS ITSELF. IT'S NOT JUST YOU. RELAX.
I'VE GIVEN OWL A RIDE BEFORE.
...I'M PRETTY SURE THE CHAIRMAN IS BAD WITH CARS...
THAT'S RIGHT.
I WAS TRYING TO DO HIM A FAVOR, AND HE ENDED UP BEING THE THOUGHTFUL ONE. HE REALLY IS VERY POLITE.
PHEW.
I'M SURE YOU'D LIKE TO SMOKE, BUT HOLD OFF FOR NOW.
UNDER-STOOD.

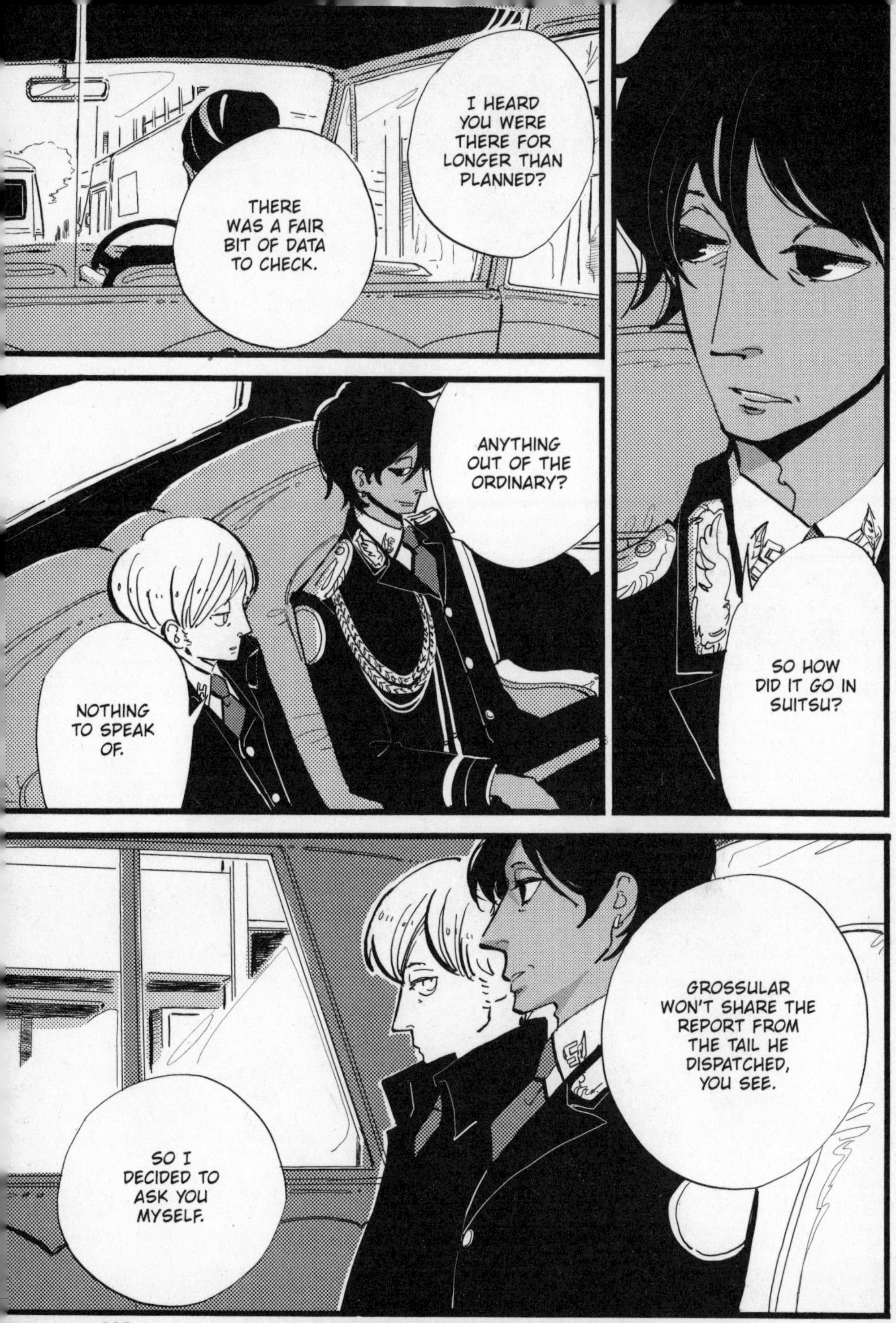

SO HOW DID IT GO IN SUITSU?
I HEARD YOU WERE THERE FOR LONGER THAN PLANNED?
THERE WAS A FAIR BIT OF DATA TO CHECK.
ANYTHING OUT OF THE ORDINARY?
NOTHING TO SPEAK OF.
GROSSULAR WON'T SHARE THE REPORT FROM THE TAIL HE DISPATCHED, YOU SEE.
SO I DECIDED TO ASK YOU MYSELF.

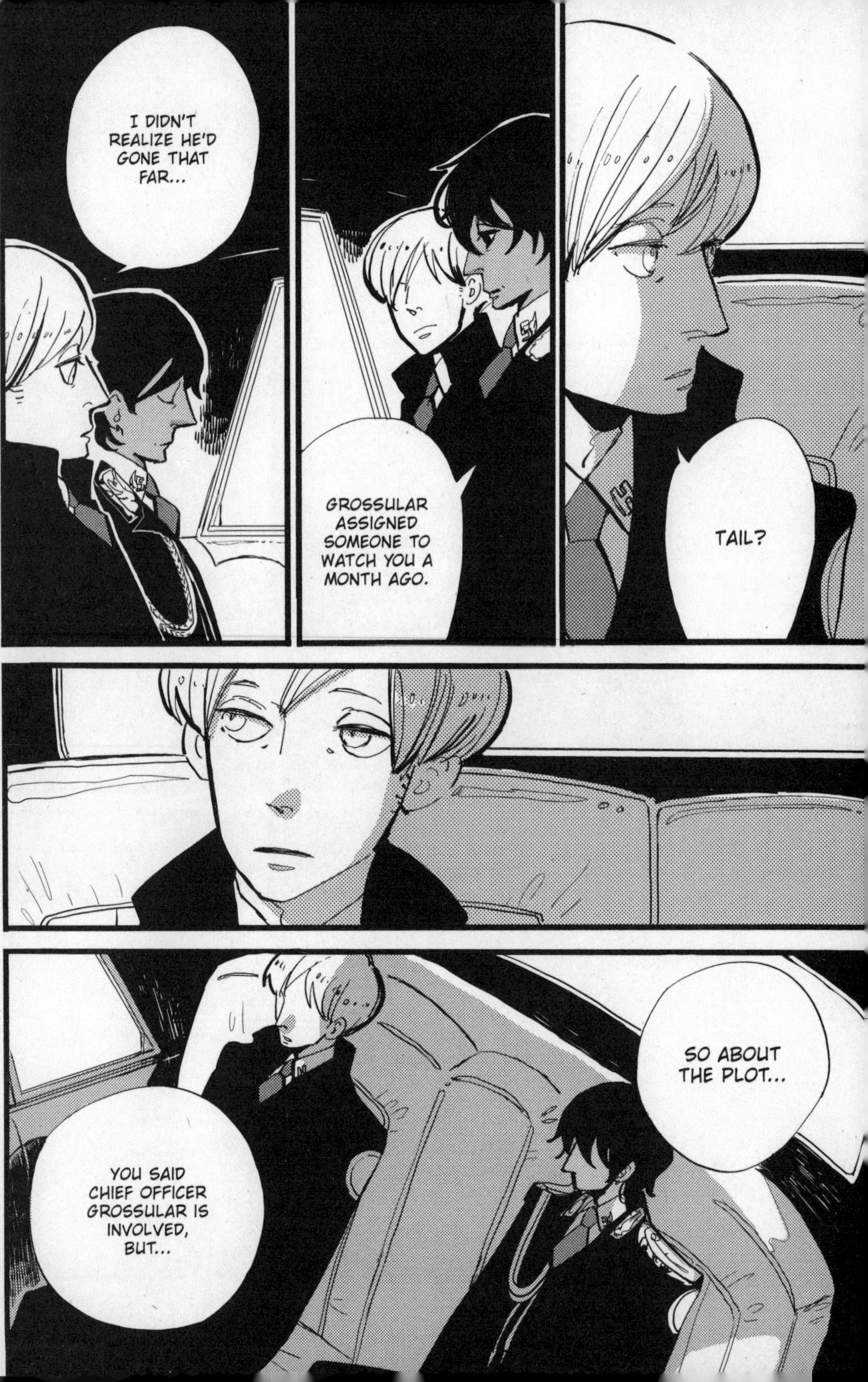
TAIL?
GROSSULAR ASSIGNED SOMEONE TO WATCH YOU A MONTH AGO.
I DIDN'T REALIZE HE'D GONE THAT FAR...
SO ABOUT THE PLOT...
YOU SAID CHIEF OFFICER GROSSULAR IS INVOLVED, BUT...

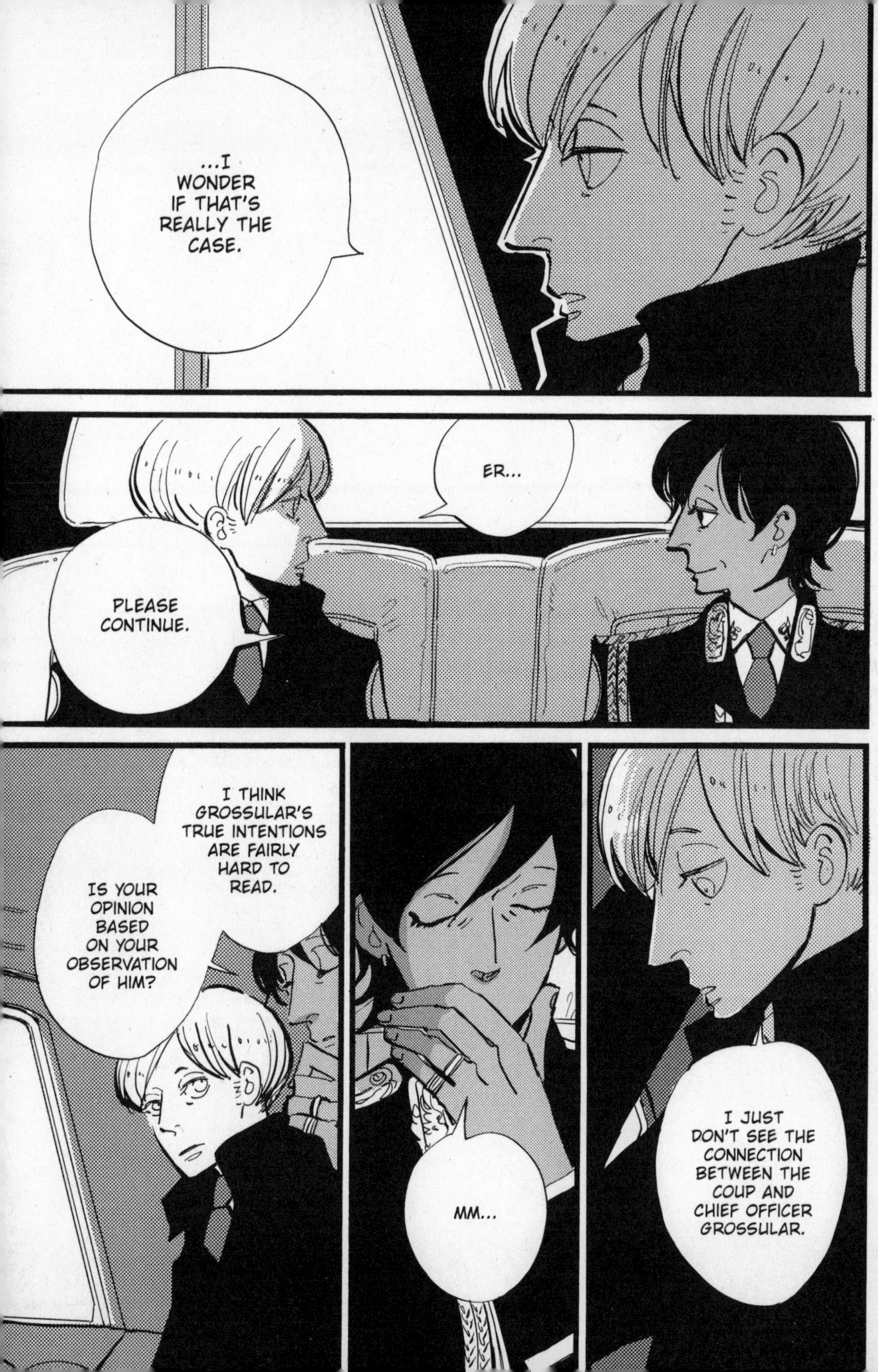
...I WONDER IF THAT'S REALLY THE CASE.
ER...
PLEASE CONTINUE.
I JUST DON'T SEE THE CONNECTION BETWEEN THE COUP AND CHIEF OFFICER GROSSULAR.
MM...
I THINK GROSSULAR'S TRUE INTENTIONS ARE FAIRLY HARD TO READ.
IS YOUR OPINION BASED ON YOUR OBSERVATION OF HIM?

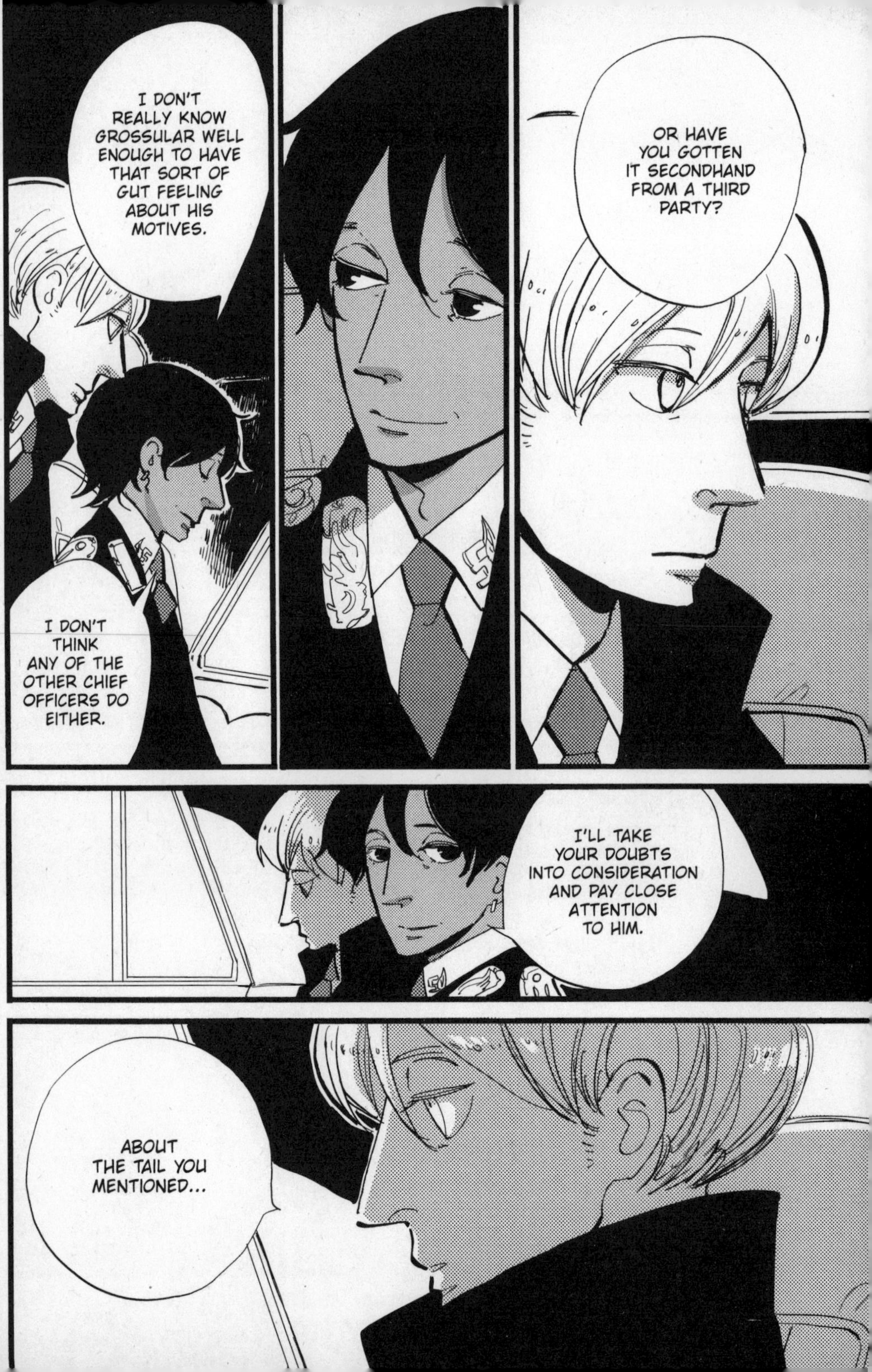
OR HAVE YOU GOTTEN IT SECONDHAND FROM A THIRD PARTY?
I DON'T REALLY KNOW GROSSULAR WELL ENOUGH TO HAVE THAT SORT OF GUT FEELING ABOUT HIS MOTIVES.
I DON'T THINK ANY OF THE OTHER CHIEF OFFICERS DO EITHER.
I'LL TAKE YOUR DOUBTS INTO CONSIDERATION AND PAY CLOSE ATTENTION TO HIM.
ABOUT THE TAIL YOU MENTIONED...

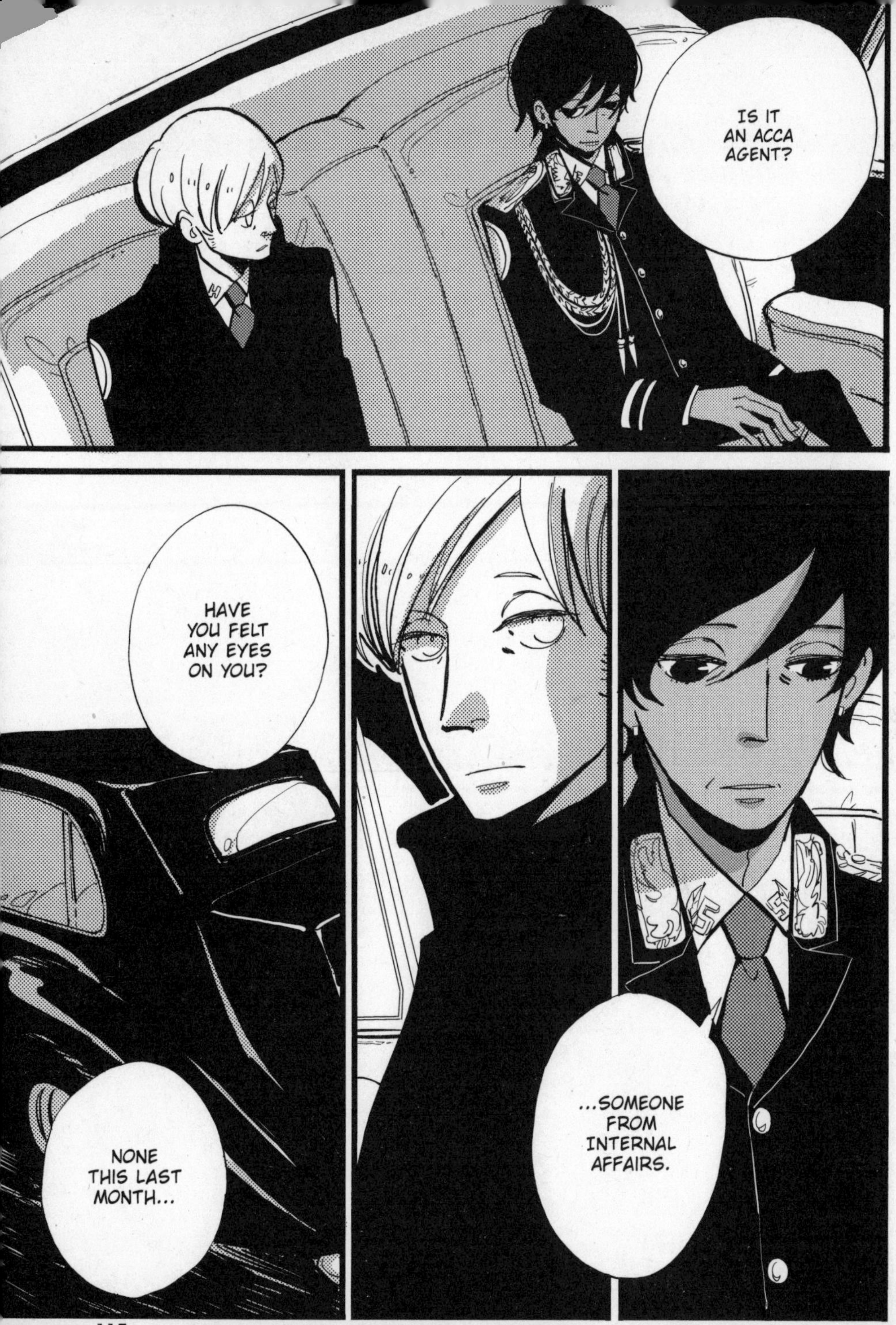
IS IT AN ACCA AGENT?
...SOMEONE FROM INTERNAL AFFAIRS.
HAVE YOU FELT ANY EYES ON YOU?
NONE THIS LAST MONTH...

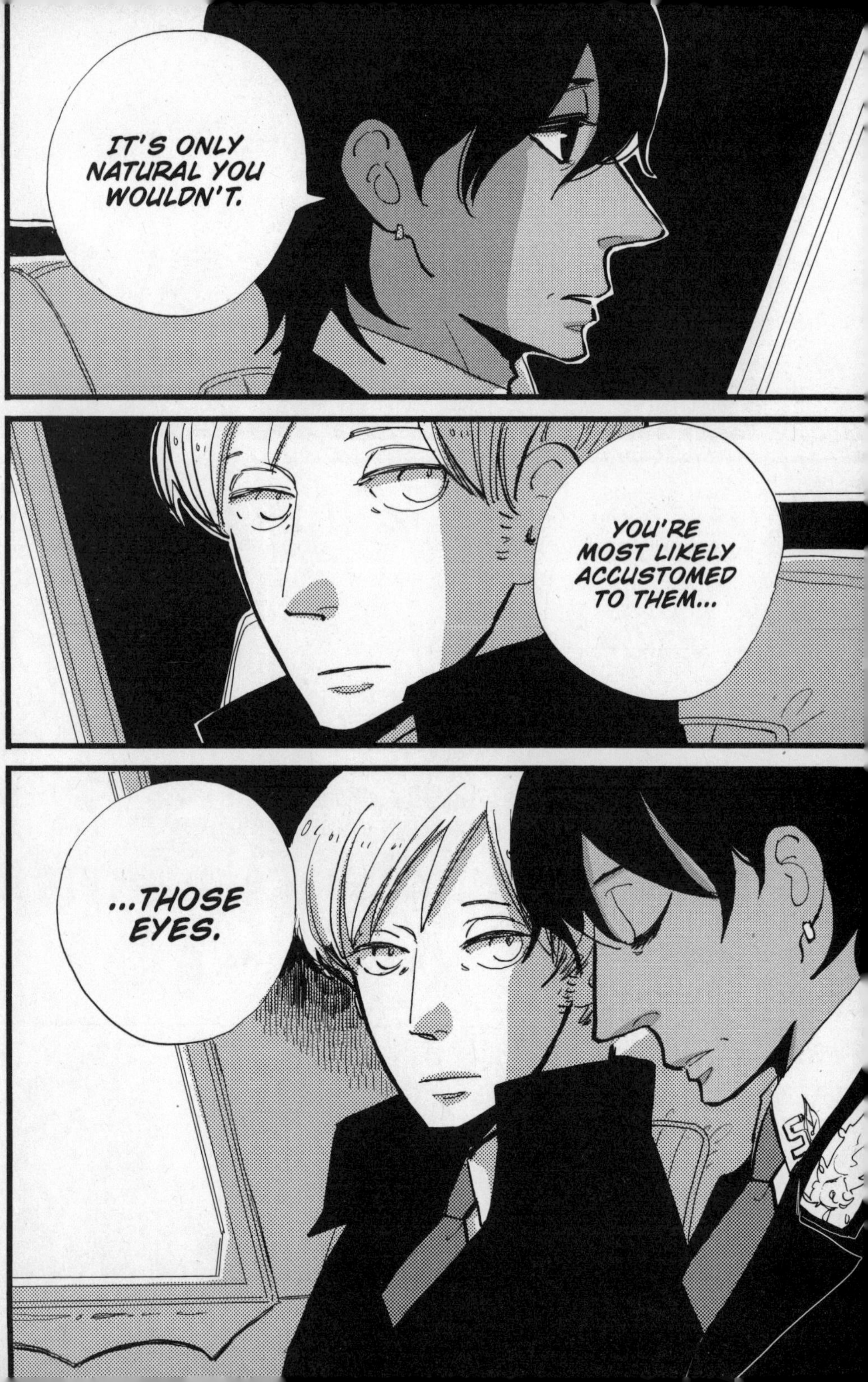
IT'S ONLY NATURAL YOU WOULDN'T.
YOU'RE MOST LIKELY ACCUSTOMED TO THEM...
...THOSE EYES.

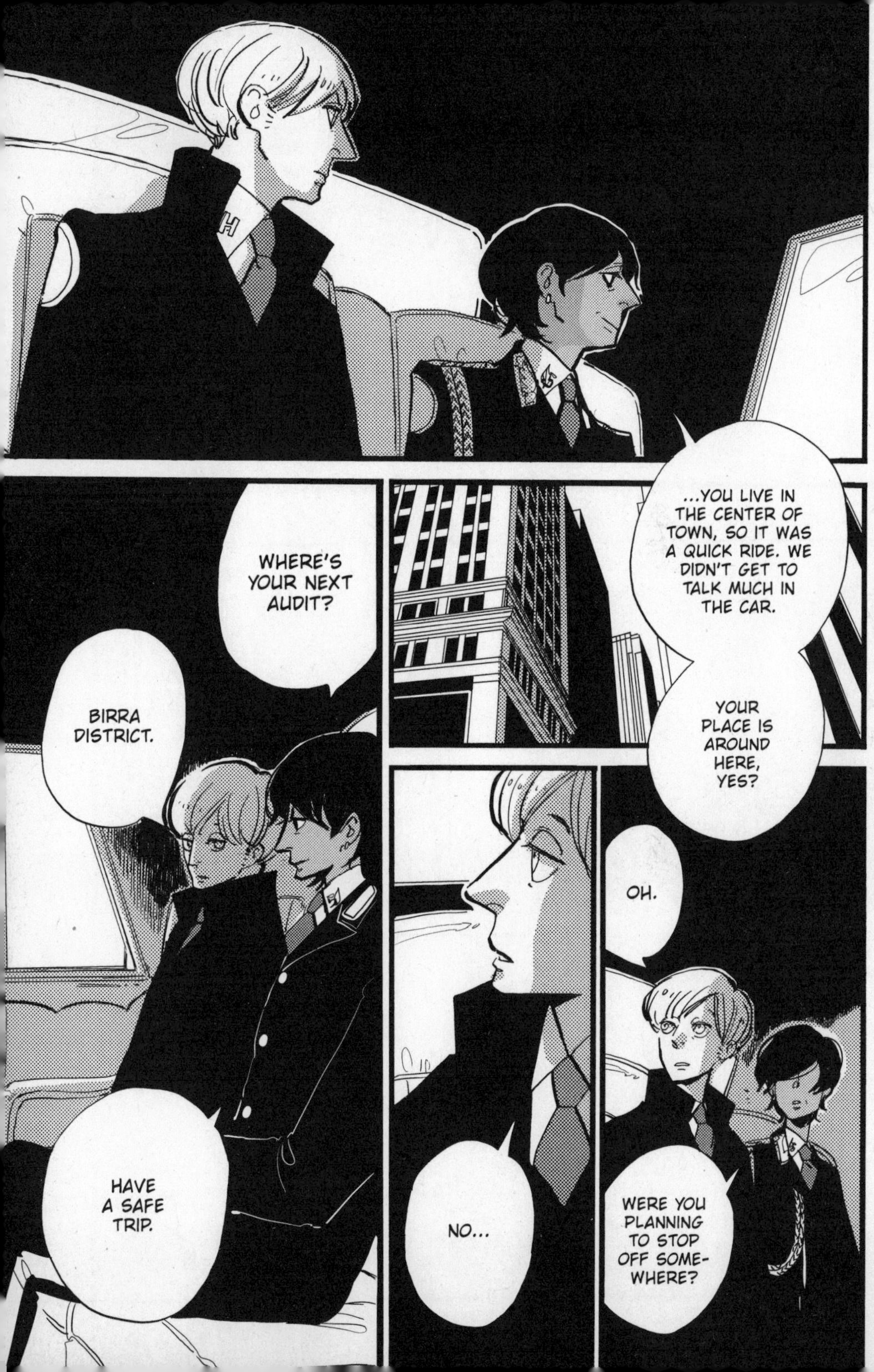
...YOU LIVE IN THE CENTER OF TOWN, SO IT WAS A QUICK RIDE. WE DIDN'T GET TO TALK MUCH IN THE CAR.
YOUR PLACE IS AROUND HERE, YES?
OH.
WERE YOU PLANNING TO STOP OFF SOME-WHERE?
NO...
WHERE'S YOUR NEXT AUDIT?
BIRRA DISTRICT.
HAVE A SAFE TRIP.

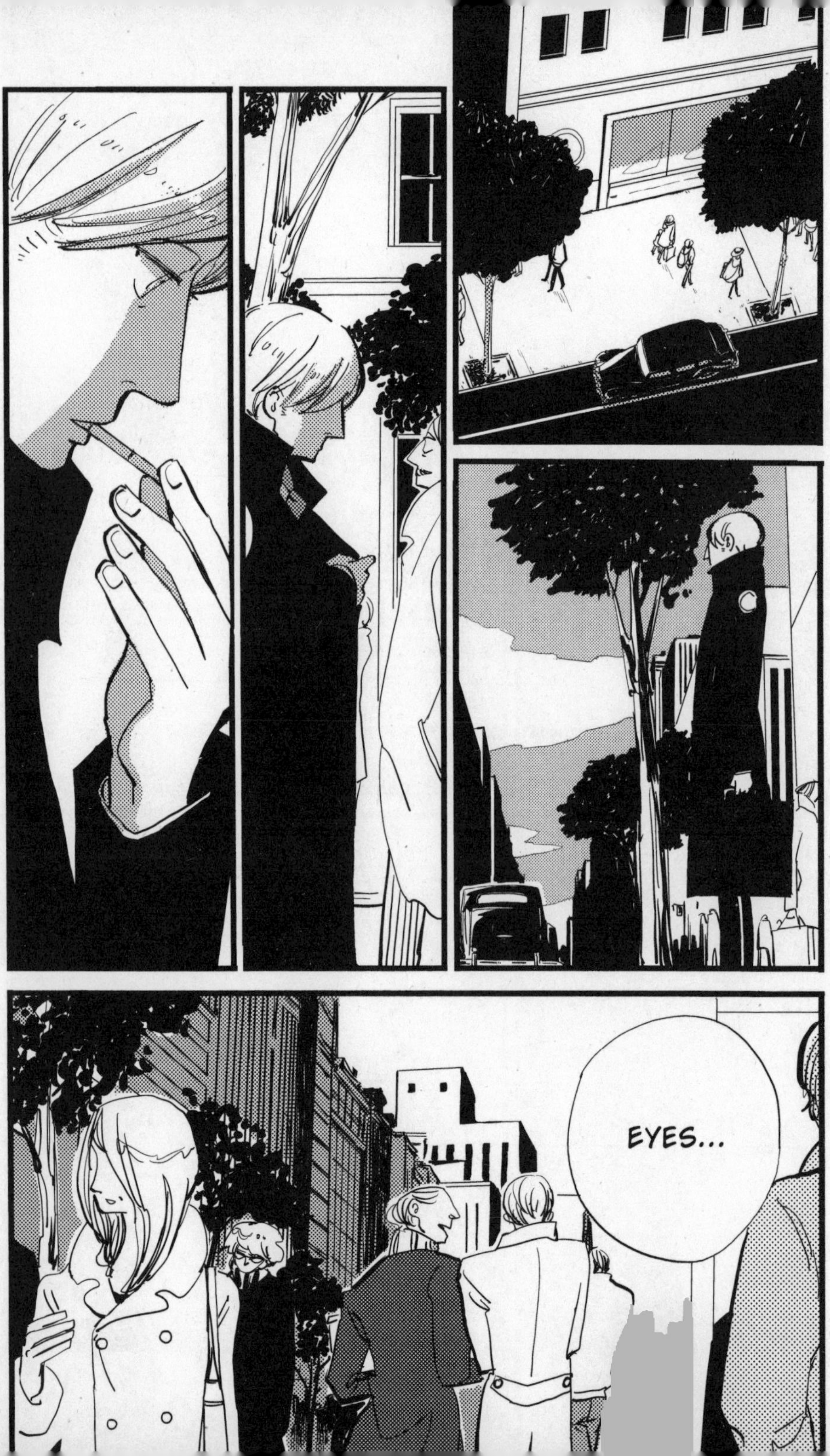
EYES...

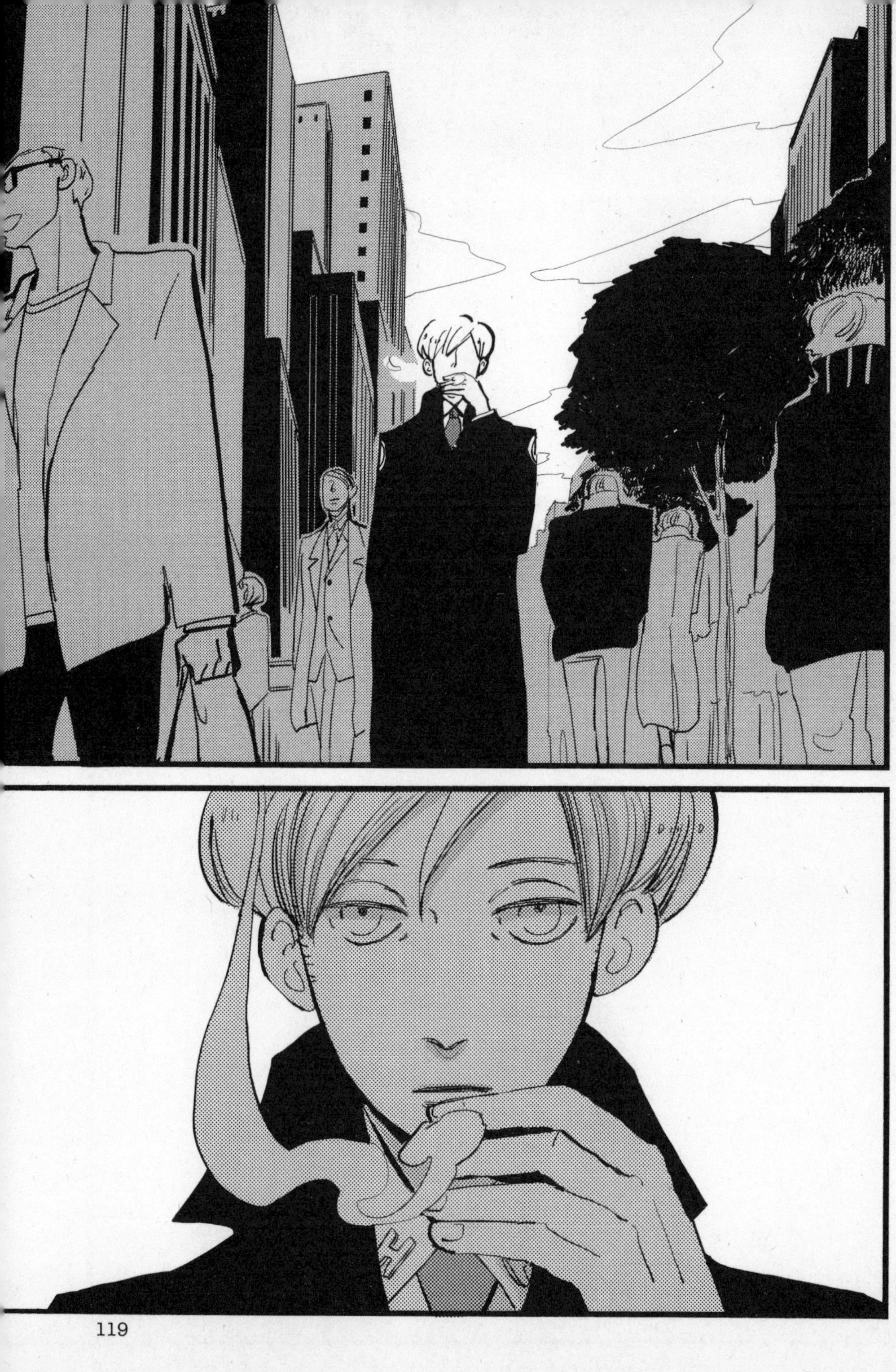

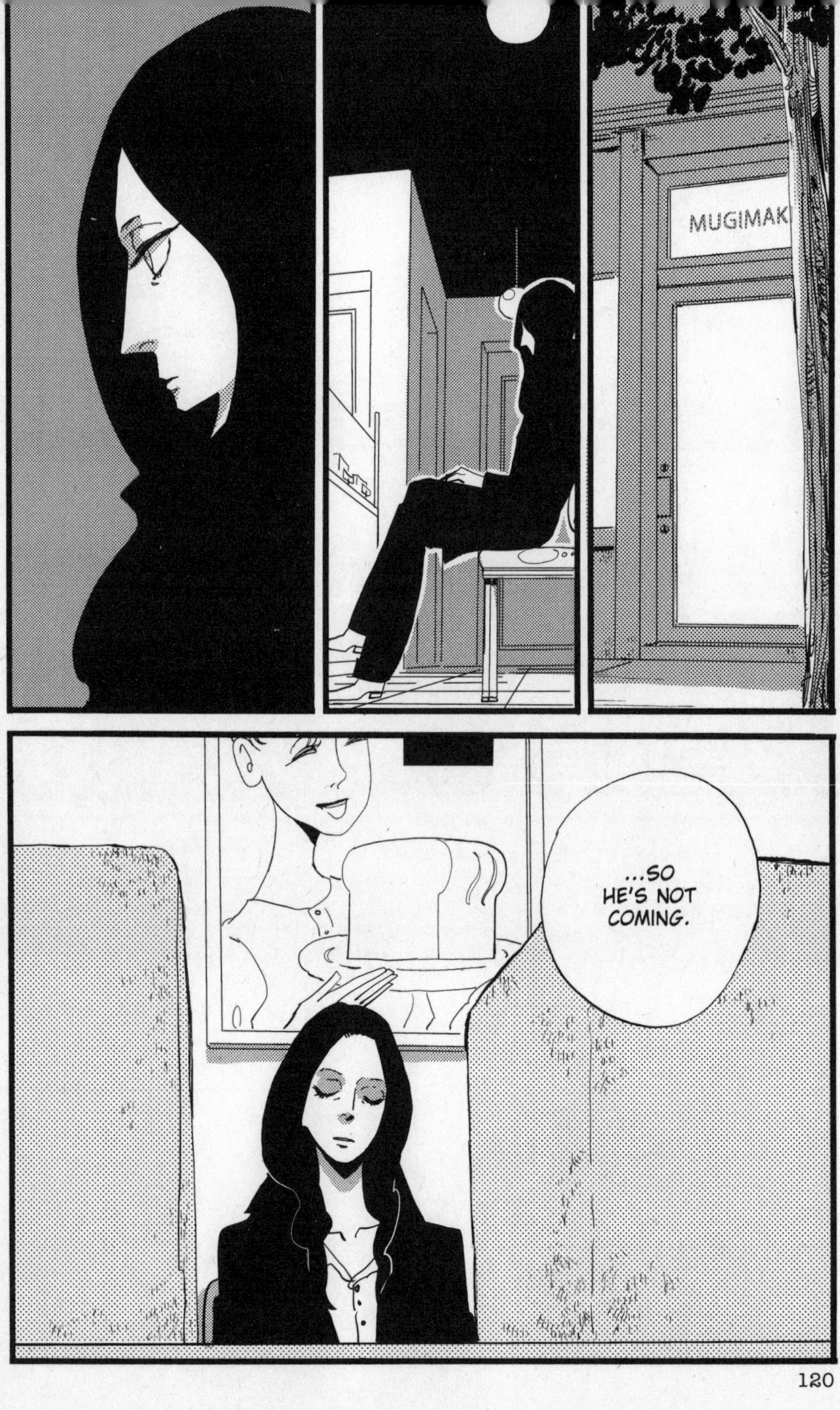
MUGIMAKI
...SO HE'S NOT COMING.

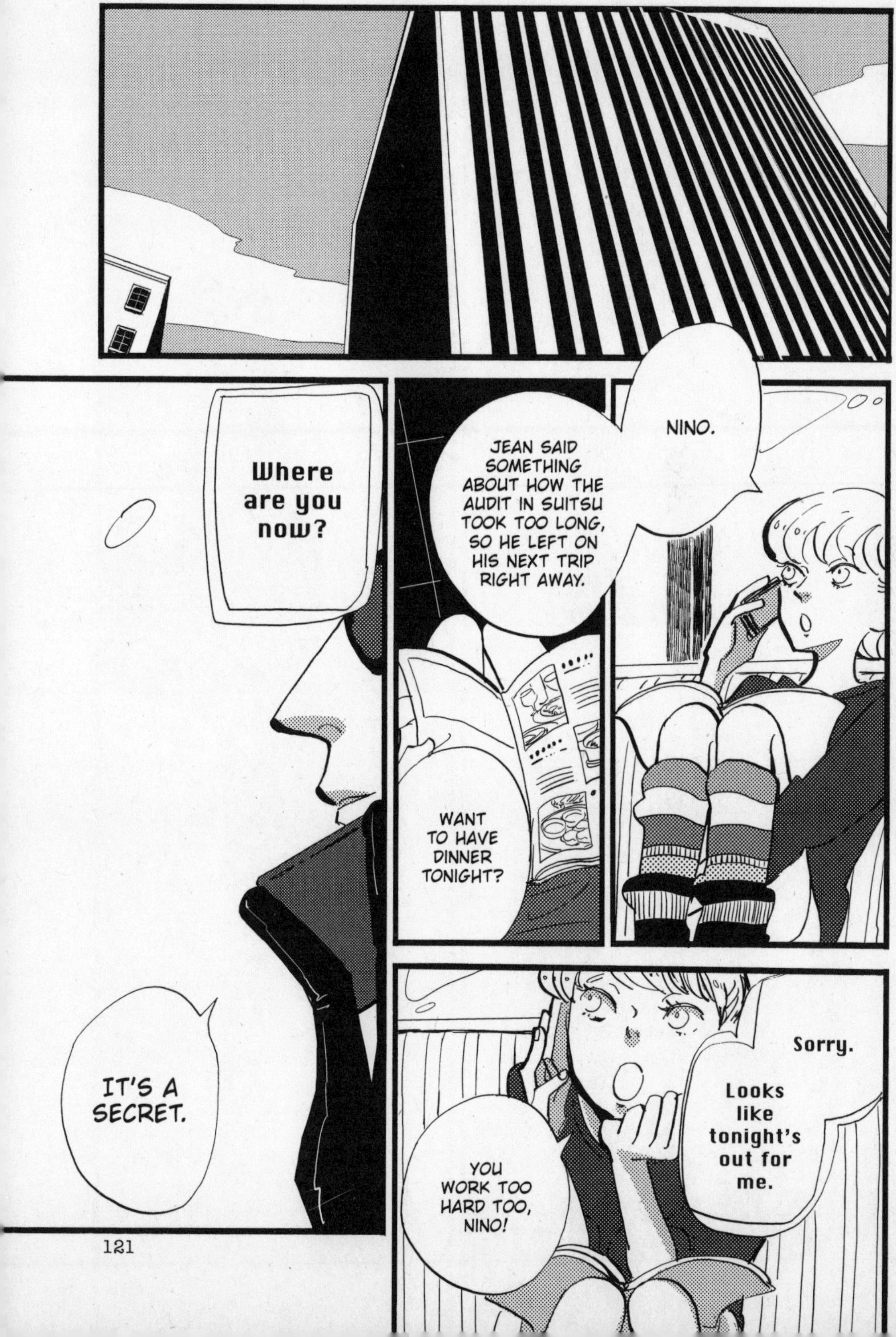
NINO.
JEAN SAID SOMETHING ABOUT HOW THE AUDIT IN SUITSU TOOK TOO LONG, SO HE LEFT ON HIS NEXT TRIP RIGHT AWAY.
WANT TO HAVE DINNER TONIGHT?
Sorry.
Looks like tonight's out for me.
YOU WORK TOO HARD TOO, NINO!
Where are you now?
IT'S A SECRET.

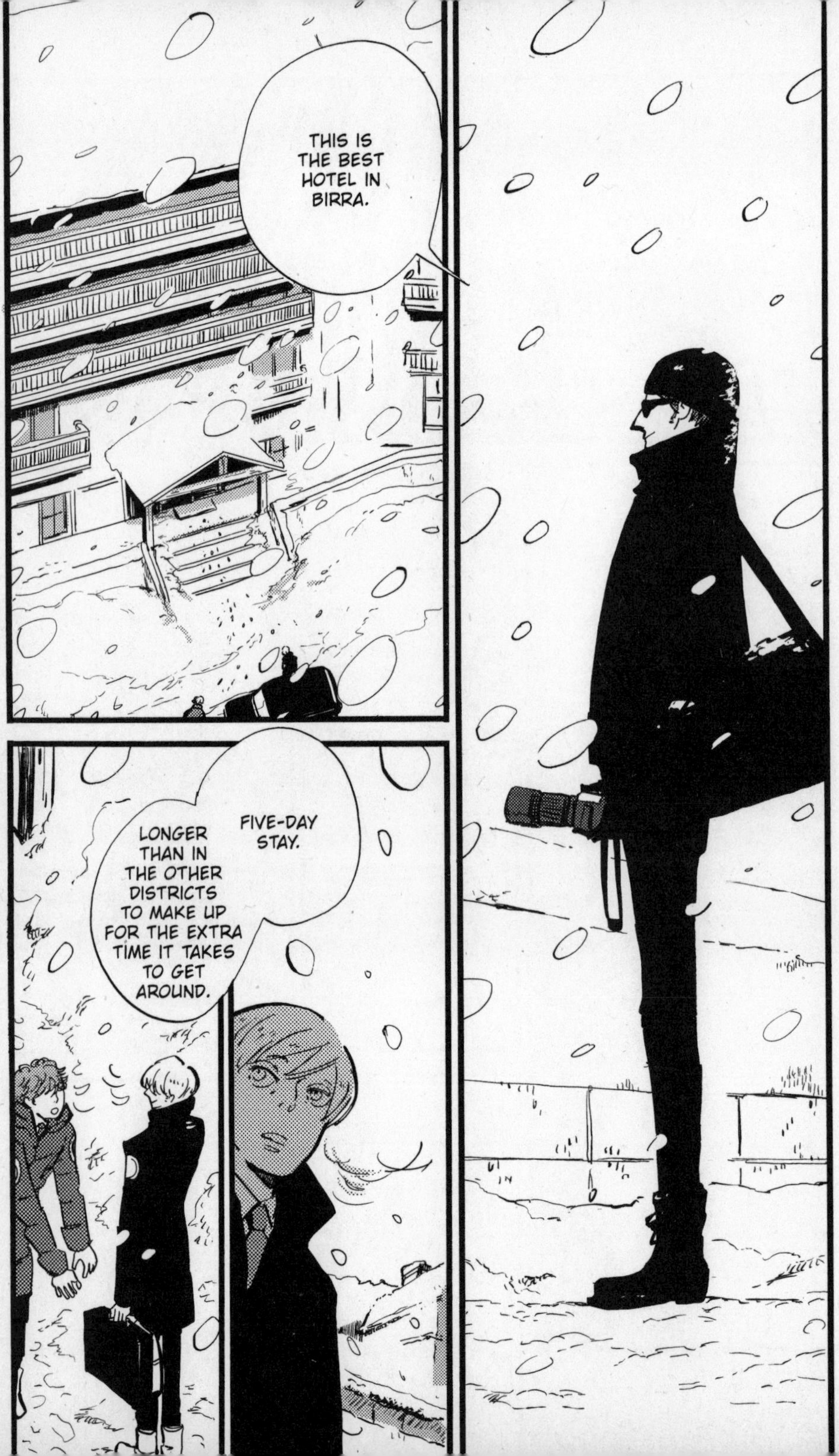
THIS IS THE BEST HOTEL IN BIRRA.
FIVE-DAY STAY.
LONGER THAN IN THE OTHER DISTRICTS TO MAKE UP FOR THE EXTRA TIME IT TAKES TO GET AROUND.

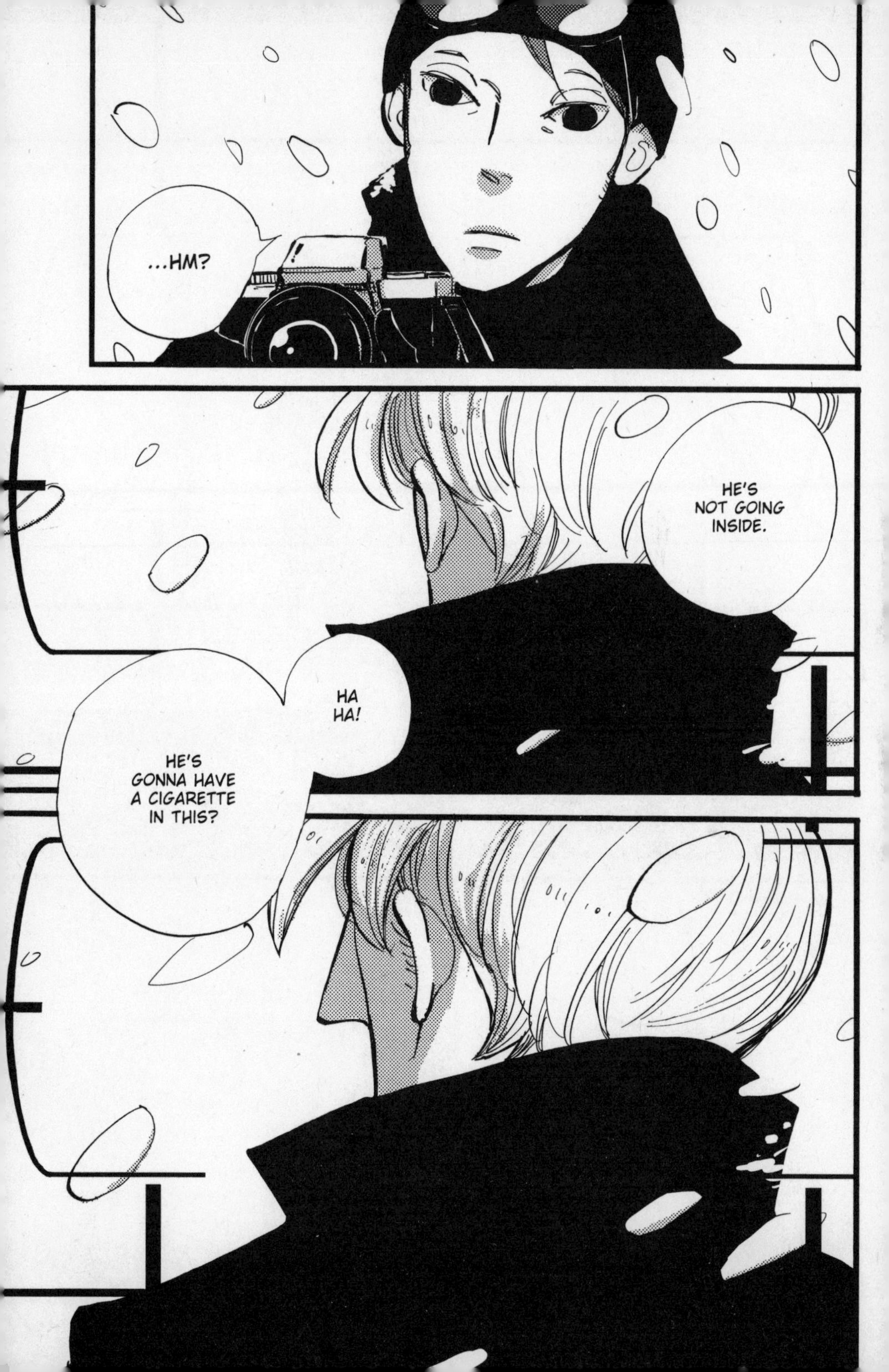
...HM?
HE'S NOT GOING INSIDE.
HA HA!
HE'S GONNA HAVE A CIGARETTE IN THIS?

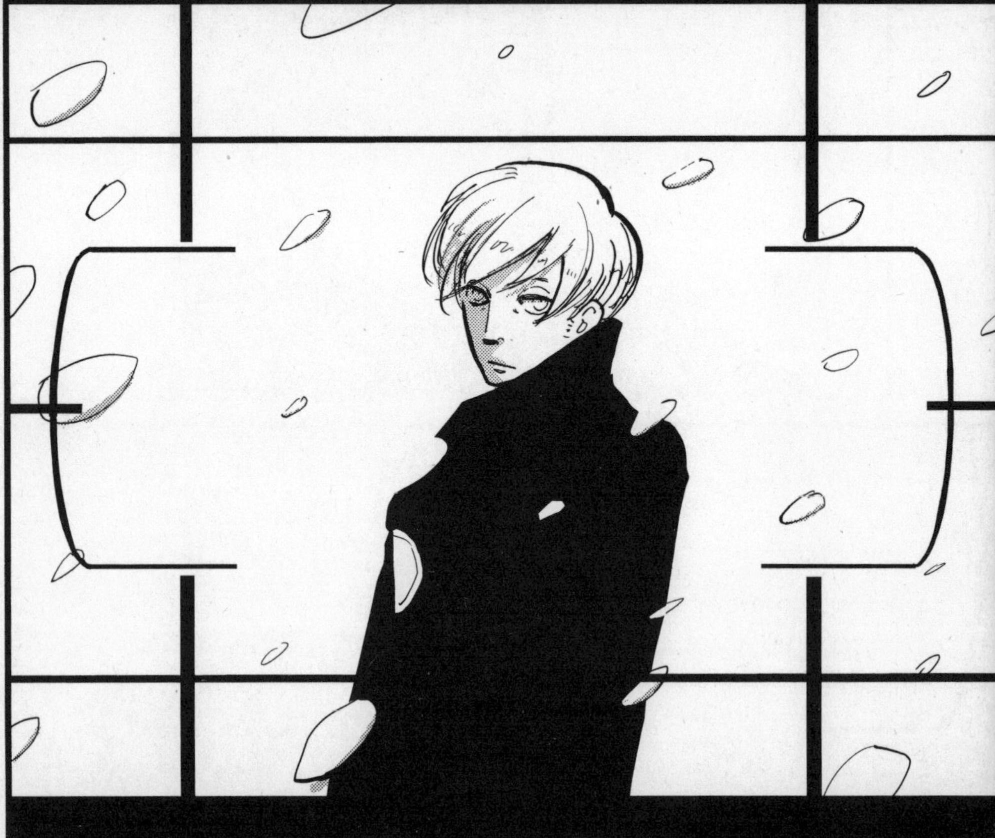
128
F 1.4

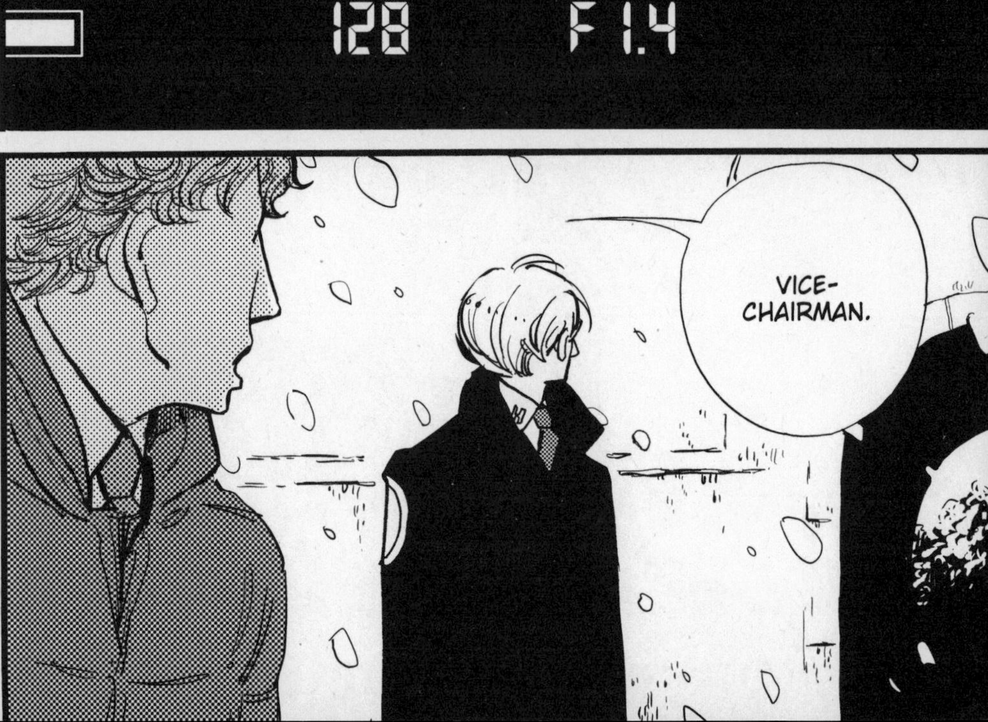
VICE-
CHAIRMAN.

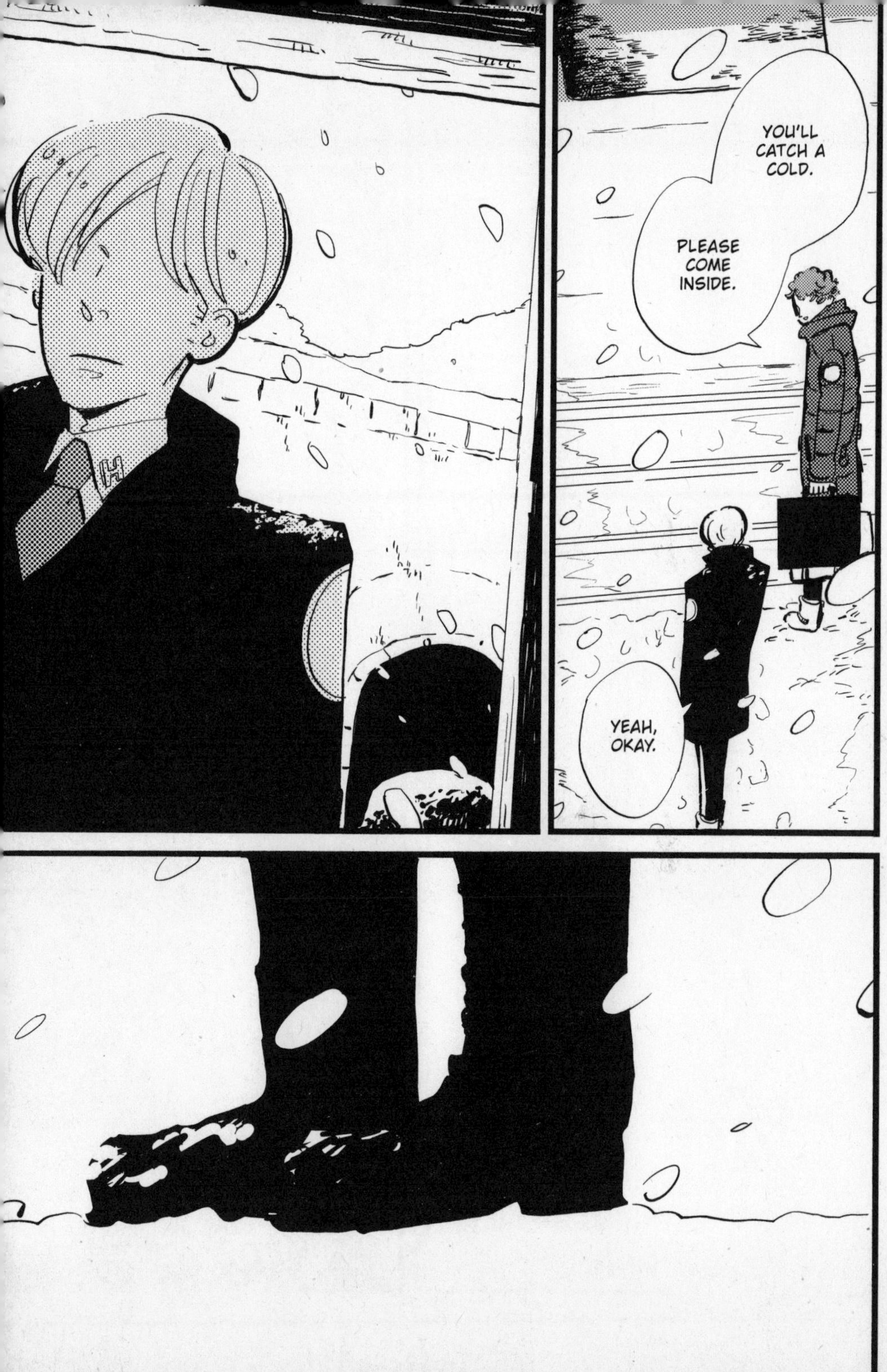
YOU'LL CATCH A COLD.
PLEASE COME INSIDE.
YEAH, OKAY.

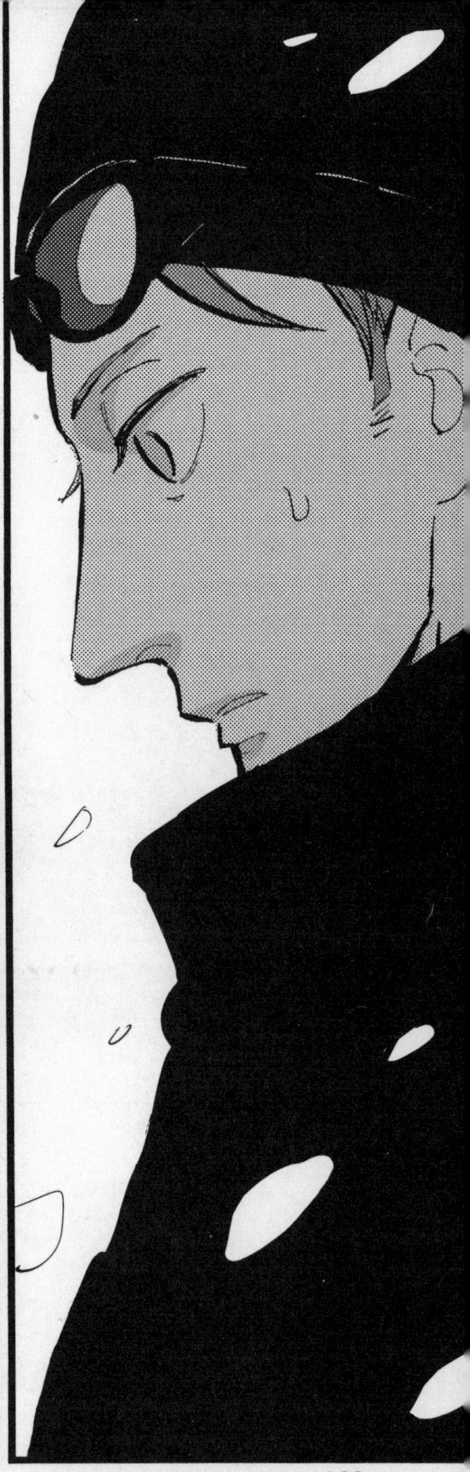

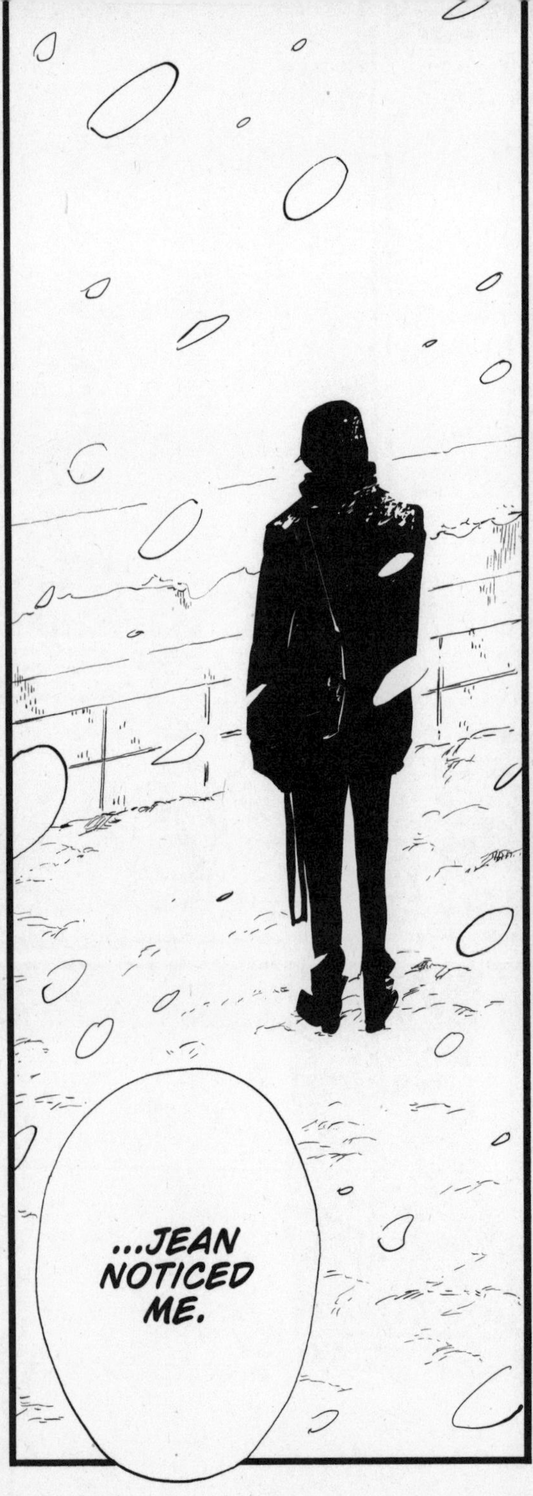
...JEAN NOTICED ME.

CHAPTER 15

Stumbling upon
a Clue in Badon

CHAPTER 16
Facing a "Friend" in Birra

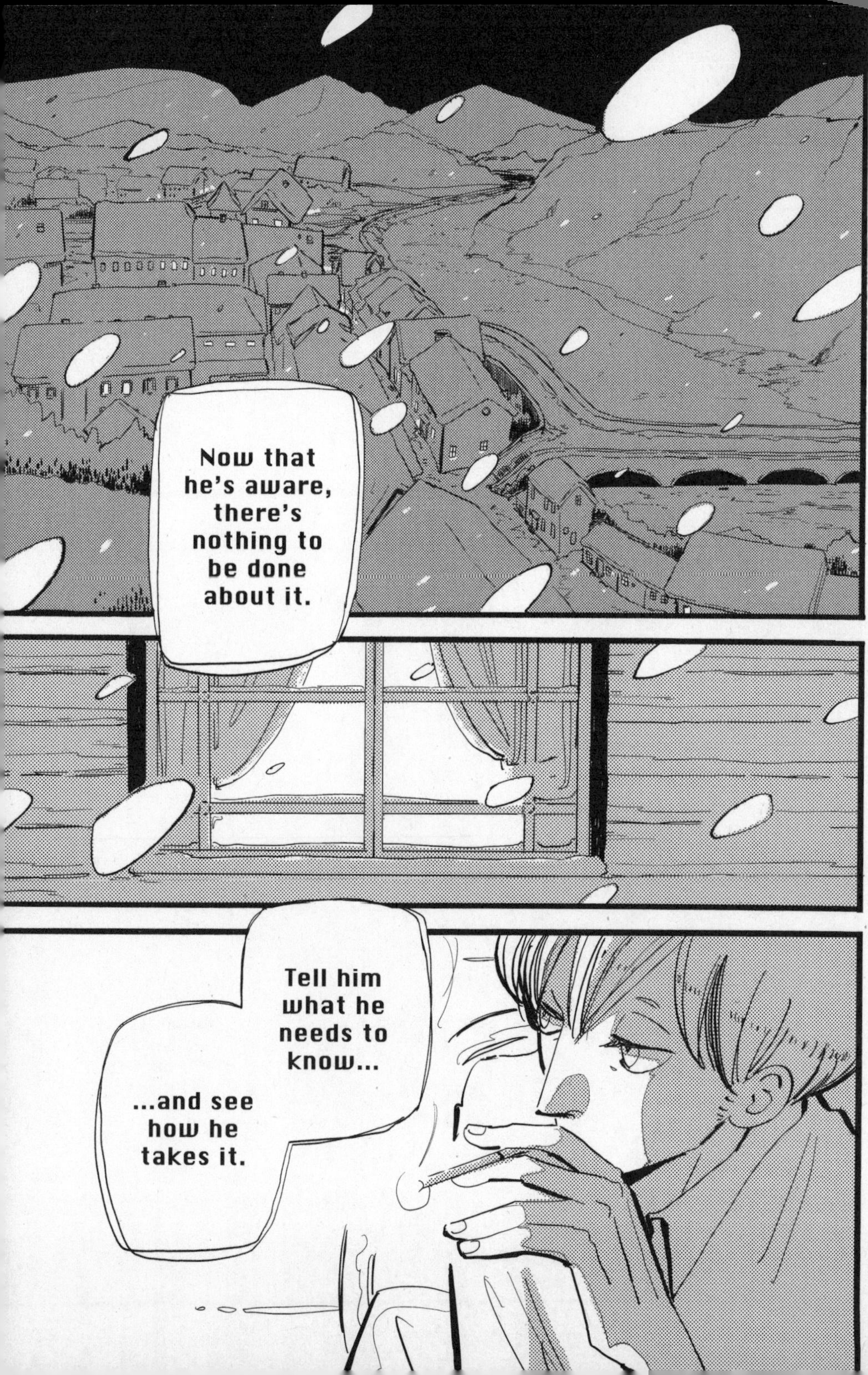
Now that he's aware, there's nothing to be done about it.
Tell him what he needs to know...
...and see how he takes it.

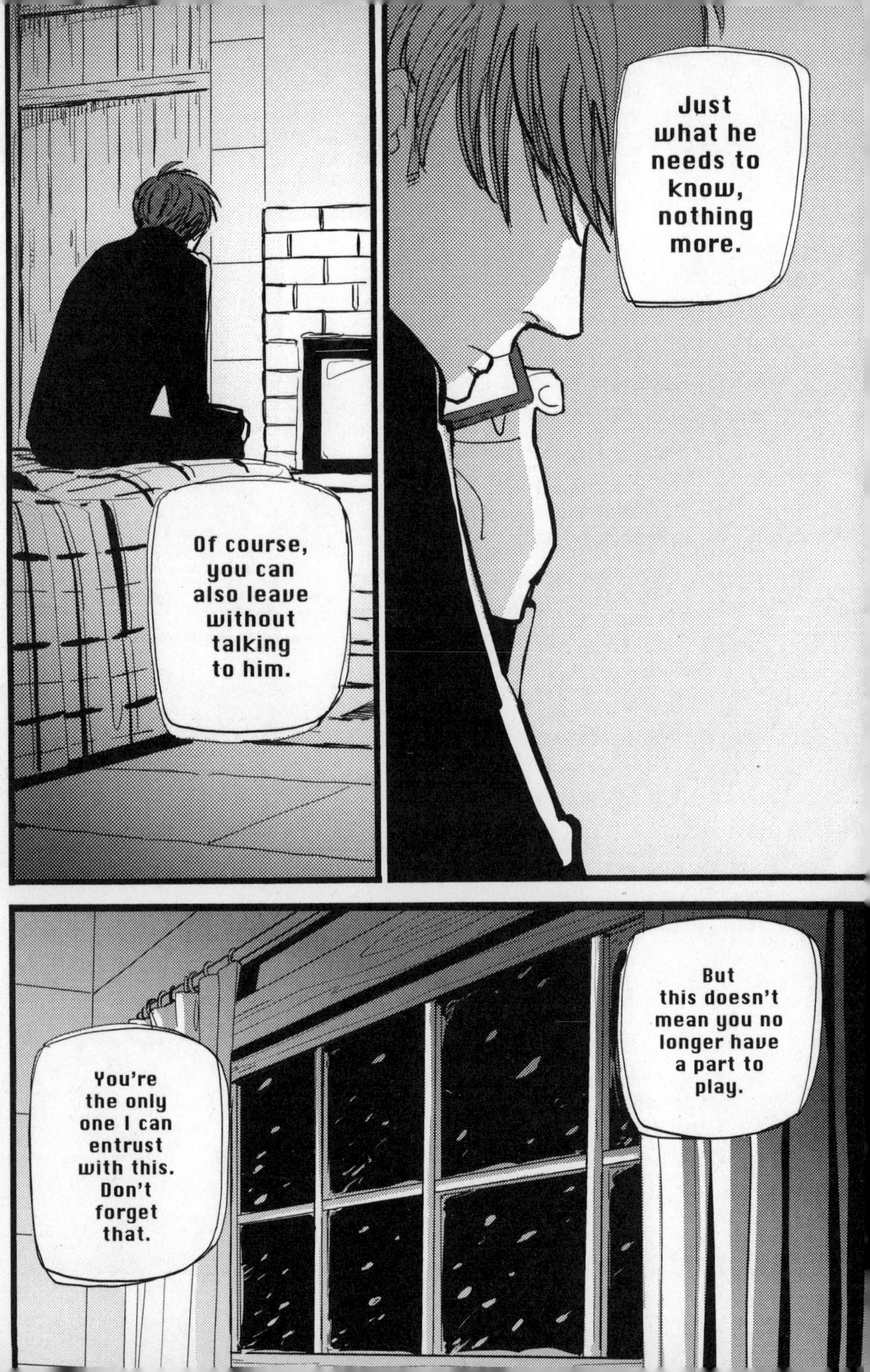
Just what he needs to know, nothing more.
Of course, you can also leave without talking to him.
But this doesn't mean you no longer have a part to play.
You're the only one I can entrust with this. Don't forget that.

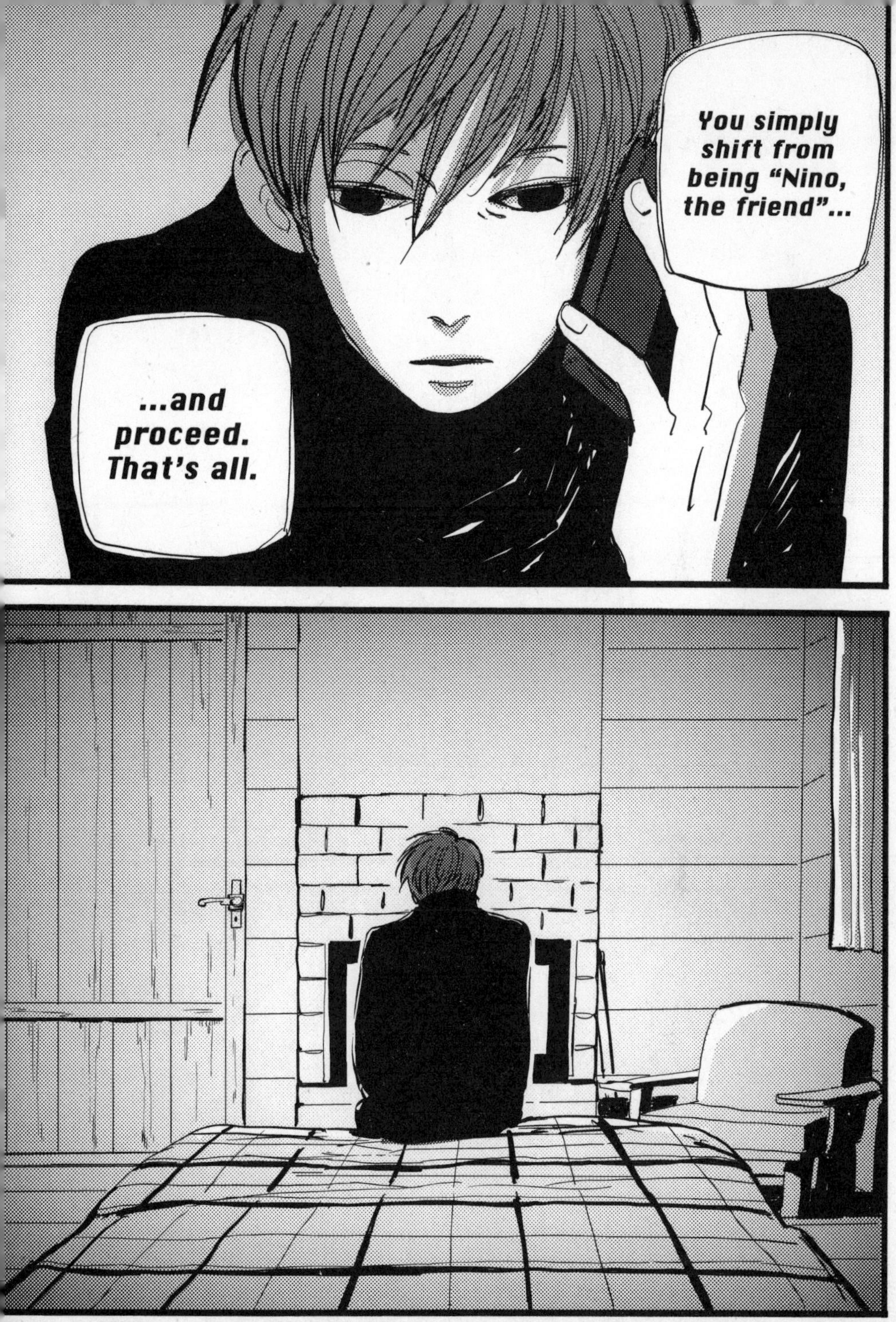
You simply shift from being "Nino, the friend"...
...and proceed. That's all.

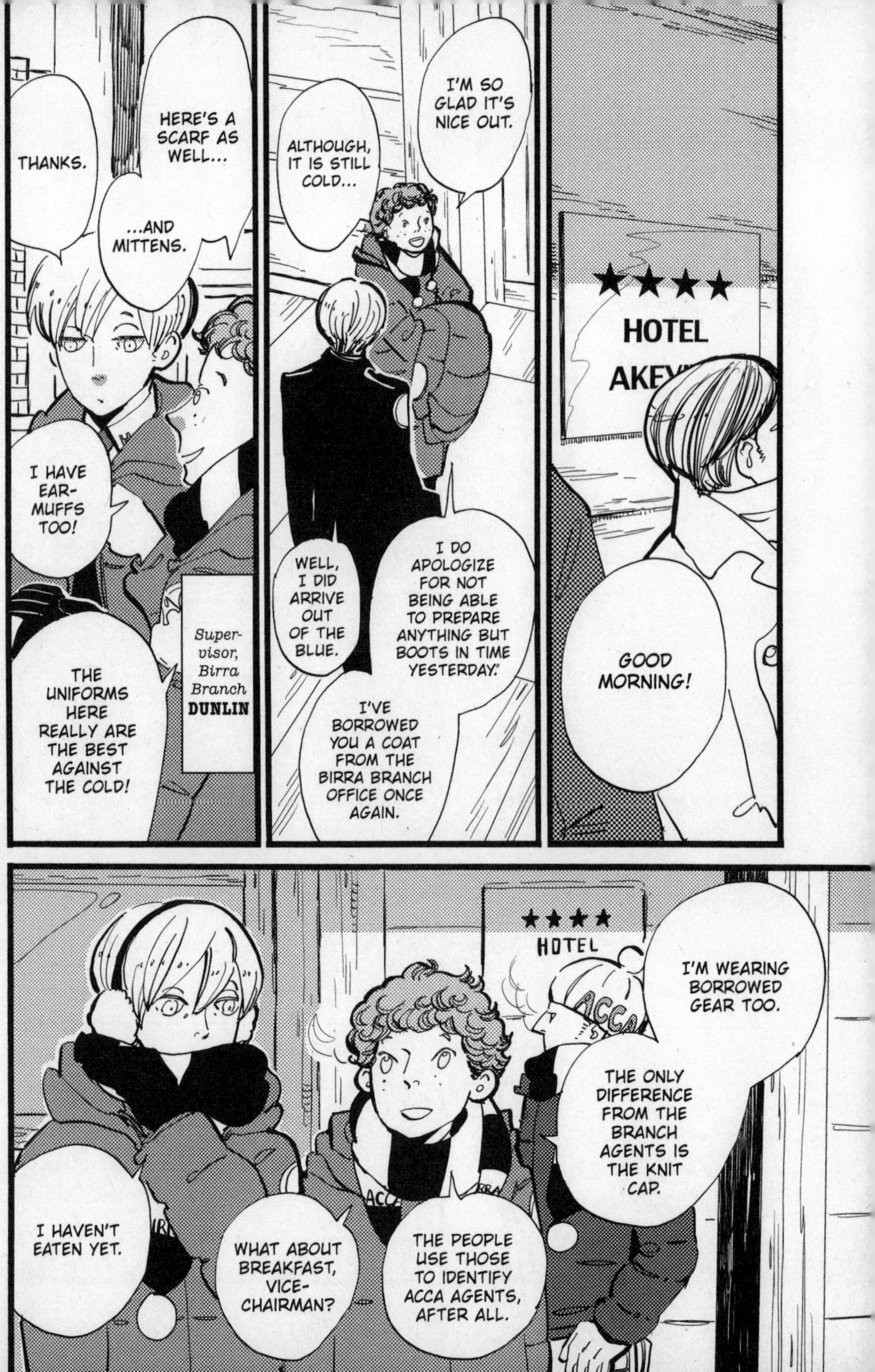
★★★★
HOTEL
GOOD MORNING!
I'M SO GLAD IT'S NICE OUT.
ALTHOUGH, IT IS STILL COLD...
I DO APOLOGIZE FOR NOT BEING ABLE TO PREPARE ANYTHING BUT BOOTS IN TIME YESTERDAY.
WELL, I DID ARRIVE OUT OF THE BLUE.
I'VE BORROWED YOU A COAT FROM THE BIRRA BRANCH OFFICE ONCE AGAIN.
HERE'S A SCARF AS WELL...
THANKS.
...AND MITTENS.
I HAVE EAR-MUFFS TOO!
Supervisor, Birra Branch DUNLIN
THE UNIFORMS HERE REALLY ARE THE BEST AGAINST THE COLD!
★★★★
HOTEL
I'M WEARING BORROWED GEAR TOO.
THE ONLY DIFFERENCE FROM THE BRANCH AGENTS IS THE KNIT CAP.
THE PEOPLE USE THOSE TO IDENTIFY ACCA AGENTS, AFTER ALL.
WHAT ABOUT BREAKFAST, VICE-CHAIRMAN?
I HAVEN'T EATEN YET.

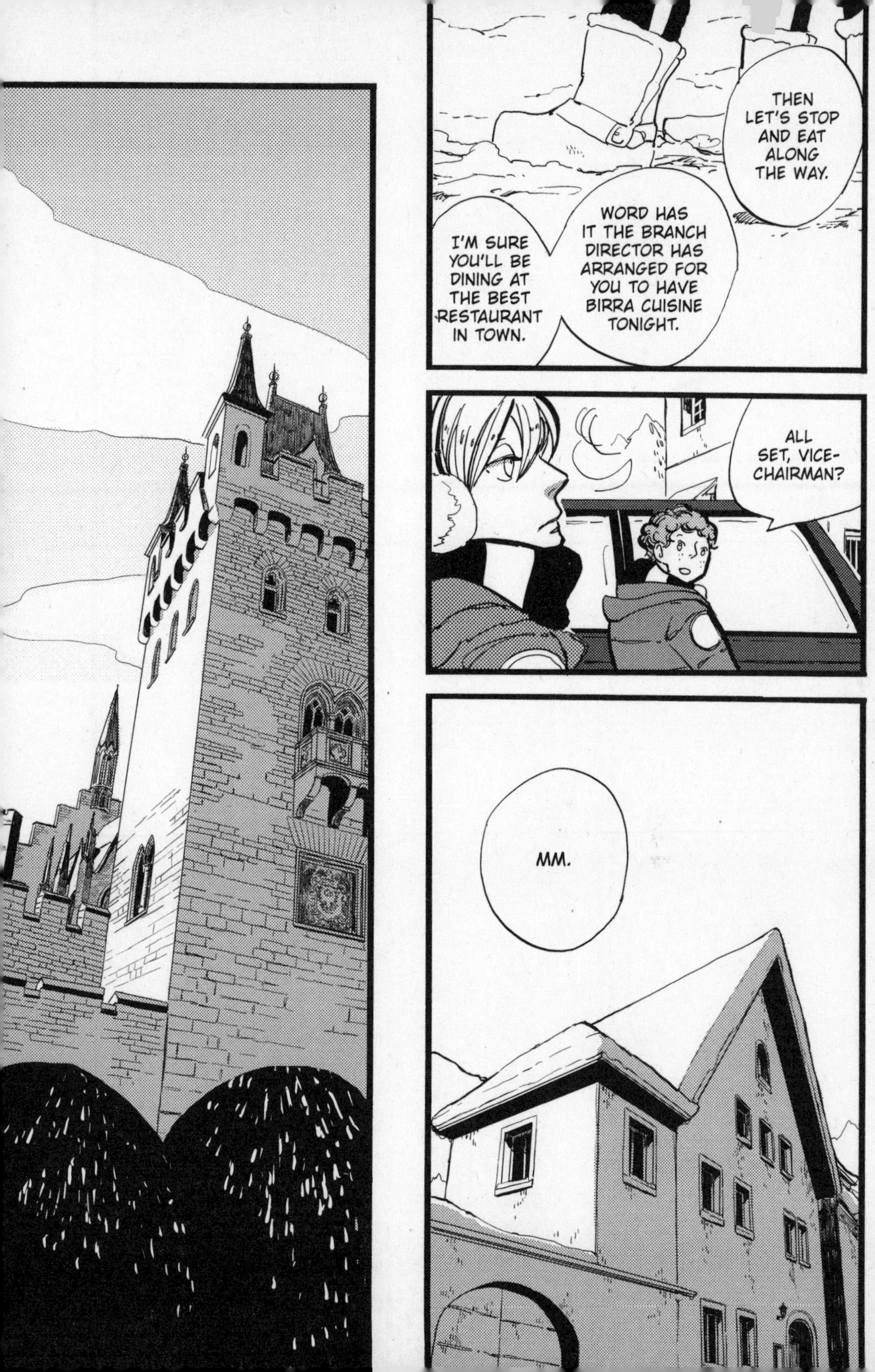
THEN LET'S STOP AND EAT ALONG THE WAY.
WORD HAS IT THE BRANCH DIRECTOR HAS ARRANGED FOR YOU TO HAVE BIRRA CUISINE TONIGHT.
I'M SURE YOU'LL BE DINING AT THE BEST RESTAURANT IN TOWN.
ALL SET, VICE-CHAIRMAN?
MM.

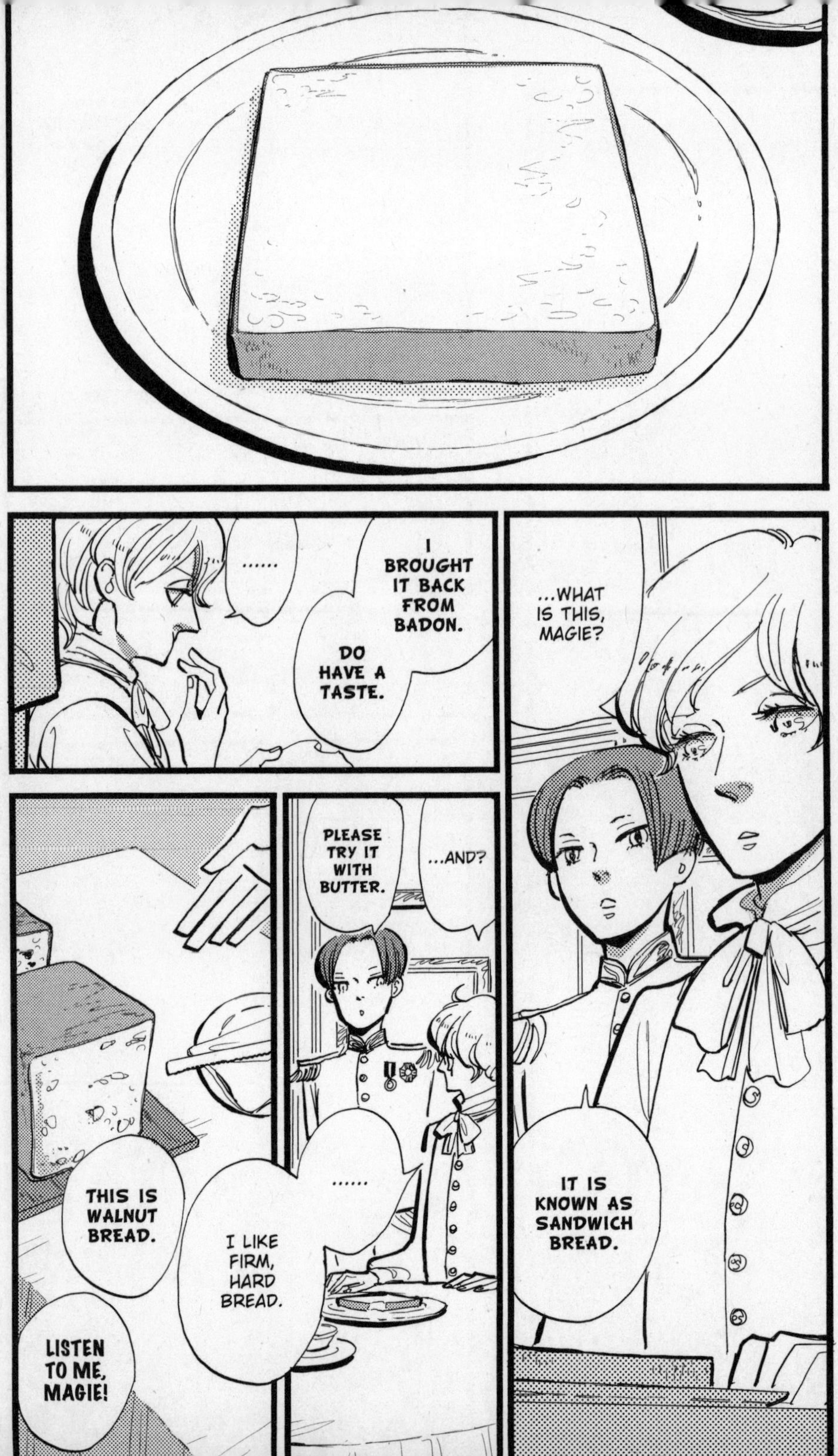
...WHAT IS THIS, MAGIE?
IT IS KNOWN AS SANDWICH BREAD.
I BROUGHT IT BACK FROM BADON.
DO HAVE A TASTE.
......
...AND?
PLEASE TRY IT WITH BUTTER.
......
I LIKE FIRM, HARD BREAD.
THIS IS WALNUT BREAD.
LISTEN TO ME, MAGIE!

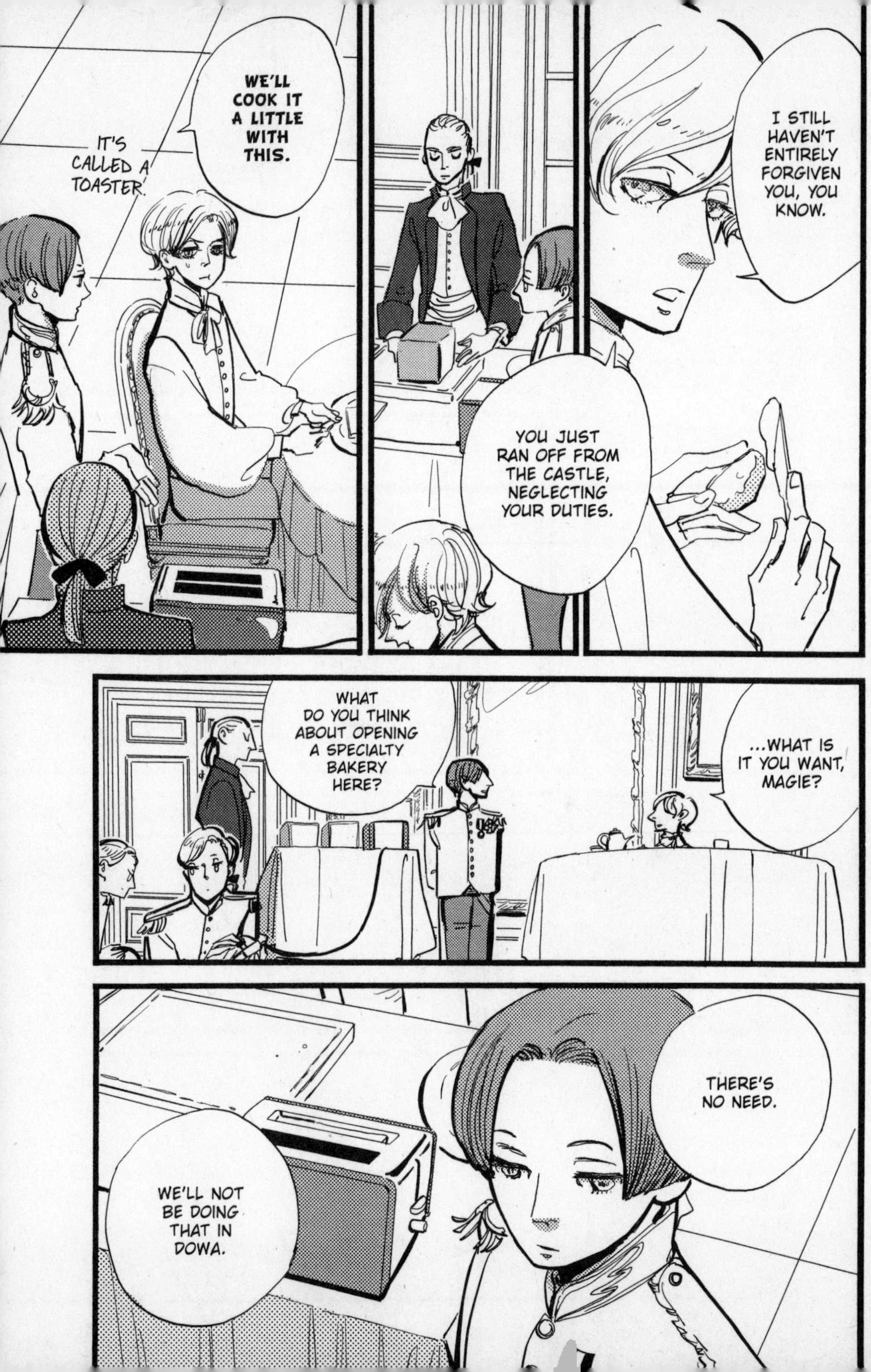
I STILL HAVEN'T ENTIRELY FORGIVEN YOU, YOU KNOW.
YOU JUST RAN OFF FROM THE CASTLE, NEGLECTING YOUR DUTIES.
WE'LL COOK IT A LITTLE WITH THIS.
IT'S CALLED A TOASTER.
...WHAT IS IT YOU WANT, MAGIE?
WHAT DO YOU THINK ABOUT OPENING A SPECIALTY BAKERY HERE?
THERE'S NO NEED.
WE'LL NOT BE DOING THAT IN DOWA.

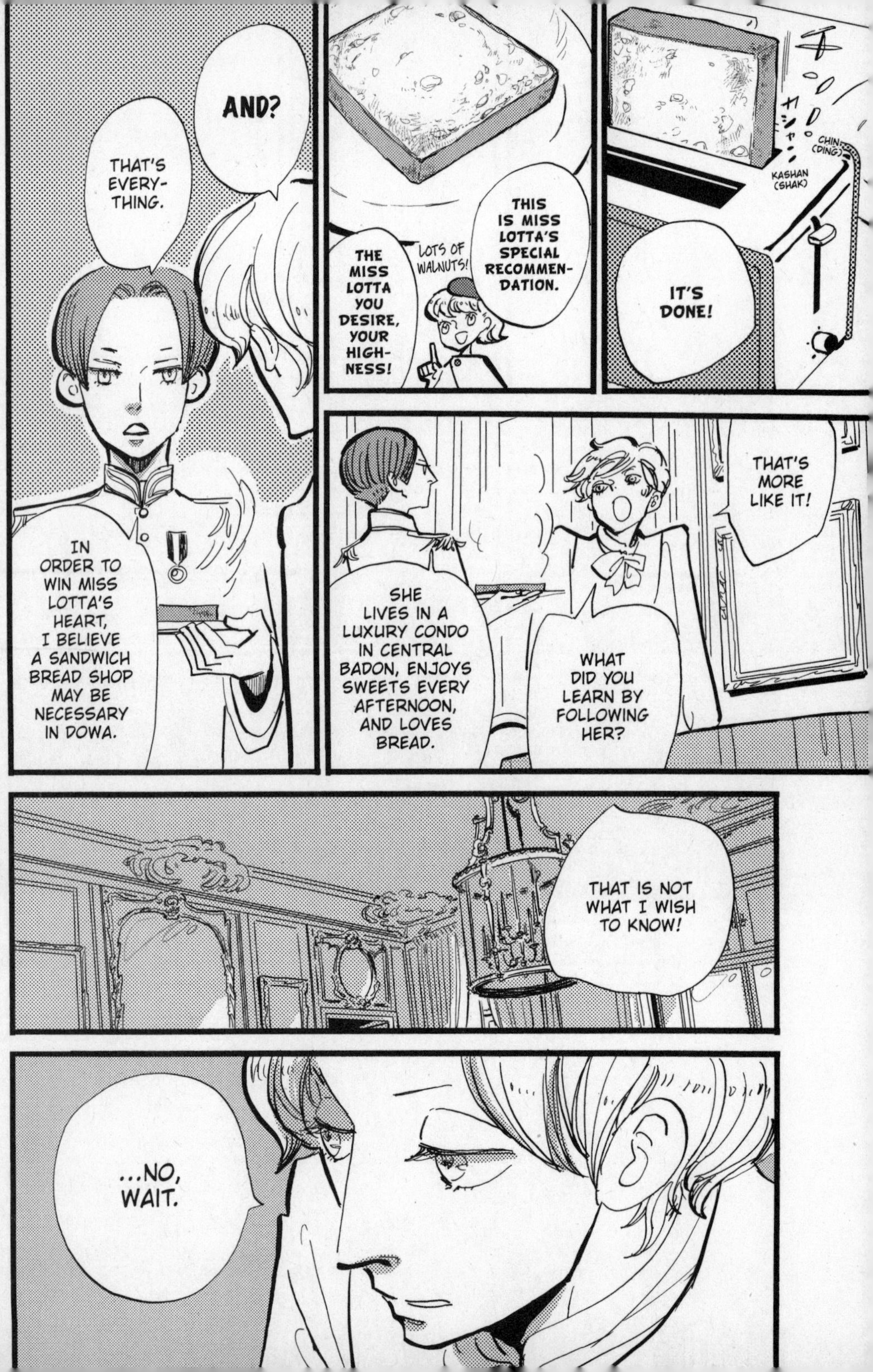
CHIN (DING)
KASHAN (SHAK)
IT'S DONE!
THIS IS MISS LOTTA'S SPECIAL RECOMMENDATION.
LOTS OF WALNUTS!
THE MISS LOTTA YOU DESIRE, YOUR HIGHNESS!
THAT'S MORE LIKE IT!
WHAT DID YOU LEARN BY FOLLOWING HER?
SHE LIVES IN A LUXURY CONDO IN CENTRAL BADON, ENJOYS SWEETS EVERY AFTERNOON, AND LOVES BREAD.
AND?
THAT'S EVERY-THING.
IN ORDER TO WIN MISS LOTTA'S HEART, I BELIEVE A SANDWICH BREAD SHOP MAY BE NECESSARY IN DOWA.
THAT IS NOT WHAT I WISH TO KNOW!
...NO, WAIT.

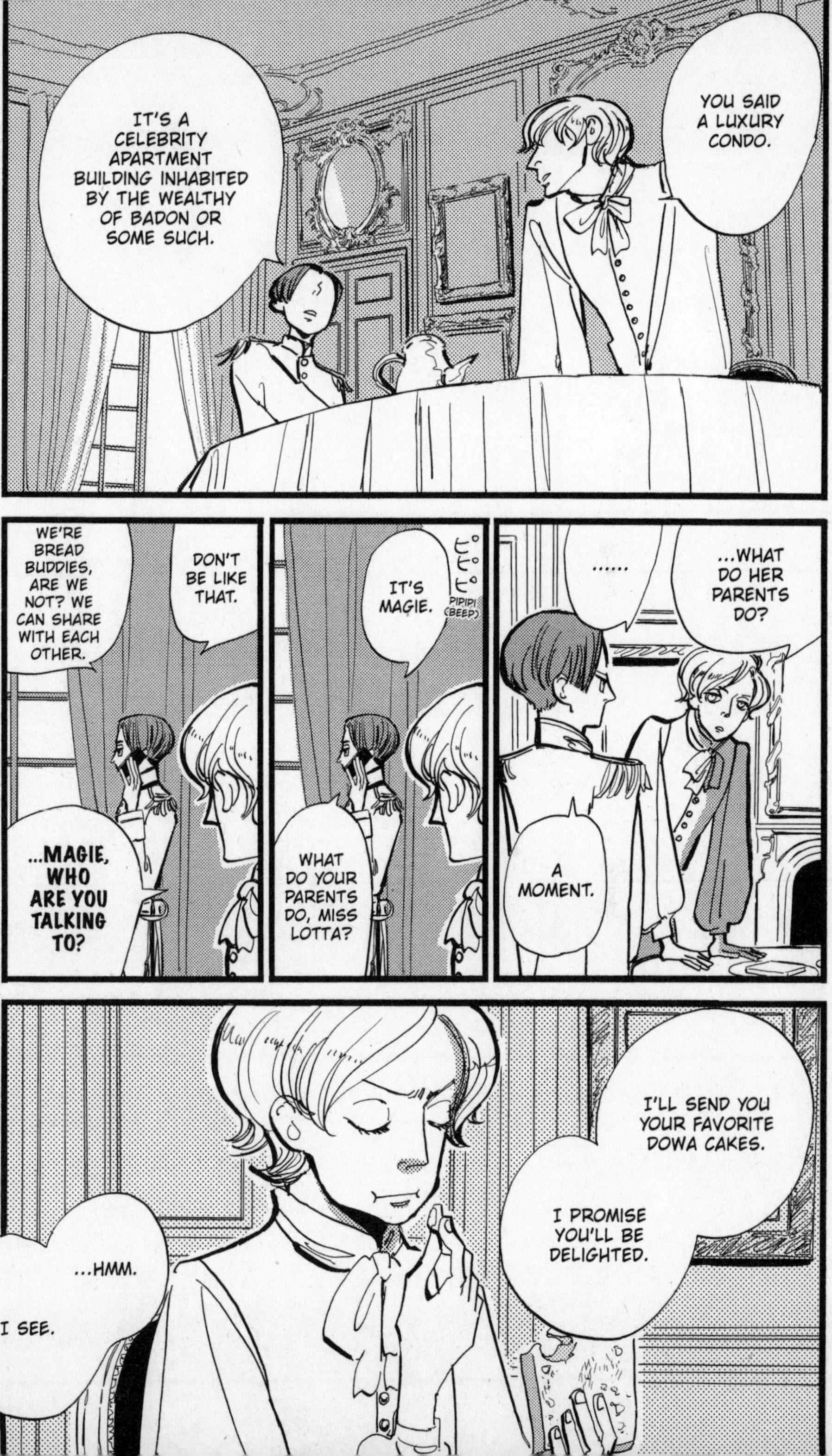
YOU SAID A LUXURY CONDO.
IT'S A CELEBRITY APARTMENT BUILDING INHABITED BY THE WEALTHY OF BADON OR SOME SUCH.
...WHAT DO HER PARENTS DO?
......
A MOMENT.
ピピピ PIPIPI (BEEP)
IT'S MAGIE.
WHAT DO YOUR PARENTS DO, MISS LOTTA?
DON'T BE LIKE THAT.
WE'RE BREAD BUDDIES, ARE WE NOT? WE CAN SHARE WITH EACH OTHER.
...MAGIE, WHO ARE YOU TALKING TO?
I'LL SEND YOU YOUR FAVORITE DOWA CAKES.
I PROMISE YOU'LL BE DELIGHTED.
...HMM.
I SEE.

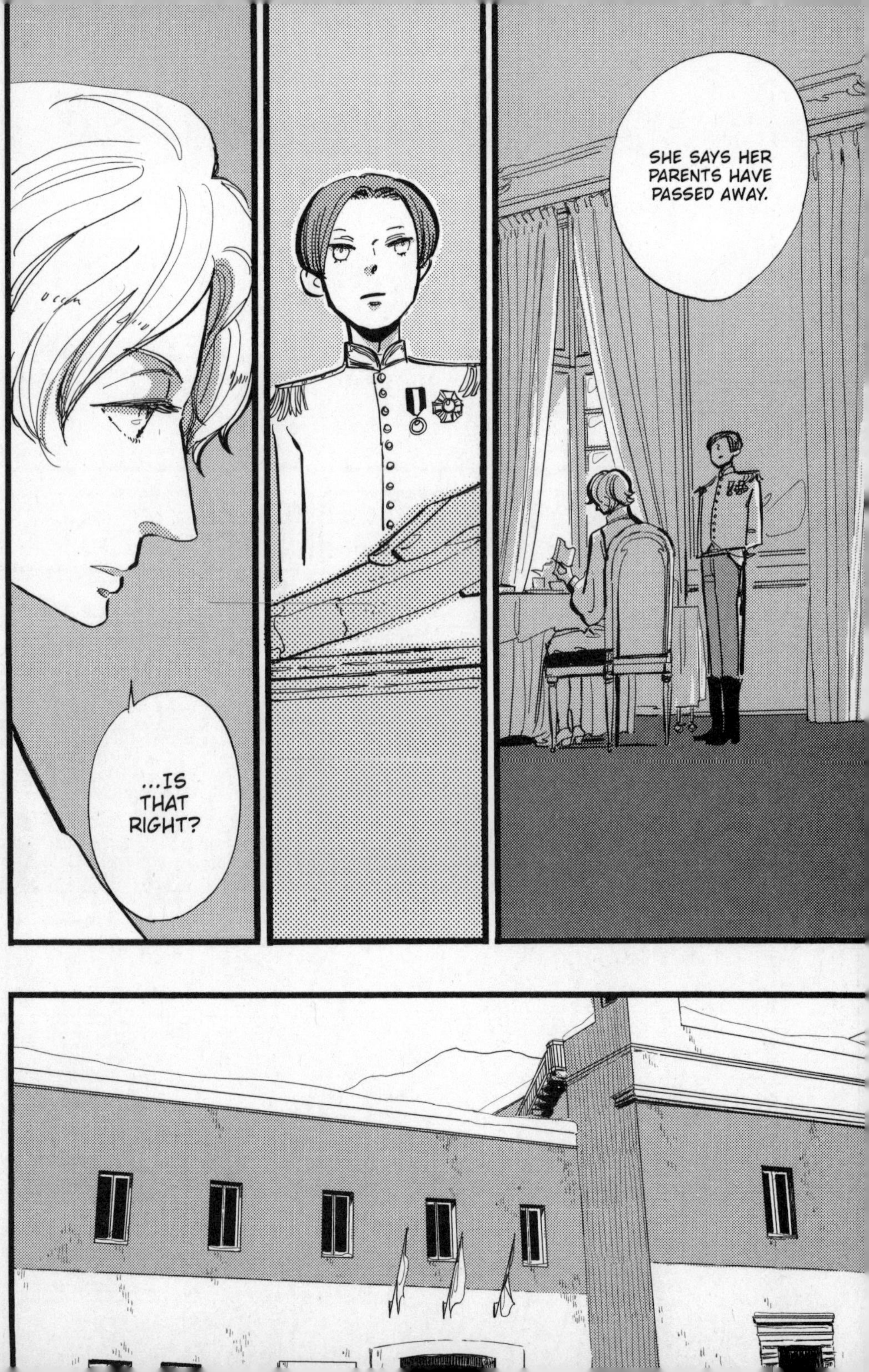
SHE SAYS HER PARENTS HAVE PASSED AWAY.
...IS THAT RIGHT?

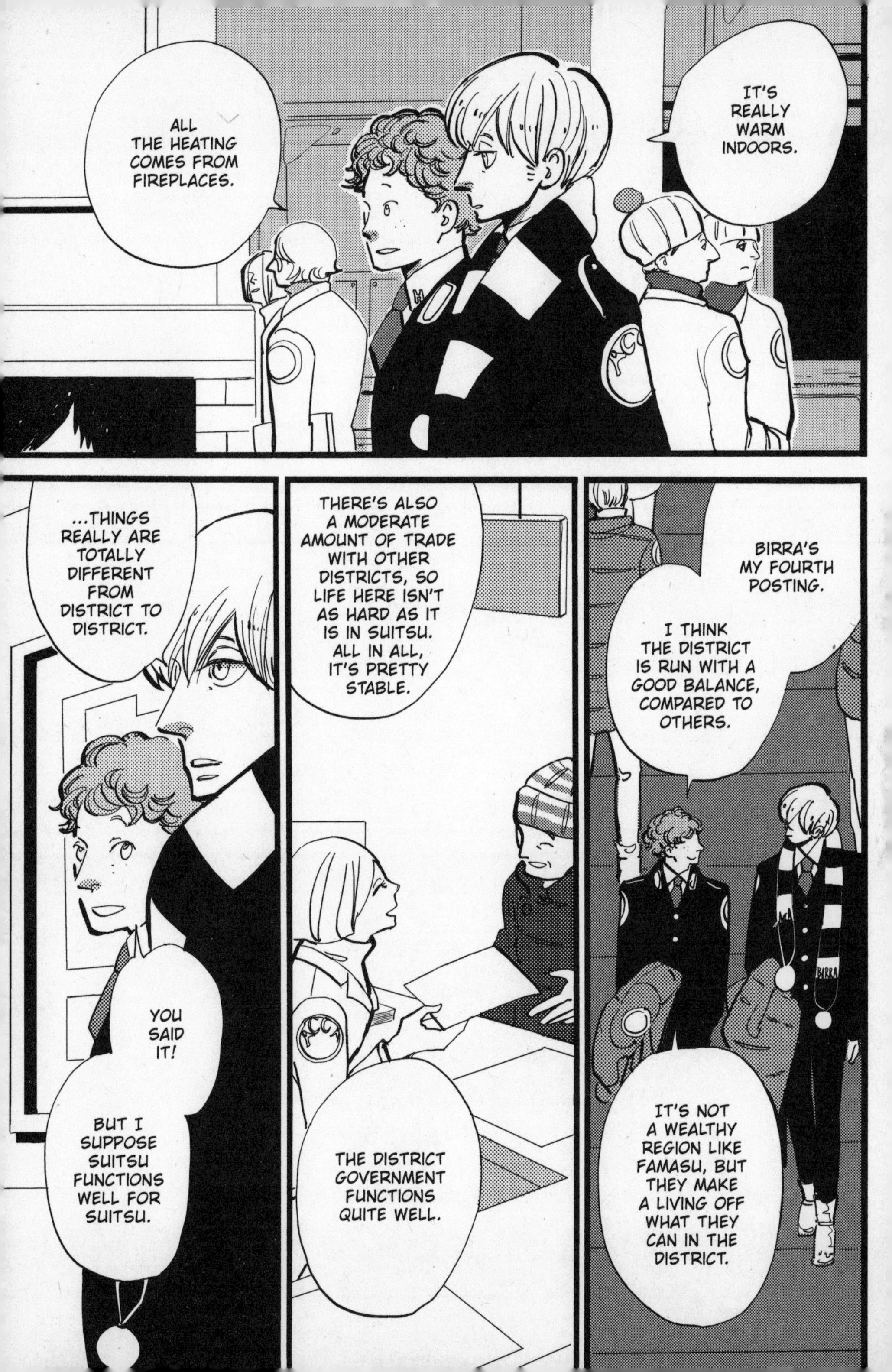
IT'S REALLY WARM INDOORS.
ALL THE HEATING COMES FROM FIREPLACES.
BIRRA'S MY FOURTH POSTING.
I THINK THE DISTRICT IS RUN WITH A GOOD BALANCE, COMPARED TO OTHERS.
IT'S NOT A WEALTHY REGION LIKE FAMASU, BUT THEY MAKE A LIVING OFF WHAT THEY CAN IN THE DISTRICT.
THERE'S ALSO A MODERATE AMOUNT OF TRADE WITH OTHER DISTRICTS, SO LIFE HERE ISN'T AS HARD AS IT IS IN SUITSU. ALL IN ALL, IT'S PRETTY STABLE.
THE DISTRICT GOVERNMENT FUNCTIONS QUITE WELL.
...THINGS REALLY ARE TOTALLY DIFFERENT FROM DISTRICT TO DISTRICT.
YOU SAID IT!
BUT I SUPPOSE SUITSU FUNCTIONS WELL FOR SUITSU.

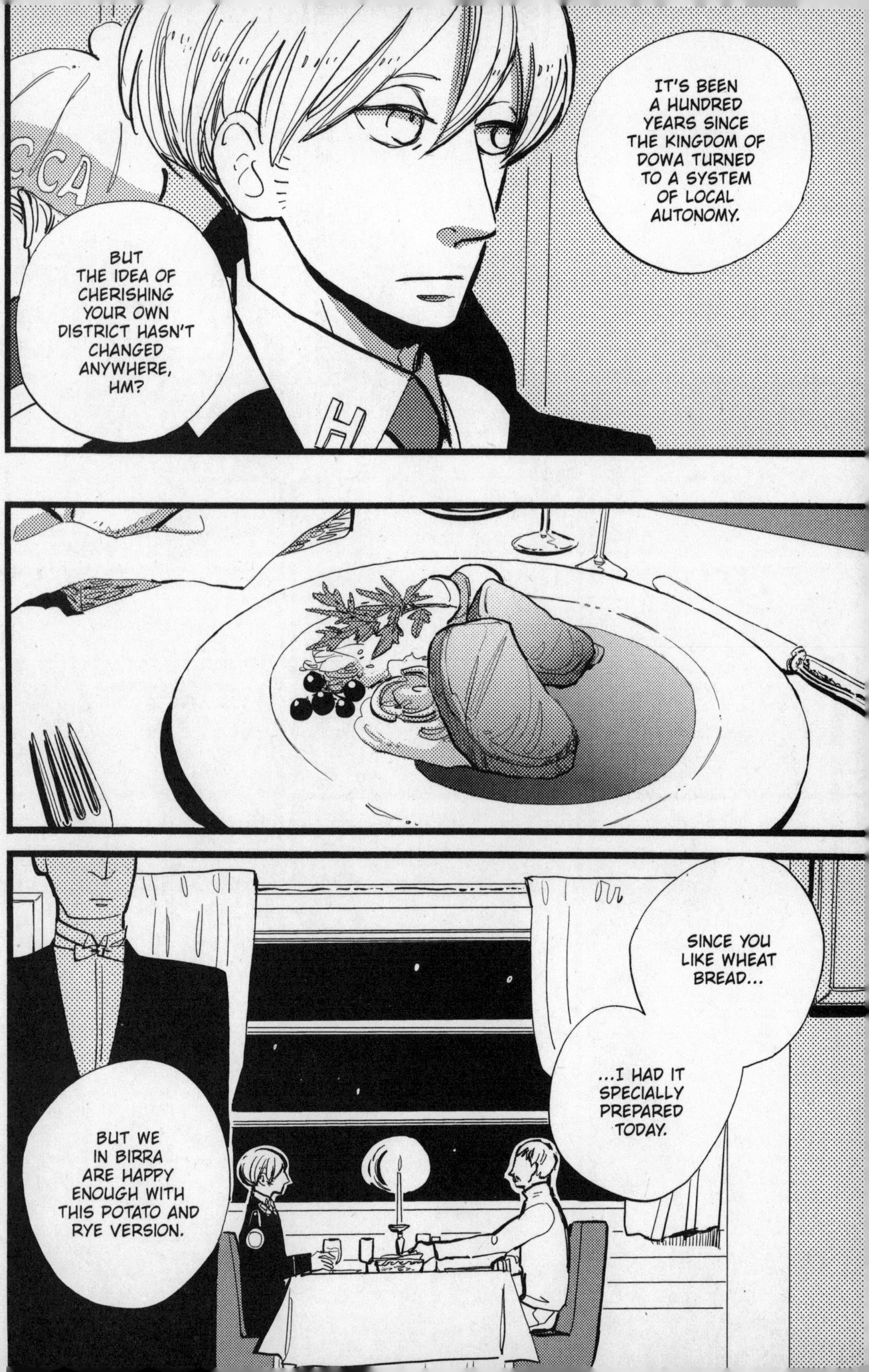
IT'S BEEN A HUNDRED YEARS SINCE THE KINGDOM OF DOWA TURNED TO A SYSTEM OF LOCAL AUTONOMY.
BUT THE IDEA OF CHERISHING YOUR OWN DISTRICT HASN'T CHANGED ANYWHERE, HM?
SINCE YOU LIKE WHEAT BREAD...
...I HAD IT SPECIALLY PREPARED TODAY.
BUT WE IN BIRRA ARE HAPPY ENOUGH WITH THIS POTATO AND RYE VERSION.

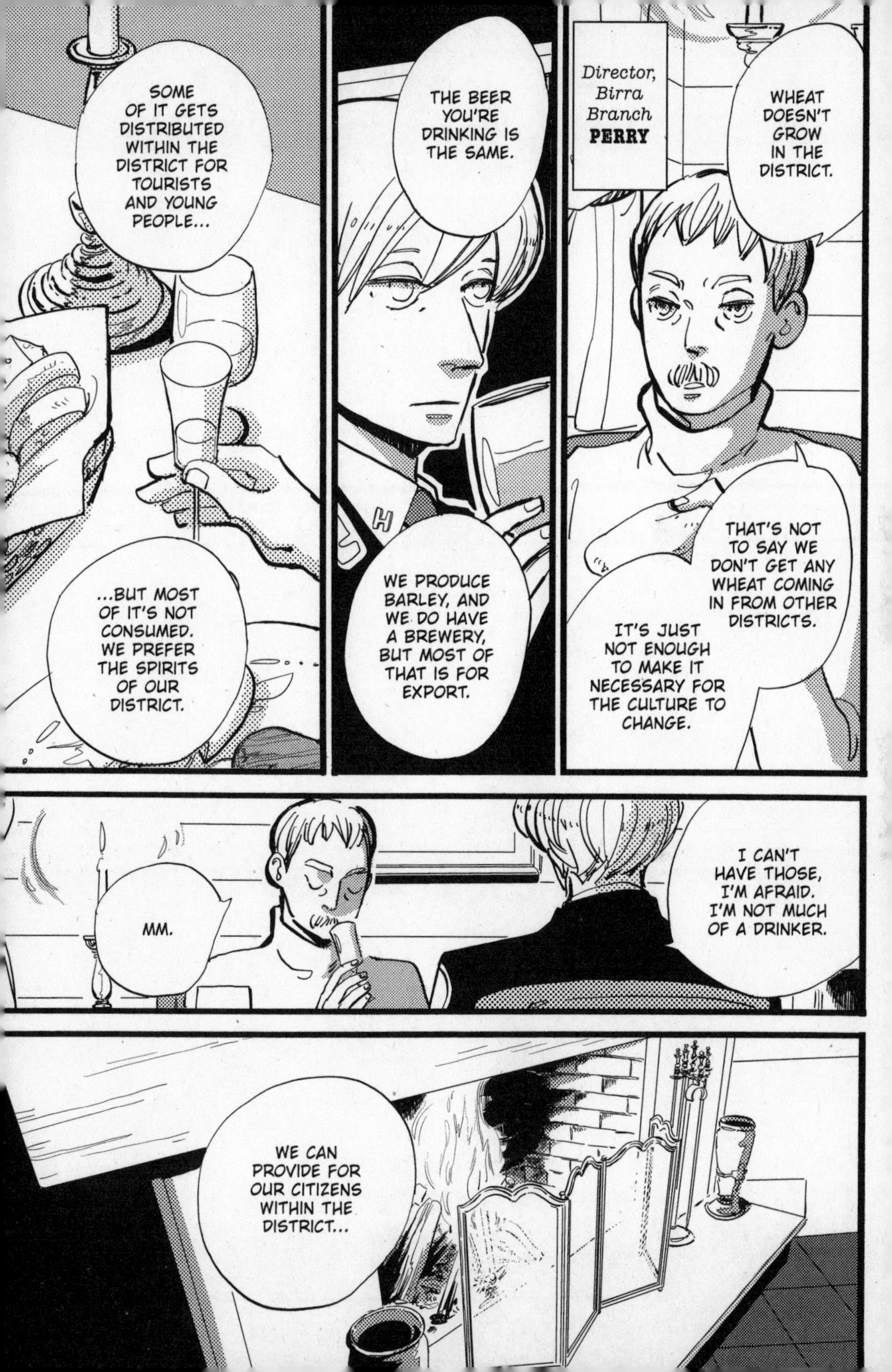

Director, Birra Branch PERRY
WHEAT DOESN'T GROW IN THE DISTRICT.
THAT'S NOT TO SAY WE DON'T GET ANY WHEAT COMING IN FROM OTHER DISTRICTS.
IT'S JUST NOT ENOUGH TO MAKE IT NECESSARY FOR THE CULTURE TO CHANGE.
THE BEER YOU'RE DRINKING IS THE SAME.
WE PRODUCE BARLEY, AND WE DO HAVE A BREWERY, BUT MOST OF THAT IS FOR EXPORT.
SOME OF IT GETS DISTRIBUTED WITHIN THE DISTRICT FOR TOURISTS AND YOUNG PEOPLE...
...BUT MOST OF IT'S NOT CONSUMED. WE PREFER THE SPIRITS OF OUR DISTRICT.
I CAN'T HAVE THOSE, I'M AFRAID. I'M NOT MUCH OF A DRINKER.
MM.
WE CAN PROVIDE FOR OUR CITIZENS WITHIN THE DISTRICT...

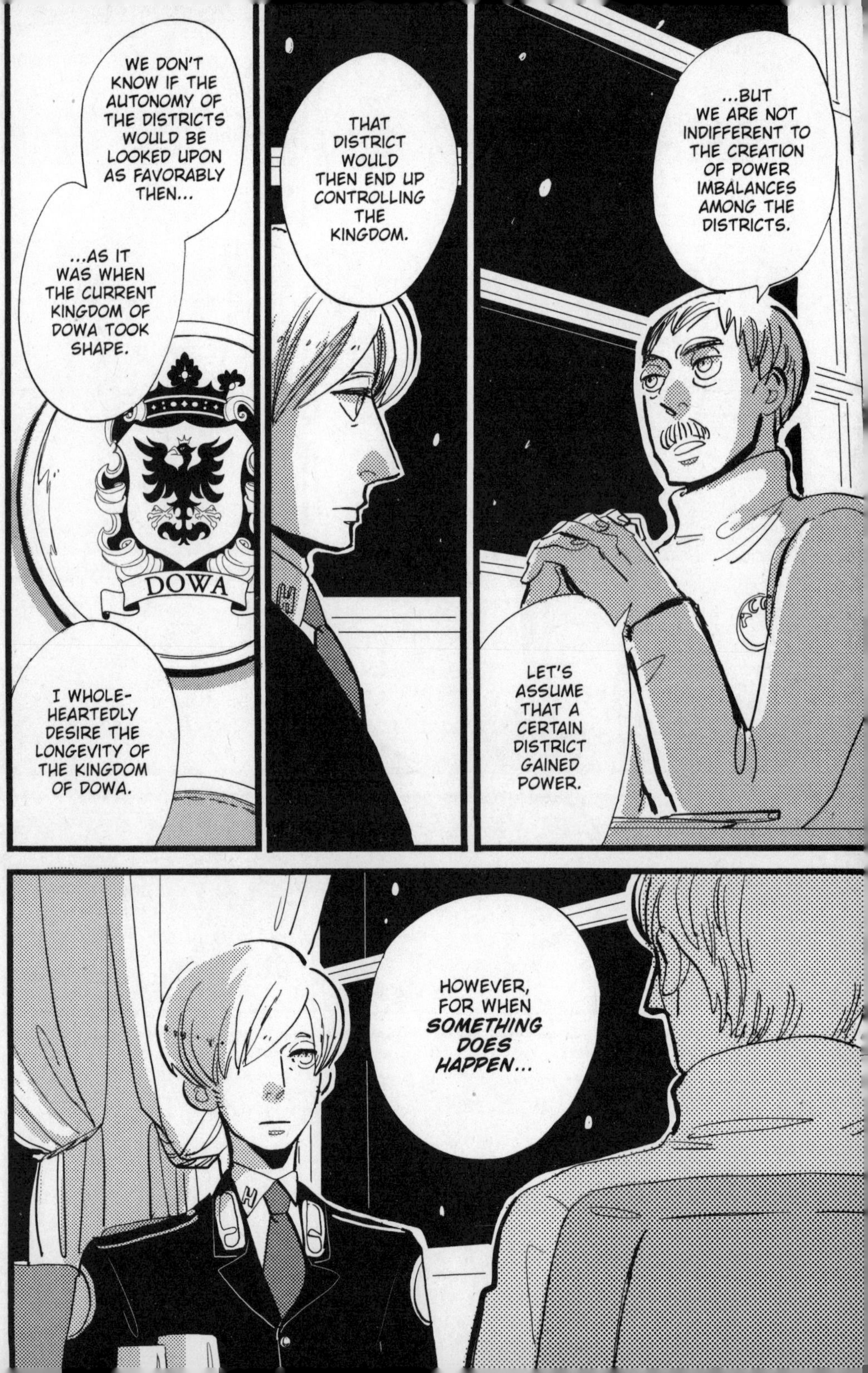
...BUT WE ARE NOT INDIFFERENT TO THE CREATION OF POWER IMBALANCES AMONG THE DISTRICTS.
LET'S ASSUME THAT A CERTAIN DISTRICT GAINED POWER.
THAT DISTRICT WOULD THEN END UP CONTROLLING THE KINGDOM.
WE DON'T KNOW IF THE AUTONOMY OF THE DISTRICTS WOULD BE LOOKED UPON AS FAVORABLY THEN...
...AS IT WAS WHEN THE CURRENT KINGDOM OF DOWA TOOK SHAPE.
DOWA
I WHOLE-HEARTEDLY DESIRE THE LONGEVITY OF THE KINGDOM OF DOWA.
HOWEVER, FOR WHEN *SOMETHING DOES HAPPEN*...

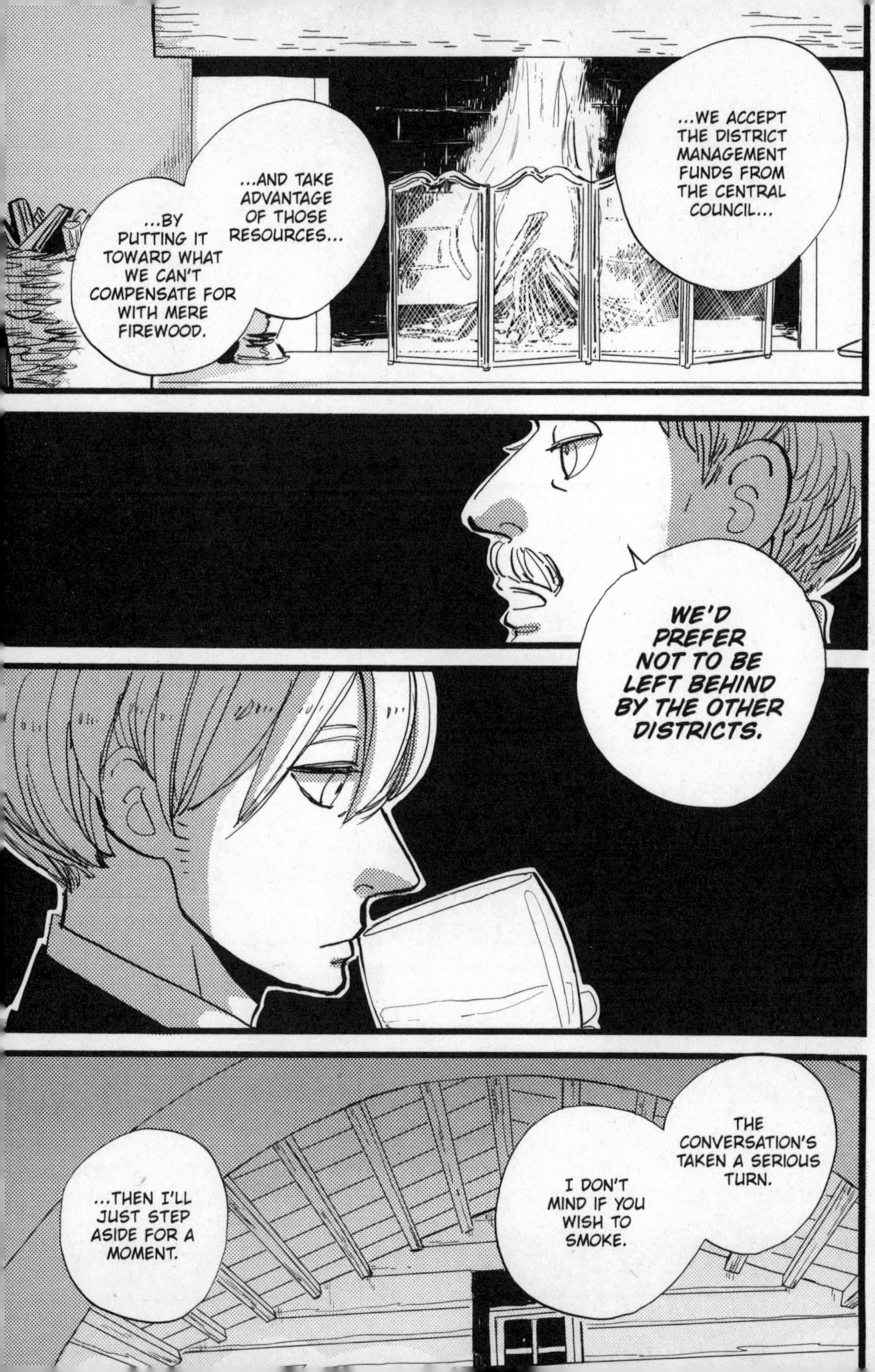
...WE ACCEPT THE DISTRICT MANAGEMENT FUNDS FROM THE CENTRAL COUNCIL...
...AND TAKE ADVANTAGE OF THOSE RESOURCES...
...BY PUTTING IT TOWARD WHAT WE CAN'T COMPENSATE FOR WITH MERE FIREWOOD.
WE'D PREFER NOT TO BE LEFT BEHIND BY THE OTHER DISTRICTS.
THE CONVERSATION'S TAKEN A SERIOUS TURN.
I DON'T MIND IF YOU WISH TO SMOKE.
...THEN I'LL JUST STEP ASIDE FOR A MOMENT.

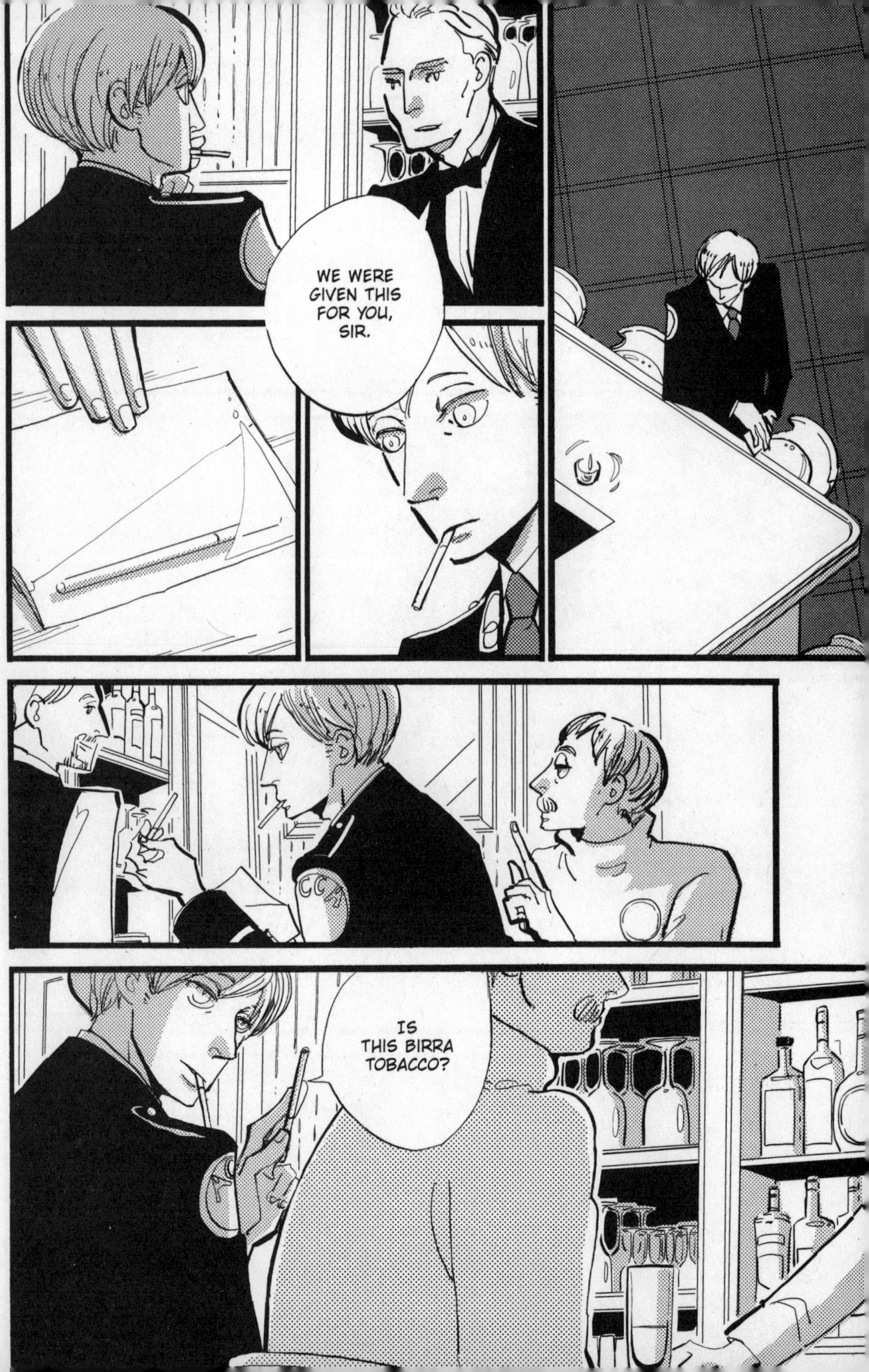
WE WERE GIVEN THIS FOR YOU, SIR.
IS THIS BIRRA TOBACCO?

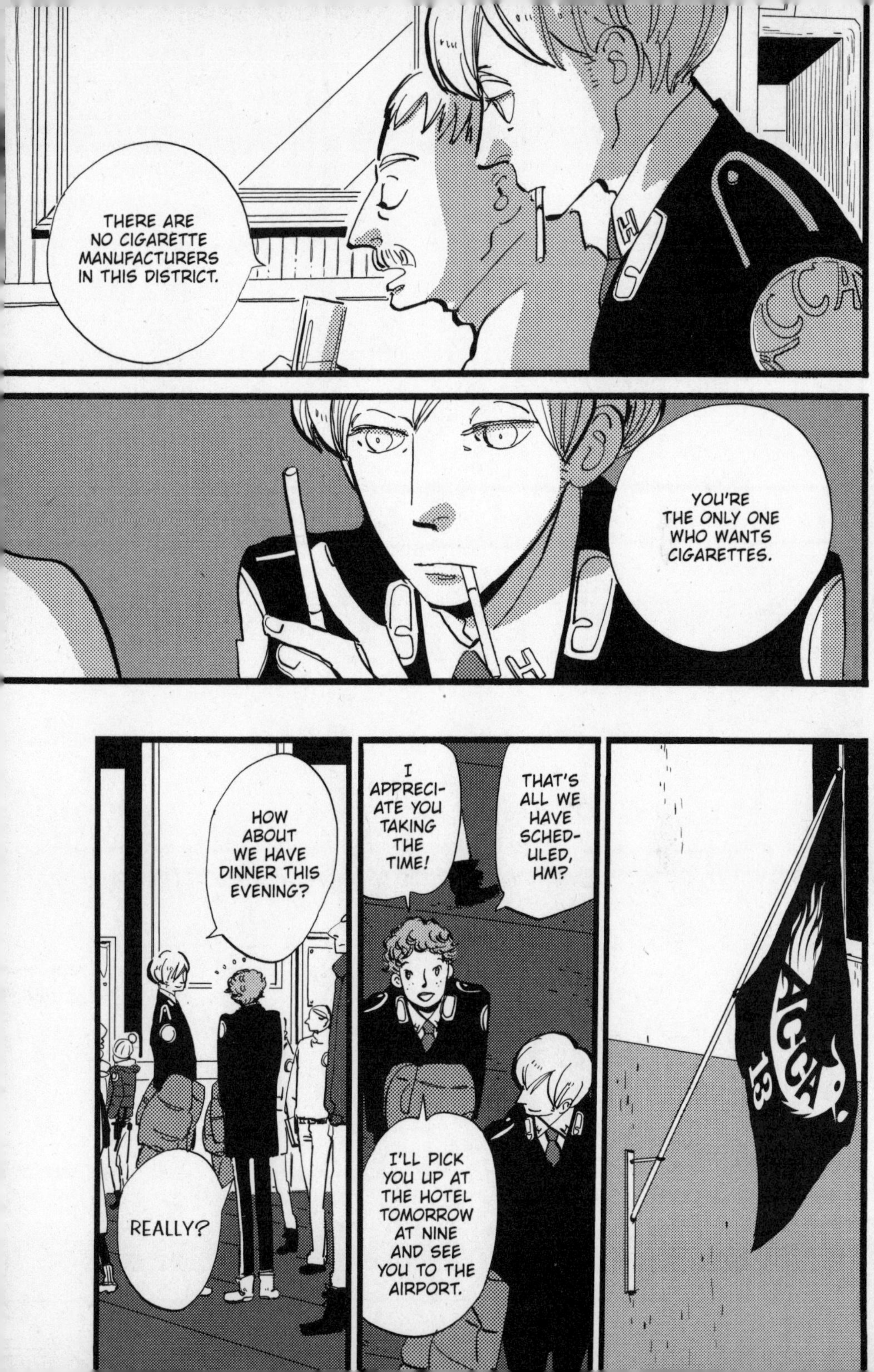
THERE ARE NO CIGARETTE MANUFACTURERS IN THIS DISTRICT.
YOU'RE THE ONLY ONE WHO WANTS CIGARETTES.
ACCA 13
THAT'S ALL WE HAVE SCHED-ULED, HM?
I APPRECI-ATE YOU TAKING THE TIME!
I'LL PICK YOU UP AT THE HOTEL TOMORROW AT NINE AND SEE YOU TO THE AIRPORT.
HOW ABOUT WE HAVE DINNER THIS EVENING?
REALLY?

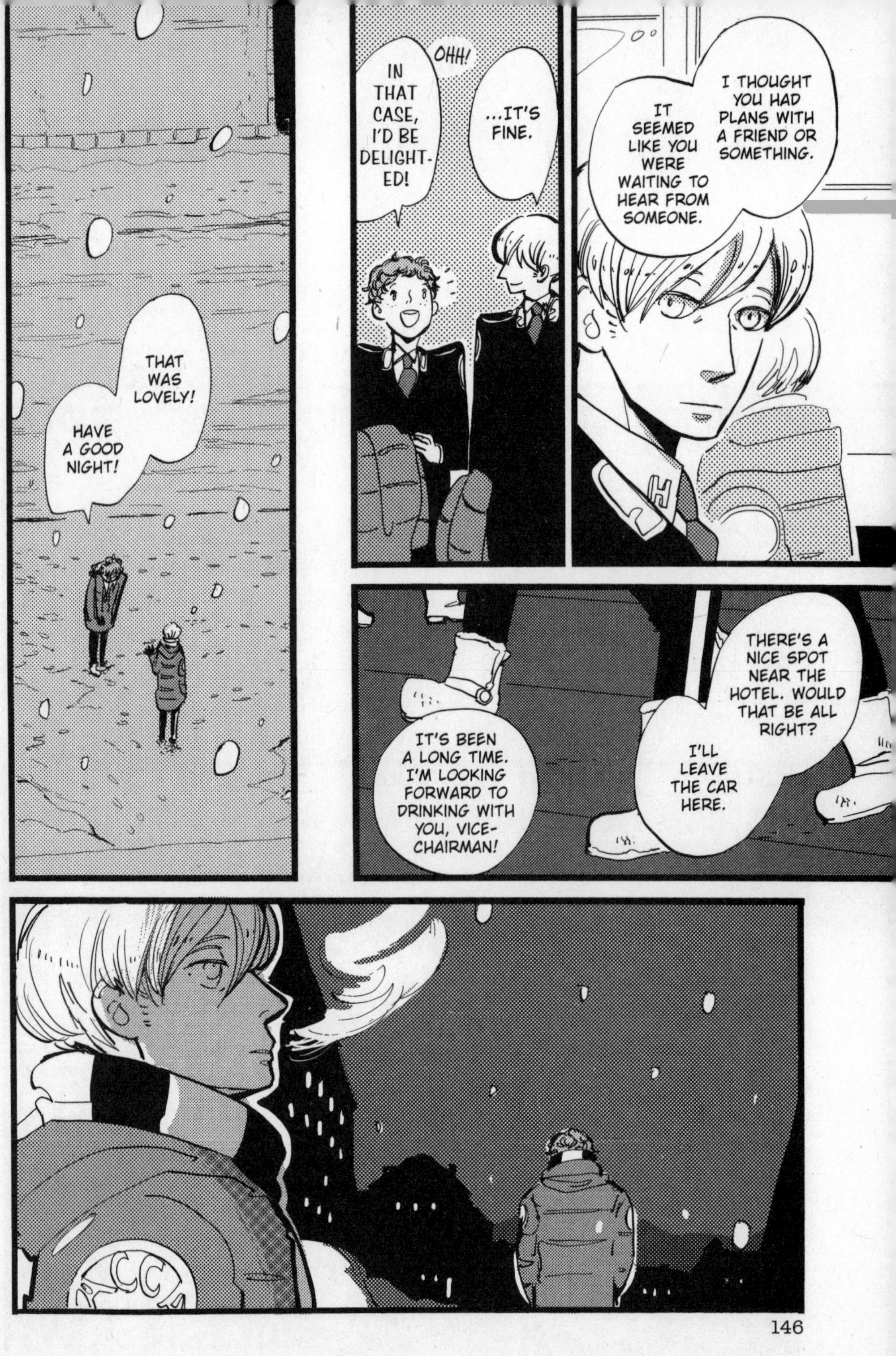
I THOUGHT YOU HAD PLANS WITH A FRIEND OR SOMETHING.
IT SEEMED LIKE YOU WERE WAITING TO HEAR FROM SOMEONE.
...IT'S FINE.
OHH!
IN THAT CASE, I'D BE DELIGHT-ED!
THERE'S A NICE SPOT NEAR THE HOTEL. WOULD THAT BE ALL RIGHT?
I'LL LEAVE THE CAR HERE.
IT'S BEEN A LONG TIME. I'M LOOKING FORWARD TO DRINKING WITH YOU, VICE-CHAIRMAN!
THAT WAS LOVELY!
HAVE A GOOD NIGHT!

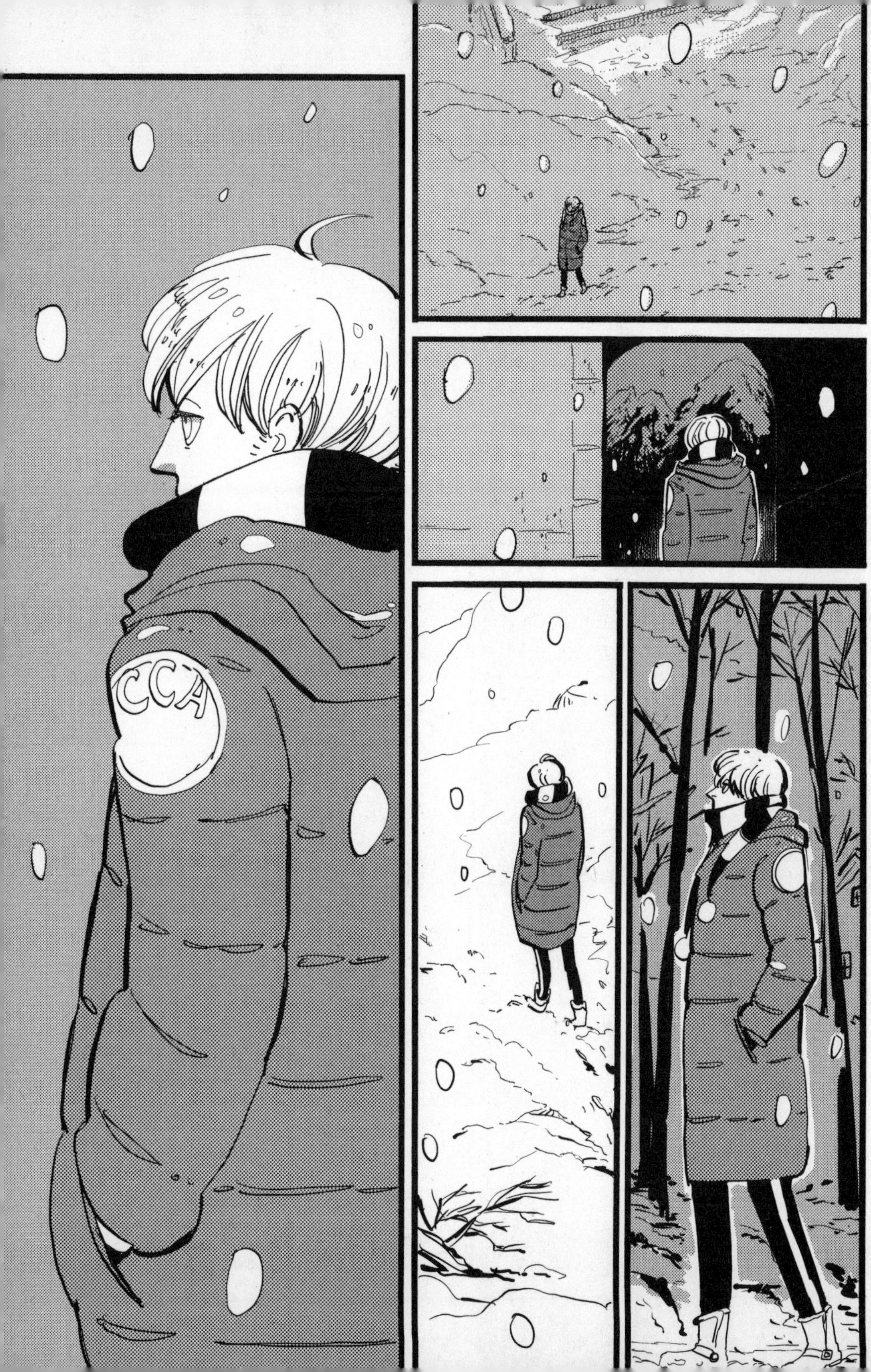
CCA

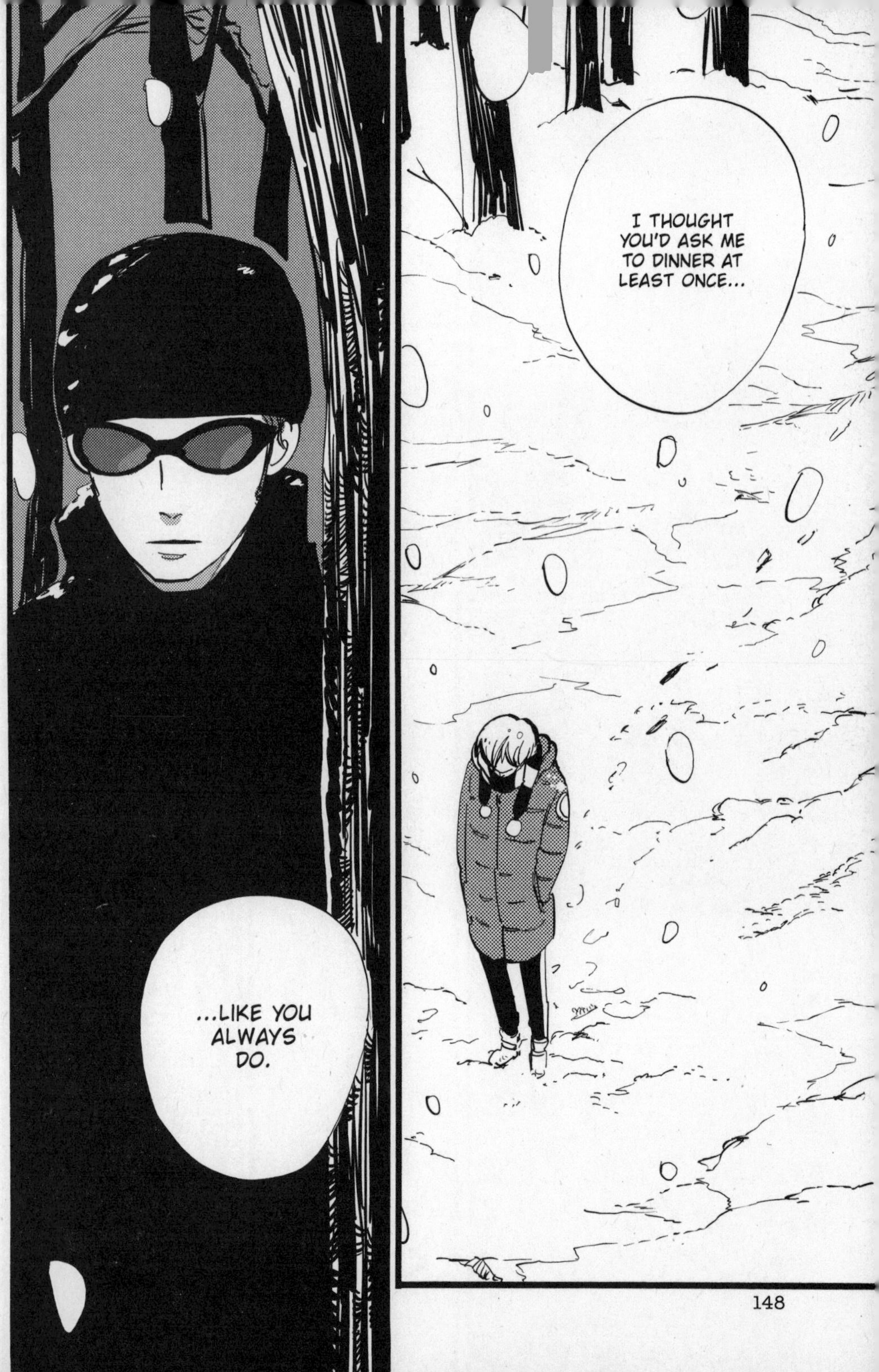
I THOUGHT YOU'D ASK ME TO DINNER AT LEAST ONCE...
...LIKE YOU ALWAYS DO.

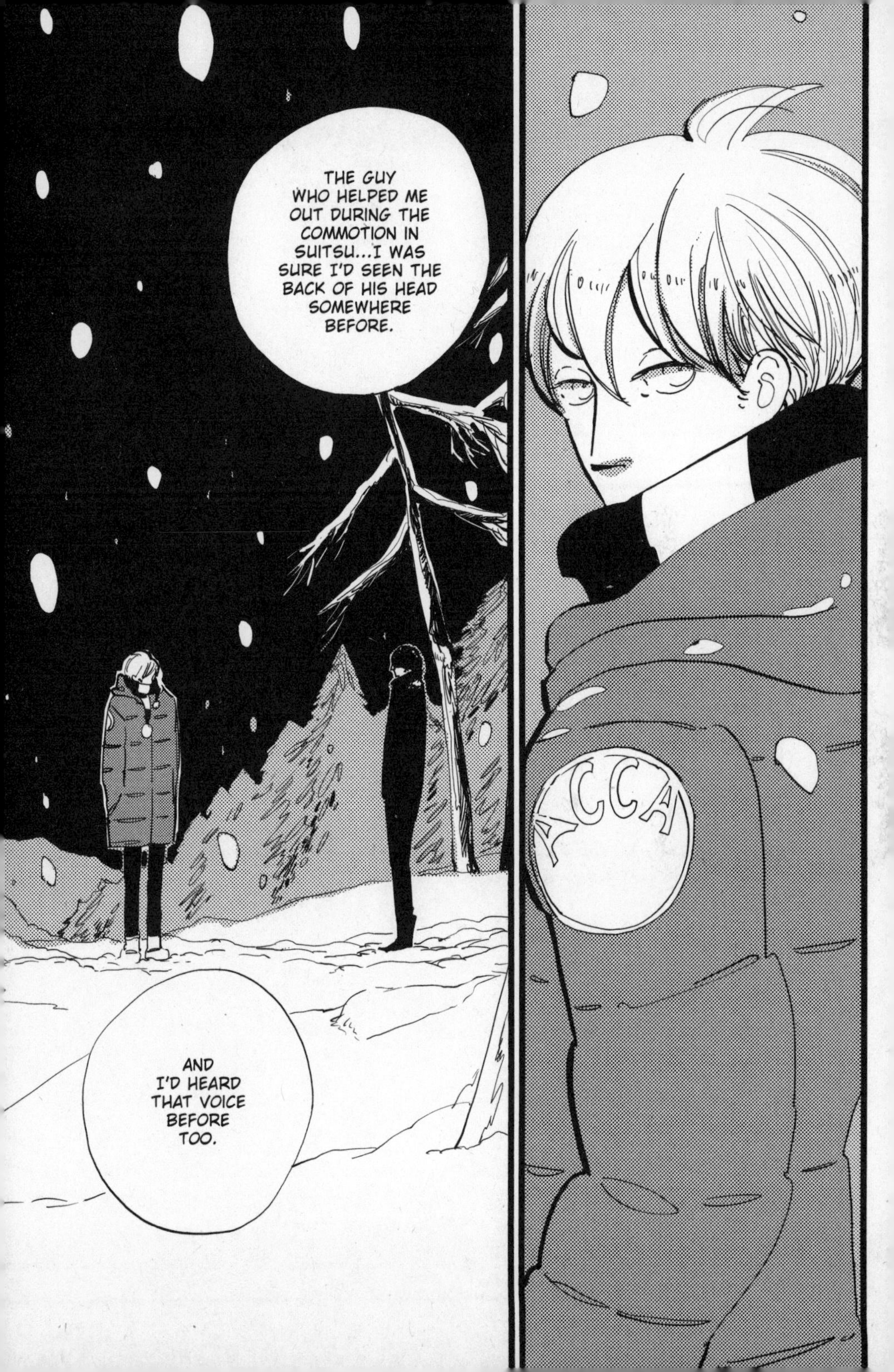
ACCA
THE GUY WHO HELPED ME OUT DURING THE COMMOTION IN SUITSU...I WAS SURE I'D SEEN THE BACK OF HIS HEAD SOMEWHERE BEFORE.
AND I'D HEARD THAT VOICE BEFORE TOO.

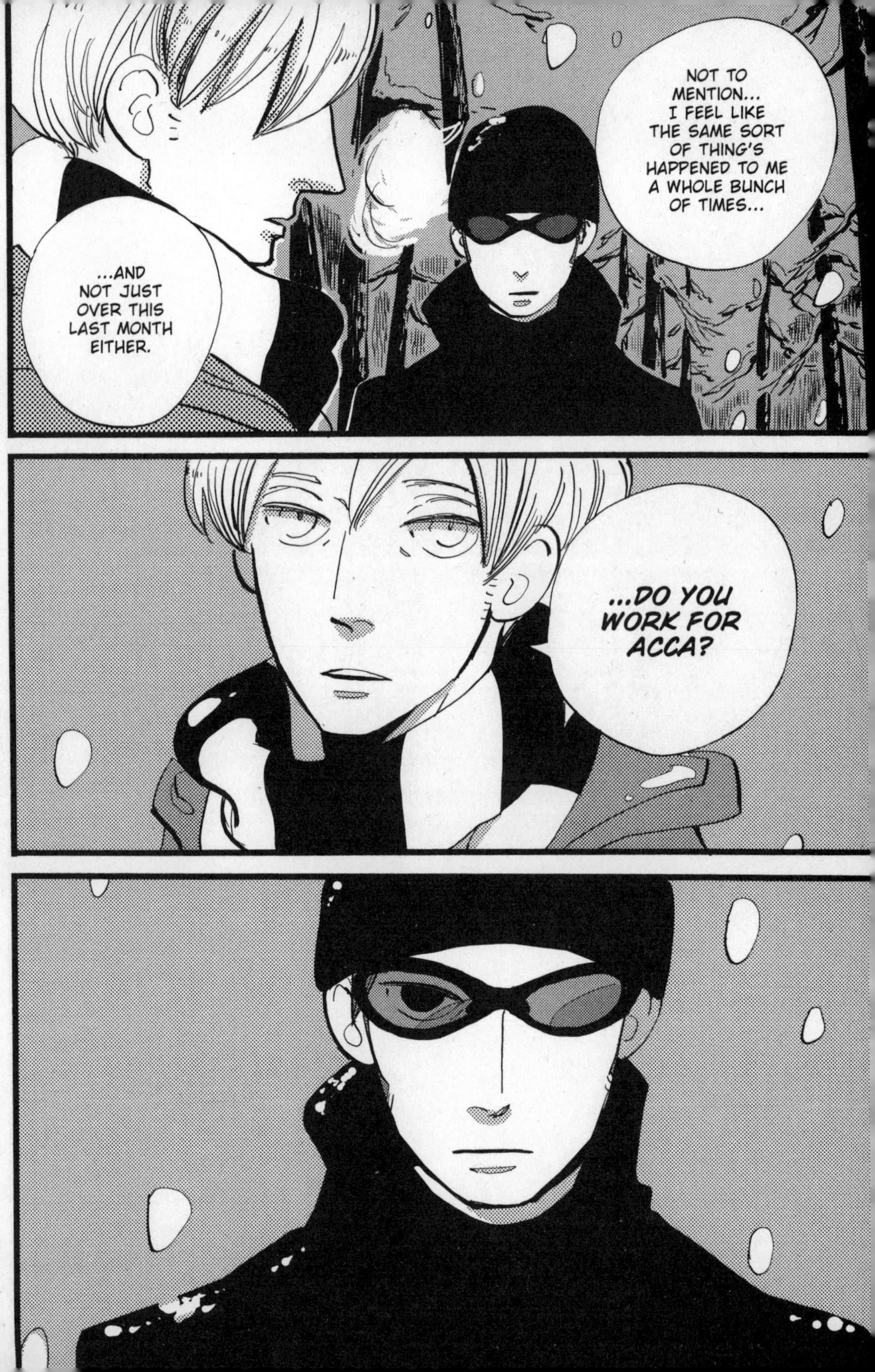
NOT TO MENTION... I FEEL LIKE THE SAME SORT OF THING'S HAPPENED TO ME A WHOLE BUNCH OF TIMES...
...AND NOT JUST OVER THIS LAST MONTH EITHER.
...DO YOU WORK FOR ACCA?

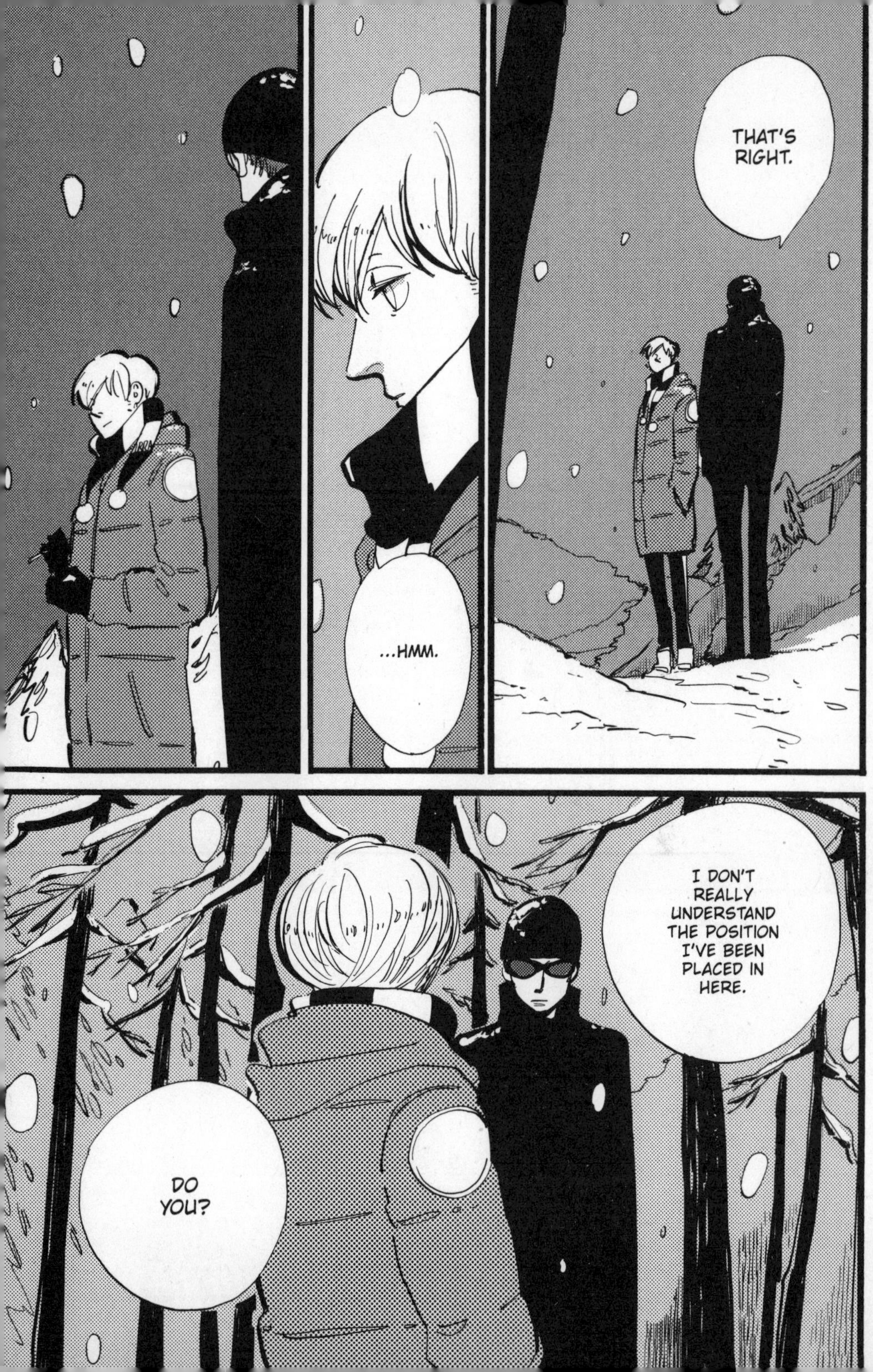
THAT'S RIGHT.
...HMM.
I DON'T REALLY UNDERSTAND THE POSITION I'VE BEEN PLACED IN HERE.
DO YOU?

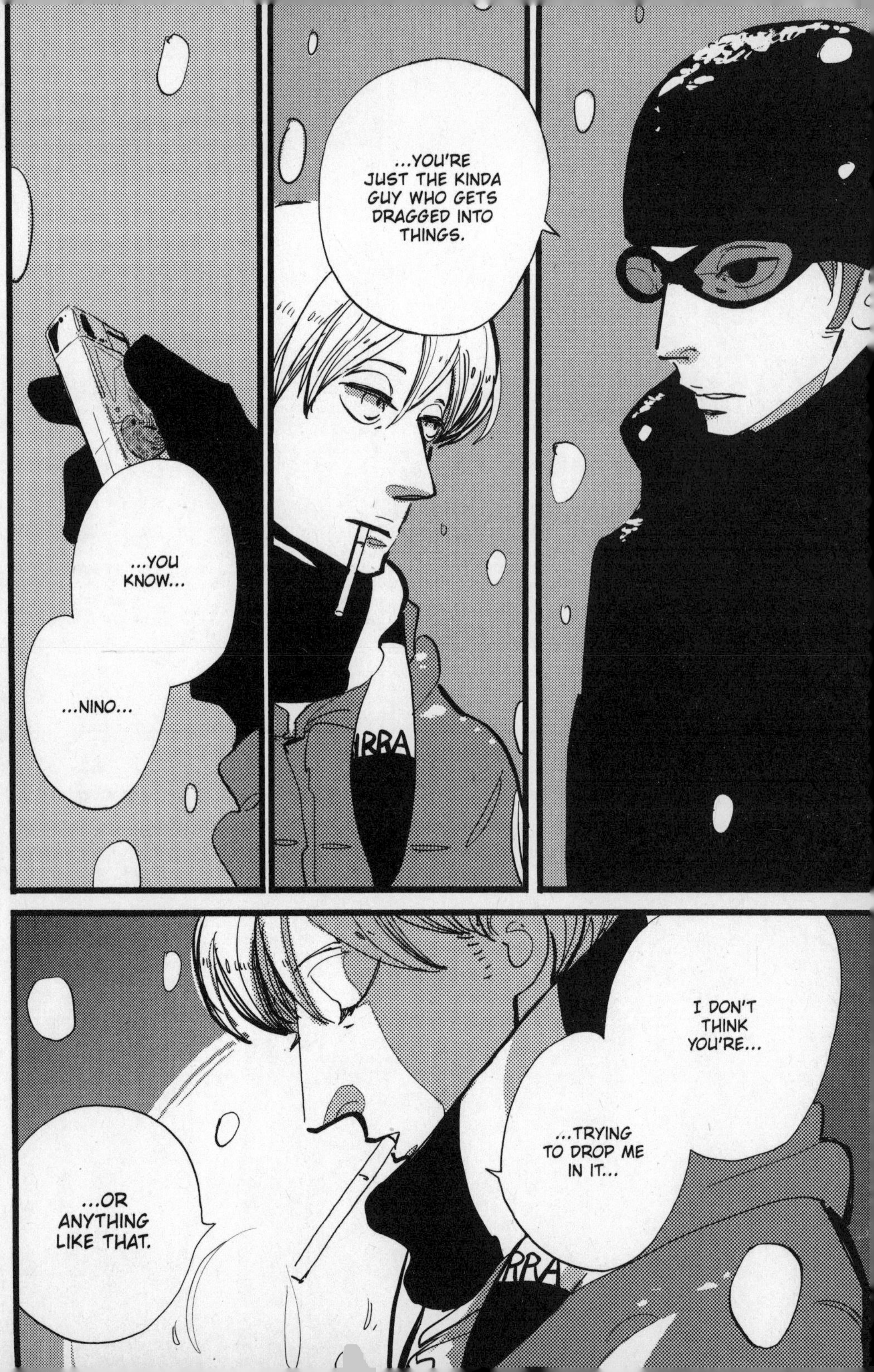
...YOU'RE JUST THE KINDA GUY WHO GETS DRAGGED INTO THINGS.
...YOU KNOW...
...NINO...
I DON'T THINK YOU'RE...
...TRYING TO DROP ME IN IT...
...OR ANYTHING LIKE THAT.

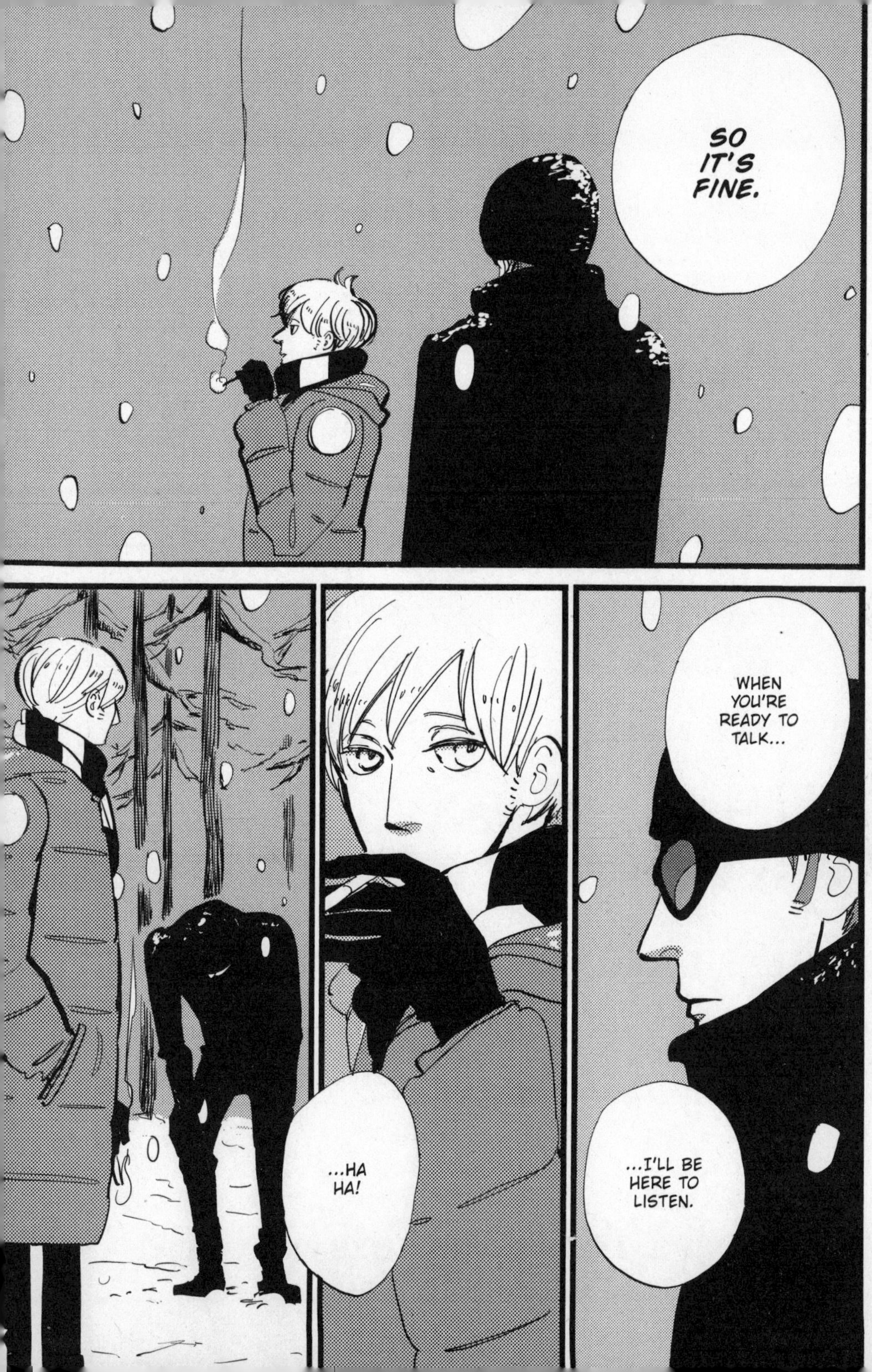
SO IT'S FINE.
WHEN YOU'RE READY TO TALK...
...I'LL BE HERE TO LISTEN.
...HA HA!

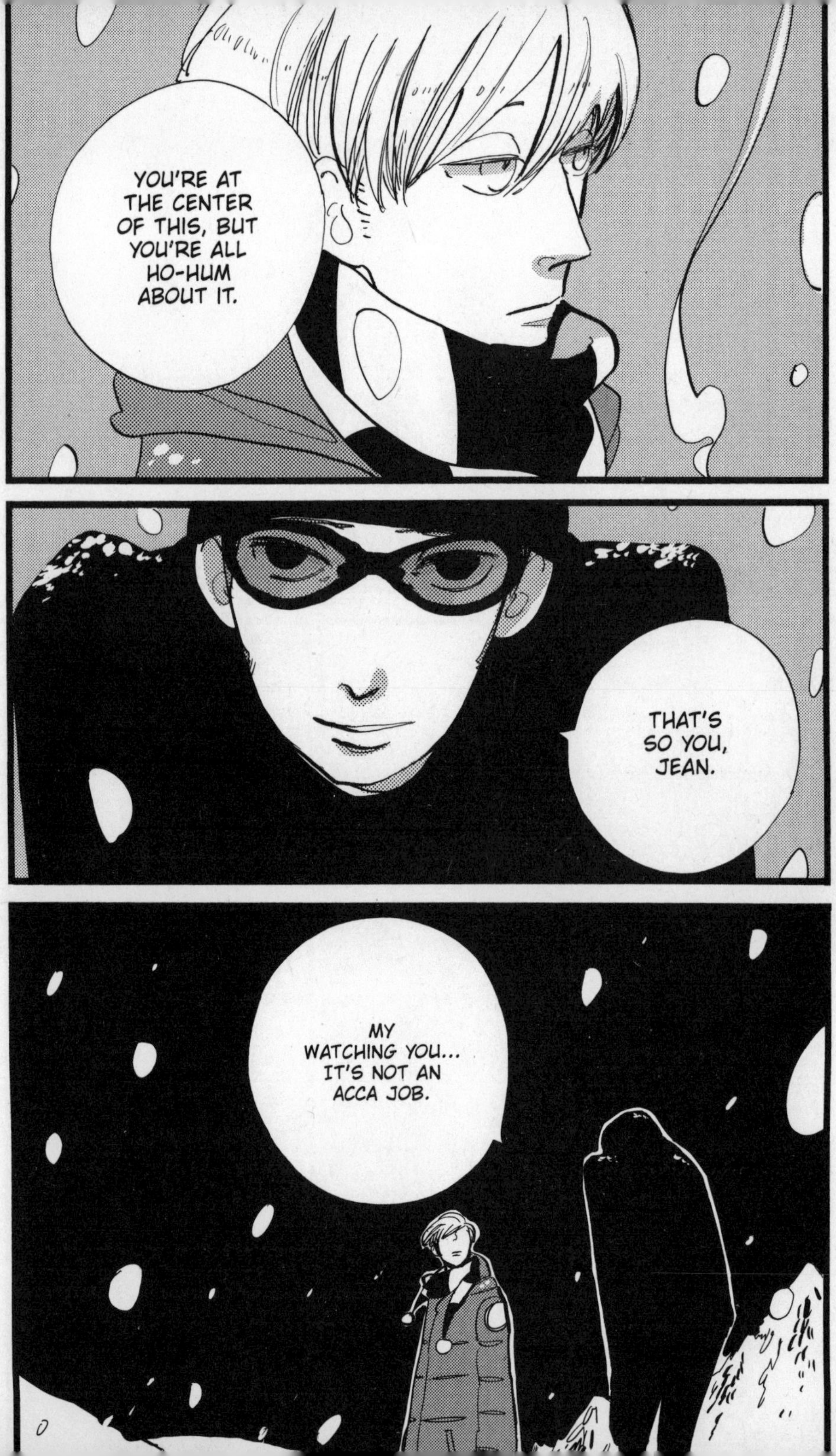
YOU'RE AT THE CENTER OF THIS, BUT YOU'RE ALL HO-HUM ABOUT IT.
THAT'S SO YOU, JEAN.
MY WATCHING YOU... IT'S NOT AN ACCA JOB.

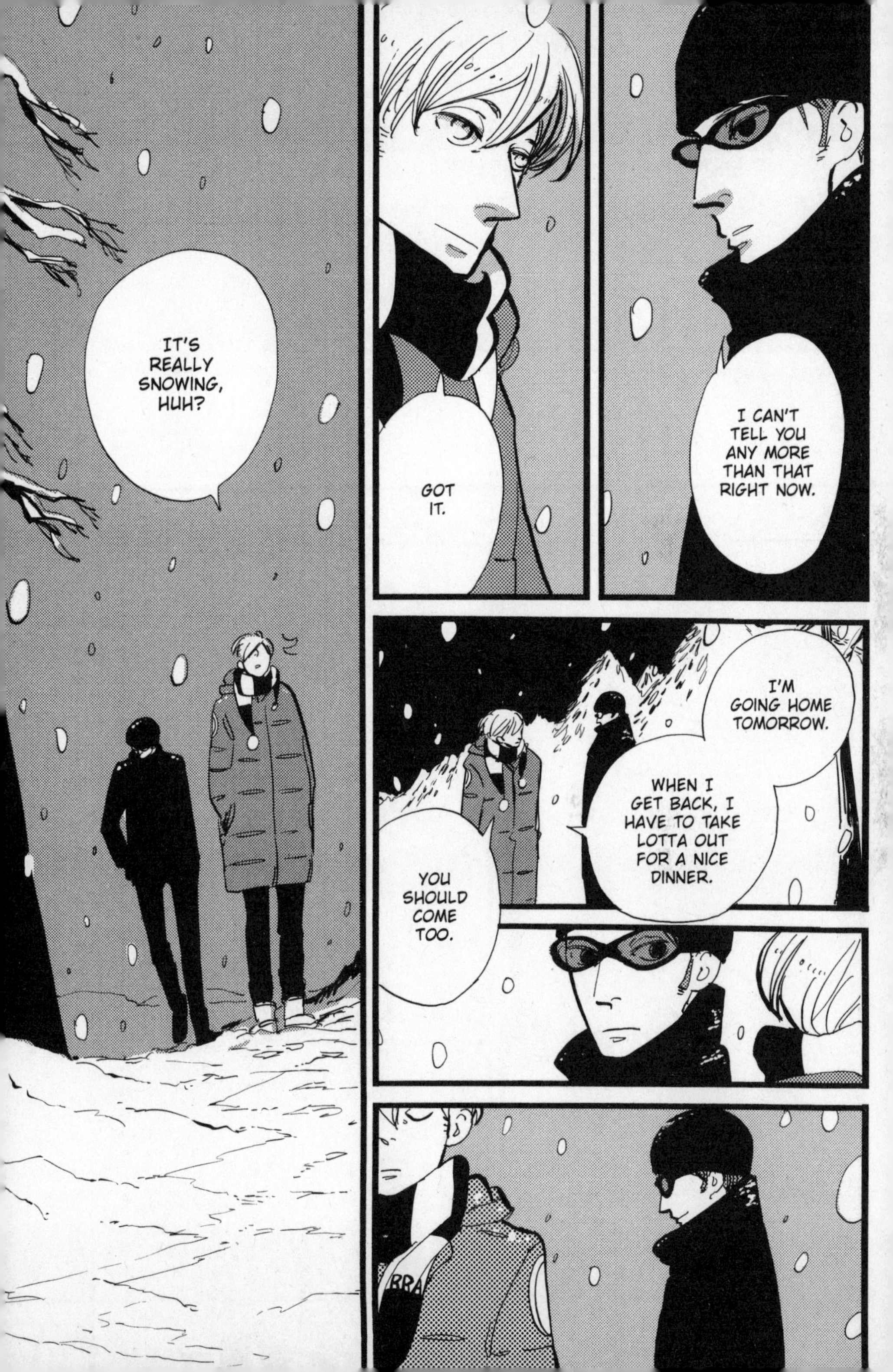
I CAN'T TELL YOU ANY MORE THAN THAT RIGHT NOW.
GOT IT.
I'M GOING HOME TOMORROW.
WHEN I GET BACK, I HAVE TO TAKE LOTTA OUT FOR A NICE DINNER.
YOU SHOULD COME TOO.
IT'S REALLY SNOWING, HUH?

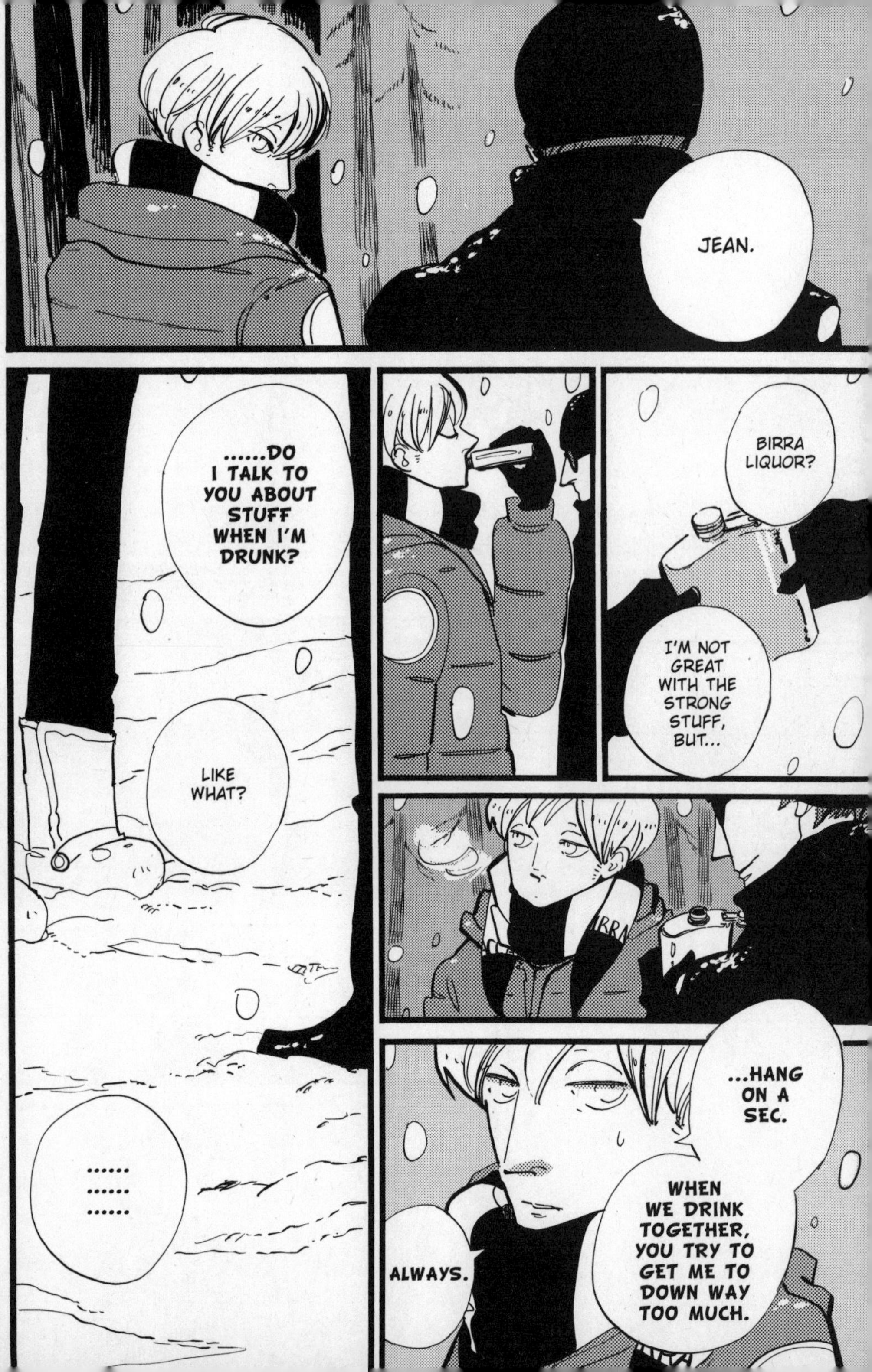
JEAN.
BIRRA LIQUOR?
I'M NOT GREAT WITH THE STRONG STUFF, BUT...
...HANG ON A SEC.
WHEN WE DRINK TOGETHER, YOU TRY TO GET ME TO DOWN WAY TOO MUCH.
ALWAYS.
......DO I TALK TO YOU ABOUT STUFF WHEN I'M DRUNK?
LIKE WHAT?
....

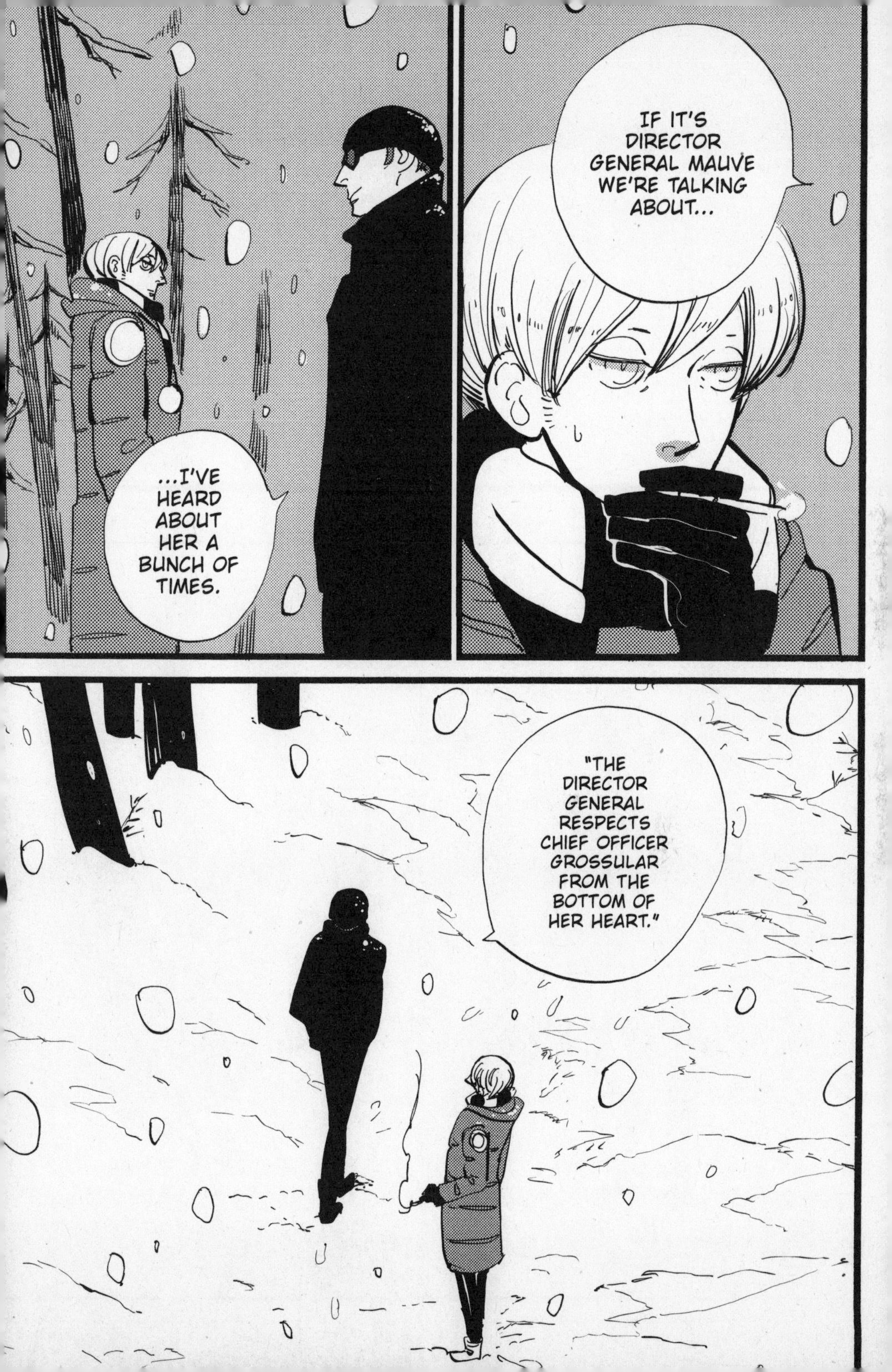
IF IT'S DIRECTOR GENERAL MAUVE WE'RE TALKING ABOUT...
...I'VE HEARD ABOUT HER A BUNCH OF TIMES.
"THE DIRECTOR GENERAL RESPECTS CHIEF OFFICER GROSSULAR FROM THE BOTTOM OF HER HEART."

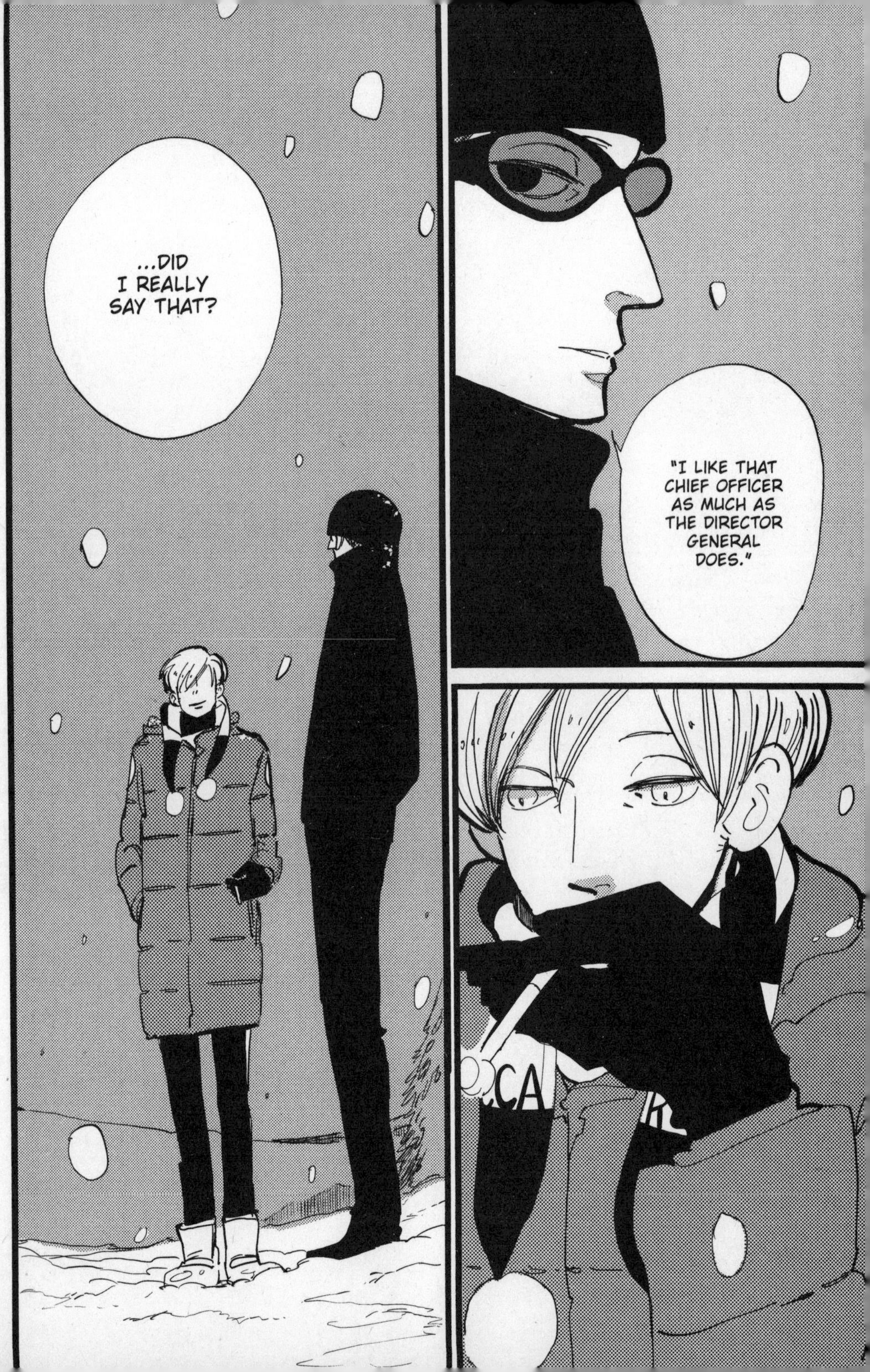
"I LIKE THAT CHIEF OFFICER AS MUCH AS THE DIRECTOR GENERAL DOES."
...DID I REALLY SAY THAT?

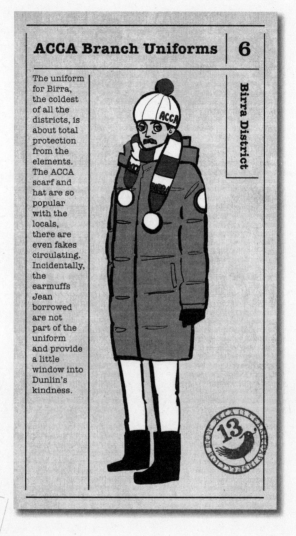

ACCA Branch Uniforms | 6

The uniform for Birra, the coldest of all the districts, is about total protection from the elements. The ACCA scarf and hat are so popular with the locals, there are even fakes circulating. Incidentally, the earmuffs Jean borrowed are not part of the uniform and provide a little window into Dunlin's kindness.

CHAPTER 16

Facing a "Friend" in Birra

PASS

DEPT. ACCA 13 TERRITORY INSPECTION

CHAPTER 17

Staring Down Train Tracks and Pride in Rokkusu

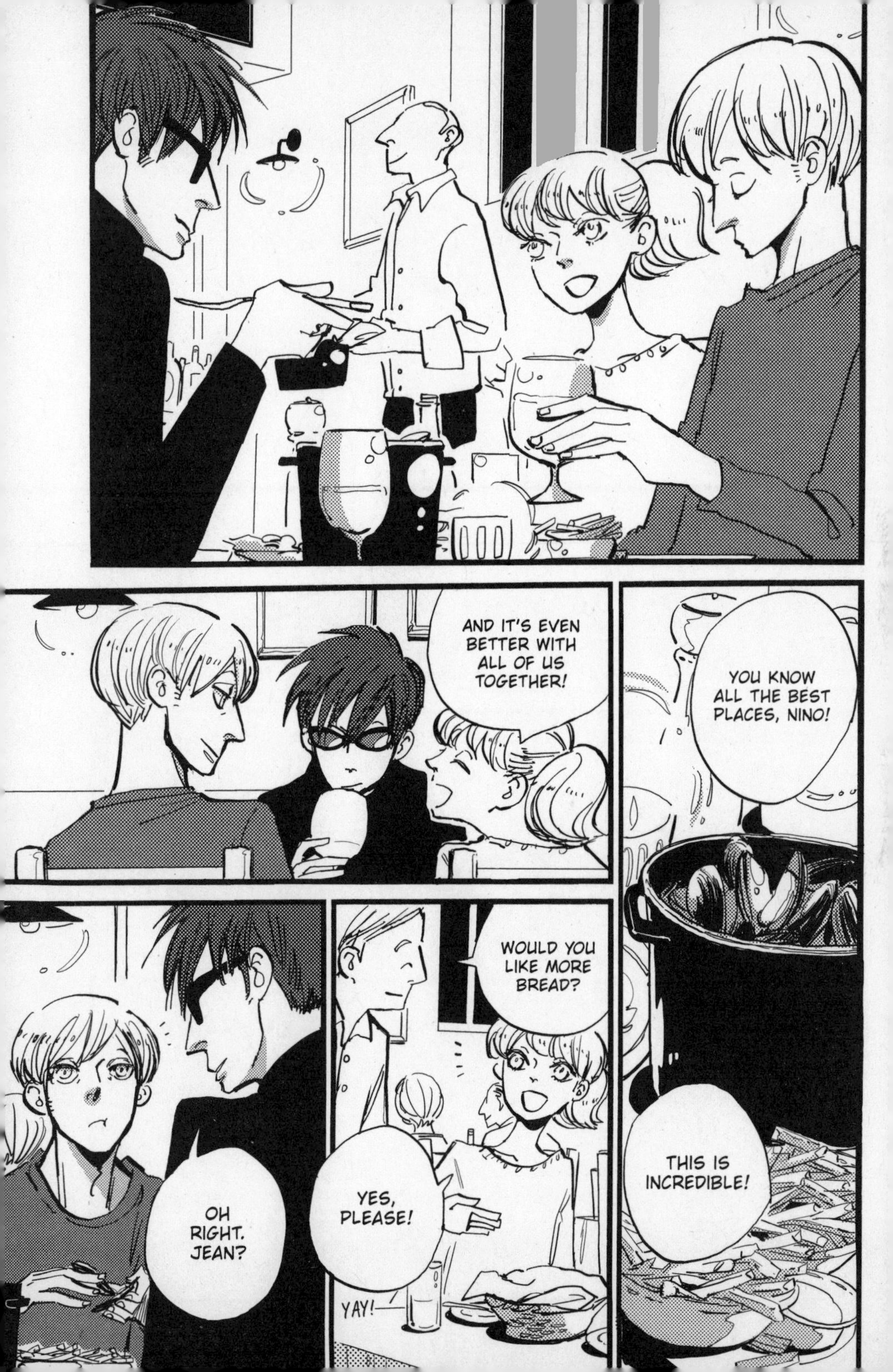
YOU KNOW ALL THE BEST PLACES, NINO!
THIS IS INCREDIBLE!
AND IT'S EVEN BETTER WITH ALL OF US TOGETHER!
WOULD YOU LIKE MORE BREAD?
YES, PLEASE!
YAY!
OH RIGHT. JEAN?

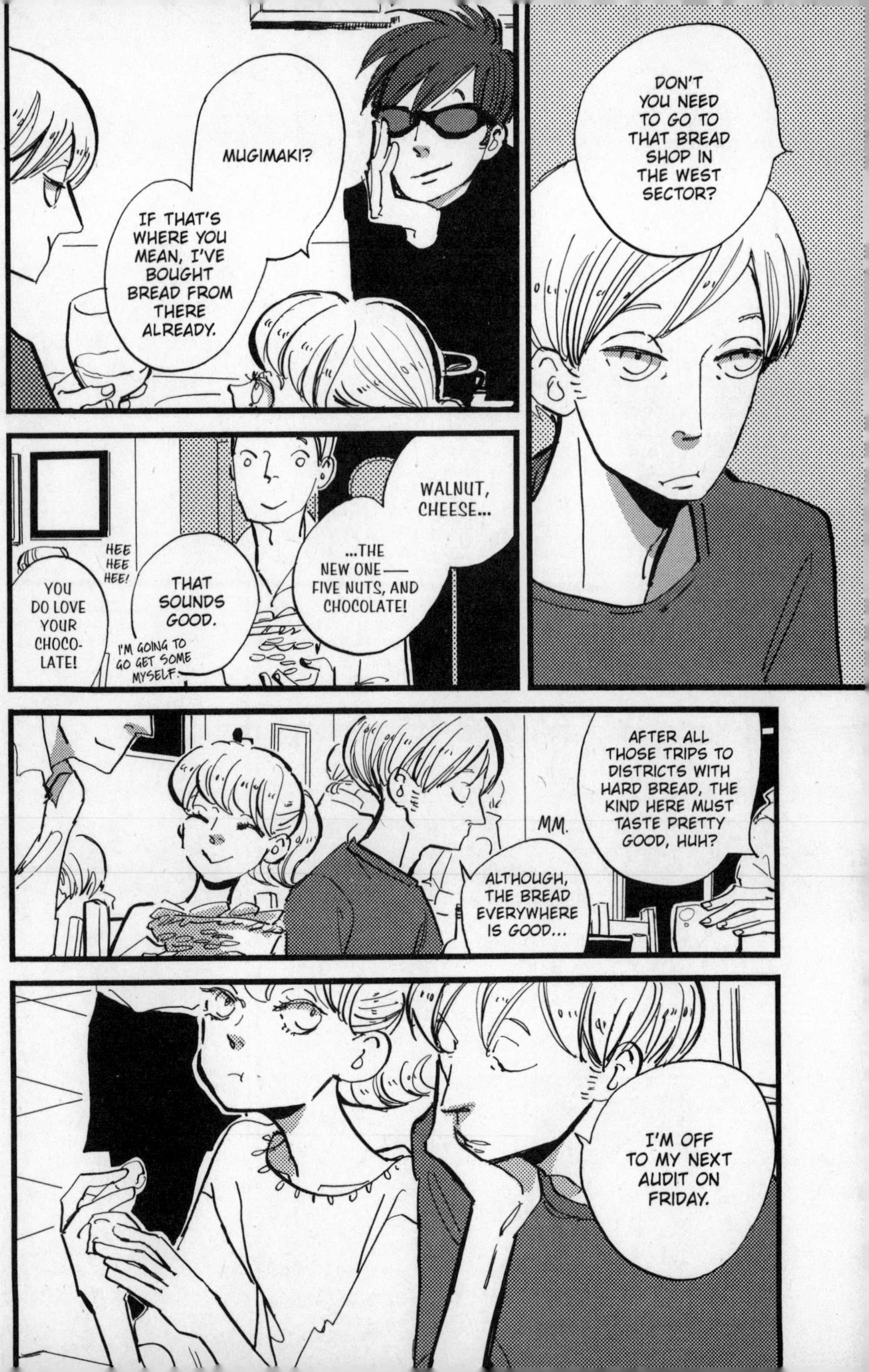
DON'T YOU NEED TO GO TO THAT BREAD SHOP IN THE WEST SECTOR?
MUGIMAKI?
IF THAT'S WHERE YOU MEAN, I'VE BOUGHT BREAD FROM THERE ALREADY.
WALNUT, CHEESE...
...THE NEW ONE— FIVE NUTS, AND CHOCOLATE!
THAT SOUNDS GOOD.
HEE HEE HEE!
YOU DO LOVE YOUR CHOCO-LATE!
I'M GOING TO GO GET SOME MYSELF.
AFTER ALL THOSE TRIPS TO DISTRICTS WITH HARD BREAD, THE KIND HERE MUST TASTE PRETTY GOOD, HUH?
MM.
ALTHOUGH, THE BREAD EVERYWHERE IS GOOD...
I'M OFF TO MY NEXT AUDIT ON FRIDAY.

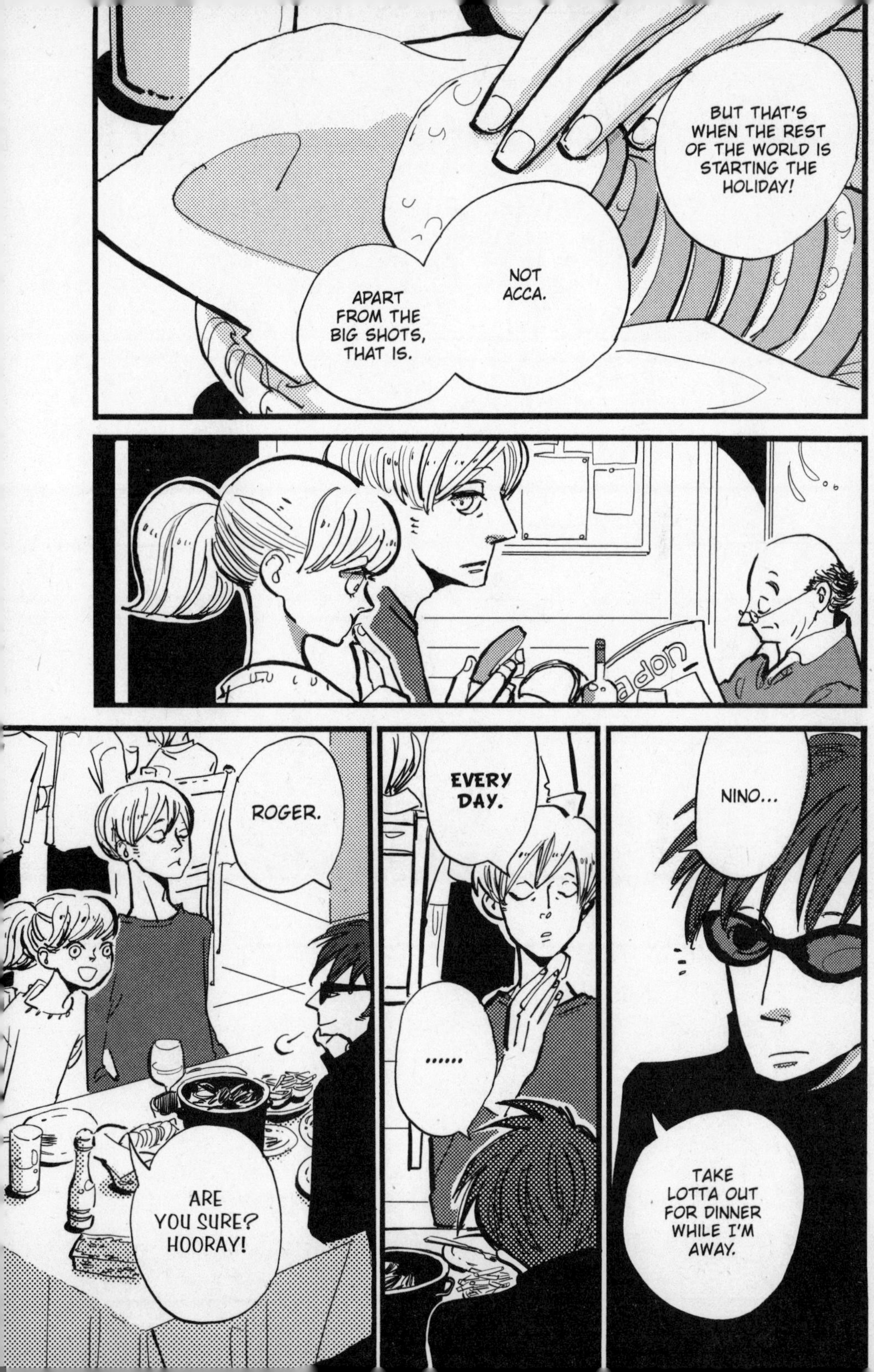
BUT THAT'S WHEN THE REST OF THE WORLD IS STARTING THE HOLIDAY!
NOT ACCA.
APART FROM THE BIG SHOTS, THAT IS.
NINO...
TAKE LOTTA OUT FOR DINNER WHILE I'M AWAY.
EVERY DAY.
......
ROGER.
ARE YOU SURE? HOORAY!

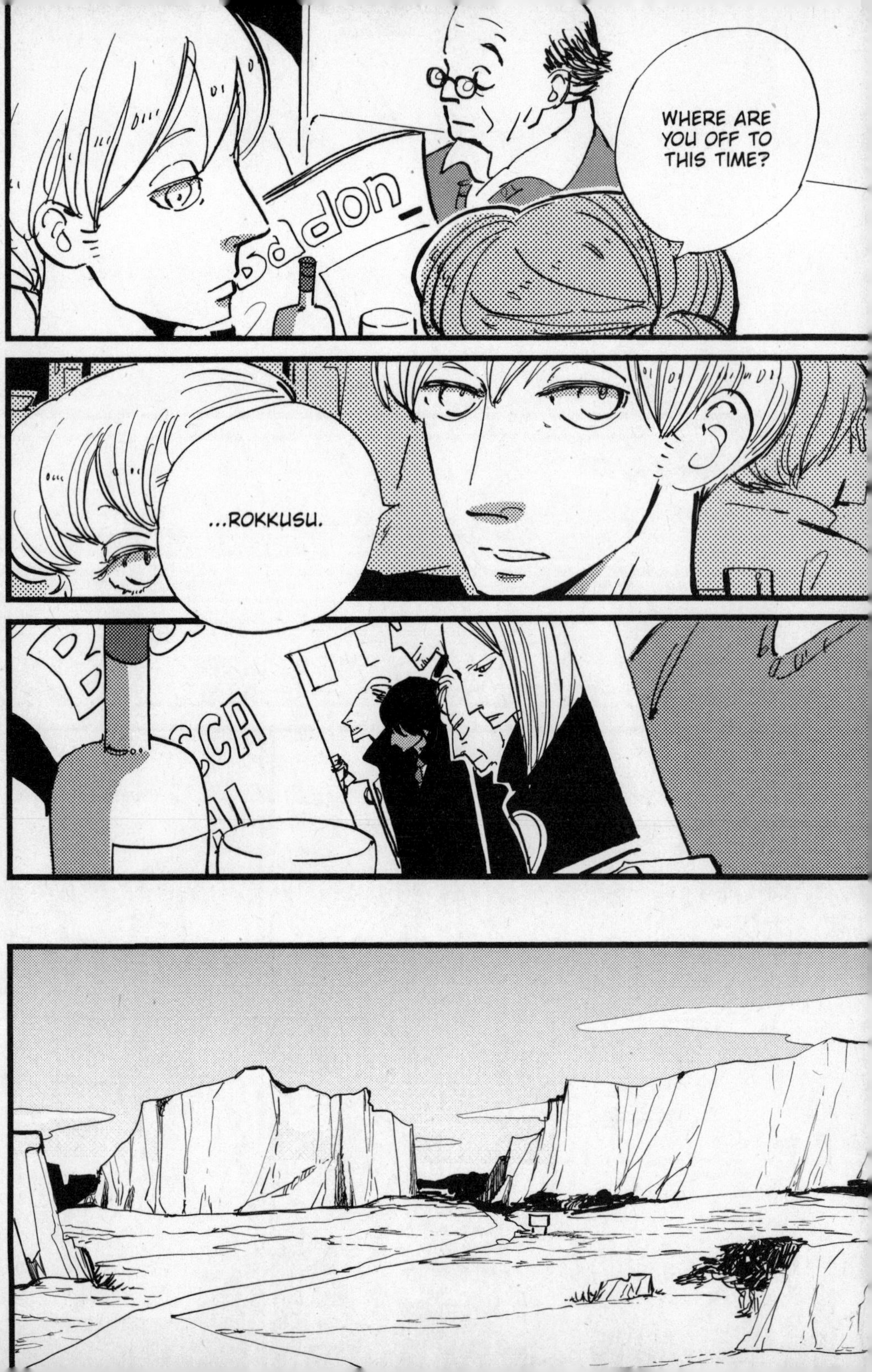
WHERE ARE YOU OFF TO THIS TIME?
...ROKKUSU.

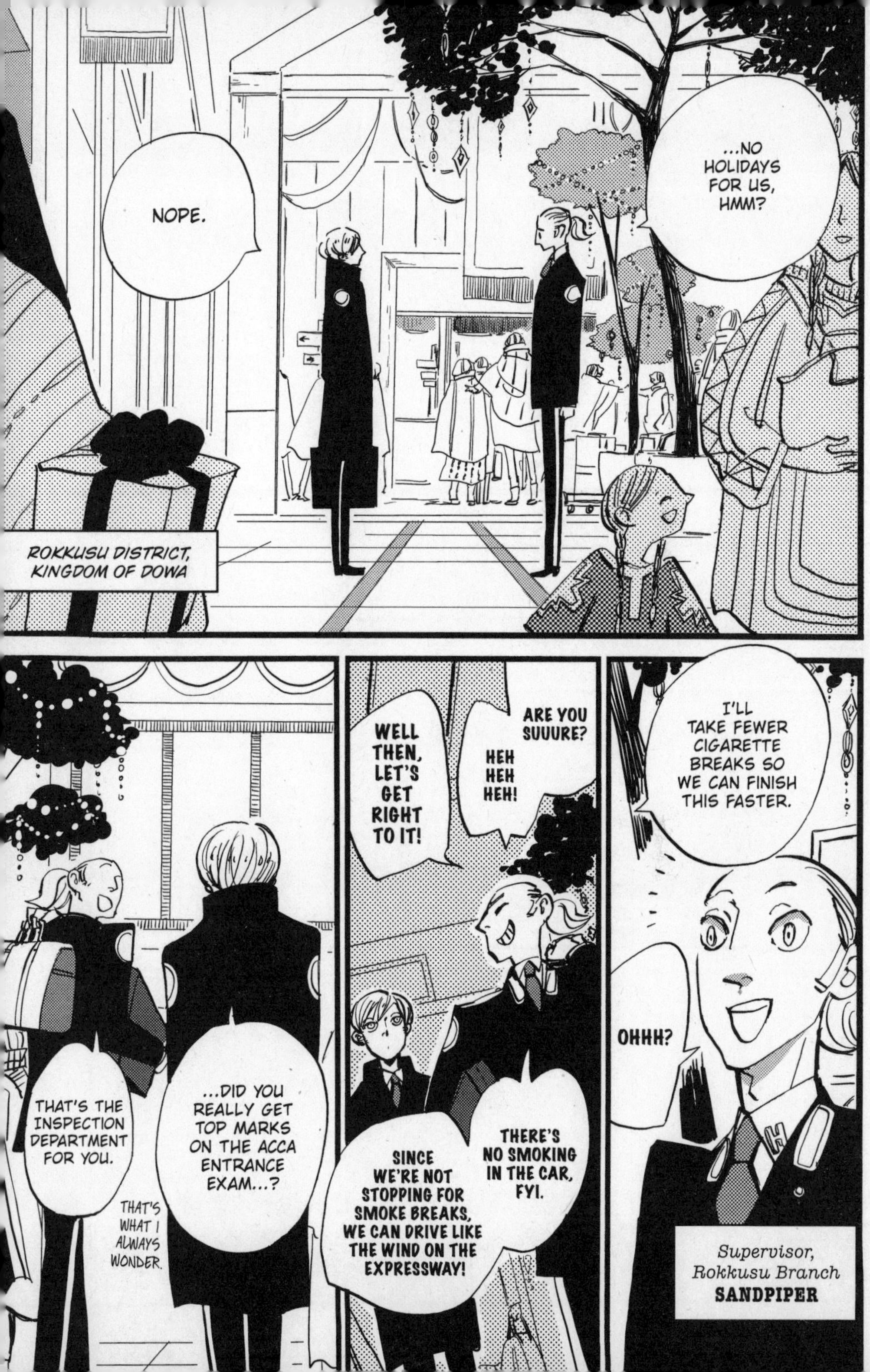
...NO HOLIDAYS FOR US, HMM?
NOPE.
ROKKUSU DISTRICT, KINGDOM OF DOWA
I'LL TAKE FEWER CIGARETTE BREAKS SO WE CAN FINISH THIS FASTER.
OHHH?
Supervisor, Rokkusu Branch SANDPIPER
ARE YOU SUUURE?
HEH HEH HEH!
WELL THEN, LET'S GET RIGHT TO IT!
THERE'S NO SMOKING IN THE CAR, FYI.
SINCE WE'RE NOT STOPPING FOR SMOKE BREAKS, WE CAN DRIVE LIKE THE WIND ON THE EXPRESSWAY!
...DID YOU REALLY GET TOP MARKS ON THE ACCA ENTRANCE EXAM...?
THAT'S THE INSPECTION DEPARTMENT FOR YOU.
THAT'S WHAT I ALWAYS WONDER.

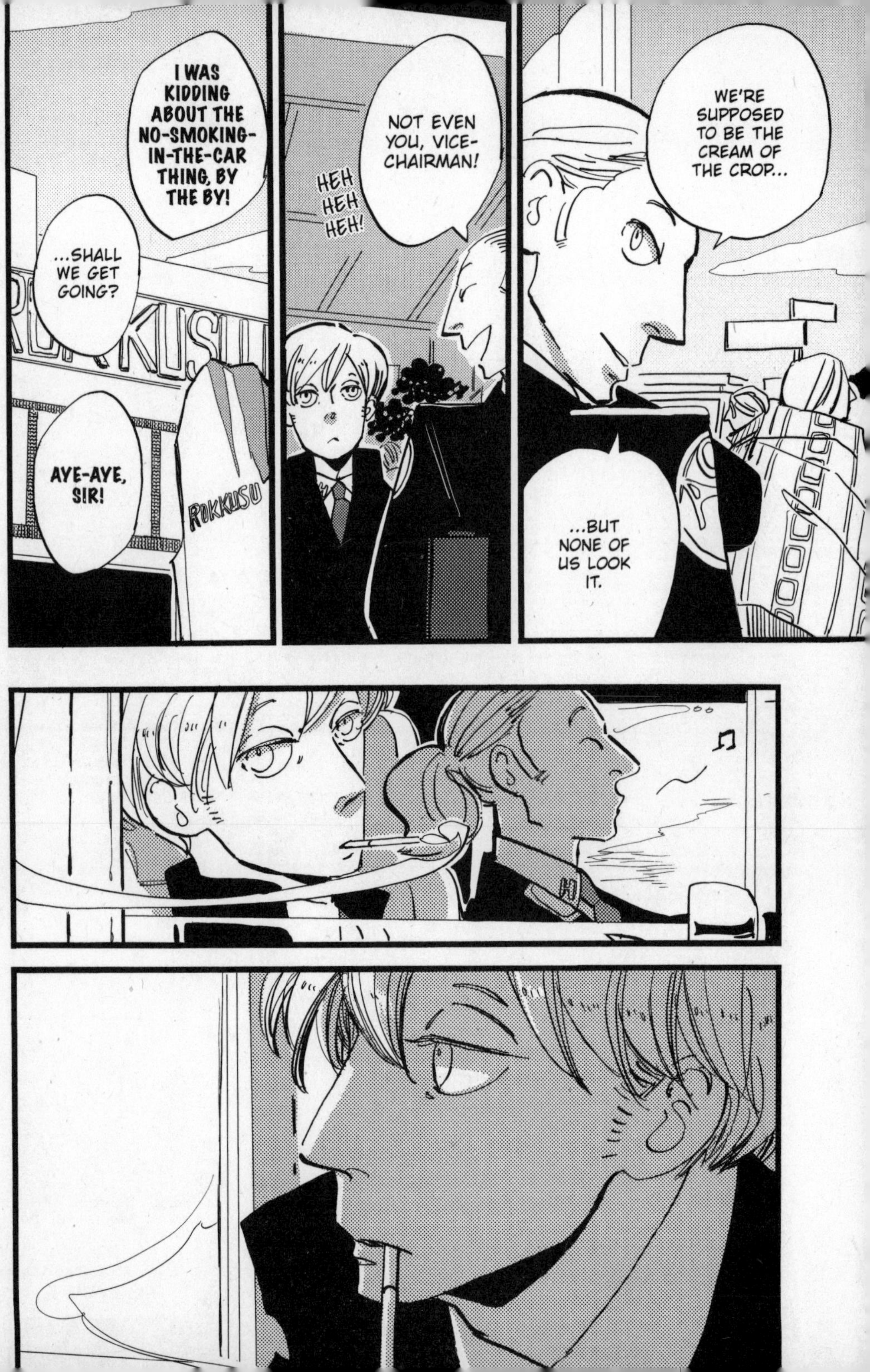
WE'RE SUPPOSED TO BE THE CREAM OF THE CROP...
...BUT NONE OF US LOOK IT.
NOT EVEN YOU, VICE-CHAIRMAN!
HEH HEH HEH!
I WAS KIDDING ABOUT THE NO-SMOKING-IN-THE-CAR THING, BY THE BY!
...SHALL WE GET GOING?
AYE-AYE, SIR!
ROKKUSU

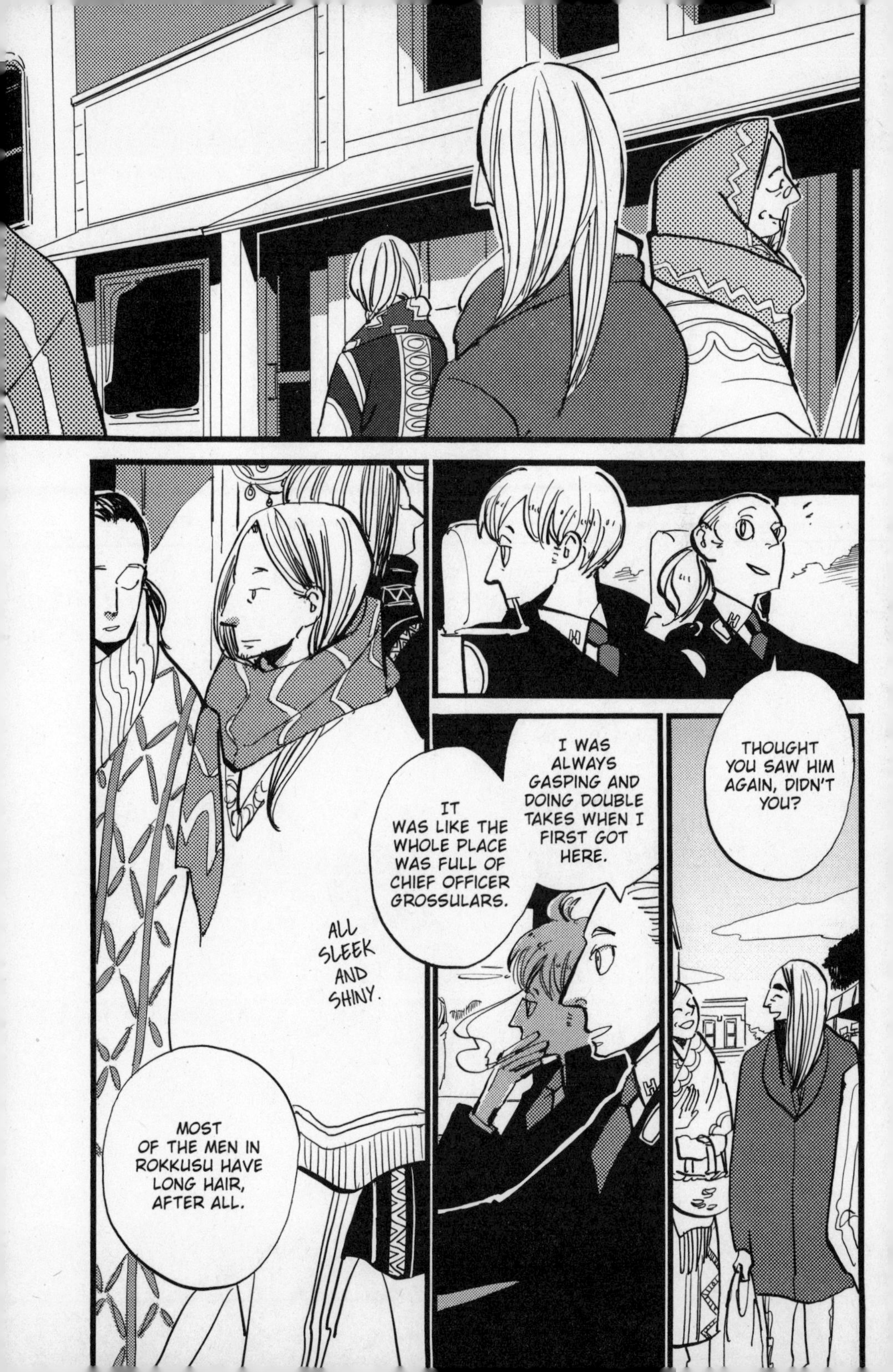
THOUGHT YOU SAW HIM AGAIN, DIDN'T YOU?
I WAS ALWAYS GASPING AND DOING DOUBLE TAKES WHEN I FIRST GOT HERE.
IT WAS LIKE THE WHOLE PLACE WAS FULL OF CHIEF OFFICER GROSSULARS.
ALL SLEEK AND SHINY.
MOST OF THE MEN IN ROKKUSU HAVE LONG HAIR, AFTER ALL.

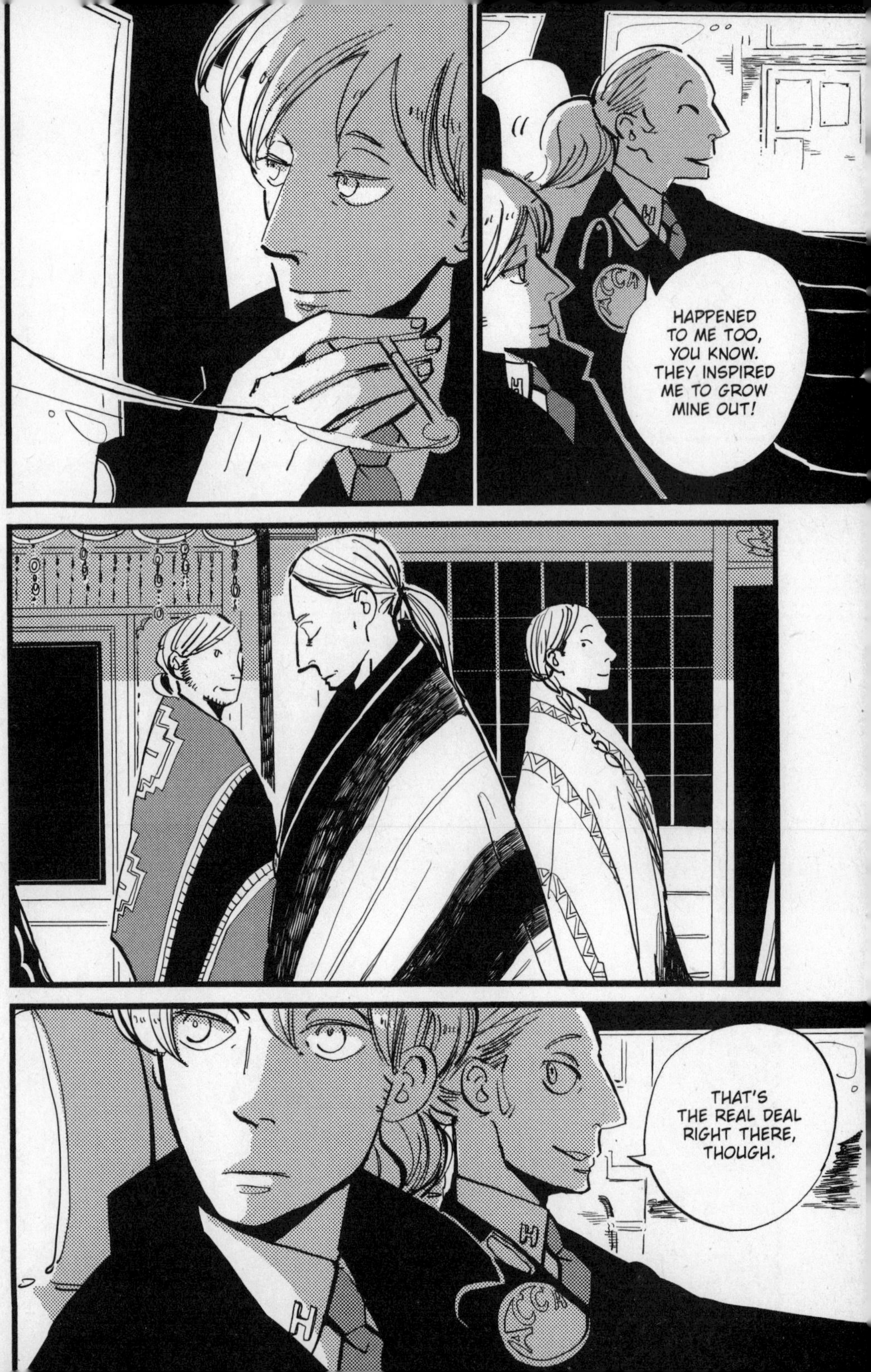
HAPPENED TO ME TOO, YOU KNOW. THEY INSPIRED ME TO GROW MINE OUT!
THAT'S THE REAL DEAL RIGHT THERE, THOUGH.

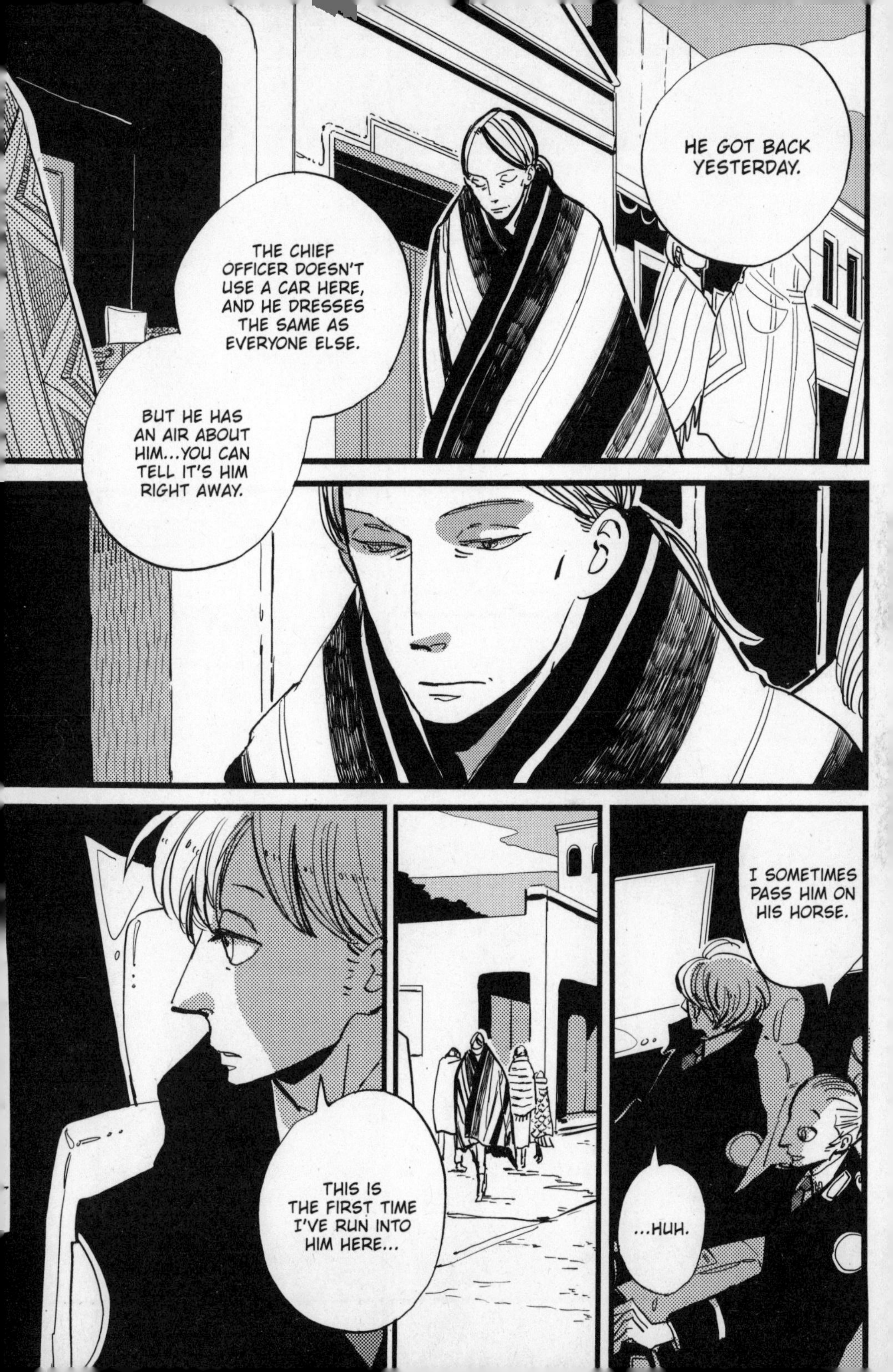
HE GOT BACK YESTERDAY.
THE CHIEF OFFICER DOESN'T USE A CAR HERE, AND HE DRESSES THE SAME AS EVERYONE ELSE.
BUT HE HAS AN AIR ABOUT HIM...YOU CAN TELL IT'S HIM RIGHT AWAY.
I SOMETIMES PASS HIM ON HIS HORSE.
...HUH.
THIS IS THE FIRST TIME I'VE RUN INTO HIM HERE...

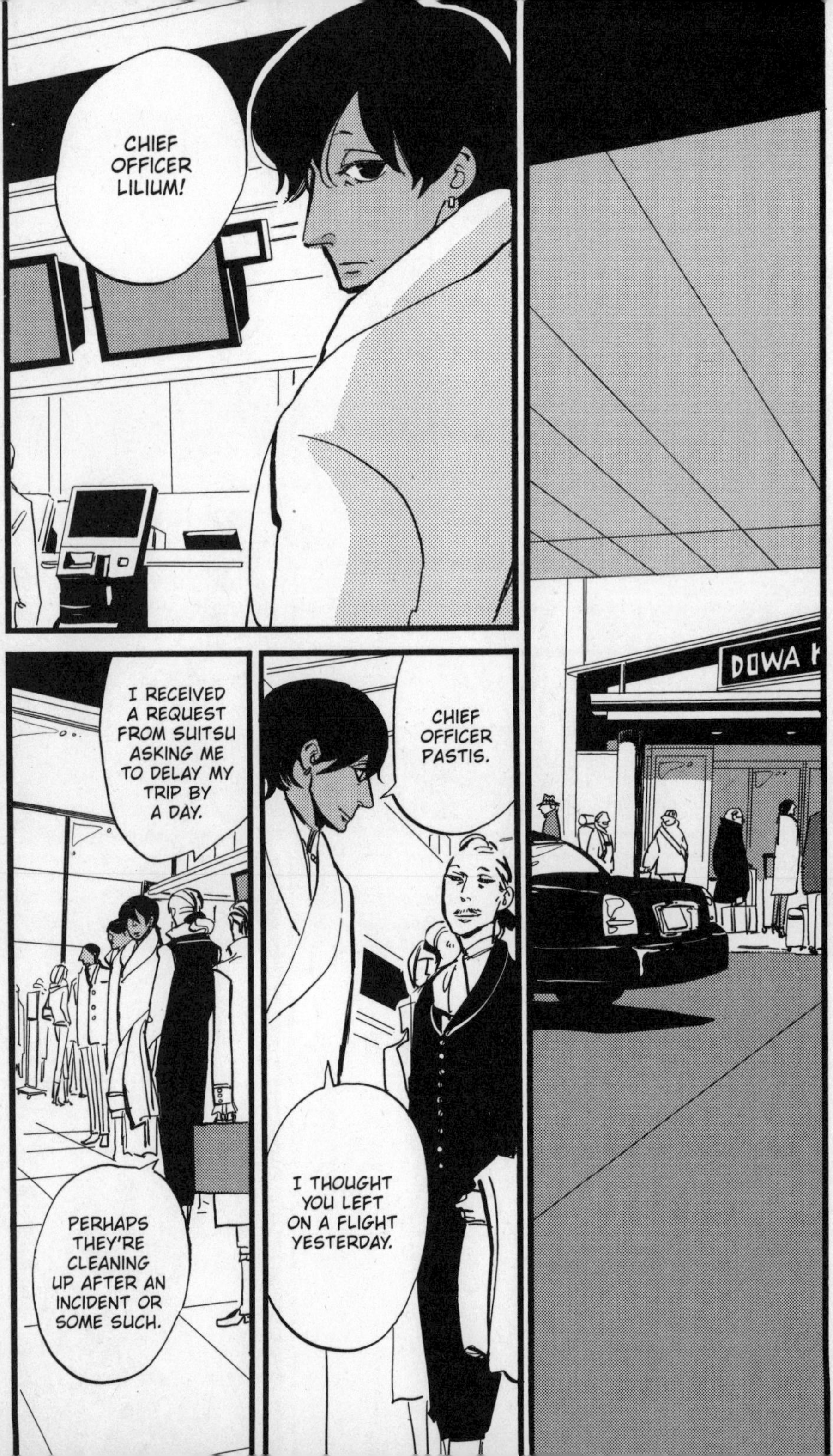
DOWA K
CHIEF OFFICER LILIUM!
CHIEF OFFICER PASTIS.
I THOUGHT YOU LEFT ON A FLIGHT YESTERDAY.
I RECEIVED A REQUEST FROM SUITSU ASKING ME TO DELAY MY TRIP BY A DAY.
PERHAPS THEY'RE CLEANING UP AFTER AN INCIDENT OR SOME SUCH.

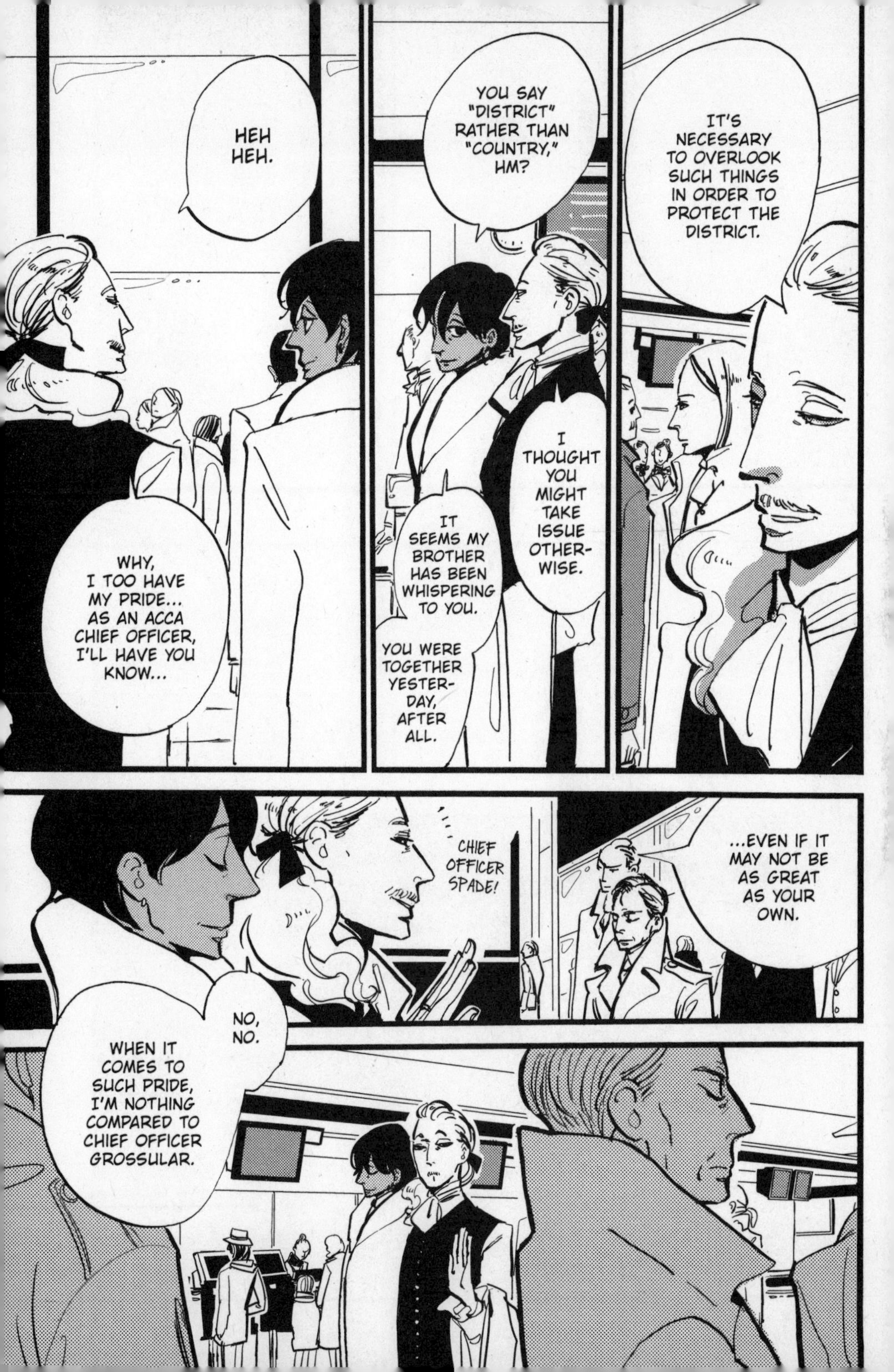
IT'S NECESSARY TO OVERLOOK SUCH THINGS IN ORDER TO PROTECT THE DISTRICT.
YOU SAY "DISTRICT" RATHER THAN "COUNTRY," HM?
I THOUGHT YOU MIGHT TAKE ISSUE OTHER-WISE.
IT SEEMS MY BROTHER HAS BEEN WHISPERING TO YOU.
YOU WERE TOGETHER YESTER-DAY, AFTER ALL.
HEH HEH.
WHY, I TOO HAVE MY PRIDE... AS AN ACCA CHIEF OFFICER, I'LL HAVE YOU KNOW...
...EVEN IF IT MAY NOT BE AS GREAT AS YOUR OWN.
CHIEF OFFICER SPADE!
NO, NO.
WHEN IT COMES TO SUCH PRIDE, I'M NOTHING COMPARED TO CHIEF OFFICER GROSSULAR.

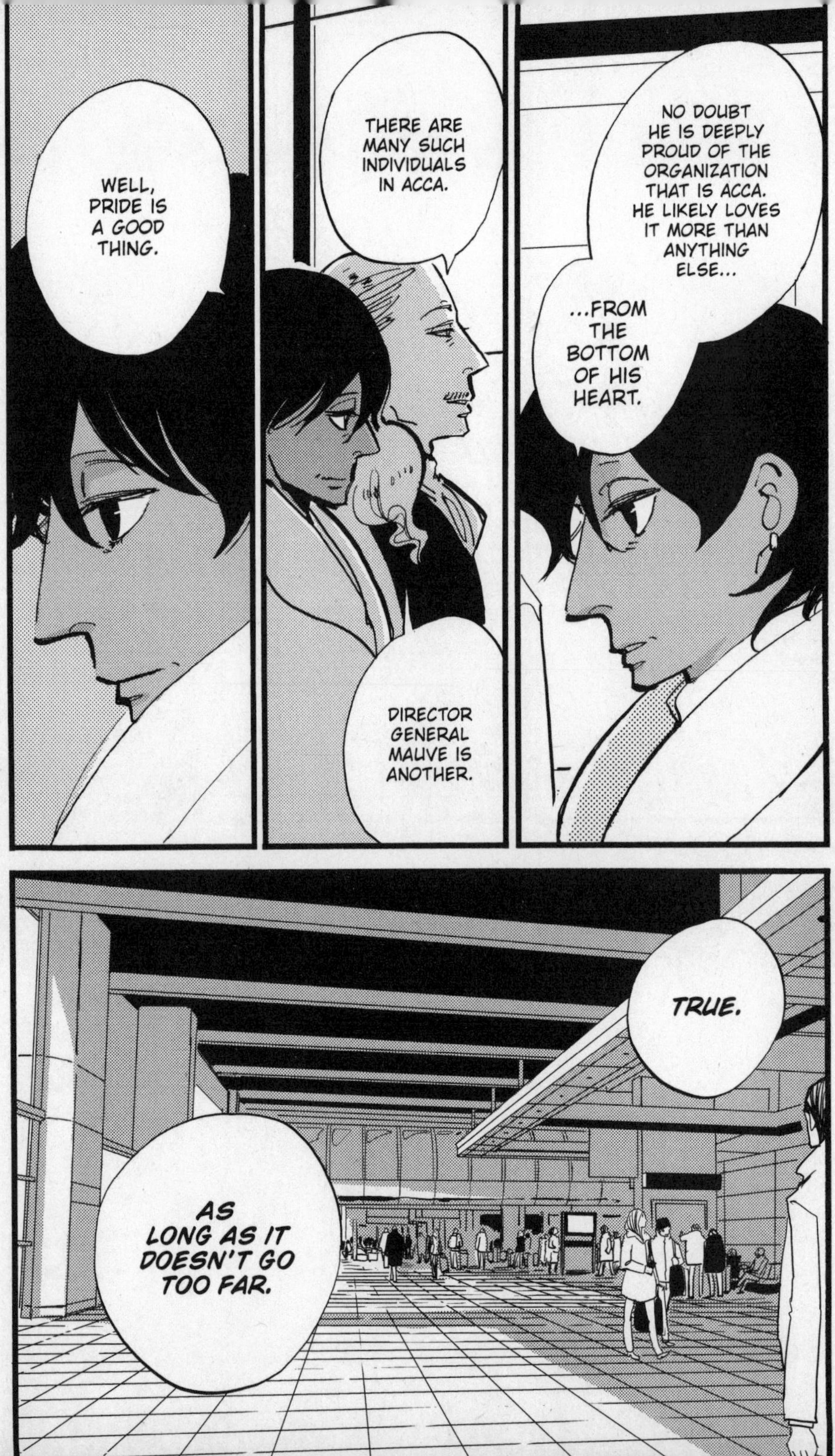
NO DOUBT HE IS DEEPLY PROUD OF THE ORGANIZATION THAT IS ACCA. HE LIKELY LOVES IT MORE THAN ANYTHING ELSE...
...FROM THE BOTTOM OF HIS HEART.
THERE ARE MANY SUCH INDIVIDUALS IN ACCA.
DIRECTOR GENERAL MAUVE IS ANOTHER.
WELL, PRIDE IS A GOOD THING.
TRUE.
AS LONG AS IT DOESN'T GO TOO FAR.

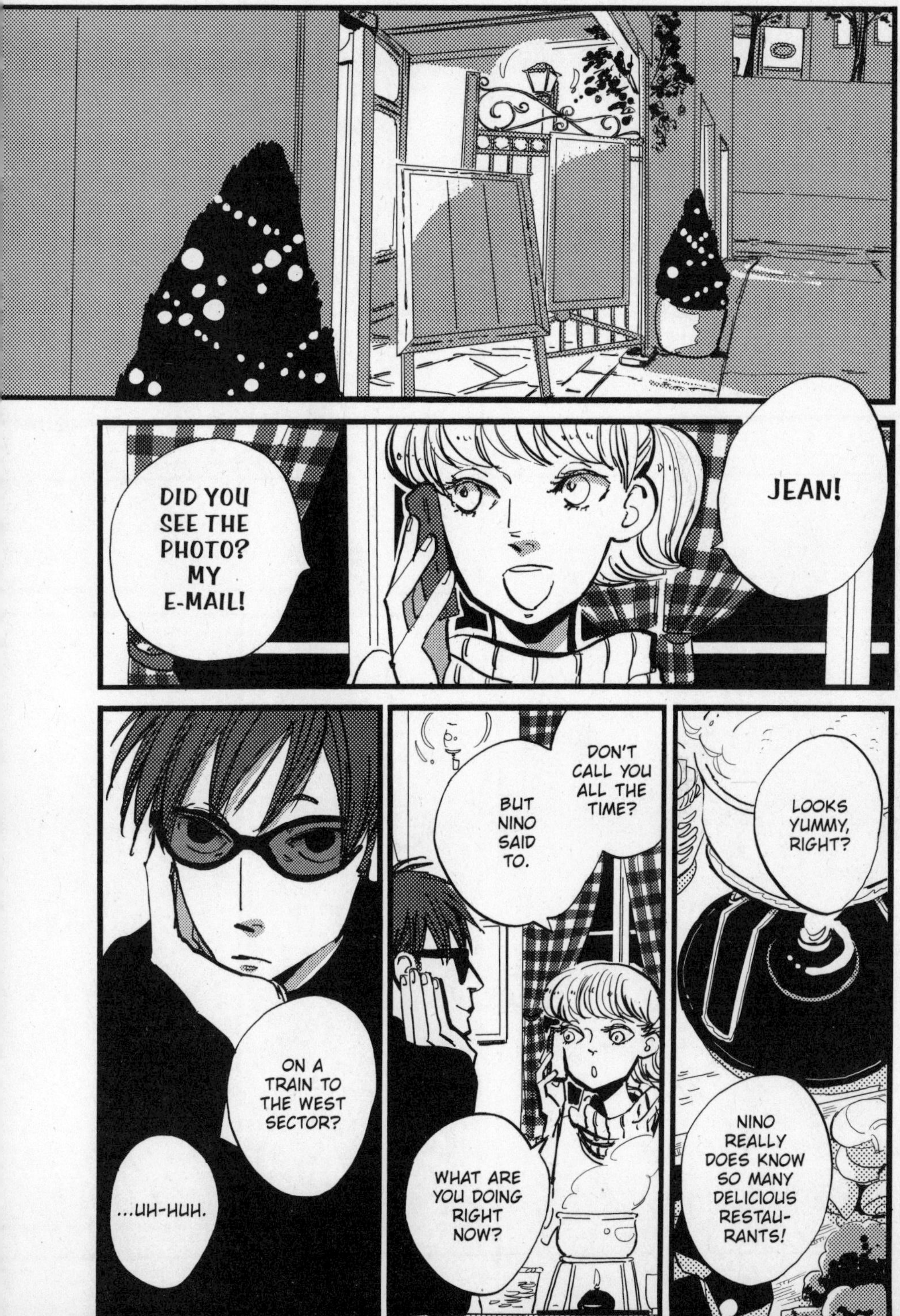
JEAN!
DID YOU SEE THE PHOTO? MY E-MAIL!
LOOKS YUMMY, RIGHT?
NINO REALLY DOES KNOW SO MANY DELICIOUS RESTAU-RANTS!
DON'T CALL YOU ALL THE TIME?
BUT NINO SAID TO.
WHAT ARE YOU DOING RIGHT NOW?
ON A TRAIN TO THE WEST SECTOR?
...UH-HUH.

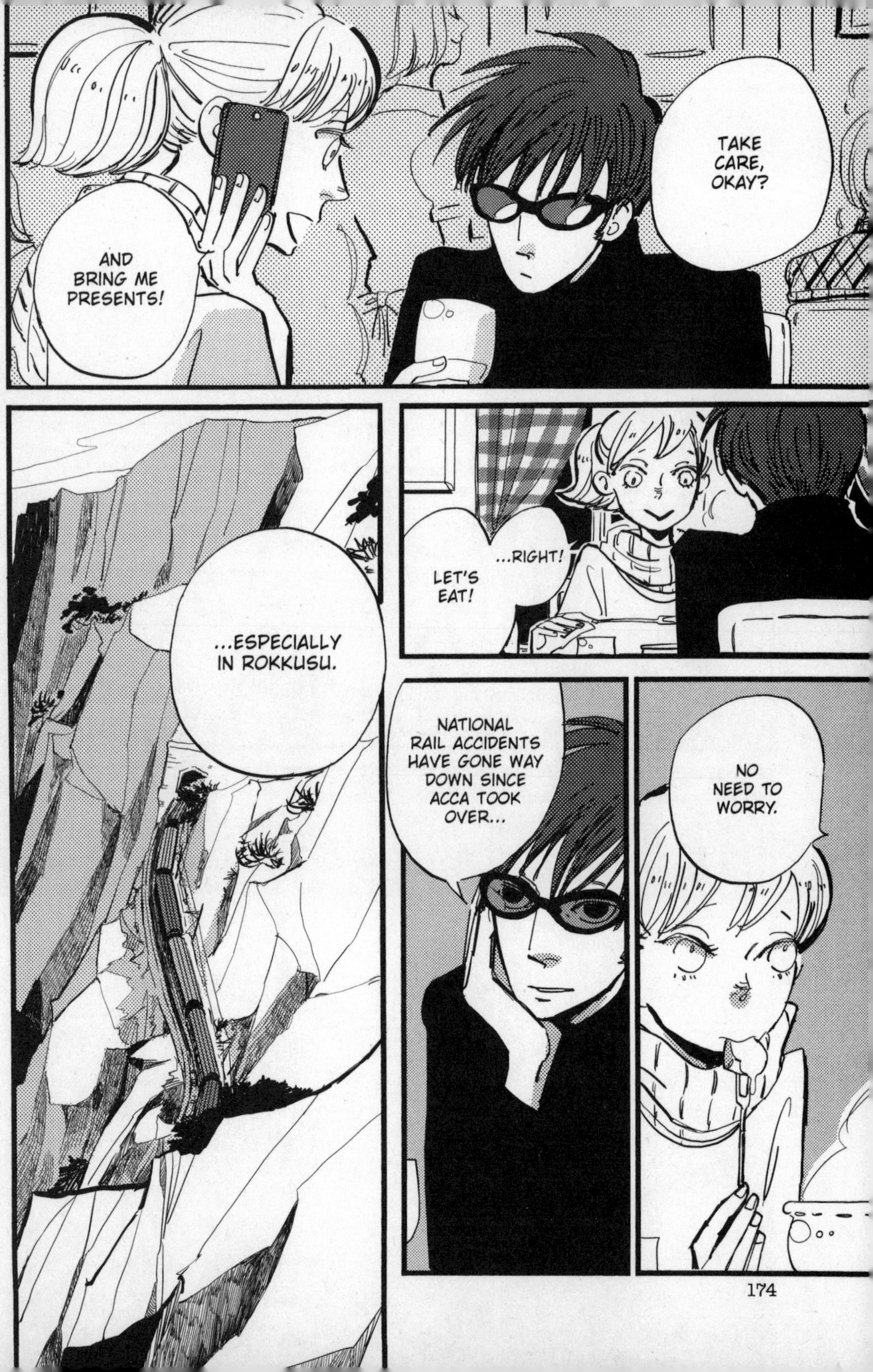
TAKE CARE, OKAY?
AND BRING ME PRESENTS!
...RIGHT!
LET'S EAT!
NO NEED TO WORRY.
NATIONAL RAIL ACCIDENTS HAVE GONE WAY DOWN SINCE ACCA TOOK OVER...
...ESPECIALLY IN ROKKUSU.

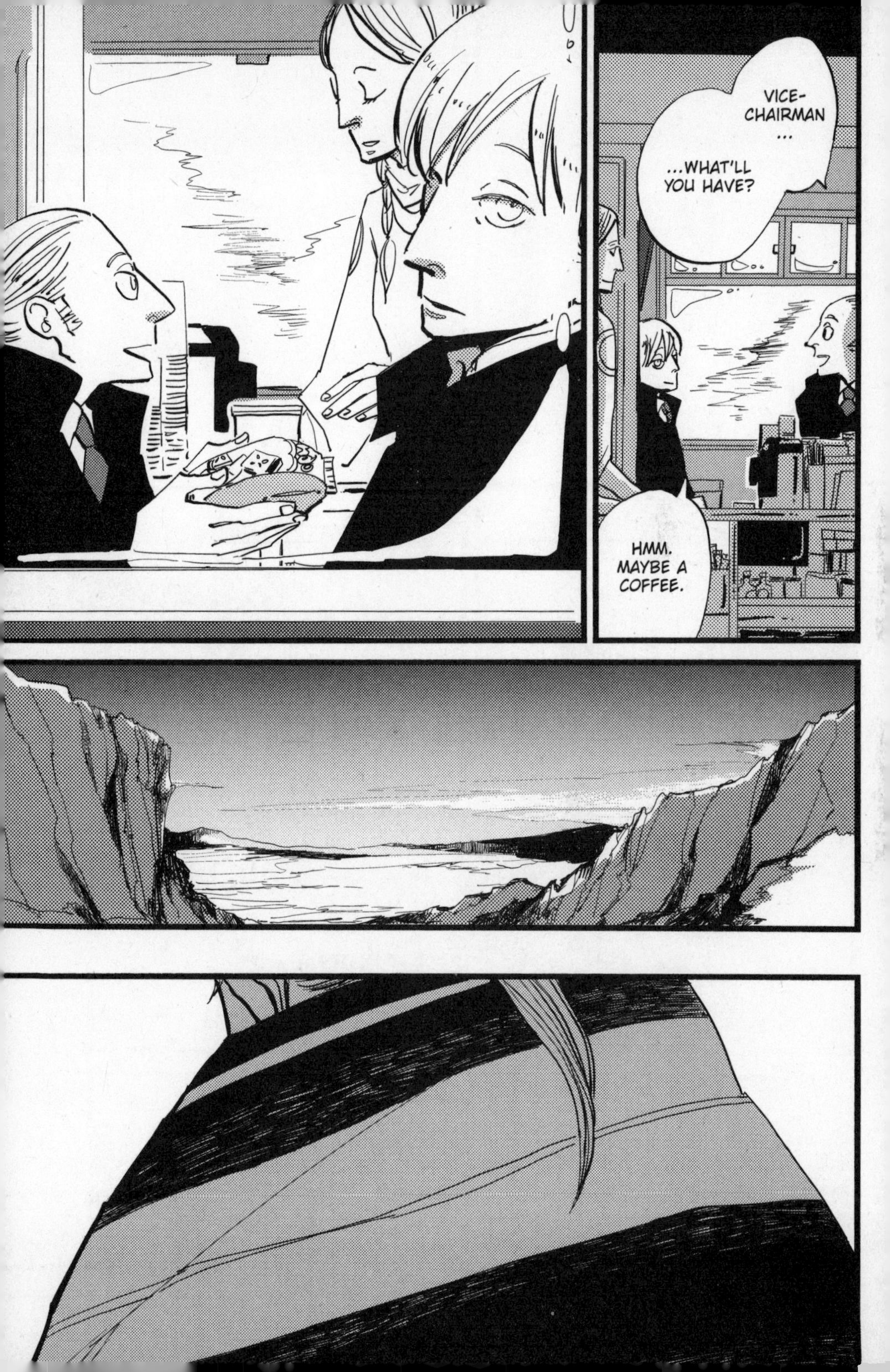
VICE-CHAIRMAN ...
...WHAT'LL YOU HAVE?
HMM. MAYBE A COFFEE.

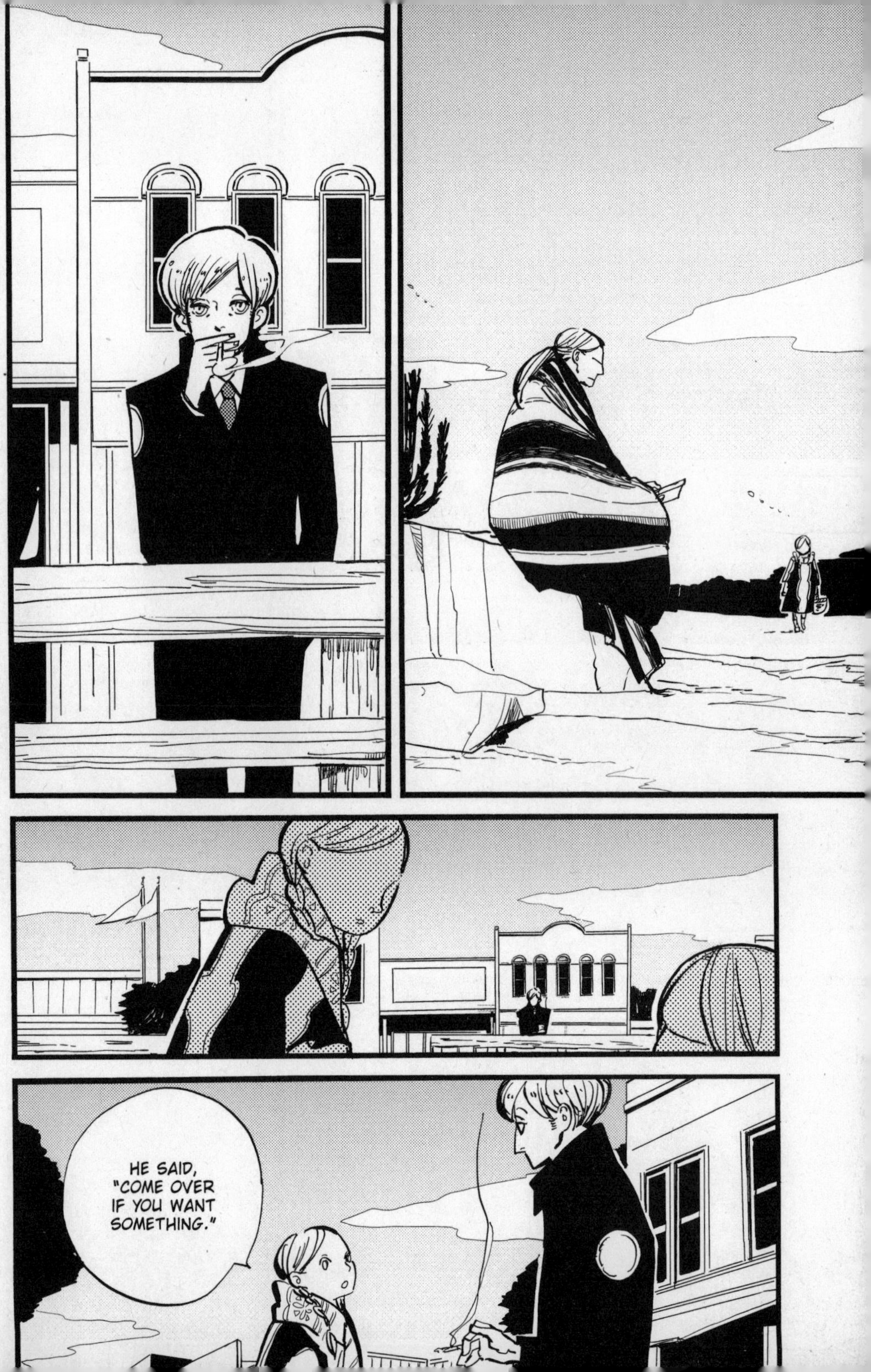
HE SAID, "COME OVER IF YOU WANT SOMETHING."

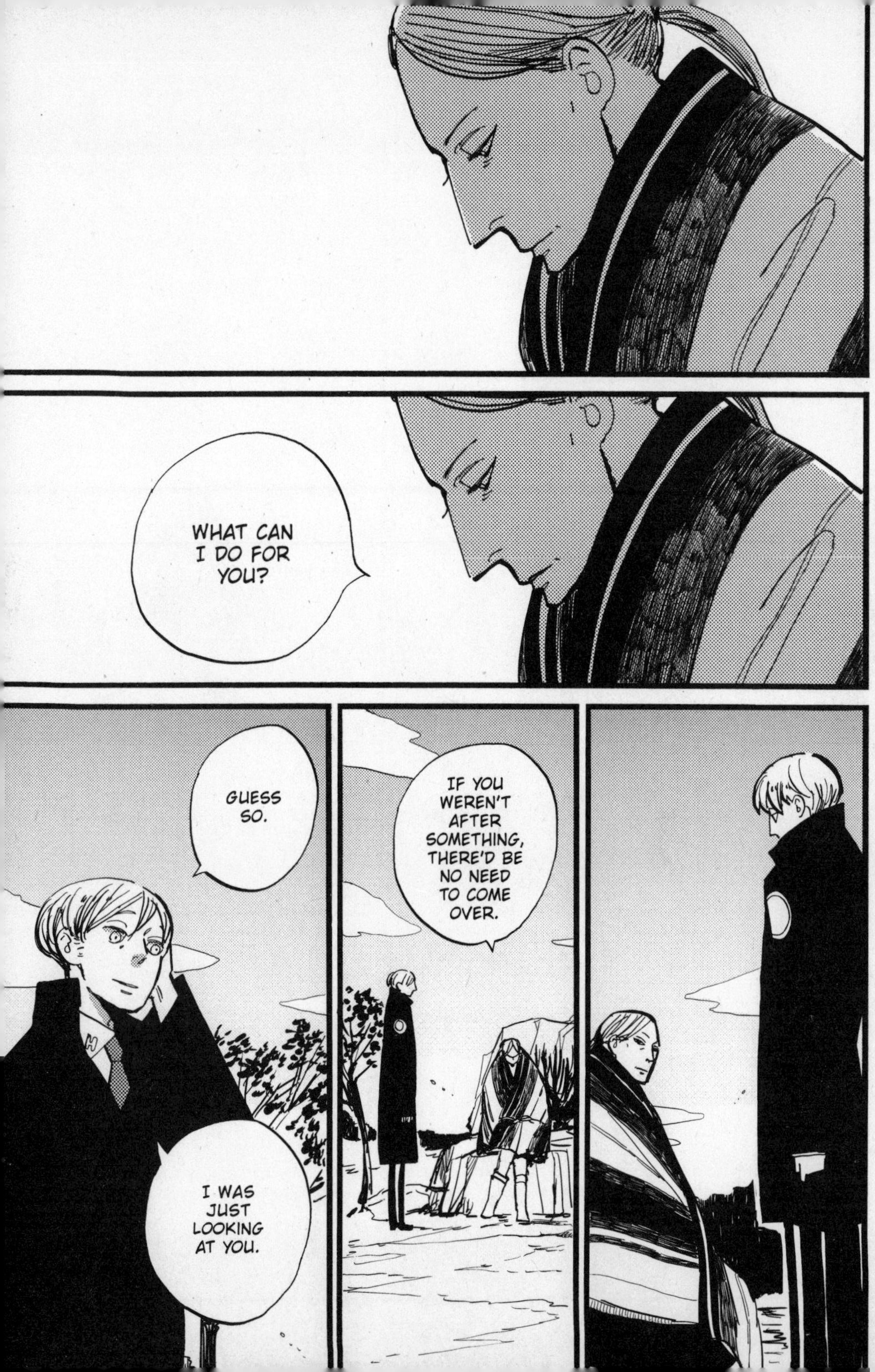
WHAT CAN I DO FOR YOU?
IF YOU WEREN'T AFTER SOMETHING, THERE'D BE NO NEED TO COME OVER.
GUESS SO.
I WAS JUST LOOKING AT YOU.

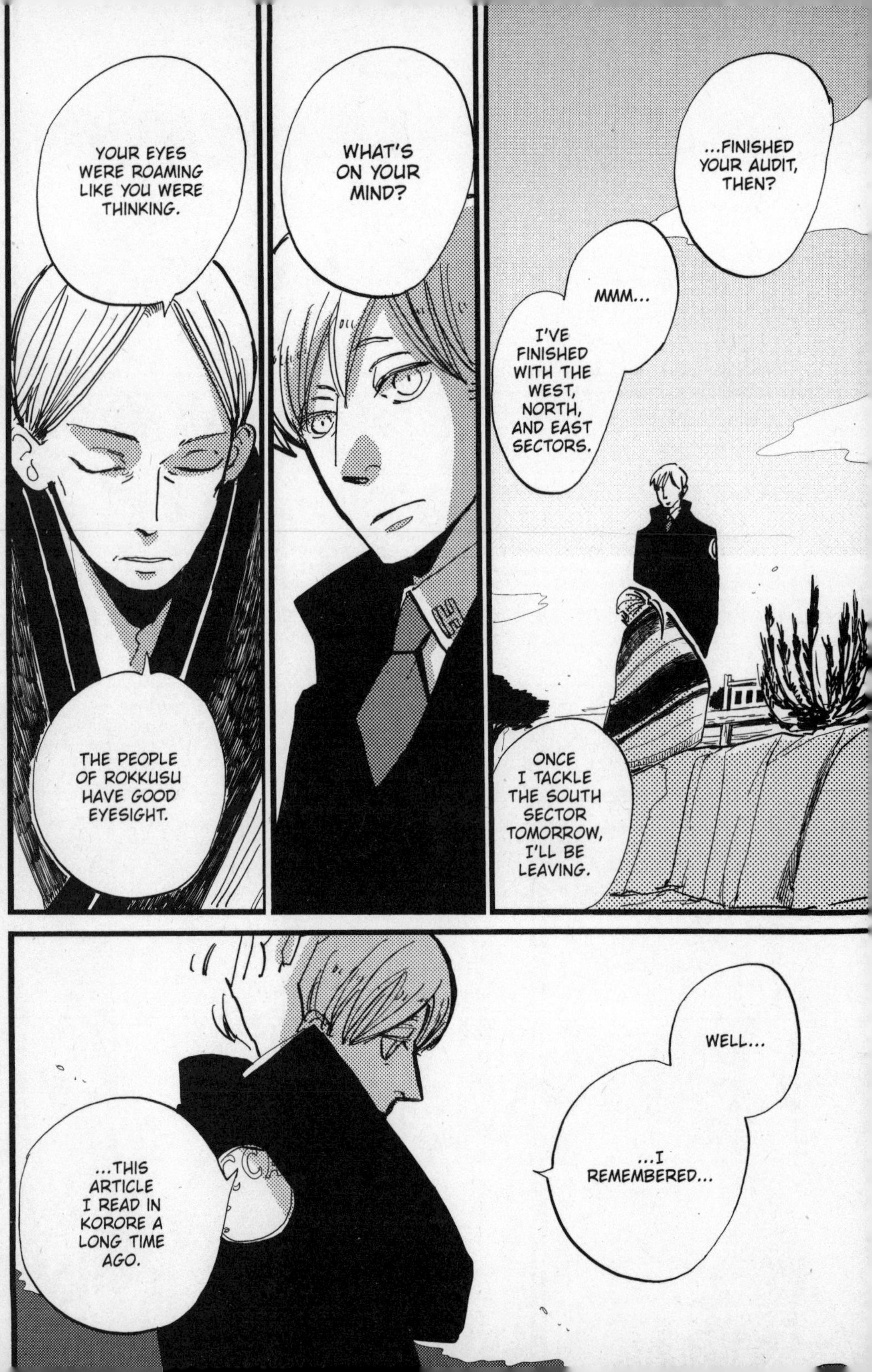
...FINISHED YOUR AUDIT, THEN?
MMM...
I'VE FINISHED WITH THE WEST, NORTH, AND EAST SECTORS.
ONCE I TACKLE THE SOUTH SECTOR TOMORROW, I'LL BE LEAVING.
WHAT'S ON YOUR MIND?
YOUR EYES WERE ROAMING LIKE YOU WERE THINKING.
THE PEOPLE OF ROKKUSU HAVE GOOD EYESIGHT.
WELL...
...I REMEMBERED...
...THIS ARTICLE I READ IN KORORE A LONG TIME AGO.

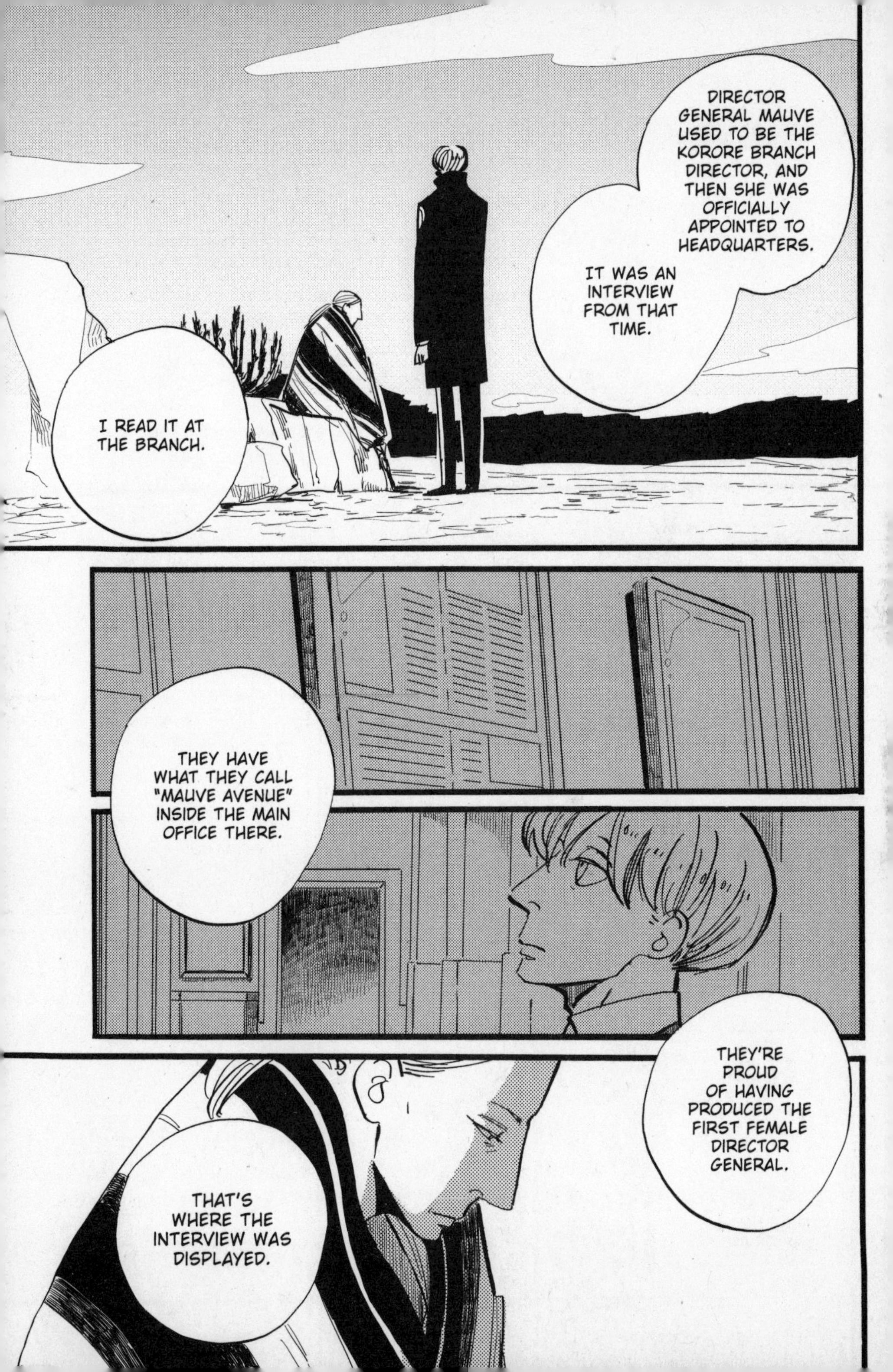
DIRECTOR GENERAL MAUVE USED TO BE THE KORORE BRANCH DIRECTOR, AND THEN SHE WAS OFFICIALLY APPOINTED TO HEADQUARTERS.
IT WAS AN INTERVIEW FROM THAT TIME.
I READ IT AT THE BRANCH.
THEY HAVE WHAT THEY CALL "MAUVE AVENUE" INSIDE THE MAIN OFFICE THERE.
THEY'RE PROUD OF HAVING PRODUCED THE FIRST FEMALE DIRECTOR GENERAL.
THAT'S WHERE THE INTERVIEW WAS DISPLAYED.

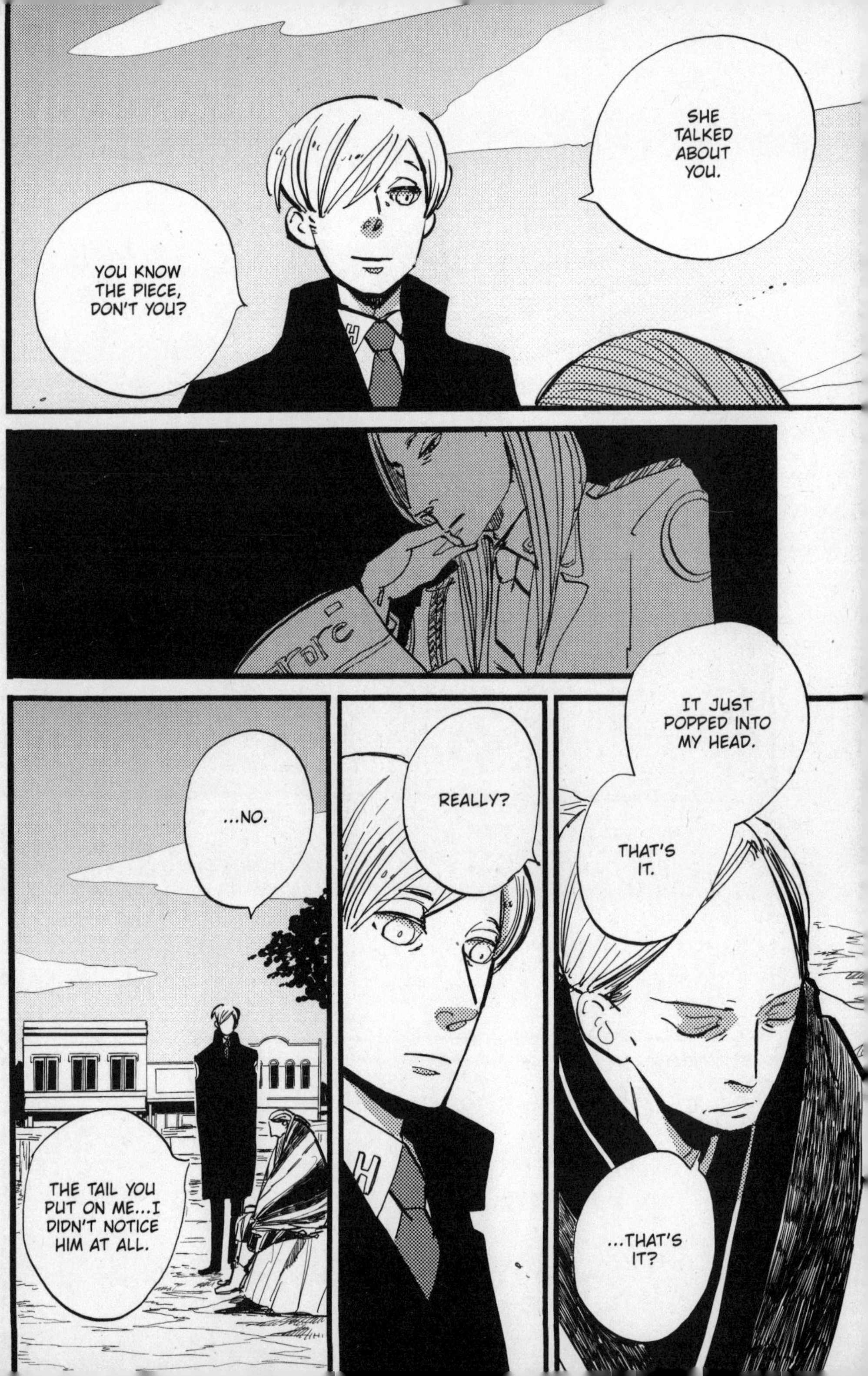
SHE TALKED ABOUT YOU.
YOU KNOW THE PIECE, DON'T YOU?
IT JUST POPPED INTO MY HEAD.
THAT'S IT.
...THAT'S IT?
REALLY?
...NO.
THE TAIL YOU PUT ON ME...I DIDN'T NOTICE HIM AT ALL.

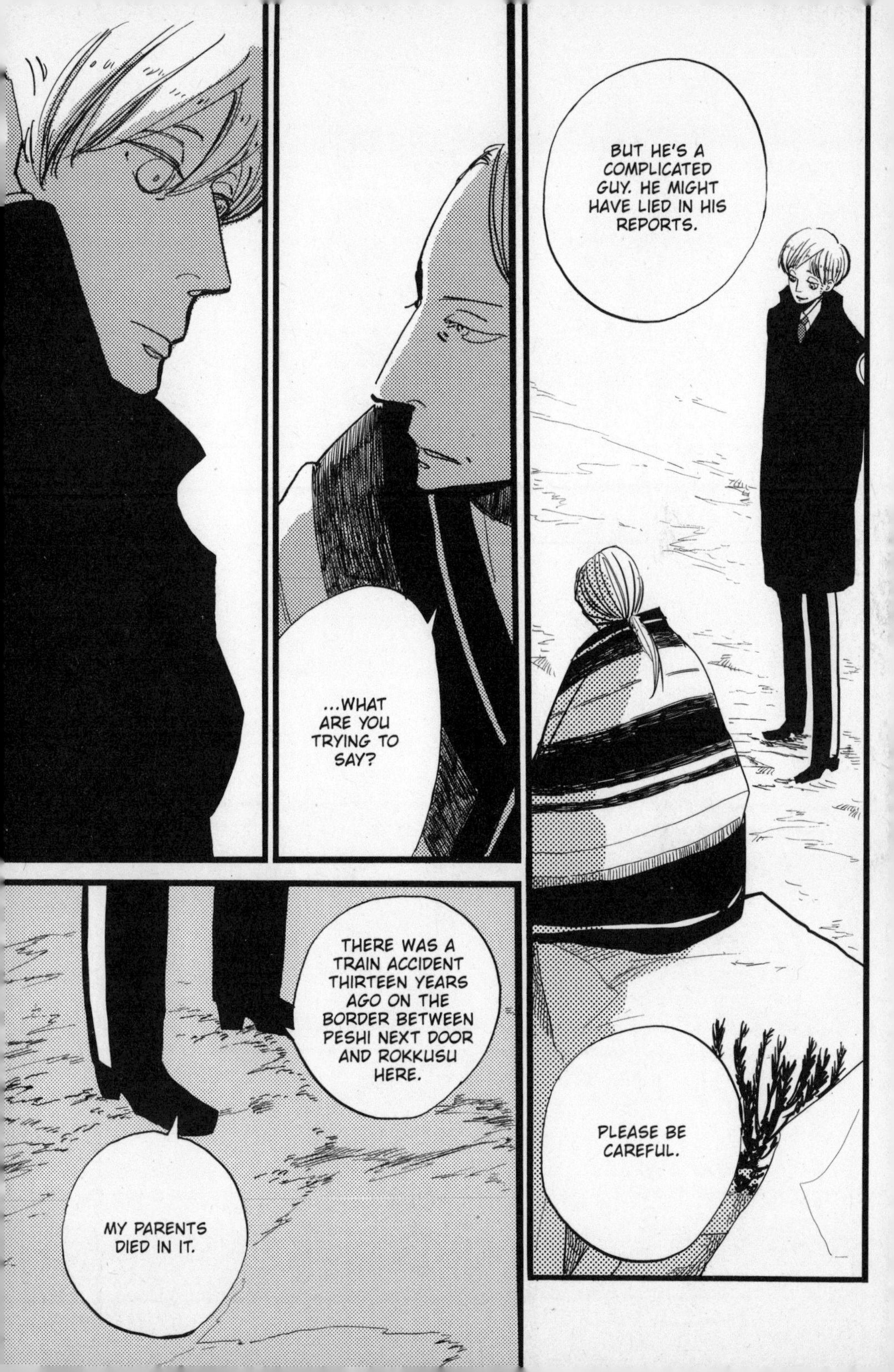
BUT HE'S A COMPLICATED GUY. HE MIGHT HAVE LIED IN HIS REPORTS.
PLEASE BE CAREFUL.
...WHAT ARE YOU TRYING TO SAY?
THERE WAS A TRAIN ACCIDENT THIRTEEN YEARS AGO ON THE BORDER BETWEEN PESHI NEXT DOOR AND ROKKUSU HERE.
MY PARENTS DIED IN IT.

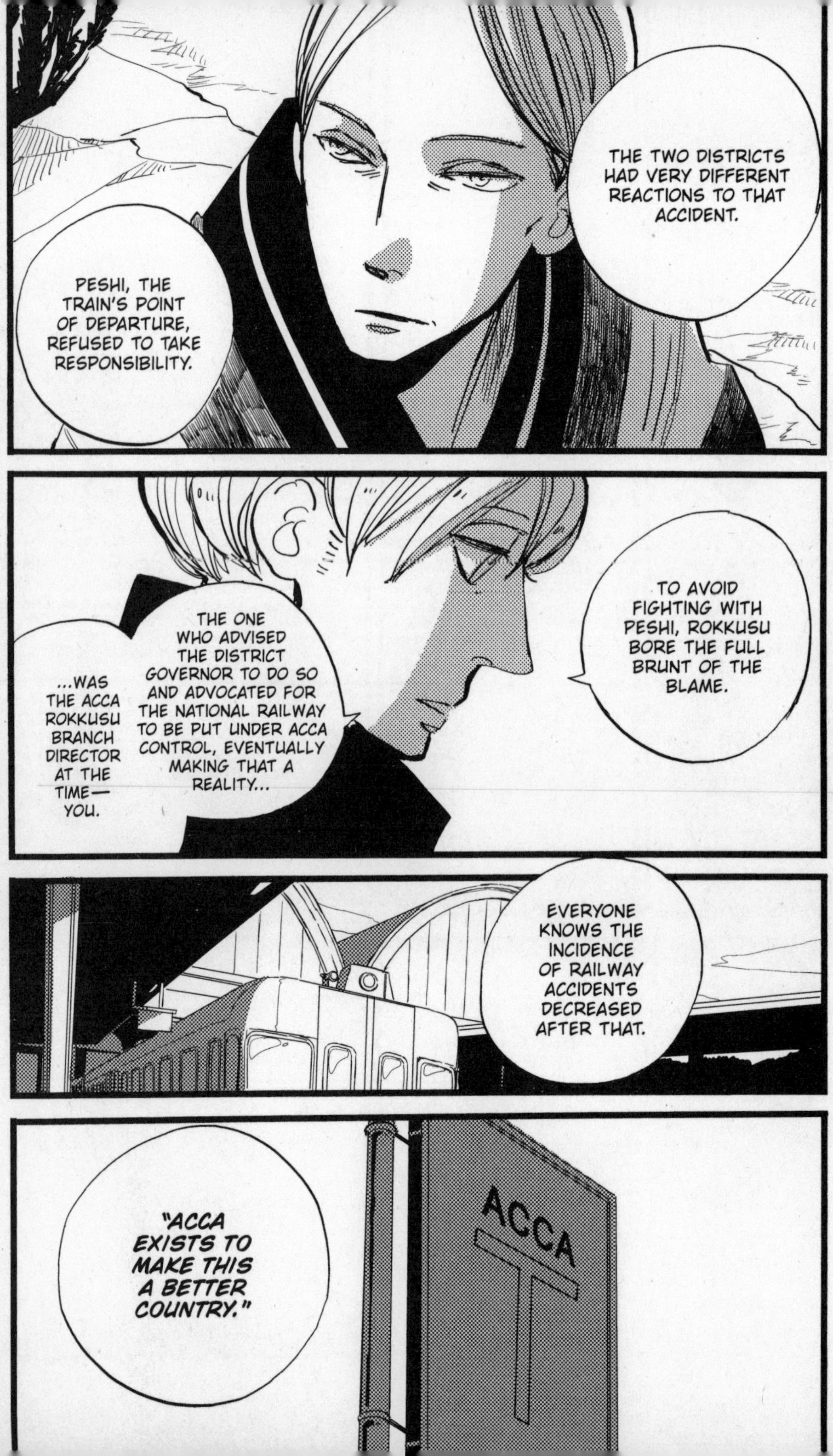
THE TWO DISTRICTS HAD VERY DIFFERENT REACTIONS TO THAT ACCIDENT.
PESHI, THE TRAIN'S POINT OF DEPARTURE, REFUSED TO TAKE RESPONSIBILITY.
TO AVOID FIGHTING WITH PESHI, ROKKUSU BORE THE FULL BRUNT OF THE BLAME.
THE ONE WHO ADVISED THE DISTRICT GOVERNOR TO DO SO AND ADVOCATED FOR THE NATIONAL RAILWAY TO BE PUT UNDER ACCA CONTROL, EVENTUALLY MAKING THAT A REALITY...
...WAS THE ACCA ROKKUSU BRANCH DIRECTOR AT THE TIME—YOU.
EVERYONE KNOWS THE INCIDENCE OF RAILWAY ACCIDENTS DECREASED AFTER THAT.
ACCA
"ACCA EXISTS TO MAKE THIS A BETTER COUNTRY."

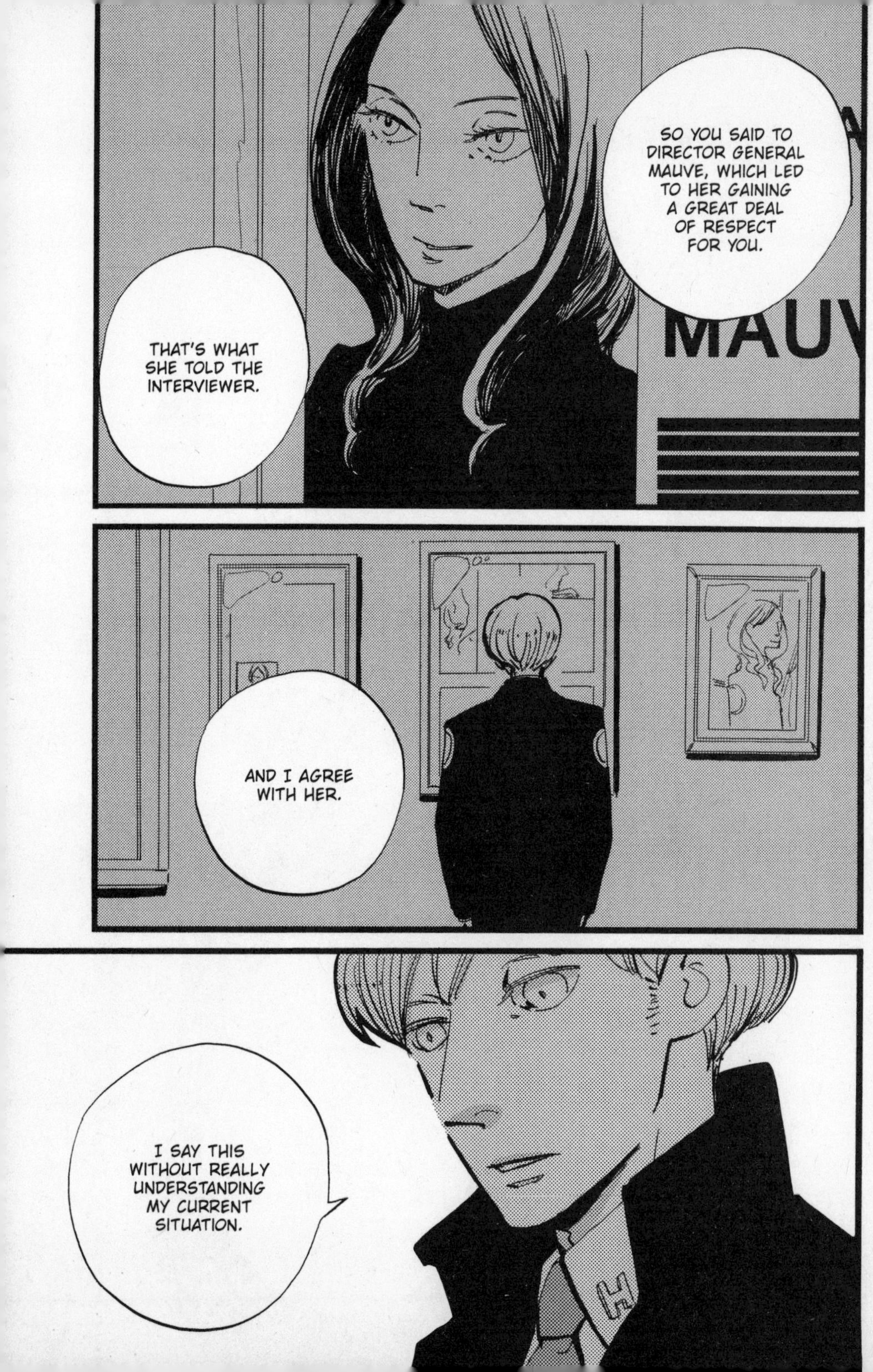

SO YOU SAID TO DIRECTOR GENERAL MAUVE, WHICH LED TO HER GAINING A GREAT DEAL OF RESPECT FOR YOU.
THAT'S WHAT SHE TOLD THE INTERVIEWER.
AND I AGREE WITH HER.
I SAY THIS WITHOUT REALLY UNDERSTANDING MY CURRENT SITUATION.

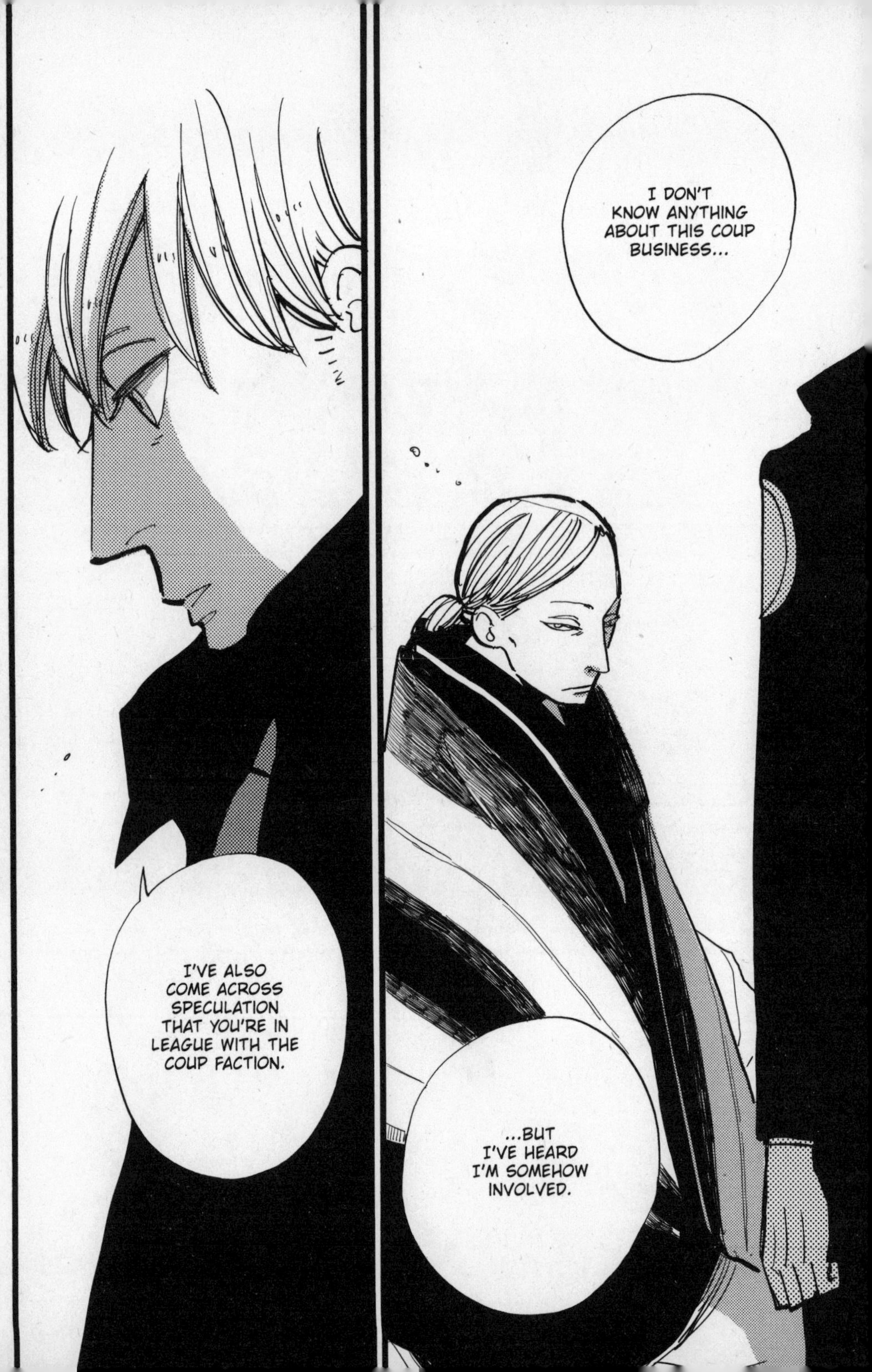
I DON'T KNOW ANYTHING ABOUT THIS COUP BUSINESS...
...BUT I'VE HEARD I'M SOMEHOW INVOLVED.
I'VE ALSO COME ACROSS SPECULATION THAT YOU'RE IN LEAGUE WITH THE COUP FACTION.

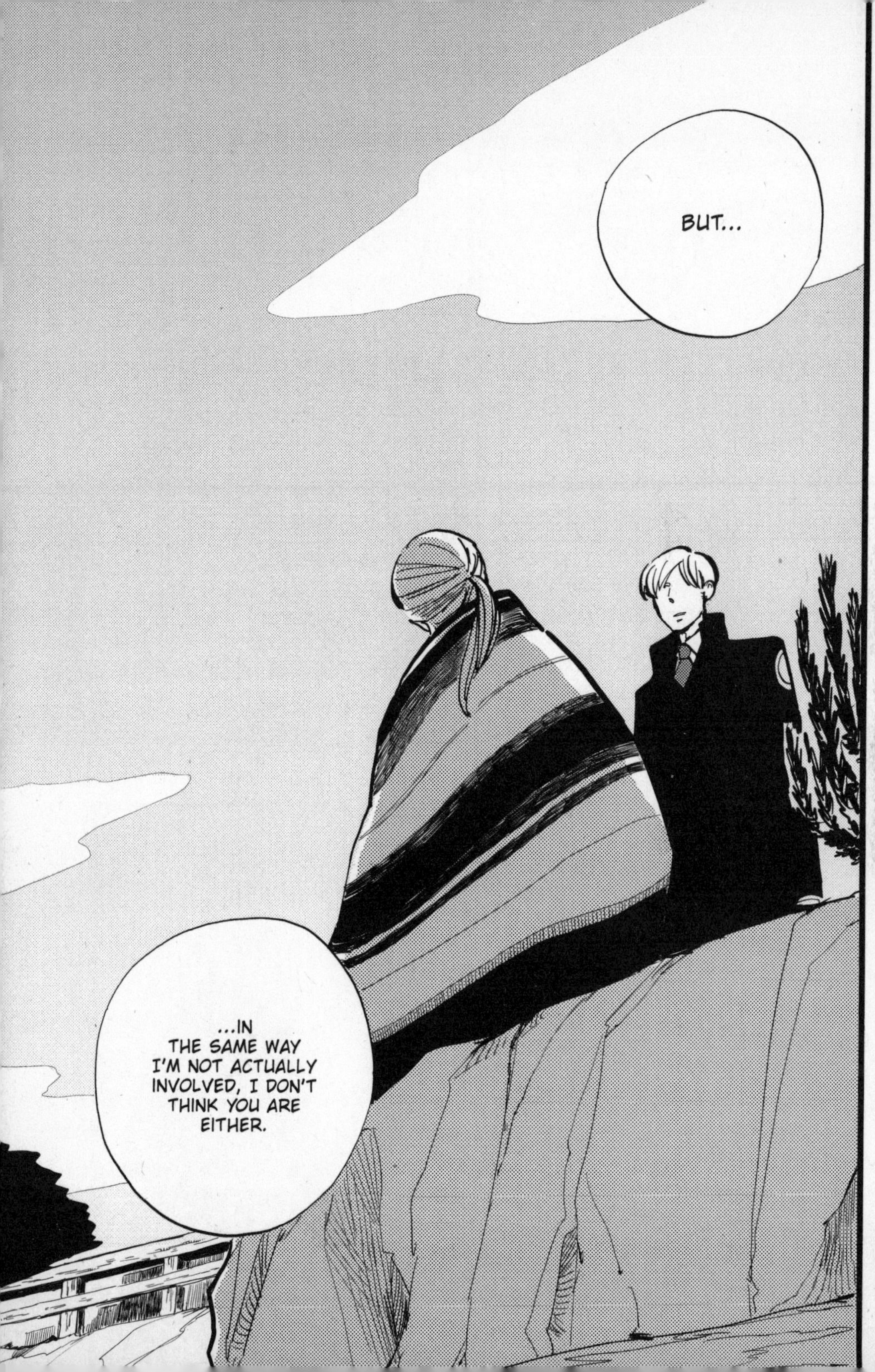
BUT...
...IN THE SAME WAY I'M NOT ACTUALLY INVOLVED, I DON'T THINK YOU ARE EITHER.

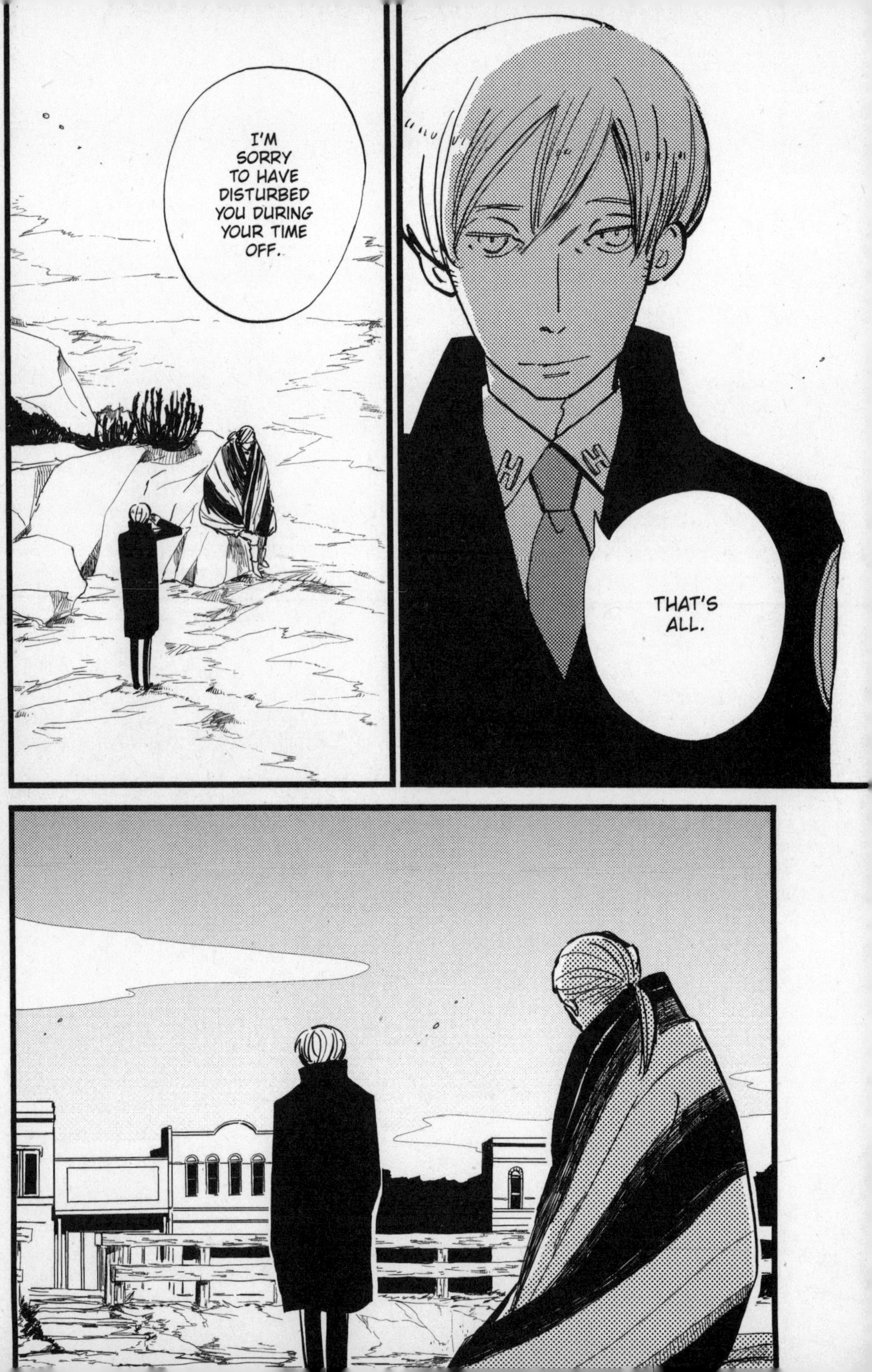
THAT'S ALL.
I'M SORRY TO HAVE DISTURBED YOU DURING YOUR TIME OFF.

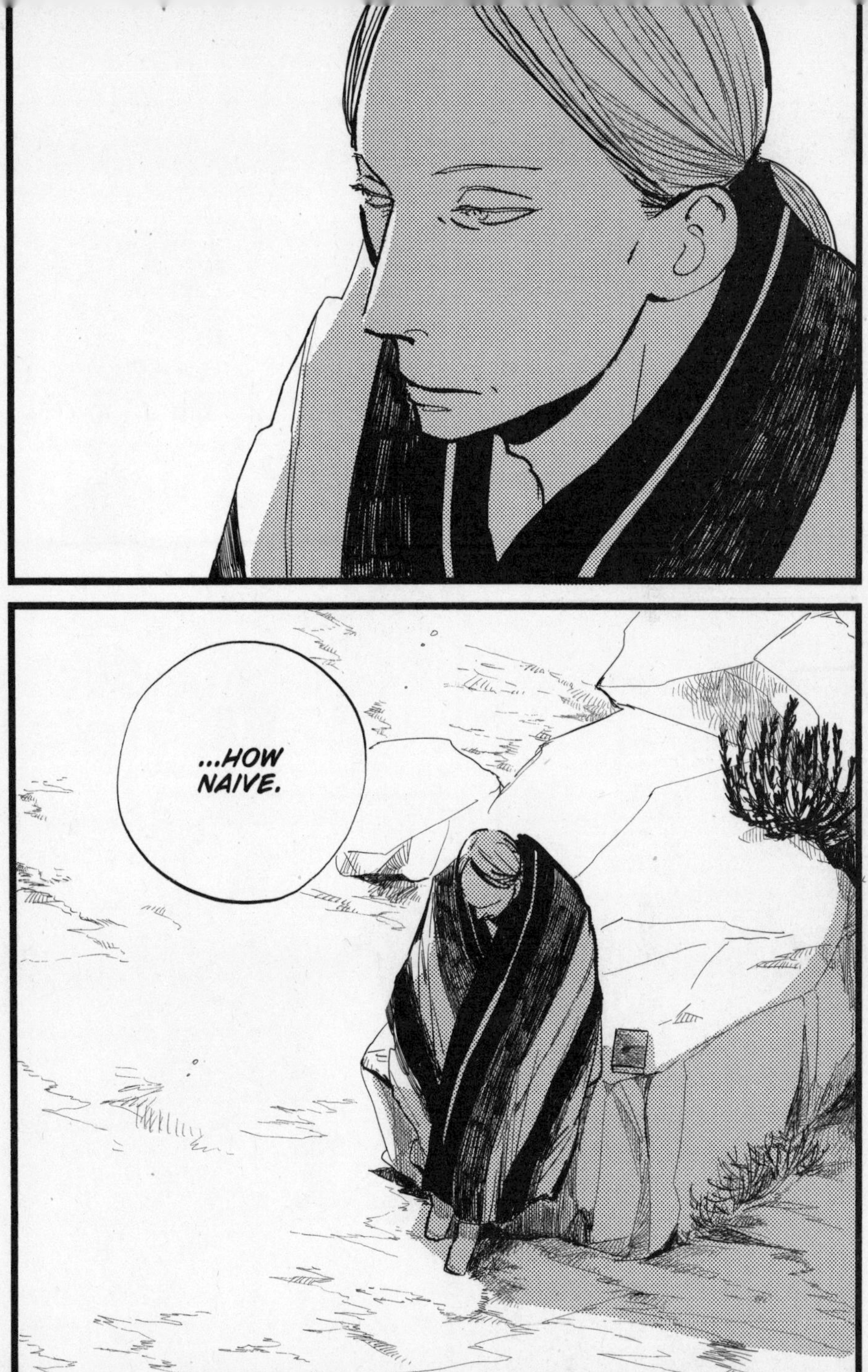
...HOW NAIVE.

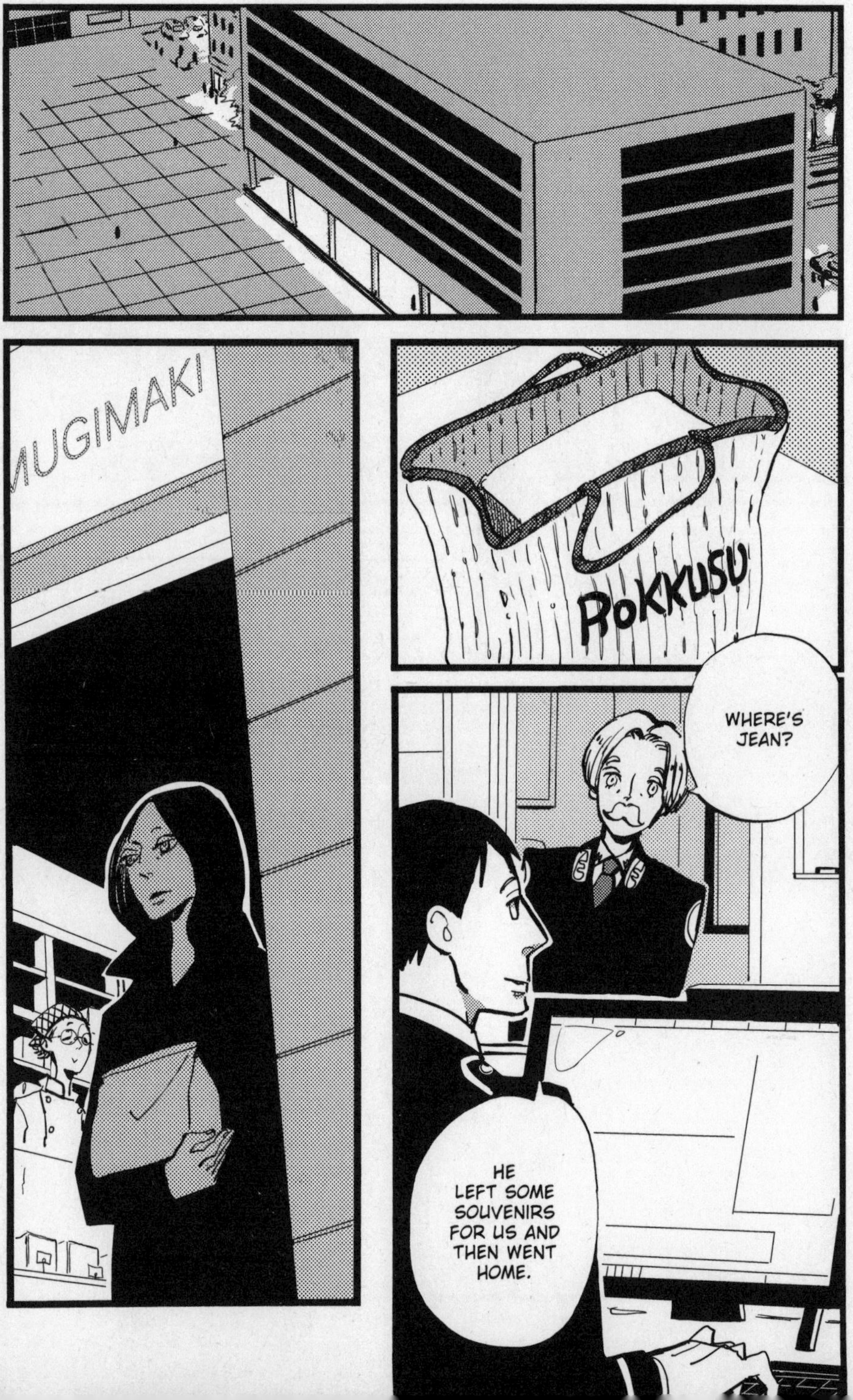
ROKKUSU
WHERE'S JEAN?
HE LEFT SOME SOUVENIRS FOR US AND THEN WENT HOME.
MUGIMAKI

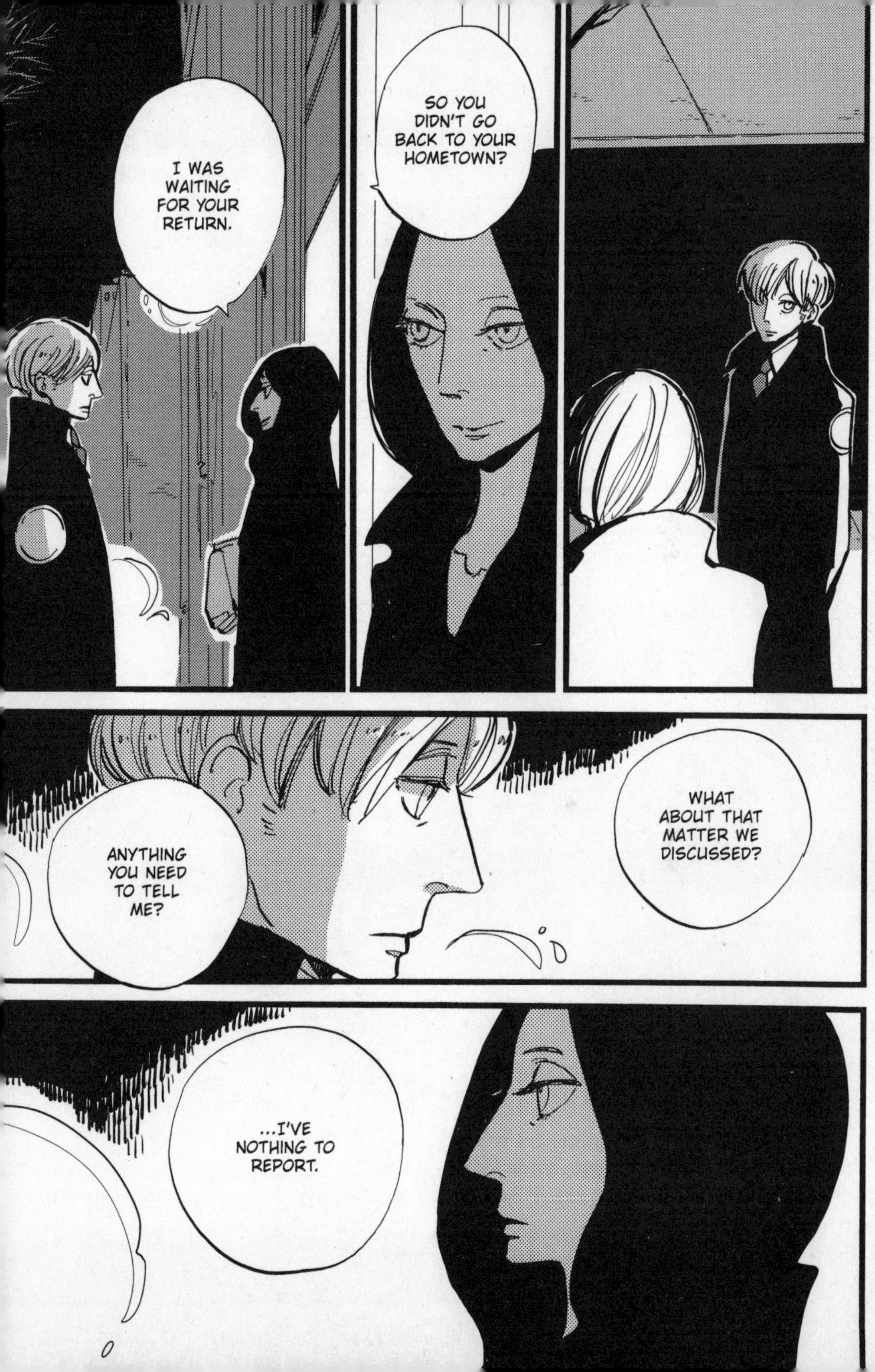
SO YOU DIDN'T GO BACK TO YOUR HOMETOWN?
I WAS WAITING FOR YOUR RETURN.
WHAT ABOUT THAT MATTER WE DISCUSSED?
ANYTHING YOU NEED TO TELL ME?
...I'VE NOTHING TO REPORT.

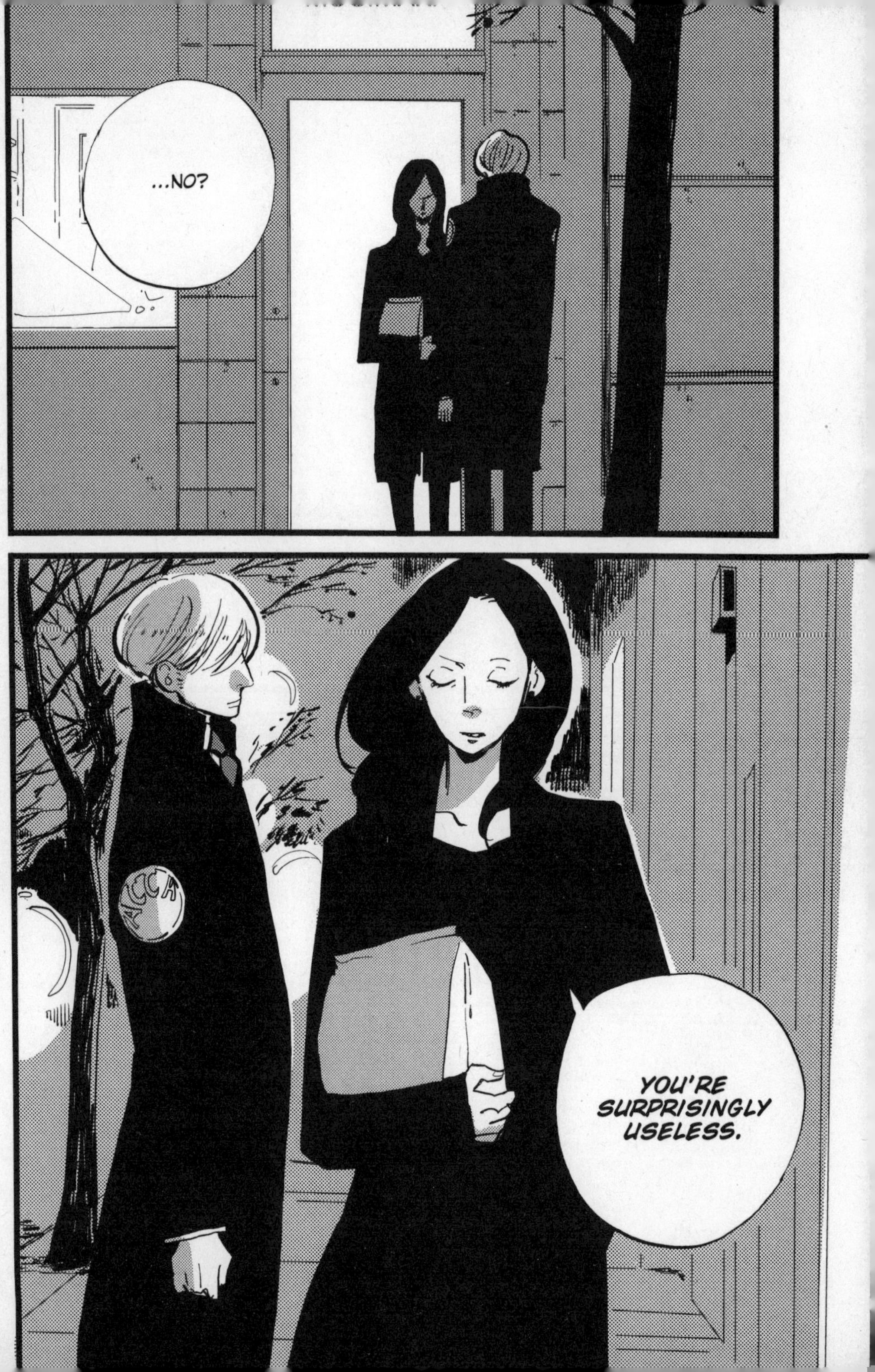
...NO?
YOU'RE SURPRISINGLY USELESS.

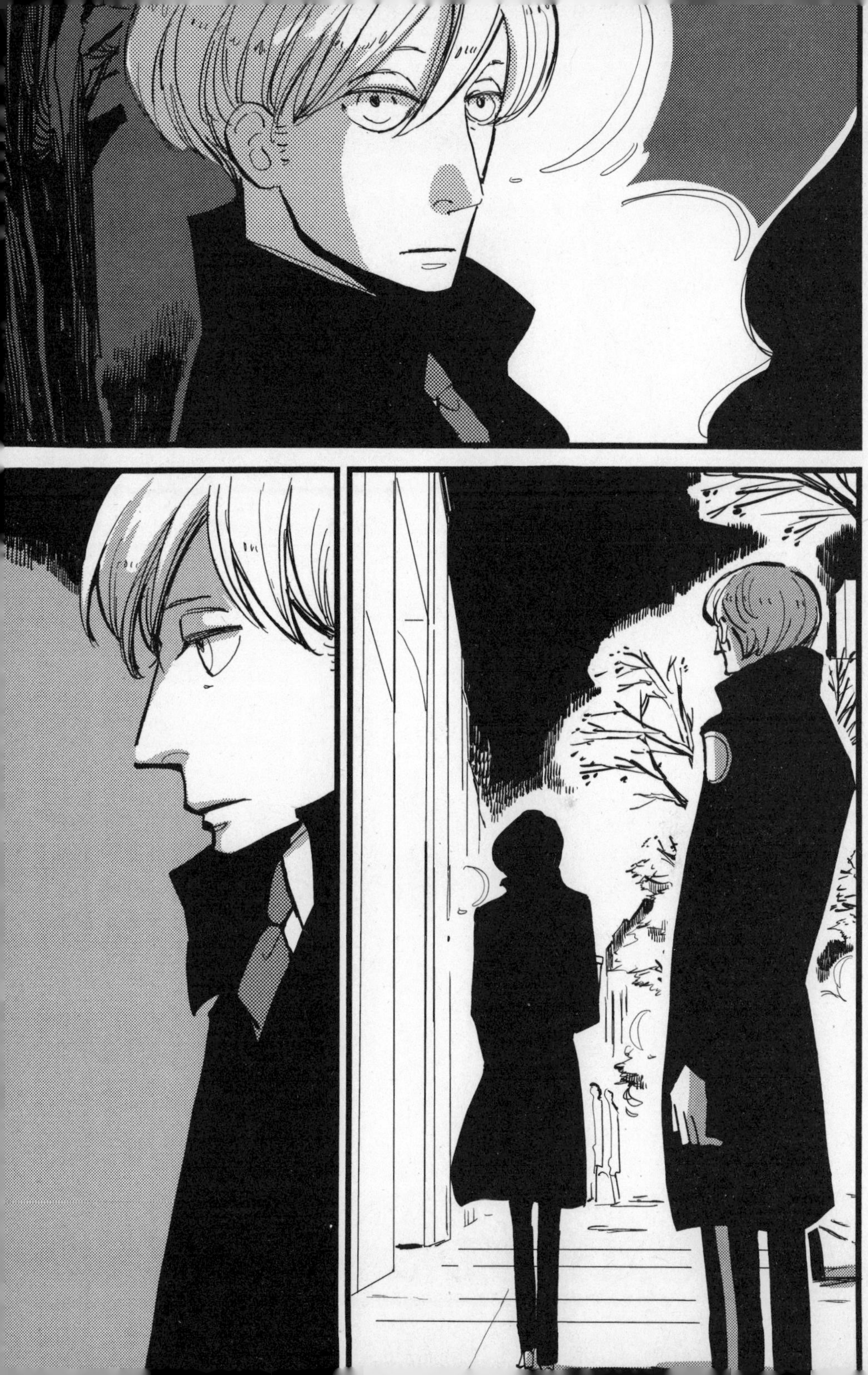

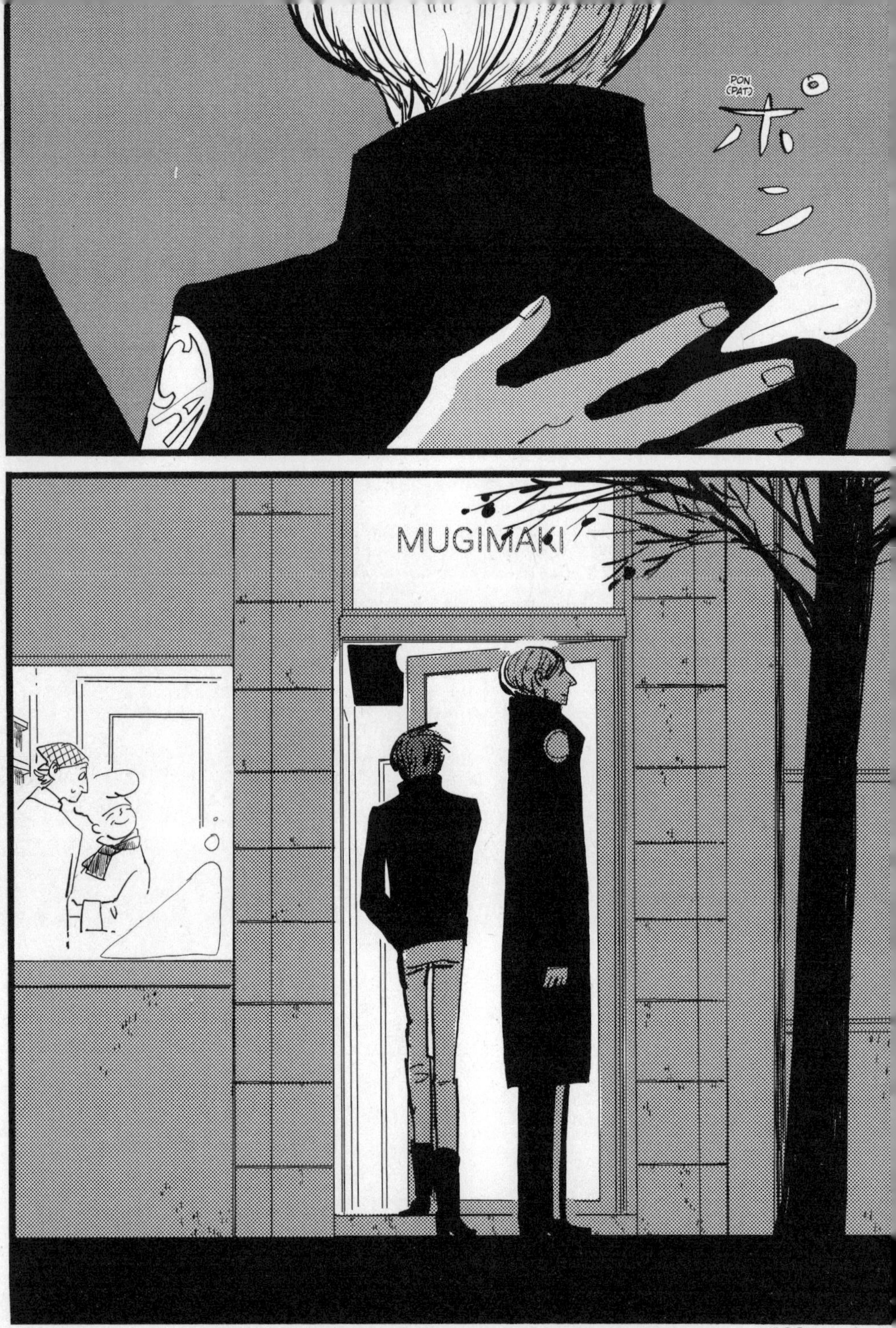
PON (PAT)
MUGIMAKI

Kingdom of Dowa

Dowa, a kingdom with regional self-government, is divided into thirteen districts, with each district having its own unique culture.

ACCA is a massive unified organization, encompassing the police department, the fire department, and medical services, among others. The organization is managed by the branches in each district, with Headquarters in the capital performing the role of uniting the thirteen ACCA branches. The Inspection Department Jean belongs to has Headquarters agents stationed at each branch and also sends a supervisor to audit at irregular intervals in order to monitor the daily operations of the branches.

Birra
Badon
Korore
Dowa
Peshi
Suitsu
Rokkusu
Yakkara
Jumoku
Pranetta
Famasu
Furawau
N
Hare

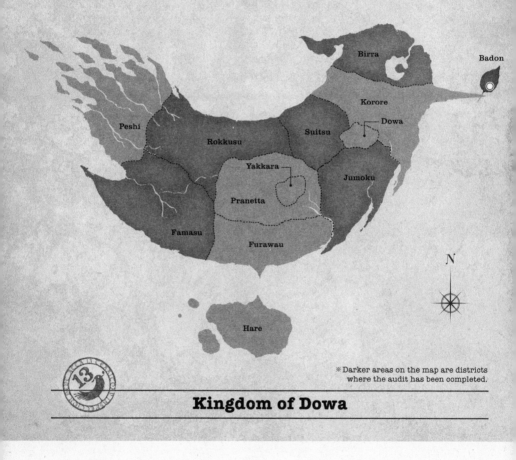

※ Darker areas on the map are districts where the audit has been completed.

Kingdom of Dowa

INSPECTION DEPT ACCA 13 TERRITORY
PASS

CHAPTER 17
Staring Down Train Tracks and Pride in Rokkusu

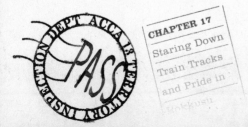

ACCA Organization Chart
(Headquarters)

ACCA Headquarters is located in the capital city of Badon. The entrance exam is more difficult than that for the individual branches, and the staff at HQ are considered "elites."

Inspection Department

Inspection Department Headquarters agents are dispatched to the ACCA branches in each autonomous district. There, they manage the data from the daily operations of each branch. Additionally, a superior agent audits each branch at irregular intervals; these audits are Jean's main duty.

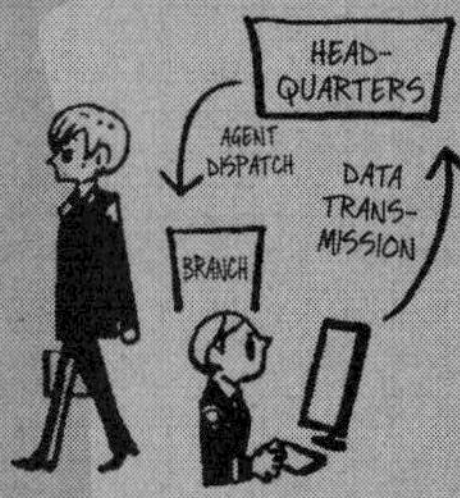
HEAD-QUARTERS
AGENT DISPATCH
DATA TRANS-MISSION
BRANCH

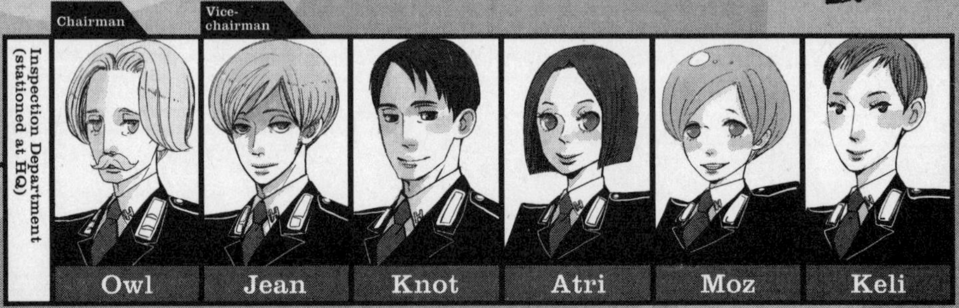
Chairman
Vice-chairman
Inspection Department (stationed at HQ)
Owl
Jean
Knot
Atri
Moz
Keli

At the Inspection Department, 10:00 A.M. and 3:00 P.M. are snack times!!! ...Apparently!

The main snacks so far—

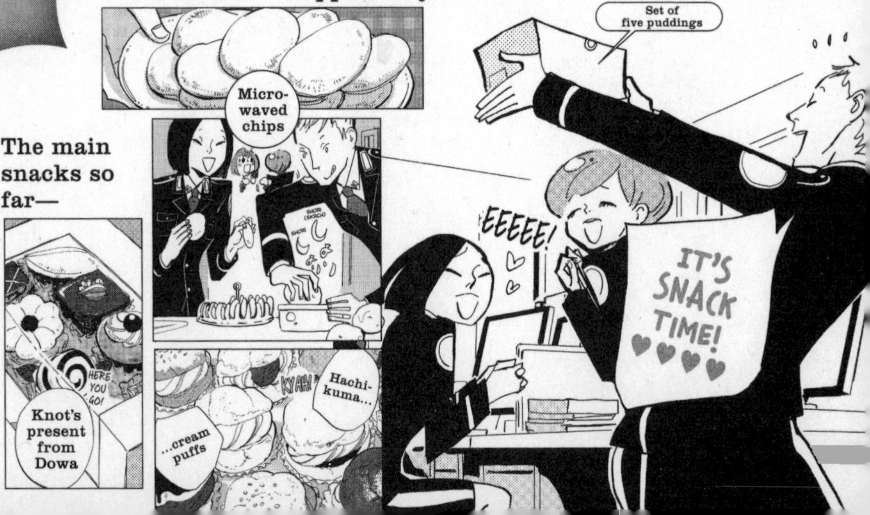
Set of five puddings
EEEEE!
IT'S SNACK TIME!
Micro-waved chips
Hachi-kuma...
KYAH!
...cream puffs
HERE YOU GO!
Knot's present from Dowa

ACCA Five Chief Officers

The top five in the organization. The five chief officers make all sorts of resolutions.

Grossular | Lilium | Spade | Pastis | Pine

Head-quarters

HQ staff focuses primarily on coordinating the thirteen branches. They also have miscellaneous duties that work toward maintaining functions within HQ.

Director General Mauve

Deputy Director General Pouchard

Internal Affairs

Operations

Public Relations

General Affairs

Data Management

et cetera ......

Undercover Internal Affairs agent, nickname "Crow"

Crow

Jean's longtime friend

Nino

The thirteen branches are unified by Headquarters.

Turn the page for the branch organization chart!

ACCA Organization Chart
(Branches)

At the ACCA branches in each district, the branch agents are people from those districts; only those in the Inspection Department are dispatched from HQ.

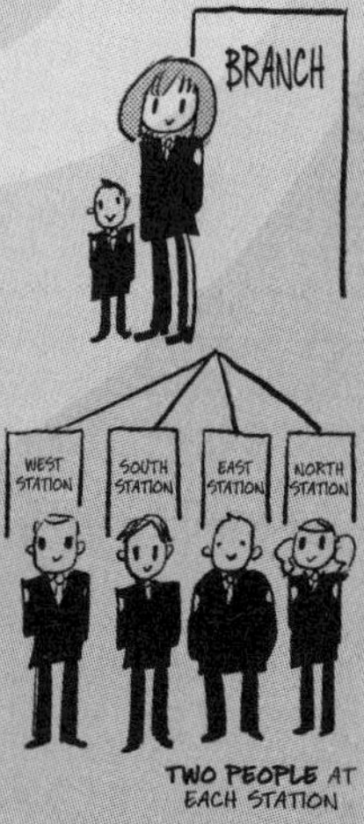

BRANCH
WEST STATION
SOUTH STATION
EAST STATION
NORTH STATION
TWO PEOPLE AT EACH STATION

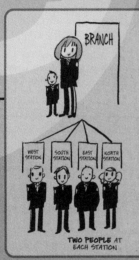

Branch Inspection Department dispatch agents

☆ At a predetermined time each day, using a dedicated line, they send data on all incidents occurring in the district for which they are responsible.

☆ A total of ten people are dispatched: the supervisor and deputy supervisor at the branch headquarters and two agents at each station.

☆ As a general rule, they are transferred to a new region every two years to prevent collusion with local agents.

A major responsibility for the supervisors is showing Jean around when he comes for an audit from HQ!

Famasu branch supervisor **Eider**

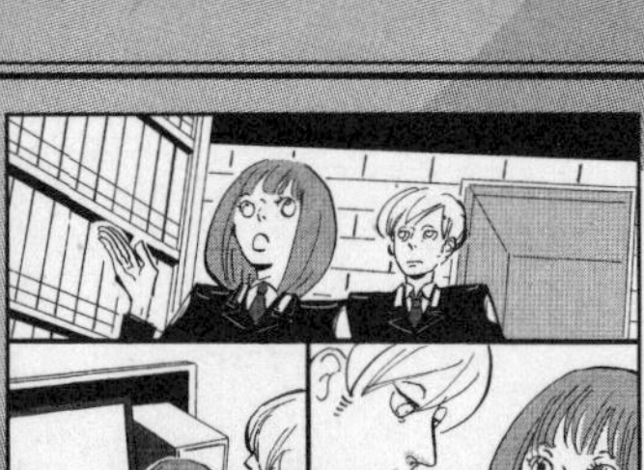

Badon branch supervisor **Grus**

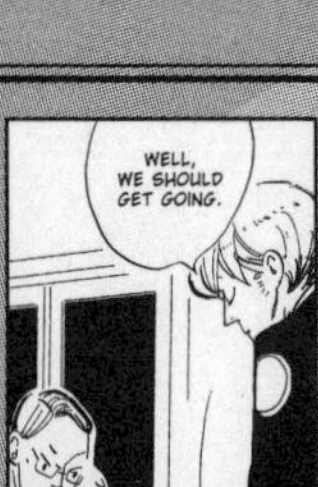

WELL, WE SHOULD GET GOING.
YES, SIR!

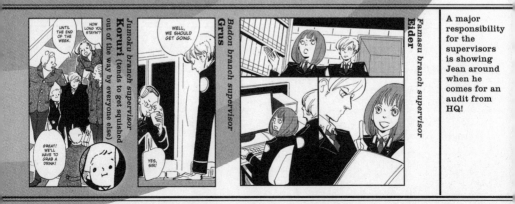

Jumoku branch supervisor **Koruri** (tends to get squished out of the way by everyone else)

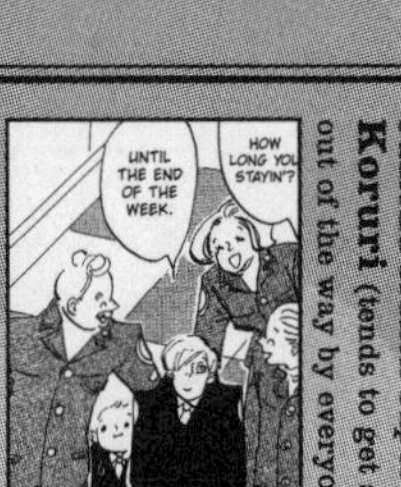

HOW LONG YOU STAYIN'?
UNTIL THE END OF THE WEEK.
GREAT! WE'LL HAVE TO GRAB A DRINK!

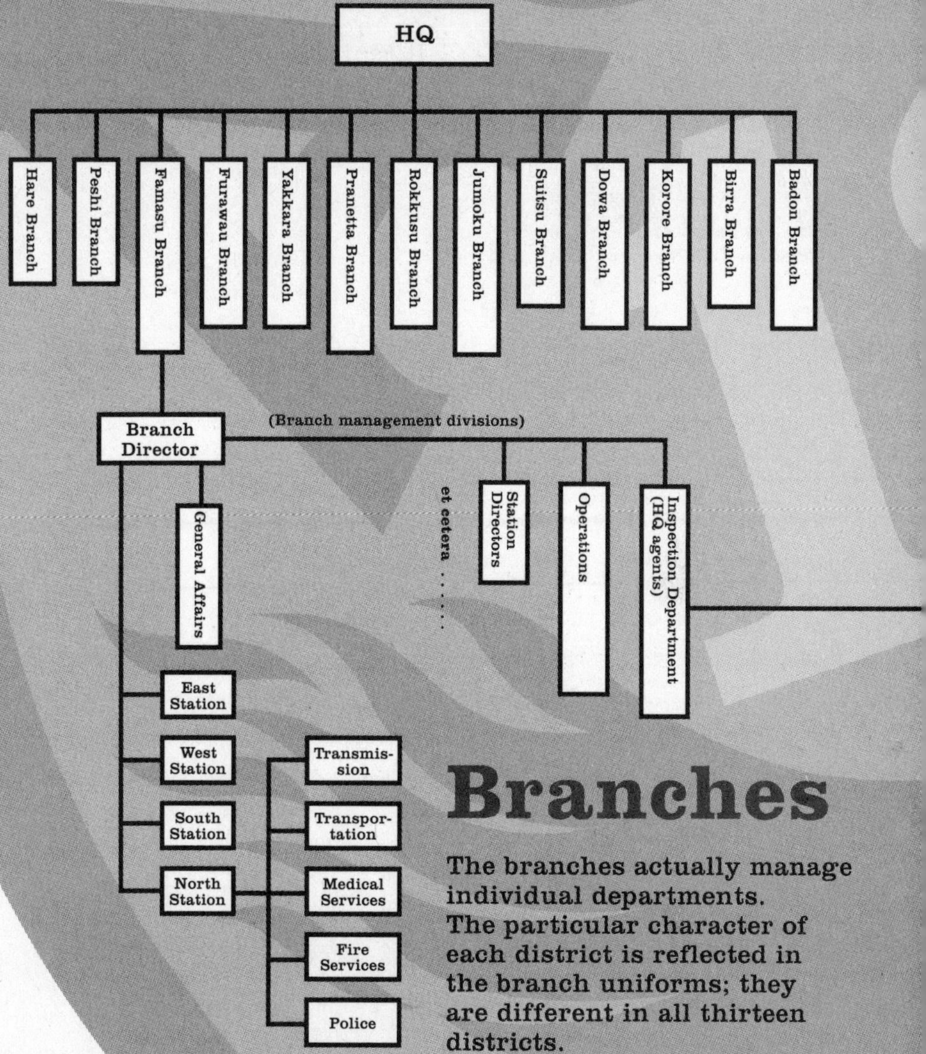
HQ
Hare Branch
Peshi Branch
Famasu Branch
Furawau Branch
Yakkara Branch
Pranetta Branch
Rokkusu Branch
Jumoku Branch
Suitsu Branch
Dowa Branch
Korore Branch
Birra Branch
Badon Branch
Branch Director
(Branch management divisions)
General Affairs
et cetera ......
Station Directors
Operations
Inspection Department (HQ agents)
East Station
West Station
South Station
North Station
Transmission
Transportation
Medical Services
Fire Services
Police

Branches

The branches actually manage individual departments. The particular character of each district is reflected in the branch uniforms; they are different in all thirteen districts.

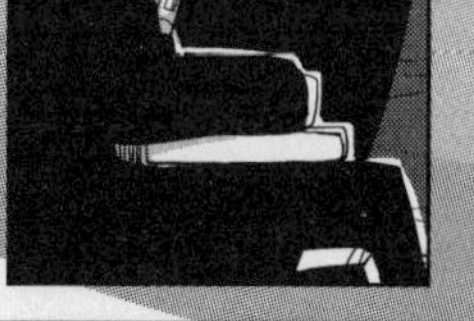
HMPH.

Suitsu branch supervisor
Warbler

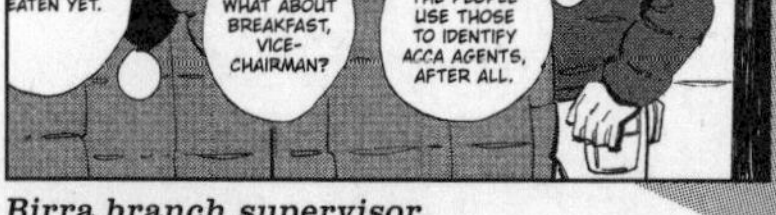
★★★★
HOTEL
I'M WEARING BORROWED GEAR TOO.
THE ONLY DIFFERENCE FROM THE BRANCH AGENTS IS THE KNIT CAP.
THE PEOPLE USE THOSE TO IDENTIFY ACCA AGENTS, AFTER ALL.
WHAT ABOUT BREAKFAST, VICE-CHAIRMAN?
I HAVEN'T EATEN YET.

Birra branch supervisor
Dunlin

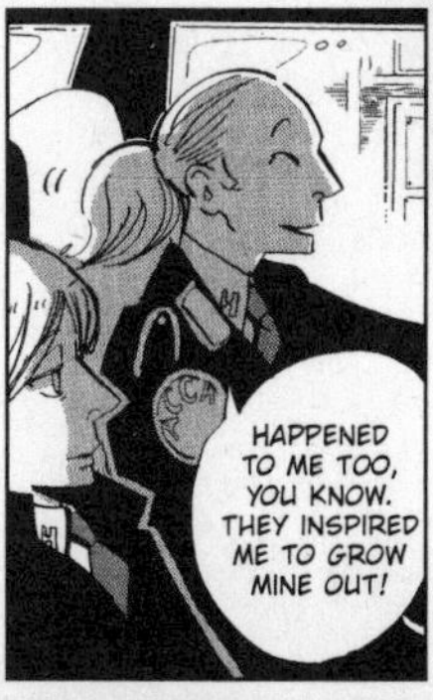
HAPPENED TO ME TOO, YOU KNOW. THEY INSPIRED ME TO GROW MINE OUT!

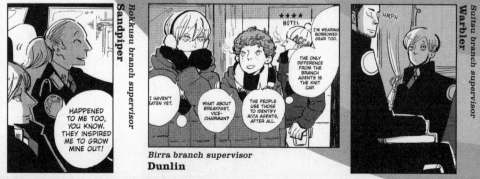

Rokkusu branch supervisor
Sandpiper

sbya

ACCA 13 TERRITORY INSPECTION DEPARTMENT

NATSUME ONO

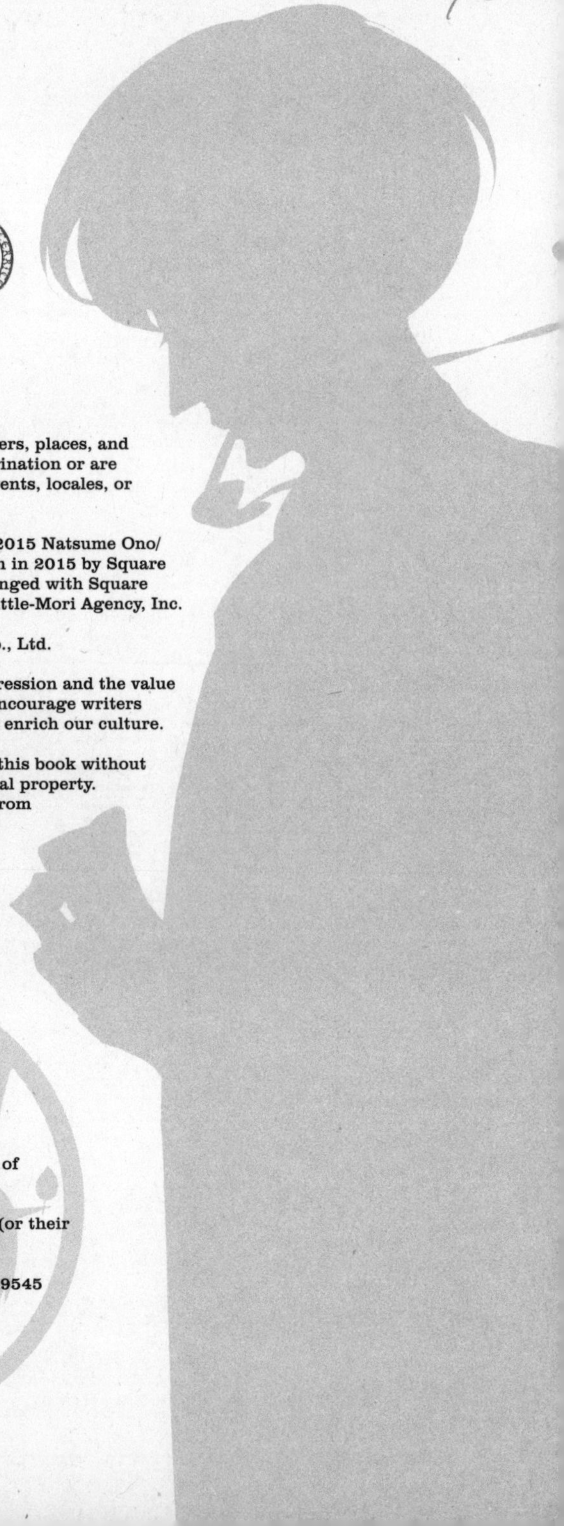

Translation:
Jocelyne Allen

Lettering:
Lys Blakeslee

ACCA JUSAN-KU KANSATSU-KA Volume 3 ©2015 Natsume Ono/ Square Enix Co., Ltd. First published in Japan in 2015 by Square Enix Co., Ltd. English translation rights arranged with Square Enix Co., Ltd. and Yen Press, LLC through Tuttle-Mori Agency, Inc.

English translation ©2018 by Square Enix Co., Ltd.

Yen Press
1290 Avenue of the Americas
New York, NY 10104

Visit us at yenpress.com
facebook.com/yenpress
twitter.com/yenpress
yenpress.tumblr.com
instagram.com/yenpress

First Yen Press Edition: June 2018

Yen Press is an imprint of Yen Press, LLC.
The Yen Press name and logo are trademarks of
Yen Press, LLC.

The publisher is not responsible for websites (or their content) that are not owned by the publisher.

Library of Congress Control Number: 2017949545

ISBNs: 978-0-316-44667-9 (paperback)
       978-0-316-44670-9 (ebook)

10 9 8 7 6 5 4 3 2 1

WOR

Printed in the United States of America